MAJOR & MR
DEFINITIVE
BATTLEFIELD GUIDE TO THE

D-DAY

NORMANDY LANDING BEACHES

TONIE AND VALMAI HOLT

"Believe me, Lang, the first 24 hours of the invasion will be decisive... for the Allies, as well as for Germany, it will be the longest day."

Field-Marshal Rommel to his aide-de-camp, April 1944.

BRITISH NORMANDY MEMORIAL
VER-SUR-MER

MAJOR & MRS HOLT'S DEFINITIVE BATTLEFIELD GUIDE

D-DAY
NORMANDY LANDING BEACHES
TONIE AND VALMAI HOLT

 PEN & SWORD BOOKS

By the same authors

Picture Postcards of the Golden Age: A Collector's Guide
Picture Postcard Artists: Landscapes, Animals and Characters
Stanley Gibbons Postcard Catalogue: 1980, 1981, 1982, 1984, 1985, 1987
Till the Boys Come Home: The First World War Through its Picture Postcards. New edition 2014
Germany Awake! The Rise of National Socialism illustrated by Contemporary Postcards
I'll be Seeing You: the Picture Postcards of World War II
The Best of Fragments from France by Capt Bruce Bairnsfather
The Biography of Captain Bruce Bairnsfather, "In Search of the Better 'Ole", his Works and Collectables
Revised edition 2001. Limpback edition 2014
Violets From Oversea: Reprinted 1999 as Poets of the Great War
My Boy Jack: The Search for Kipling's Only Son: Revised limpback edition 2001, 2007, 2008, 2009
Holts' Battlefield Guidebooks: Normandy-Overlord/Market-Garden/Somme/Ypres
Visitor's Guide to the Normandy Landing Beaches
Battlefields of the First World War: A Traveller's Guide
Major & Mrs Holt's Concise Guide to the Ypres Salient
Major & Mrs Holt's Battle Maps: Normandy/Somme/Ypres/Gallipoli/MARKET-GARDEN
Major & Mrs Holt's Definitive Guide to the Ypres Salient + Battle Map
Major & Mrs Holt's Defintive Guide to the Somme + Battle Map
Major & Mrs Holt's Battlefield Guide to Gallipoli + Battle Map
Major & Mrs Holt's Battlefield Guide to MARKET-GARDEN (Arnhem) + Battle Map
Major & Mrs Holt's Definitive Guide to the Normandy D-Day Landing Beaches
Major & Mrs Holt's Battlefield Guide to the Western Front – North
Major & Mrs Holt's Battlefield Guide to the Western Front – South
Major & Mrs Holt's Pocket Battlefield Guide to Ypres & Passchendaele
Major & Mrs Holt's Pocket Battlefield Guide to the Somme 1916/1918
Major & Mrs Holt's Pocket Battlefield Guide to Normandy Landing Beaches/D-Day

* * *

First published in Great Britain in 1999,
This 8th Updated Edition 2019
PEN AND SWORD MILITARY
an imprint of
Pen & Sword Books Ltd
47 Church Street
Barnsley, South Yorkshire S70 2AS
Text copyright © Tonie and Valmai Holt, 2019

ISBN 978 152675 790 6

Typeset by Chic Graphics

Printed and bound in India by Replika Press Pvt. Ltd

Pen & Sword Books Ltd incorporates the imprints of Pen & Sword Aviation, Pen & Sword Family History,
Pen & Sword Maritime, Pen & Sword Military, Wharncliffe Local History, Wharncliffe True Crime, Wharncliffe
Transport, Pen & Sword Discovery, Pen & Sword Select, Pen & Sword Military Classics, Leo Cooper,
Remember When, The Praetorian Press, Seaforth Publishing and Frontline Publishing

For a complete list of Pen & Sword titles please contact
PEN & SWORD BOOKS LIMITED
47 Church Street, Barnsley, South Yorkshire, S70 2AS, England
E-mail: enquiries@pen-and-sword.co.uk   Website: www.pen-and-sword.co.uk

CONTENTS

List of ITINERARY Maps

List of BATTLE Maps

Legend for Maps

● Bunkers
● Demarcation Stones
○ Memorials
● Museums

▲ Place names
○ Sites of Special Interest
● War Cemeteries

List of DIAGRAMS

ABBREVIATIONS

Abbreviations used for military units are listed below. At intervals the full name of a unit is repeated in the text in order to aid clarity. Other abbreviations and acronyms are explained where they occur.

AB	Airborne	Inf	Infantry
ABMC	American Battle Monuments Commission	LCVG	Landing Craft Vehicle and gun
AEAF	Allied Expeditionary Air Force	LCVP	Landing Craft Vehicle and Personnel
Armd	Armoured	Pl	Plaque
Bde	Brigade	LEC	*Liberté, Egalité, Citoyenneté*
BEF	British Expeditionary Force	Mem	
Bn	Battalion	Lib	Liberation/Liberators
Brig	Brigadier	Lt	Lieutenant
Can	Canadian	LZ	Landing Zone
Cdo	Commando	Maj	Major
Cdr	Commander	Mem	Memorial
C-in-C	Commander-in-Chief	MoH	Medal of Honour
Civ	Civilian	Mus	Museum
Col	Colonel	NTL	*Normandie Terre-Liberté Totem*
Com Déb Mon Sig	*Comité du Débarquement Monument Signal*	OP	Observation Post
Coy	Company	Para	Parachute
Cpl	Corporal	Pfc	Private First Class
CWGC	Commonwealth War Graves Commission	PIR	Para Inf Regiment
		Pl	Plaque
DD	Duplex Drive	Prov	Provisional
Div	Division	Regt	Regiment
DSC	Distinguished Service Cross	RM	Royal Marine
DZ	Dropping Zone	RUR	Royal Ulster Rifles
Eng	Engineer	RV	Rendezvous
FOO	Forward Observation Officer	Sgt	Sergeant
FFL	*Forces Françaises Libres*	SGW	Stained Glass Window
Fr	French	SOP	Standard Operational Procedure
GC	George Cross		
Gen	General	Sp	Special
Ger	German	Spt	Support
GIR	Glider Infantry Regiment	Sqn	Squadron
Gren	Grenadier	WN	*Wiederstandsnest*
Indep	Independent		

INTRODUCTION

The wind of change has been blowing along the Normandy Beaches. The air was calm when we conducted our first tour of the D-Day sites more than 40 years ago - little had then changed since the completion of the beautifully landscaped war cemeteries, the erection of the first memorials and museums.

FROM THE 40TH TO THE 75TH ANNIVERSARIES

By the time we wrote our first slim guidebook to the area in 1983 the breeze was getting up in preparation for the first major commemoration of the Landings on the **40th Anniversary in June 1984**. We were honoured to be involved in the organisation of the events with the Calvados and Manche Departmental Tourist Committees, were appointed consultants to the cities of Portsmouth and Southampton, to Townsend Thoresen Ferries and British Airways and were able to take a major advisory role in the planning process.

Recommended circuits were signed, sites were landscaped and car parks built. Many new memorials were erected, existing museums were improved and new ones opened. The gallant band of British veterans formed the Normandy Veterans' Association and started to visit in their thousands, as did many American and Canadian Veterans. Ties were renewed between regiments and the towns and villages they liberated.

The actual anniversary was a right royal event, attended by the Heads of State of all the participating nations, and well covered in the media. A new awareness of the historical significance of the Normandy Landings and of the sacrifice of the men and women who took part in them was aroused on both sides of the Atlantic. School parties and family groups, and parties of non-veterans also started to visit Normandy and the various tourist authorities began to recognise the significance of battlefield tourism to their economy.

Over the next thirty-five years the subtle change from 'pilgrimage' to 'tourism' that had taken place in other major battlefield areas like Ypres and the Somme progressed apace in Normandy. As well as the specialist military history guided tour groups that had proliferated since we pioneered battlefield tours in the late 1970s came the general tourists, content with a less in-depth visit. Each anniversary saw more investment and more memorials and museums (such as the ambitious *Mémorial* at Caen in 1988). The **50th Anniversary** saw the impressive statues of Generals Eisenhower and Montgomery (at Bayeux and Colleville-Montgomery respectively) and the setting up of *Normandie Terre-Liberté* (qv) routes. The **55th Anniversary** saw the inauguration of many more major memorials and the Airborne Museum at Pegasus Bridge, followed in 2003 by the JUNO Beach Centre at Courseulles. Some of the extraordinarily well-preserved remnants of Hitler's Atlantic Wall defences like the Batteries at Longues, Azeville, Crisbecq etc were progressively restored and more elements opened to the public.

The wind had gained strength after Stephen Spielberg's epic film, *Saving Private Ryan* in 1998, followed by *The Band of Brothers* in 2001. By the time of the build-up for the **60th Anniversary** in June 2004 it had reached hurricane proportions. The event was seen by the organisers as 'The Last Hurrah' for the sadly dwindling and ageing number of veterans and a varied and imaginative programme of commemorative events was planned for them. These took the form of many diverse happenings in addition to the traditional laying of wreaths, veterans' parades and the awarding to them of commemorative badges, parachute drops and displays of military vehicles. Street parties, lunches, dinners, Glenn Miller dances, international concerts, fireworks, childrens' races, commemorative walks and bike rides, photographic and art exhibitions, the participation of many communes in 'My village tells its story' events, dramas and film shows, debates and symposia, readings of letters and diaries, aerobatic displays, the naming of ships, militaria fairs, the recreation of wartime houses and military camps, and the naming of many streets, squares and roundabouts to regiments or individual veterans.

The *Comité du Débarquement* (qv) created a special *Normandie Mémoire 44* Committee to co-ordinate the events. *Normandie-Mémoire* (qv) continued and has gone from strength to strength as an organisation dedicated to preserving the memory of the historic events of the summer of 1944 in Normandy and of those who sacrificed their lives. It is concerned with the quality of the museums, memorials and other important sites and encourages visits through the Normandy Pass (qv). See **www.normandiememoire.com**

Many regiments and divisions erected what they expect to be their final monuments, statues and plaques so that the number of over 300 existing memorials swelled considerably. As well as the traditional bronze statues (like 'Iron Mike' at la Fière and the 51st Div Highlander at Château St Côme) came many French/International sculptures in the more modern medium of Inox (stainless steel), several of them commemorating Peace rather than military achievement or sacrifice.

This development marked another change in the direction of the wind. The name 'Memorial' was progressively being used in the names of new museums (like the *Mémorial* at Caen, with its by-line '*Un Musée pour la Paix*). They became 'Peace', rather than 'Battle' or 'War' museums. The dove replaced the rifle in memorials and one example of this trend is the striking bronze pistol with the knotted barrel outside the Caen *Mémorial*. The flamboyant silver-coloured female figure at Grandcamp Maisy symbolises Peace and the concept of political correctness is creeping through museum displays. More changes were apparent with the hand-over of ownership and direction of the important museum at Bayeux which in 2006 re-opened with completely new exhibits and which is run by the *Mairie* of Bayeux. The following year the direction of the Arromanches Museum, one of the first major museums to open, passed from the *Comité du Débarquement* to the *Mairie* of Arromanches.

In the flurry of renovation of many sites a certain sanitised air has been the inevitable result of making them accessible to the thousands of new visitors without damaging the historic infrastructure. This is evident, for instance, in the vastly enlarged car park area and reception centre (a joint American-French project) at Pointe du Hoc. Atmosphere and the original battlefield feel has to be sacrificed to the need for preservation for future generations and the desire to make their significance more easily understood by the casual visitor. Presentations in museums are becoming more 'high-tech' to appeal to the all-important younger generation.

Another unprecedented development was the opening in 2007 of the splendid Visitor Centre beside the American Normandy Cemetery at St Laurent which with its historical displays has had a considerable impact on local museums.

Far from the **60th** being the last great commemoration as anticipated, the **65th Anniversary** saw yet more new memorials, notably the fine US Naval statuary group at UTAH Beach, the Memorial to Easy Coy (Band of Brothers) 506th PIR, at Brécourt Manor and the '*Coup de Main*' Memorial in the grounds of the Pegasus Memorial Museum.

The event was not without controversy The British Government, insisting that commemorations should be supported on 25th, 50th, 60th and 100th anniversaries, but not on 65th, was late in the day in agreeing to fund the 800 veterans who were fit enough to make the pilgrimage. Diplomatic feathers were somewhat ruffled when it appeared that Pres Sarkozy had invited Pres Obama to what he called 'the main Franco-American event' but not HM Queen Elizabeth. Prince Charles stepped into the breach at the last moment by attending and the British veterans were given a right royal welcome wherever they appeared, as were their American and Canadian Allies. 1940s military vehicles cabbied happily along the beaches and the coastal towns, services were held, wreaths were laid, *vins d'honneur* were drunk, fireworks blazed, concerts rang out – all in a wonderful spirit of *entente cordiale and* genuine gratitude.

Later a frequently occurring phenomenon was the erection of plaques and memorials to men who survived the 1944 campaign but who either settled in, or frequently visited, their old stamping grounds (e.g. Harold Pickersgill (qv), Bill Millin (qv), Daniel Robinson (qv); Robert Murphy (qv) 'Dick' Winters of 'Easy' Coy)....

Considerable investment continued to be made in improving and expanding existing sites, e.g. the UTAH Beach Museum, the Merville Battery and the Ste Mère Eglise Airborne Museum.

REVISED AND EXPANDED EDITIONS

Over the following ten years of intensive visits and research we made some fundamental changes and major innovations to reflect advances in technology and visitors' requirements and methods of navigation. The proliferation of new sites of interest were included.

Firstly we expanded and remodelled the Itineraries, increasing them from 5 to 6. With a few exceptions, Itineraries 1 and 2 cover the US Landings at UTAH and OMAHA Beaches and the US Airborne and Ranger Operations. Itinerary 3 covers Bayeux, Arromanches & GOLD Beach. Itinerary 4 covers the Canadian Operations, Carpiquet to JUNO Beach. Itinerary 5 covers the Allied Commando Operations/SWORD Beach to Caen. Itinerary 6 covers Pegasus Bridge and British Airborne Operations.

The most important of all the sites of interest on these Itineraries are now listed, with their GPS Latitude & Longitude location and a photograph (although we are confident that our readers will, as always, point out some that we have not discovered).

The inclusion of Lat & Long locations reflect the modern desire to proceed directly to one's personal area of interest using satnav. It is then possible to create one's own itinerary, dipping in and out of our recommended routes for historical background as required.

We now direct you to the **HOW TO USE THIS GUIDE SECTION** to help you get the most out of using this new format guide, whether on the ground or from the comfort of your armchair. It really is worthwhile reading that section before travelling.

The book has consequently expanded to some 360 pages and, mindful that users called the previous edition, *The Bible*, we have had the temerity to call it the 'Definitive' guide to the areas covered. There can never be the 'Complete' guide: historians and regimental associations will always continue to strive to commemorate those who sacrificed so much for our freedom and who have still not been honoured with a memorial. However in attempting to create a record of the memorials to those who gave so much in the struggle to liberate Europe, we have limited our reach to approximately the line of the planned advance for D-Day and only strayed over it when it seemed wrong not to do so. Even so we have listed almost 500 memorials.

THIS 2019 75TH ANNIVERSARY UPDATED EDITION

The 75th Anniversary will obviously mark the last great hurrah by the dwindling band of D-Day Veterans and any major changes in the area. The Normandy Veterans' Association disbanded in October 2014, and the D-Day & Normandy Fellowship in January 2018.

N.B. However the reader must be aware of the fact that, as these updates are being made, the outcome of BREXIT negotiations is still ongoing and may have a major impact on the future of battlefield touring in France.

KEEPING THE FLAME OF REMEMBRANCE ALIGHT

Despite all the innovations and change of emphasis in the area, the flame of remembrance still burns brightly in the towns and villages of Normandy, liberated in 1944 after four years of enemy occupation. Their gratitude and welcome to pilgrims and students of those momentous days remain as warm as ever, despite the suffering and destruction of life and property they endured during the Battle for Normandy. The region is a place of great natural beauty with many gourmet delights. We hope that this book will help you to enjoy your visit or your trip down memory lane as well as making it an emotional and rewarding experience.

Tonie and Valmai Holt
Woodnesborough, Kent, 2019.

THE AUTHORS
Opening the Doors to the Battlefields

Tonie and Valmai Holt are acknowledged as the founders, in the 1970s, of the modern battlefield tour. Their company, Major & Mrs Holt's Battlefield Tours, covered battlefields worldwide.

Valmai Holt took a BA (Hons) in French and Spanish and taught History. Tonie Holt took a BSc (Eng) and is a graduate of the Royal Military Academy, Sandhurst and of the Army Staff College at Camberley. Both are Fellows of the Royal Society of Arts and Science, early members of The Western Front Association, Honorary Members of the Guild of Battlefield Guides and Life Members of the Last Post Association.

In 1984 they acted as consultants to the cities of Portsmouth and Southampton, The Département of Calvados and British Airways to co-ordinate the 40th Anniversary of the D-Day Landings, and subsequently were appointed ADCs to Congressman Robert Livingston of Louisiana for services in support of American veterans. In the 1980s they took over the organisation of the Royal British Legion Pilgrimages.

Writing together and doing all their own research, they combine male and female viewpoints allowing military commentaries to be linked with the culture of the period under study. Their *Major & Mrs Holt's Battlefield Guides* series encapsulates over 40 years of work.

In 2014 they were awarded the Department of the Somme's Centenary Medal *'for opening the door to the battlefields'* and service to tourism and in November 2017, they were honoured by The Last Post Association and the City of Ieper.

In March 2018, they celebrated their Diamond Wedding Anniversary.

The Authors, Tonie and Valmai Holt.

How To Use This Guide

This book is designed to guide the visitor around the main sites and features, memorials, museums and cemeteries of the D-Day Landing Beaches, and to provide sufficient information about those places to allow an elementary understanding of what happened where. It makes extensive use of veterans' and participants' memories. The majority of the boxed 'D-Day Memories' were told to the authors personally, for the most part on the ground itself.

PRIOR TO YOUR VISIT

Read the following sections carefully and mark up the recommended maps (see below). There is no doubt that a better picture of what happened on D-Day, and why it happened, can be obtained from a general understanding of the background to the invasion. Therefore, the traveller is advised to read the Historical Summary below and the brief introductory passages at the beginning of each itinerary before setting out on the tour.

GPS REFERENCES – LATITUDE AND LONGITUDE

The completion of the motorway link from the Channel ports and the fast rail services from Paris have made it possible for brief visits to be made to the Normandy area when, owing to a lack of time on the ground, what might be described as 'digital touring' is the order of the day i.e. the visitor wishes to go from specific place to place rather than take particular routes and to follow a sequential story. Thus we have now provided decimal Latitude and Longitude references for all the memorials in the text so that by using their GPS visitors can move quickly and surely from place to place. However, if the visitor has the time, we recommend that as far as possible the suggested itineraries should be followed as each one forms a continuous story which adds to the general understanding of what happened.

CHOOSING YOUR ROUTES

If You Wish to Visit a Particular Place

Use the index at the back of the book to locate what you wish to visit. You can now go directly there using a GPS. If it is a particular grave, find the location from the Commonwealth War Graves Commission/American Battle Monuments Commission (see below) before you set out.

If You Just Want to 'Tour the Beaches' or 'Drop Zones'

By and large the beaches landed on by the Americans (UTAH and OMAH) are covered in Itineraries One and Two, by the Canadians (JUNO) in Itinerary Four and the British, French and Belgian (GOLD and SWORD) in Itineraries Three and Five. Airborne Operations are covered in Itineraries One, Two and Six. See Battle Map 1.

THE ITINERARIES/MILES COVERED/DURATION/MAP REF/LAT & LONG/PIC REF/RWC/OP/TOURIST OFFICES/RESTAURANTS

A PERSONAL NOTE FROM THE AUTHORS: There is an immense amount of factual information given in this book to help the visitor locate each site described, resulting in a certain degree of initial apparent complication in the headings for the stops. Also, in order to be able to include almost 200 more pictures covering all visits made off the main itinerary, we have introduced Group Picture Pages which hold up to a dozen small pictures. Please read this section very thoroughly before setting out and all will be made clear! When planning your route, please study the summaries of the various itineraries at the beginning of each battlefield tour as this will help you decide whether you wish to take any of the deviations from the main itinerary.

TRAVEL INSTRUCTIONS are indented and written in italics to make them stand out clearly.
Tourist Offices, Hotels/Restaurants & Cafés are indicated in a **distinctive typeface** to make them stand out clearly.
ODOMETER. It is absolutely essential to set your mileage trip to zero before starting and to make constant reference to it. Distances in the headings are given in miles because the trip meters on British cars still operate in miles. Conversion to kilometers may be done by dividing by 5 and multiplying the result by 8. Distances within the text are sometimes given in kilometres and metres as local signposts use those measures.

MAIN ITINERARIES

There are six **Main Itineraries**, which need not be taken in any particular sequence, nor travelled in the directions given in this book, though it will ease navigation if they are. The composition of the **Main Itineraries** is based upon what the authors, in many years of conducting interested groups around the area, have found to be the places that most people have asked to see.

Each itinerary is preceded by an historical account which should be read before, or concurrently, with setting out. The itineraries cover the five Landing Beaches and the areas of the US and British Airborne Operations. Details of the routes are given at the beginning of each timed and measured itinerary. The times stated do not include stops for refreshments or the Extra Visits or N.B.s (see below).

In the heading for each Main Itinerary stop is the name of the site, a running mileage total, how long you may wish to stop there, its Map reference to the relevant ITINERARY MAP, (e.g. **MAP It1-2**), its **GPS Lat & Long** ref, (e.g. **49.40115 -1.36331**) and an indication (**R/WC**) if there are refreshment and toilet facilities. **OP** indicates an Observation Point from which features of the battlefield may be seen.

EXTRA VISITS

Although the Main Itineraries cover the most 'popular' sites and may be taken by ignoring any suggested deviations, there are many memorials and places of interest that can be seen during a visit. Indeed some visitors' interests may lie outside the normal touring areas and therefore within the area of our 'D-Day Boundary' (qv) we have attempted to list all the memorials in place at the time of writing.

Thus, in addition to the Main Itineraries, *Extra Visits* are described to sites of particular interest which lie near to the recommended routes. They are **shaded grey** so that they stand out clearly from the main route. Generally these offer a circuit route that returns the traveller to the main itinerary. Estimates of the round trip mileage and duration are given. The collective headings list all the stops in this particular Extra Visit, each with its Map, Lat & Long & Picture Ref.

N.B.s. Other deviations from the main route to points of interest which do not have a circuit but are 'there and back' trips are prefaced by 'N.B.' These are slightly indented and boxed and the Map, Lat & Long & Picture Refs are given.
Note that N.B.s sometimes occur within Extra Visits!

PICTURES for these sections only are arranged on '**GROUP PICTURE PAGES**' (up to 4 pages per Itinerary) which are headed, for example, 'Group Picture Page Itinerary One-1' etc. The captions for these pictures are listed in a box near the picture page and are numbered GPPIt1-1/1 [Group Picture Page Itinerary One, page 1, picture 1] etc.
Typical location information for an *Extra Visit* or an **N.B.** site is: 'Map It2-B/Lat & Long: 49.31226 -1.26139/GPPIt2-1/6'.

MAPS/LOCAL ROUTE SIGNS

In-text Maps

Itinerary Maps. These show the recommended stops for all the different Itineraries. Main Itinerary stops are numbered (1, 2, 3,...). Extra Visit and N.B. stops are indicated by letters (A-Z, then a-z.) They are followed by a Legend describing each stop.

Battle Maps. These show the landing and battle details of the invading air and sea-borne forces relevant to each Itinerary.
Major & Mrs Holt's Battle Map of the Normandy D-Day Landing Beaches (1:116,000), coloured, double-sided (Side 1: SWORD, JUNO, GOLD, 6th BR AB Ops. Side 2: US Airborne Ops, UTAH, OMAHA). Grid and alphabetical indexes showing Memorials, Museums, War Cemeteries, Bunkers, Assault formations; D-Day objective line; actual 6 June line; Points of Interest; Personalities; Contours etc. Packaged with this book.

Michelin 231 (1:200,000), covers the whole Normandy area, and 303 (1:1.500,00), which covers the Départements of Calvados and la Manche, are recommended.

IGN *(Institut Géographique National)* produce more detailed maps (1:25,000) of the Landing Beaches.

CWGC Michelin Map overlaid with CWGC Cemeteries. Contact CWGC e-mail: casualty.enq@cwgc.org

Local Route Signs. *Normandie Terre-Liberté*

The *Départements* of Calvados, La Manche and the Orne have signed eight recommended local routes for what is described as an open-air museum of memory in Normandy, Land of Liberty. Their white directional signs all carry the logo of a seagull in flight and at 100 important sites well-researched, informative blue signboards called *Normandie Terre-Liberté* - **NTL Totems,** describe the other sites in the section and summarise what happened at the site in French and in English. The sections are:-

1. Overlord – *L'Assaut* (The Assault)
Pegasus Bridge/SWORD/JUNO/GOLD Beaches

2. D-Day – *Le Choc* (The Onslaught)
Bayeux/Port-en-Bessin/OMAHA Beach/Pointe du Hoc/UTAH Beach

3. *Objectif – un Port* (Objective - a Port)
US Airborne/UTAH Beach to Cherbourg

4. *L'Affrontement* (The Confrontation)
The British break-out round Caen/Panzers in the Bocage

5. Cobra – *Percée* (Operation COBRA/The Breakout)
From Cherbourg to Avranches. Patton's tanks on Liberty Highway

6. *Le Contre-Attaque* (The Counter-Attack)
Last German offensive at Mortain. The Panzers Retreat

7. *L'Encerclement* (The Encirclement)
From Alençon to l'Aigle. Gen. Leclerc's tanks progress.
8th German Army encircled.

8. *Le Dénouement* (The Outcome)
From Caen to l'Aigle. The Polish, Canadian and British close the Falaise Gap.
End of the Battle of Normandy.

New panels headed **'mob e'** on each Totem describe how by holding your mobile phone close to the Totem you will be able to access 20 archive films and extra information.

A descriptive leaflet, *The D-Day Landings and the Battle of Normandy EXPLORATION AND EMOTION,* produced by *Normandie Mémoire* describing the **NTL Totem** routes and other sites is available from all main tourist offices.

HISTORICAL SUMMARY
BACKGROUND TO NORMANDY

Pre-1940

The name 'Normandy' derives from the Norsemen who invaded the area in the ninth century. The land they occupied was known as *Neustrie* (Kingdom of the West), one of three Frankish Kingdoms founded by Childeric in 567. It was inhabited by Celtic, Iberian and Gallic tribes who had already been conquered by the Romans in 50BC. The quarrelsome tribes were subdued by Roman rule and an uneasy peace, broken only by the warring Francs and Carolingians, reigned - until the Norman invasion.

The story of the most famous Norman of all, William the Bastard (also known as 'the Conqueror'), is charted in the famous Bayeux Tapestry - a *must* when visiting Normandy (see Bayeux entry below). When William invaded England in 1066 it was with the greatest invasion fleet and force the world had ever known. The fleet and force that invaded, in the opposite direction, in 1944 was also the greatest invasion fleet and force the world had hitherto known. The irony of the conjunction of these two historical landmarks is recorded in the Latin inscription on the Bayeux Memorial: *Nos a Gulielmo victi victoris Patriam liberavimus* ('We, once conquered by William, have now set free the conqueror's native land').

After the Normans it was the English who were to be Normandy's next invaders - during the 100 Years' War. As in 1944, the proximity of Normandy's fine beaches to the English coast attracted invaders, such as Edward III and Henry V. The last battle in Normandy of the 100 Years' War took place in 1450 in Formigny (on what is now the N13 behind OMAHA beach). It is marked by a splendid memorial that was knocked over by a Sherman tank in 1944, but now once more proudly dominates the town's crossroads.

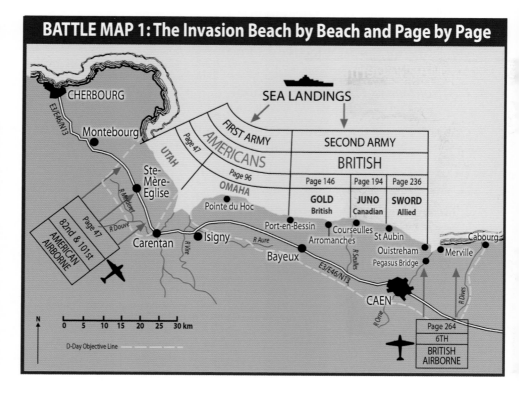

BATTLE MAP 1: The Invasion Beach by Beach and Page by Page

From then until the German Occupation in 1940, the province flourished. Its temperate climate and good soil fostered successful agriculture and dairy farming. Its plentiful seas offered a rich harvest of seafood. The province's reputation for rich gastronomy encouraged tourism, which developed in the 1890s with the rail link to Paris and the burgeoning of smart resorts like Cabourg, Deauville and Trouville. For Normandy it was truly the beginning of the *Belle Epoque,* and royalty, high society and the artistic *monde* savoured its clear air, beautiful sandy beaches and fine Romanesque and Norman architecture. It was to remain so until the Fall of France in 1940.

The Occupation 1940-44

For the four years until June 1944, the phlegmatic Normans by and large evolved a comfortable *modus vivendi* with their German occupiers. The quality of the German troops during the occupation was generally poor. There was a high percentage of under- or over-age soldiers and convalescents. Many of them were non-German. Most Normans settled for a quiet life with them - glad of the money they could make by supplying much-appreciated dairy produce, cider and Calvados. Underneath the sleepy surface, active members of the Resistance worked by day and, more often, by night. Forbidden radios, tuned to the BBC, picked up the message which was to announce the Allied Invasion.

This message was the first verse of Paul Verlaine's *Chanson d'Automne* (Autumn Song). The first three lines,

Les sanglots longs
Des violons
De l'Automne

(The long sobs of autumn violins)
was broadcast on 1 June. On 5 June, the next three lines,

Blessent mon coeur
D'une longueur
Monotone

(Wound my heart with a monotonous languor)
followed. It signalled that the invasion would take place in 48 hours.

BATTLE MAP 2: German Defences and the Assault by Beaches

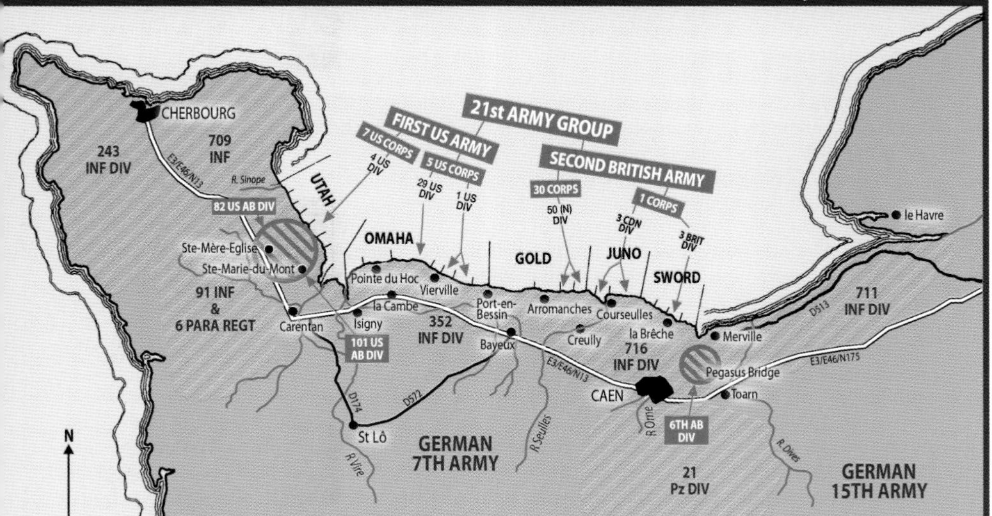

In one of the strangest coincidences in the story of the D-Day landings, another famous poet, Lord Byron (1788-1824), wrote in *Don Juan,*

'Twas on a summer's day – the sixth of June:
I like to be particular in dates.
Not only of the age, and year, but moon;
They are a sort of post-house, where the Fates
Change horses, making History change its tune,

Then spur away o'er states,
Leaving at last not much besides chronology,
Excepting the post-orbits of theology.
'Twas on the sixth of June, about the hour
Of half-past-six – perhaps still nearer seven ...

In actual fact he was probably writing about the attack on the Turkish fort of Imail by the Russian General Suvarov in 1790 during the reign of Catherine the Great!

From 6 June 1944

As a reprisal, and in a certain amount of panic, when the Germans realised the scale of the landings, they executed (by shooting) all the male Resistance workers in Caen Prison except two - a youth of only 16 and a man whose name was wrongly recorded by the Germans, who thus did not call him out to be shot. The killings started on the evening of 6 June and continued the next day. Over eighty men were executed.

The Normans certainly paid dearly for their liberation. As well as these Resistance executions, thousands of civilians were killed over the next seventy or so days in Allied bombings and bombardments and in the fierce fighting between the invaders and occupiers.

In Caen alone, starting with an incendiary bomb raid on 6 June and continuing to its liberation on 9 July, at the very lowest count 2,000 (and it could have been as many as 5,000 as records were impossible to keep in those fearsome days) civilians were killed. Thousands more were injured and made homeless.

Lives were lost, homes were destroyed, albeit on a lesser scale, all along the landing beaches. Valuable farm land was scarred and pitted. Livestock was killed in profusion. One of the most vivid memories of many D-Day veterans is the pathetic sight of bloated cows, their legs up-turned, and the dreadful stench of rotting animals. Yet, today the French welcome returning veterans with genuine warmth.

'At one of the wine receptions,' wrote John Slaughter, veteran of the US 29th Division, returning to Normandy in September 1988 for the unveiling of his Divisional Memorial at Vierville, 'many of the locals would shake hands and say, "Thank you for what you did". This is after we tore hell out of their homes and villages. After three years of living under the Boche iron boot we were their liberators. I now have a different perspective of the French.'

Memorials are on the whole well maintained, ceremonies are well attended, by local people and Resistance workers and Free French standard bearers, often delightfully out of step, standards sometimes less than rigidly held, beret and *Gauloise* both at a jaunty angle, but with hearts in a very correct place.

Although of only small significance, there was another side to the coin. There was an element of collaboration during the occupation. Some British veterans recall being met by fierce sniper fire, which turned out to be from young Frenchmen. After the invasion many female fraternisers had to be ignominiously shaved, tarred and feathered. Returning German veterans are still sometimes greeted with more than cordial enthusiasm in some households - notably, it is reported, when members of 12th SS Panzer attended the burial of Obersturmführer Michael Wittmann in La Cambe German Cemetery in May 1983.

But these were rare cases and the spirit of remembrance and gratitude fostered by the unceasing efforts of the *Comité du Débarquement* (qv) and by other commemorative associations (see below), and by individual French men and women seems as strong as ever.

Great Anglo/American/Canadian-French ceremonies are held every fifth year. But each 6 June and on the successive days into July that mark their liberation, small French *Communes* - like Hermanville with its 'H.M.S.' *(Histoire, Mémoire, Souvenir)* Association and private individuals - like Bernard Saulnier, the Amfréville farmer who for many years held 'open house' for British commandos - welcome returning veterans. *L'Entente Cordiale* is alive and well and manifest along the Normandy battlefields and beaches.

Background To The Invasion

Blitzkrieg - War begins

At dawn on Friday 1 September 1939 Operation WEISS (White) began. Almost fifty German divisions, including six Panzer divisions, supported by over fifteen hundred aircraft, invaded Poland. It was the start of World War II. In Britain general mobilisation was proclaimed. The French went a stage further and instituted martial law.

The German *Blitzkrieg* (lightning war) was overwhelmingly successful. The basic tactic was a close co-operation between tanks and aircraft with a rapid movement deep into enemy territory to sever the defending army from its supplies and communications. The original concept of *Blitzkrieg* has been attributed to both General Hans von Seeckt of the Reichswehr in the 1920s and to Captain Basil Liddell Hart in the 1930s, but its formidable exponents in September 1939 were two German Army Groups: North, commanded by Colonel General Fedor von Bock, and South, commanded by Colonel General Gerd von Rundstedt.

The progress of one formation in particular stood out as a prime example of *Blitzkrieg* at its most formidable - the advance of the XIX Panzer Corps commanded by General Heinz Guderian.

It was all over by 5 October when the last Polish troops surrendered near Warsaw. The Russians too had marched into Poland on 17 September and in accord with their non-aggression pact the Germans and Russians divided Poland between them. Then the Germans and the Russians stopped. The Phoney War began.

The Phoney War

President Roosevelt sent emissaries from America to investigate the possibility of a negotiated settlement. The BEF went to France and the European nations eyed each other across the Franco-Belgian borders and prepared for war. Eight months later, after the period known as the 'Phoney War', or the *Sitzkrieg*, the Germans struck again.

Dunkirk

On Friday 10 May 1940 in Operation GELB (Yellow) seventy-seven German divisions, including ten Panzer divisions and two airborne divisions, invaded Belgium, Holland and Luxembourg. Three Panzer Corps, one of which was Guderian's XIX, struck east through the Ardennes forests outflanking the French in the Maginot Line.

That same day the BEF, strung along the Belgian border, advanced into Belgium to take up positions along the Dyle River under a plan that Field Marshal Montgomery later described as a 'dog's breakfast'. In England the 'Pilgrim of Peace', Neville Chamberlain, resigned, and Winston Churchill became Prime Minister

The German *Blitzkrieg* worked again. Confused by the speed of the German advance, and with no proper liaison between British, Belgian and French commanders, the Allied response was ineffective. The BEF withdrew to the Channel and at Dunkirk between 26 May and 4 June a quarter of a million British soldiers were evacuated - among them the 3rd Division's commander, Major General Bernard Law Montgomery.

Two weeks later General Erwin Rommel's 7th (Ghost) Panzer Division entered the port of Cherbourg in Normandy as British troops were being evacuated under the covering fire of the French cruiser *Courbet*. His division had covered over 140 miles the previous day. At the end of the same week, the French signed an armistice in Marshal Foch's old railway carriage at Compi gne. Adolf Hitler went on a sightseeing tour of Paris. Now he was ready to turn his eyes towards Britain.

Alone

One of the planks of Adolf Hitler's rise to power was his insistence that all he wanted to do was to redress the wrongs inflicted upon Germany by the Treaty of Versailles after World War I. In addition, he claimed, he did not want to go to war with Britain.

At the end of June 1940 various overtures for a negotiated peace were made by Berlin to London. Lord Halifax, the British Foreign Secretary, was 'strictly forbidden to entertain any such suggestion' by Prime Minister Churchill. Hitler had overlooked the fact that Britain's new leader was a descendant of Marlborough and not inclined to give in.

Even before the fall of France, the Prime Minister had told the nation, 'We shall defend our island whatever the cost may be'. The Germans, distrustful of their new ally Russia, planned to attack her, but first, since they would not negotiate, the British had to be dealt with. Southern England had to be invaded.

The Battle of Britain

The German plan for the invasion of Britain, Operation SEALION, could not be implemented until the Royal Air Force had been destroyed.

Hitler's directive for the invasion began, 'The landing operation must be a surprise crossing on a broad front extending approximately from Ramsgate to a point west of the Isle of Wight ...', and, as an essential preparation to the invasion, the directive continued, 'The English Air Force must be eliminated.'

The task fell to the Luftwaffe under Reichsmarschall Hermann Goering and he had little doubt that it could be achieved. The Germans had over three thousand combat aircraft available while the British had less than half that number. Allowing for the fact that the British had to spread their aircraft in anticipation of attacks anywhere in the South of England and the Germans could concentrate theirs, the odds against the RAF were much greater than 2:1.

The Luftwaffe offensive against the Royal Air Force began on 'Eagle Day', 13 August 1940 and by 5 September the RAF, its bases badly damaged and losing pilots and planes faster than they could be replaced, was on the point of collapse. Then, in retaliation for air raids on Berlin, Hitler changed his plans and ordered an all-out offensive on London. The pressure on the RAF eased. Planes and airfields were repaired. Knowing, too that the Germans' target was London, the RAF could now concentrate against their enemy and even up the odds. Radar (Radio Aid to Detection and Ranging) and ULTRA helped too. German air losses increased. Daylight bombing was replaced by less costly night attacks and then, when it became clear that Britain could not be defeated quickly, Operation SEALION was cancelled. It was 17 September 1940.

The Battle of Britain had been won, the Invasion had been stopped. Now came the Blitz.

The Blitz

The bombing of London and other industrial cities and ports in Britain was a night-time terror which lasted from September 1940 until May 1941. During this period 39,600 civilians were killed and 46,100 injured.

On Sunday 22 June 1941, Germany launched her invasion of Russia - Operation BARBAROSSA. The Luftwaffe, needing every available aircraft - including bombers - on the Eastern Front for what was expected to be only a 6-month campaign, turned its attention away from Britain. The Blitz was over.

Before the end of the year Winston Churchill spoke in secret to his Combined Operations Staff about another cross-Channel invasion. This one, however, would be going in the opposite direction to SEALION and would eventually be called OVERLORD.

COUNTDOWN TO OVERLORD

1941

March	The Lend-Lease Act was passed in America, and President Roosevelt immediately declared that the defence of Great Britain was vital to the defence of the United States. Thus, every form of support for Britain short of American intervention began.
June	Hitler invaded Russia in Operation BARBAROSSA.
October	Winston Churchill told Lord Louis Mountbatten and his Combined Operations Staff to prepare plans for 'our great counter-invasion of Europe'.

'The Führer at the Atlantic Wall'.

key to the defeat of an Allied invasion lay with the German armoured divisions - but they did not agree how the divisions were to be used and this aggravated the normally complex commander/subordinate relationship into a strained and inefficient chain of command.

Rommel had taken over Army Group B in February 1944 with responsibility for the defence of an area stretching from Holland to the Atlantic coast of France. He divided his force into two - Seventh Army West of the River Orne and Fifteenth Army East (see Map 2). In his opinion the only place to stop the invasion was on the beaches and he demanded that control of the nine armoured divisions in Panzer Group West be given to him so that an immediate counterstroke could be launched against a landing. To carry out his plan he needed to hold the armour close behind the likely landing areas and with such a long coastline to defend it would use up almost all of the German armour.

Guderian did not like the idea of committing armoured formations to the defence of a particular landing area. In his opinion, it could lead to disaster, because if they guessed wrongly about where the invasion would come it would be difficult to correct their mistake. Von Rundstedt held a quite different opinion. He believed that a landing could not be prevented and that the bulk of the armour should be held well back until the true direction of any landing was clear, when a massive and decisive counterstroke could be made.

Hitler, although he favoured Rommel's belief that the first 48 hours after a landing would be the most critical, compromised, and did not give control of the Panzers to his favourite general. Instead, three of the nine Panzer divisions were placed under Rommel's direct command while the remainder, although technically under von Rundstedt, could not be released without the Führer's authority.

The chain of command was made even more complex because the C-in-C West had no operational authority over the Luftwaffe or the Navy, and formations in Army Group B could, and did, receive orders from three different headquarters - Rommel's, von Rundstedt's and Hitler's.

Ironically, in Führer Directive No 40 of 23 March 1942, which was entitled 'Command Organisation on the Coasts', Hitler had said, 'The preparation and execution of defensive operations must unequivocally and unreservedly be concentrated in the hands of one man.' It was fortunate for the Allies that Hitler did not follow his own orders.

In all, Rommel's command had thirty-nine Infantry Divisions and three Panzer divisions at the time of the landings. 21st Panzer was just south of Caen, moved there from Rennes in April to support the 7th Army. The other two Panzer divisions, one west of Paris, the other near Amiens, were to support the 15th Army in the Pas de Calais. In May 1944 Rommel had asked OKW to move the four reserve Panzer divisions nearer to the coast. Von Rundstedt protested and the request was denied.

When the Allies landed, Rommel had only one Panzer division available in the area, the 21st, and that was at the extreme eastern end of the invasion area, behind Caen and the British beaches.

The Infantry

German divisions were classified into four categories, mainly according to their degree of mobility. These categories were: 'capable of full attack', 'limited attack', 'full defence' or 'limited defence'. But mobility could mean a unit equipped with anything from bicycles via horses to motor transport, and the mobility of Army Group West was very limited.

As an example, 243rd Division was converted to a nominal attack division from being a static division in late 1943 by issuing four of its six battalions with bicycles, but the indigenous artillery regiment and anti-tank battalion never received their planned motor transport.

709th Division alongside and to the east of 243rd Division (see Map 2), and whose area included the small village of Ste Mère Eglise on the N13 Cherbourg to Carentan road, was also to be upgraded from a defence to an attack category. That had not been done by June.

More than half of Army Group West was made up from 'ear-nose-and-throat' soldiers, those who were unfit for anything other than static service, perhaps too old, perhaps recovering from wounds. Some formations were units broken on the eastern front and reformed with a mixture of unreliable conscripts - Poles, Russians and Italians.

Yet, by contrast, there were good and experienced soldiers peppered amongst the pack and one of the most highly trained formations was brought in by Rommel. That was the 6th Parachute Regiment. The average age of its soldiers was 17 1/2 years and each one had done at least nine jumps, several in darkness.

Rommel's energetic thickening of the Atlantic Wall defences was not confined to under-water obstacles, mines and concrete. He thickened the defenders too. Reserve infantry was brought forward, sacrificing defence in depth for manpower on the beaches, where he felt it was most needed. Every man in forward units had his own defensive position to go to. In February 1944 he brought the 352nd Division, a 'full attack' formation, from St Lô, and placed it in the area from Arromanches to Carentan. It sat behind the beach the Allies called OMAHA.

Between Rommel's arrival in Normandy in 1943 and 6 June 1944, the German infantry defences, despite all the handicaps imposed by Allied bombing, poor mobility, unfit and unwilling soldiers and differences between commanders, had improved beyond measure. An invasion could not be certain to succeed even though the Allies, thanks to Bletchley Park's breaking of the Enigma codes, which the Germans used to protect all their command radio traffic, knew all of the major German dispositions.

Rommel

In February 1944 Rommel took command of Army Group B under the C-in-C West, von Rundstedt, though he had the right of direct access to Adolf Hitler. His task was to check and progress the Atlantic Wall defences and he rapidly set out on a tour of inspection, beginning in Denmark and then going on to the Scheldt and to the Somme, working south-west across Normandy towards Brest.

To his dismay he discovered that the concrete emplacements that were to form the backbone of the Wall were far from complete and he immediately ordered that other defensive works be instituted on the beaches. These included large wooden stakes with explosive mines or shells

Typical beach obstacles 1944:
Belgian Gate, Tetrahedrons,
Czech Hedgehogs.

attached to them, concrete and metal structures designed to stop landing craft, Czech hedgehogs (large three-dimensional six-pointed stars made by welding or bolting three pieces of angle-iron together), concrete tetrahedrons for anti-tank defence and a variety of other underwater mined obstacles whose purpose was to delay an invading force long enough for it to come under direct fire from the defenders.

Between December 1943 and May 1944, Rommel toured furiously. At first he looked at his whole frontage and then, in February and March 1944, repeated the process, paying particular attention to the area of the Pas de Calais. In April and May he travelled extensively in Normandy, exhorting his men to the utmost effort. Fields that might be used for glider landings were dotted with upright stakes placed sufficiently close together to act as anti-airlanding obstacles - these would become known to the Allies as Rommel's Asparagus.

Rommel's efforts in Normandy immediately before the Allied Invasion may just have been coincidence, or prompted by Hitler's spring inspiration that the Allies would land on the Brittany and Cotentin Peninsulas. On 6 May Hitler insisted that the defences on the Normandy coast and in the area of Cherbourg should be strengthened. Rommel told the 7th Army, and the 91st Division was diverted from Nantes to Normandy with, under command, 6th Para Regiment and other units. Their role was plainly stated - defence against airborne landings.

Thus, barely a month before two US airborne divisions were due to drop on the Cotentin, behind the beach code-named UTAH, it was reinforced by troops whose main role was anti-airlanding.

On 9 May Rommel noted in his daily report, 'Drive to the Cotentin Peninsula which seems to have become the focal point of the invasion'. He drove to Houlgate on the coast to the east of Merville, then to Caen for a briefing by senior officers, including the commander of 21st Panzer Division. After lunch he toured the area covered by 716th Infantry Division whose beaches the Allies called GOLD, JUNO and SWORD. Next he visited the concrete casemated naval battery at Longues and then via Grandcamp and Isigny went on to St Lô for dinner.

On 20 May at his HQ at La Roche Guyon, 30 miles west of Paris, Rommel interviewed two British Commando officers who had been captured in the 15th Army area during a raid exploring beach obstacles. They should have been turned over to the SS but Major General Speidel, Rommel's Chief of Staff, brought them to Rommel who sent them on to a prisoner-of-war camp, which probably saved their lives. What the Field Marshal did not find out was that their names were Lieutenant Roy Woodbridge and Lieutenant George Lane and that their unit was No 10 (Inter-Allied) Commando. Just over 2 weeks later No 10 Commando landed on SWORD Beach near Ouistreham. Forty years later George Lane re-visited La Roche Guyon and stood on the same spot where the Field Marshal had interviewed him.

On 3 June Rommel went to see von Rundstedt to talk over his proposed visit to Germany during 5-8 June, when he intended to ask Hitler for two more armoured divisions to be transferred to Normandy.

At 0600 hours on 4 June, in rain and wind, Rommel left for Germany. He was going home for his wife's birthday

Two Very Curious Things

In 1812 the Prussian military philosopher Carl von Clausewitz wrote a paper which led to the formulation of twelve principles of war that he believed were essential to success. One of them was 'Surprise'.

Clearly the **Deception Plan** which was designed to fool the Germans into thinking that the invasion would come across the shortest sea route towards Calais and not towards Normandy was how the Allies were going to achieve 'Surprise'. But two very curious things happened before D-Day that must have given them great concern that the secret had been leaked. The curious things were: -

ONE: On 2 May 1944, barely a month before D-Day, the answer to a clue in the *Daily Telegraph* **crossword** was "Utah". Then on the 22nd of May the answer to a clue in the crossword was "**Omaha**". On the 27th of May an answer was "**Overlord**". Then on the 30th an answer was "**Mulberry**" (the codeword for the floating harbours that were to be towed across the Channel).

Finally, on 1 June an answer was "**Neptune**" (this was the Naval codeword for the invasion). Startled by the public appearance of so many secret invasion codewords two MI5 men visited the compiler, Leonard Dawe, the Headmaster of Strand School in Effingham, but apparently found no evidence of espionage. One explanation was given many years later by a former pupil of Dawe's who said that the Headmaster allowed boys to help him with the crossword and that he, the boy, had learned the words from Canadian and American soldiers camped near the school. What do you think?

TWO: The Deception Plan was designed to mislead the Germans into both when and where the invasion would take place. 'When' was difficult to conceal. Indeed on 18 May German radio broadcast that, 'The invasion will come any day now'. So they were expecting it. But they were not certain 'where' it would be. Yet on 27 May, the day that the *Telegraph* crossword contained the word "Overlord", the magazine John Bull published their 'Old Bill' cartoon by the famous First World War cartoonist Captain Bruce Bairnsfather. Old Bill is pointing to a map of

That's where Eisenhower's goin' to land.'

Europe drawn on the side of a cow and is saying to his companion, "If yer asks me mate, that's where Eisenhower's going to land, right there!" He is pointing to the middle of the Normandy Landing Beaches. Very curious.

SOME D-DAY STATISTICS

The following tables are an amalgam from German, American and British sources and do not claim any absolute accuracy. They are designed only to give a comparative indication of factors that, relative to one another, help to put what happened into perspective.

ALLIED & GERMAN AIR & SEA STRENGTHS EFFECTIVE IN THE INVASION

D-Day *only*	Allied	German
Small ships and landing craft	4,270	3
Warships	600	NIL
Available Bombers	2,200	70
Available Fighters	5,000	90

AMERICAN LANDINGS AND CASUALTIES

D-Day *only*	82nd AB*	101st AB*	UTAH	OMAHA
Total landed	7,000	6,600	23,250	34,250
Total casualties	1,240	1,260	210	3,880

BRITISH AND CANADIAN LANDINGS AND CASUALTIES

D-Day *only*	GOLD	JUNO	SWORD	6AB*
Total landed	25,000	21,500	29,000	6,000
Total casualties	413	925	630	1,200

Note: casualties include killed, wounded and missing.
* Airborne Brigades

STOP PRESS

This section lists several of the most important new memorials, changes in museums and Visitors' Centres etc in the Itinerary stops since the last updated edition of this book, with the name, the GPS and page number of each stop featured. There is also a listing of other major Museums with their websites so that the reader can check for news, opening times etc.

Hotels and restaurants also change, so it is advisable to check in advance with the relevant local Tourist Office.

In the heading of existing Itinerary stops which include such changes there is a Red Square ■ and number directing them to the listing below. It replaces the usual black spot. It also occasionally appears mid-paragraph.

■ No. 1. BRITISH NORMANDY MEMORIAL
MESSAGE FROM NICHOLAS WITCHELL,
Trustee/Secretary Normandy Memorial Trust

It has taken 75 years but, finally, there is to be a national memorial on the D-Day beaches dedicated to the part played by the United Kingdom in securing the freedoms of western Europe.

Alone among the major wartime allies, Britain has not had its own D-Day/Normandy memorial. In the words of HRH the Prince of Wales such a national memorial is "long overdue". To address that omission and, most importantly, to fulfil the ambitions of the remaining Normandy Veterans, the Normandy Memorial Trust was formed in 2016.

The support of the British government was secured through a grant of £20 million from the LIBOR fund.

The trust retained the architect Liam O'Connor, creator among other things of the acclaimed Bomber Command Memorial in London, and asked him to design the memorial.

Work was begun to bring together the names of the 22,442 servicemen and women under direct British command who lost their lives in the landings and in the subsequent Battle of Normandy. This has been an original and important piece of historical research. All the names will be inscribed on the memorial.

An outstanding site was identified on a hillside overlooking "Gold Beach" in the town of Ver sur Mer. The choice of site was overwhelmingly endorsed by Normandy Veterans consulted by the trust.

The site's spectacular position above Gold Beach has meant that it is subject to tight environmental and planning restrictions. The trust has been working closely with the local and regional authorities to secure the necessary planning permissions.

The formal inauguration of the site is scheduled to take place on 6 June 2019 as part of the 75th Anniversary of D-Day. The French President and British Prime Minister have publicly committed themselves to attend this ceremony when a Foundation Stone will be laid and the "D-Day Sculpture" by British sculptor David Williams Ellis will be unveiled.

Construction work will begin after the inauguration. It's hoped to have the Memorial in place for June 2020.

At the same time the trust has launched a public appeal, "the 22,442 campaign" to raise the further funding needed to complete the memorial to the standard that is appropriate.

The D-Day anniversary is a significant moment for Europe to look back and reflect on its recent history. The British Normandy Memorial will help to ensure that future generations are fully aware of the sacrifice made by Britain so that Europe might be free from tyranny.

For more details or if you want to support the British Normandy Memorial please go to www.normandymemorialtrust.org

See artist's impression of the Memorial on double spread title page.

■ *No. 2. The D-Day Story (previously Portsmouth D-Day Museum), Clarence Esplanade. Page 28*
Opened in March 2018 under the new name of the D-Day Story, there has been a £5m revamp of the D-Day Museum, which includes three new exhibition galleries, a café and shop.

Some important exhibits have been conserved, such as the Overlord Embroidery, landing craft and beach armoured recovery vehicles (BARVs), and it also includes objects not previously displayed, like the pencil used by Lt Cdr John Harmer to sign the order for Force G – the Naval forces that went to Gold Beach. He shaved off part of the pencil end to create a flat surface upon which he wrote, "This pencil started the invasion".

According to Jane Mee, head of Portsmouth City Council Museums, the aim of the new Museum is to involve the remaining Normandy Veterans in telling their stories and to ensure the D-Day Story maintains the international significance it deserves as the event begins to pass from living memory into history. It also enables new audiences to engage on a personal level with the remarkable events of the D-Day Landings through a unique and dramatic film using archive material to bring back memories of the wartime years.

Contact: Tel: 023 9288 2555. E-mail: theddaystory@portsmouth.gov.uk See website for opening hours and more info: www.theddaystory.com

Interior of D-Day Story Museum, Portsmouth showing REME Beach Armoured Vehicle (BARV) named Vera (based upon a Sherman which was built in Ohio) which took part in the D-Day Landings.

■ *No. 3. US Airborne Musée, Ste Mere Eglise. Opening of Douglas C47 'Argonia' Hangar. Lat & Long: 49.40834 -1.31537. Page 56.*
Note that there have been many new features in the Museum, including the high tech **'Histopad'** which transports the visitor to take part in the dramatic events of June 1944 through an interactive tablet using archive film, photos, maps etc. Bricks may be purchased

to honour individual veterans on a commemorative wall, part of the Reagan Legacy, see www.Reaganlegacyfoundation.org
Contact: Tel: (0)2 33 41 41 35. See website for opening hours and more information: https// www.airborne-museum.org

■ *No. 4. Higgins Boat Memorials, UTAH Beach Museum. Lat & Long: 49.40318 -1.9619. Pages 79-84.*
On 6 June 2015 a statue of Andrew Jackson Higgins was unveiled in the Museum beside an original of his invention, the Landing Craft Vehicle Personnel (LCVP). These are small, wooden, flat-bottomed boats which can operate in 2 ft of water so troops can land directly on a beach.

Thousands of Higgins's boats were used along 5 landing beaches in Normandy on 6 June 1944, causing Gen Eisenhower to proclaim Higgins as 'The man who won the war... If Higgins had not designed and built these LCVPs we never could have landed on an open beach. The whole strategy of the war would have been different.' On the beach is a Memorial showing 3 bronze figures running off an LCVP with a small memorial to Higgins beside.

Note the new features in the Museum including the interactive guide using your own iphone or tablet (in 9 languages) and the film 'Victory Beach' with many moving personal stories.
Contact: for opening times and news: www.utah-beach.com

Flight Engineer of C47 'Argonia', John J. Ginter, standing beside the aircraft, tells his emotional recollections of 5 June 1944 to Tonie Holt in June 1983.

American troops running off a Higgins Boat on Utah Beach. Inset, Bust of Andrew Jackson Higgins.

Artist's impression of D-Day Experience, Dead Man's Corner.

■ *No. 5. Dead Man's Corner/D-Day Experience/Paratrooper Militaria Emporium, St Côme. Lat & Long: 49.32857 1.26841. Pages 100 & 107.*

To the original Dead Man's Corner building has been added the D-Day Experience site. See https://dday-experience.com This moving, interactive experience tells the story of the flight and drop through the eyes of 101st AB Col Wolverton. He also introduces historical objects such as Gen Eisenhower's jacket etc. In the grounds are artillery and defence equipment and an Airborne Wall where visitors may sponsor commemorative stones for individual paratroopers. Work is ongoing.

■ *No. 6. Normandy Victory Museum. Lat & Long. 49.30440 -1.19303. Page 109.* Parc d'Activités on A10 Airfield, PA La Fourchette, Ave du Cotentin, 50500 Catz. **Contact**: Director Kevin Meyer. Tel : + (0)2 2371 7494. E-mail: info@normandy-victory-museum.com Website: www.normandy-victory-museum.com

Opened in May 2017 on the WW2 A10 Airfield, this new Museum replaces the Normandy Tank Museum which was based on the collection of ex-Air France pilot and collector extraordinaire Patrick Nerrant and his sons Patrick and Olivier which opened on 31 July 2013 and closed in 2016. Many of their aeroplanes and tanks were sold and the museum now concentrates on **Life under the Occupation** and the **Battle of the Hedges**, with some fascinating dioramas and show cases with 10,000 genuine items on display (including an Enigma machine) 100 mannequins and 20 vehicles. Rides in an armoured vehicle are still offered and there is an 'A10 Restaurant' and boutique.

Entrance to Normandy Victory Museum, with M4 Sherman Tank.

■ No. 7. Normandy Overlord Museum – Omaha Beach. Lat & Long: 49.34768 -0.85668. Page 137

At roundabout by avenue leading to the American National Cemetery, St Laurent. Inaugurated 5 June 2013 in the presence of British and US Normandy Veterans, this vast, architect-designed building houses the private collection of L'Aigle farmer, Michel Leloup, who was 15 years old at the time of the D-Day landings. The collection consists of 20,000 items, as diverse as small personal objects, uniforms and ephemera to large and rare (some unique) examples of great tanks, armoured vehicles, landing craft, V1 Flying bomb, reconnaissance plane, artillery pieces, soft skin vehicles, Bailey Bridge, all expertly restored. The mannequins in this Museum are extraordinarily life-like, notably a figure of "Monty". Large landscaped grounds with open-air exhibits and parking space. Well-stocked boutique. Videos, audio guides and computer graphics. Michel died in 2011, but his project has been beautifully realised and presented by his son, Nicolas, curator and custodian. **A new extension opens in 2019.** **Contact:** for current opening times and news, see www.overlordmuseum.com E-mail: n.leloup @overlordmuseum.com Tel: + (0) 2 31 22 00 55

Amphibious Sherman Tank, Normandy Tank Museum, Catz.

■ No. 8. Piper Bill Millin Statue, Colleville-Montgomery. Lat & Long: 49.29304 -02875. Page 252.

Sadly, our dear friend Bill, died on 18 August 2010, age 88, so did not see the fine tributes paid to him on 8 June 2013 on the occasion of the unveiling of his splendid bronze statue, sculpted by Gaëtan Ader. A large crowd, including Normandy Veterans, RBL Veterans, local dignitaries, led by project initiator Serge Athenour, came to witness the unveiling as Serge ceded his position as President of the Piper Bill Millin D-Day Association to Bill's son, John. Several Pipe Bands added Scottish colour to the proceedings which terminated with the fly past of a Spitfire.

The fine statue to Piper Bill Millin, Colleville-Montgomery, sculpted by Gaëtan Ader.

■ No. 9. NATIONAL ARBORETUM, Nr Alrewas, Staffs. Lat & Long 52.7311 -1.7227.

Opened May 2001 in a 150-acre site, it now contains over 350 Memorials and is increasingly the site of national commemorative events.

On 4 July 2013 a Memorial to Combined Operations (GPS 52.7311 -1.7227) was unveiled in the NMA by Gen Sir Richard Barrons, Cdr Joint Forces Command in the presence of 35 WW2 Veterans. Unfortunately the memorial began to deteriorate and on 24 September 2014 a **Normandy Campaign Memorial** was unveiled by HRH the Duke of Gloucester to commemorate the 70th Anniversary of D-Day in the presence of some 600 veterans and guests. Designed by sculptor Ian Stewart, the Memorial is

Normandy Campaign Memorial, National Arboretum with Parade Marshal for Standards.

based on the geographical undulations of the Normandy coastline. It was funded by the Spirit of Normandy Trust and the Normandy Veterans' Association.

Contact: For opening hours and news, see www.thenma.org.uk Tel: 01288 245100. E-mail: info@thenma.org.uk

75th D-DAY ANNIVERSARY COMMEMORATIONS

For events in the UK and in Normandy consult:

MOD. https://www.gov.uk/government/news/d-day-75-events-to-mark-75th-anniversary-of-normandy-landings-announced

RBL. https://www.britishlegion.org.uk/community/d-day-75

WEBSITES OF OTHER IMPORTANT MUSEUMS
FOR LATEST NEWS, OPENING TIMES ETC.

■ *No. 10.* Arromanches Musée du Débarquement: www.musee-arromanches.fr Page 174
■ *No. 11.* Bayeux Battle of Normandy Memorial: www.bayeuxmuseum.com Page 156
■ *No. 12.* Caen Mémorial: www.memorial-caen.fr Page 39
■ *No. 13.* JUNO Beach Centre: www.junobeach.org Page 224
■ *No. 14.* Merville Battery: www.batterie-merville.com Page 292
■ *No. 15.* Musée le Mur de l'Atlantique: www.museegrandbunker.com Page 256
■ *No. 16.* Pegasus Memorial Museum: https://musee.memorial-pegasus.com Page 277
■ *No. 17.* Pointe du Hoc Visitor Centre: www.abmc.gov/news-events/news/pointe-du-hoc-visitor-center Page 120

CREDITS

For information and for providing images for this Stop Press Section, we acknowledge the invaluable help of:

a. Severine Diaz, Directrice of the UTAH Beach Museum. (Higgins Boat images).

b. Danielle Duboscq www.normandyours.com and Trevor Standefer www.american-dday-tours.com trevor.standefer@gmail.com, a French-American who, as well as running in-depth tours of the American Sector, also caters for the British Sectors. (Research/information).

c. Philippe Pramil of AMI 76 French Modelling Assoc. (Normandy Victory Museum Image).

d. Ben Revell of the Lincoln Branch Royal Signals Assoc. (Normandy Campaign Memorial National Arboretum Image).

e. D-Day Story, Portsmouth. (Interior of Museum Image).

Approach One

PORTSMOUTH – CHERBOURG / CAEN

Portsmouth

As a prelude to a visit to the Normandy Beaches, an overnight stay in the interesting city of Portsmouth is thoroughly recommended. Known as 'The Waterfront City', its 800 years of history are excellently recorded and presented in the city's numerous museums, preserved sites and famous ships.

The Romans, the Normans, Henry VIII, Lord Nelson, Conan Doyle, Palmerston, Dickens - all made their mark. In 1944 Portsmouth was the area from which Force 'S' and Force 'J' set sail, and in the area beyond Havant, west to Christchurch and including Winchester, was the pre-Invasion assembly area of XXX BR Corps.

The troops were confined in sealed camps and security was, in theory, very tight. Throughout the area vast dumps of supplies, vehicles and ammunitions mushroomed. Local airfields were humming with activity. More than 11,000 aircraft - Typhoons, Mosquitos and Thunderbolts - were massing to provide air cover and undertake bombing raids. Bomber Command was to drop 5,000 tons on coastal batteries in Normandy in 7,500 sorties. Parts of the mysterious caissons which were to make up the revolutionary Mulberry harbours were being assembled. It was all a secret difficult to keep from observant locals.

In 1941 Churchill's advice to Mountbatten was 'The South Coast of England is a bastion of defence against Hitler's invasion; you must turn it into a springboard to launch an attack.' On 5 June 1944 that order became reality. Portsmouth is proud of its vital role in that springboard and today preserves the memory in its many well maintained museums.

Southwick House.

Portrait of Admiral Bertram Ramsey which hangs next to the Map Room.

VISITOR Information Centres

Visitor number is 02392 826722.

There are visitable centres at **The Hard** (at the entrance to the Historic Dockyard) and at **Southsea Seafront** (next to Blue Reef Aquarium). They can book hotels, provide information and literature on entertainment, events, sports, museums, harbour trips, tours and guides to historic Portsmouth, and Southsea.

■ *No. 2. D-Day Museum, Clarence Esplanade*

This is a *must* before crossing the Channel to Normandy. Housed in a modern, custom built exhibition area, its centrepiece is the impressive Overlord Embroidery. It is comparable to the Bayeux Tapestry in its concept. It was commissioned by Lord Dulverton, designed by Sandra Lawrence and made by the Royal School of Needlework in 1968, who took 5 years to complete the 83m (272ft) long embroidery. It depicts the preparations for Operation OVERLORD, the 6 June Invasion and the Battle for Normandy. When Bill Millin, Lord Lovat's piper who piped the Commandos over the beaches, first saw the embroidery he pointed out a mistake. He had been pictured wearing a steel helmet - the Commandos wore berets. The picture was changed. There is an audio-visual theatre showing the D-Day Landings, and exhibits using modern techniques. **Open: daily** (except 24-26 December) but opening times vary with the seasons. Tel: 02392 827261 e-mail: mvs@portsmouthcc.gov.uk website: www.ddaymuseum.co.uk Entrance fee payable. Access for the disabled.

Vivien Mallock Statues

In the road in front of the Museum are two fine bronze statues, one a 7 foot high figure of Field Marshal Montgomery wearing his field-marshal's uniform with his favourite flying jacket over it, with one thumb tucked informally into the pocket, the other hand holding his army commander's orders for the day. Monty was garrison commander in Portsmouth (1937-38), he planned his D-Day strategy in a house on the outskirts of the city and left Portsmouth to land in Normandy with the British invasion force. The other is a 6 foot 1 inch high figure of a seated, 18 year old boy soldier, called 'Ted' by the sculptress, who symbolises "every mother's son" reading a letter from home. The plinth is inscribed with the poignant quatrain

> Decades of easy peace may go their way
> And tide, and time, may drift us far apart,
> But you who shared our savage yesterday
> Will hold the highest places in our heart.

Commissioned by Portsmouth City Council, they were unveiled by the Duke of Kent on 4 June 1997. Monty cost £15,000 and Ted £18,000. Funds were raised by the Normandy Veterans Association and other veterans' associations, individuals and the business community. The statue of Monty is identical to that in Colleville-Montgomery (qv). The statues were all sculpted by Vivien Mallock (qv), wife of Colonel Russ Mallock, a member of the Airborne Trust which commissioned the fine bronzes which are a striking feature on sites in Normandy. They took three months to research and complete. Vivien's studio adjoins the Thruxton MFH Art Foundry of Mike Fry, who cast the figures of all these personalities of the Normandy Campaign. Vivien sculpted the last bust of HM Queen Elizabeth, the Queen Mother, in 2001.

Portsmouth Historic Dockyard.

Recorded Infoline Tel: 02392 861512/Visitor Centre Tel: 02392 722562. Website: www.historicdockyard.co.uk – for details of opening times/ticket prices to the following:
The Royal Naval Museum/HMS *Victory*/*Mary Rose* Museum/HMS *Warrior* 1860/HMS *M33* (last Gallipoli 'Monitor')
Action Stations/Harbour Tours
Old Portsmouth Fortifications
Contact the Visitor Information Centres for details of guided walks.

Portchester Castle
Open: daily (except 24-26 December, 1 January) but opening times vary according to season.
Tel: 02392 378291.
Portsmouth Cathedral (St Thomas's)
D-Day memorial window, unveiled by the Queen Mother on 6 June 1984.
Burma Star Window. Cathedral Book Shop. Tel: 02392 823300. Website:
www.portsmouthcathedral.org.uk **Open: daily** between services.
Royal Marines Museum, Eastney
A marvellous museum, with relevance to the Normandy Campaign - over 17,500 Royal
Marines took part in the Landings - on board ship and on land.
Open: daily 1000-1700 (except 24-26 December) Tel: 023 925 19354. E-mail:
info@royalmarinesmuseum.co.uk website: www.royalmarinesmuseum.co.uk
Royal Navy Submarine Museum, Gosport
Open: daily 1000 hours (except 24 December – 1 January) Tel: 023 925 10354. E-mail:
admin@rnsubus.co.uk website: www.nmrn.org.uk/submarinemuseum
Southsea Castle (shares car park with D-Day Museum)
Open: daily October-March, opening times vary with the seasons. Tel: 023 928 41625. E-mail:
info@southseacastle.co.uk website: www.southseacastle.co.uk
Southwick House: D-Day Wall Map
The D-Day Map Room may be visited BY STRICT APPOINTMENT ONLY with "Flagship
Training". Tel: Mr Bill Todd on 023 9228 4404.

In 1941 Southwick House was requisitioned as a wartime residence and the School of
Navigation moved there. The Action Information Training Centre was built in 1943 and the first
control room completed in 1944.

On 26 April 1944 Admiral Sir Bertram Ramsay, Naval Commander for Operation
OVERLORD, established his headquarters in Southwick House and by 1 June Montgomery
parked his famous caravan in the grounds.

It was from the house at 0415 hours, 5 June, that General Eisenhower said, 'Let's go' - the
signal to commence the mighty invasion. In the run up to D-Day the Supreme Commander had
been making daily shuttles between here and his main headquarters at Bushey Park via his Air
Headquarters at Stanmore. His driver was the English girl Kay Summersby, the former model for
the Worth fashion house, with whom it was rumoured he was having an affair. In her book, *Past
Forgetting*, written when she was dying of cancer and when one might imagine she would have
no motivation to hide the truth, Kay asserts that they were indeed lovers. Whatever the truth of
the matter she paints a picture of a charming and very human Commander-in-Chief and gives an
insight into the overwhelming pressures that lay on the shoulders of just one man. These
pressures led to Eisenhower writing in his own hand a note accepting full responsibility for the
failure of the invasion. Oddly he dated it July 5, an indication perhaps of the inner turmoil he
must have been undergoing. The note said -

'Our landings in the Cherbourg - Havre area have failed to gain a satisfactory foothold and
I have withdrawn the troops. My decision to attack at this time and place was based upon
the best information available. The troops, the air and the Navy did all that Bravery and
devotion to duty could do.

If any blame or fault attaches to the attempt it is mine alone.'

The great D-Day Wall Map, on which the progress of the Invasion was to be charted, was made
of plywood by the Midlands toy company, Chad Valley, in May. The two men who installed the
map were not allowed to go home after they had completed their work, despite the fact that the
area displayed ranged from Norway to Spain, but were held there without access to the outside
world until the invasion was under way! It can still be seen, with the D-Day weather maps, in
the Map Room here, together with a painting by war artist Norman Wilkinson of the assault

5TH/6TH JUNE 1944

Just after midnight on 5th June, the first paratroopers and gliders land.
Seaborne commandos led by the piper of their Brigadier Lord Lovat link up
with the paratroopers on the afternoon of 6th June.

Panel 17 of the D-Day Tapestry, showing the action at Pegasus Bridge in the D-Day Museum, Portsmouth.

Sculpture of a WW2 soldier by Vivien Mallock outside the D-Day Museum, Portsmouth.

forces going into GOLD Beach and other action scenes. The map and the room fell into disuse after D-Day and it was not until the war was over that the operations room was restored. One of the best impressions of the atmosphere of the room during its heyday can be obtained from the painting *Headquarters Room* by the official war artist Barnett Freedman. The adjoining room has been converted into a memorial to Admiral Sir Bertram Ramsay.

THE CHANNEL CROSSING

DUE TO THE UNCERTAINTY OF THE EFFECT OF BREXIT ON DEPARTURE TIMES ETC PLEASE CONSULT THE RELEVANT WEBSITE/TEL NO.

BRITTANY FERRIES

Reservations/Prices/Sailing Times - Tel: 0330 159 7000. E-mail: reservations@brittanyferries.com
Website: www.brittanyferries.co.uk
On all Ferry Services there is a choice of restaurants/bars/Duty Free shopping. Check-in 30 minutes before departure.
Portsmouth-Caen. From Continental Ferryport off the M27 Motorway.
The ferry actually arrives at the Port of Ouistreham (qv). Then take the D514 to Caen (approximately 10 minutes).
Portsmouth-Le Havre. Crossing time: 5 hours 30 mins.
Ferry Service. Crossing Time: 6-7 hours. .
Normandie Express High Speed Service. Crossing time 3 hours 45 minutes.
Poole-Cherbourg. From the Terminal off B3068 from the M3/M27/A31/A35 (avoiding the lifting bridge).
Ferry Service. Crossing time: 5 hours 15 minutes.
High Speed Service. Crossing Time: 2 hours 15 minutes.
Portsmouth-Cherbourg. Crossing time: 5 hours 15 minutes.

Ferry Service: Crossing time: 5 hours.
Normandy Express Service. Crossing time: 3 hours.

FRENCH DRIVING REQUIREMENTS.
For current rules, consult the RAC site https://www.rac.co.uk/drive/travel/country/France/

Cherbourg

Cherbourg is not included in any of the Itineraries as it did not figure in the D-Day Landings on 6 June. However, it was a vital factor in the invasion planning and is therefore briefly described here. Cherbourg is at the tip of the Cotentin Peninsula. It can be visited at the end of the Channel crossing to Cherbourg in Approach One or as an Extra Visit from Valognes in Itinerary One.

That a major port should be included in the landing beaches area was always a vital factor. The beaches of Normandy were particularly suitable as they included two - Cherbourg and le Havre - although following the lessons of Dieppe neither was in the initial assault area. Both were considered vital to the success of OVERLORD, as Cherbourg alone was not considered capable of supporting the twenty-nine combat divisions to be put in the lodgement area. At first it was thought that Cherbourg should be taken by the eighth day by the Americans who had landed by sea at OMAHA and UTAH, and those who were due to drop behind UTAH. The US 1st Army's main task was 'to capture Cherbourg as quickly as possible'.

That Cherbourg and le Havre were spared from heavy Allied air attacks in the spring of 1944 was a clue to the Germans that the invasion might take place on the beaches between them. Hitler ordered strong defences in this area, envisaging some 40 strongpoints facing the sea and 80 covering the land approach, and this was enthusiastically implemented by Rommel although neither port received the two heavy gun batteries that German Navy plans had specified they should have. Troops were ordered into the Cotentin in May, but few defensive positions in the area were completed, especially the *Zweite Stellung* (Second positions) due to be constructed as a further defensive line a few kilometers in from the coast, which Rommel ordered to be abandoned in May in order to concentrate on defences further forward.

When the strength of German reinforcement of the Cotentin was appreciated, probably from information supplied from Bletchley Park, the date for taking the port was revised to D+15, i.e. 21 June.

Following the invasion, the Americans reached Valognes, on the N13 road, a bare 13 miles from Cherbourg, on 19 June. Hitler had flown from Berchtesgaden to meet von Rundstedt and Rommel on 17 June at Soissons. Sensing defeat, a furious Hitler pronounced that 'Cherbourg be held at all cost'.

Between 25,000 and 40,000 Germans, including Todt Organisation and naval personnel, were locked in the peninsula as the US V11 Corps swung around from Barneville on the west coast of the peninsula, to which they had fought after landing at UTAH, and headed directly north for Cherbourg. During 20 June, the Germans hastily reformed their 'Landfront' into four regimental *'Kampfgruppen'*. All were understrength and weary, their combat efficiency low.

On 21 June the US 8th and 12th Infantry Regiments had fought their way into the edges of the main Cherbourg defences. One of their first missions was to flush out a suspected V1 weapon launching site near Bois de Rondou (to the right of the N13 on the D56 at le Mesnil au Val). Remnants of the installation can still be seen today.

On the evening of 21 June US VII Corps was ready for the final assault. Cherbourg's capture had become even more vital because of a heavy four-day storm in the Channel which blew up on 19 June and which seriously disrupted troop and supply landings on the captured beaches.

The artificial harbour at OMAHA was completely destroyed and Admiral Hall, the naval commander at OMAHA, decided not to attempt to rebuild it. General Collins ordered a renewed attack on Cherbourg, which should be 'the major effort of the American army', with 'air pulverization'. The air attack with four squadrons of RAF Typhoons, followed by six squadrons of Mustangs plus twelve groups of US 9th Air Force fighter bombers, went in at 1240 on 22 June, their object to demoralise the enemy. The bombing went on continuously for an hour and involved 375 aeroplanes. The previous night General J. Lawton Collins commanding VII Corps broadcast a message demanding the surrender of Cherbourg by 0900 hours the following morning. General von Schlieben, commanding the mixed force *Gruppe von Schlieben* defending Cherbourg, ignored the 0900 hours 22 June ultimatum. The assault went in.

The US 9th Division with the 60th Infantry and the 47th Infantry attacked on the right. The 79th Division attacked along the axis of the N13 up to the Fort du Roule. The 4th Division was to seal off the city from the east.

General Schlieben's command post was in a vast underground command bunker in the rue Saint Sauveur. On 22 June he received a message from Hitler, 'It is your duty to defend the last bunker and leave to the enemy not a harbour but a field of ruins'. 'Reinforcement is absolutely necessary,' replied the unimpressed General to Rommel.

The fighting nevertheless continued through 23 June, when the outer ring of fortresses was penetrated. On 24 June US VII Corps entered the city itself. Losses were heavy. Lieutenant-Colonels Conrad Simmons (Commander 1st Bn 8th Infantry) and John W. Merrill (Commander 1st Bn 22nd Infantry) were killed, together with many of their men. On 25th June, General Omar N. Bradley brought down a naval bombardment on the Cherbourg batteries from three battleships, four cruisers and screening destroyers. The ships did not escape damage, and during a three-hour duel the battleship *Texas* and the cruiser *Glasgow* were hit with a total of 52 naval casualties.

Schlieben radioed, 'Loss of the City is unavoidable... 2,000 wounded without a possibility of being moved... Directive urgently requested.' Rommel replied, 'You will continue to fight until the last cartridge in accordance with the order from the Führer.'

That day **Corporal John D. Kelly**, who after three attempts took an enemy pill box, and **Lieutenant Carlos C. Ogden**, who destroyed an 88mm enemy gun, were both awarded the **Medal of Honour**. The fort was finally reduced on 26 June. That day too, General Schlieben's underground bunker was discovered in Saint Sauveur. A German prisoner was sent in to ask for surrender. Schlieben declined, but a few rounds from a tank destroyer into the tunnel entrance brought out not only General Schlieben but Admiral Hennecke, Naval Commander Normandy, and some 800 Germans. The next day Schlieben's deputy, General Sattler, formally surrendered the fortress of Cherbourg to Colonel Smythe, Commander of the 47th Infantry Regiment.

The last of the outlying gun batteries fell on 30 June and work on clearing the harbour began immediately with over 100 mines being found in about two weeks, for the loss of three minesweepers and seven other small vessels. The 47th had trained before D-Day in the Alresford area near Winchester and had adopted a dog named Hambone Jr as their mascot. Sadly he died before the Regiment left for France so they buried him with a stone grave marker which says, 'Here lies Hambone Jr, faithful friend of the 47th Inf Regt, 9th Div US Army, May 1944.' The marker is beside the river at Alresford at a walk known as The Dean, which is hard to find. There is a Plaque on the wall of No 50 Broad Street commemorating the HQ of the 47th and a Memorial in Soke Gardens to Capt Robert Cogswell who prevented his B17 from crashing into the village in September 1943.

A D-DAY MEMORY

JOHN TOLD US THIS STORY IN CHERBOURG ON THE 40TH ANNIVERSARY

Lt J.J. Whitmeyer. 9th US Infantry Division. Participated in the capture of Cherbourg.

"I was at that time a lieutenant in the Infantry. We had a schedule about a week or so to go from UTAH Beach to Cherbourg. I think it was due to fall ... in about a week and actually Cherbourg was emptied on the 26th of June and I think the history records may even show that it was captured on the 27th. There was a sergeant in the 314th Infantry, who at that time was a private, who was the first man accredited for mounting the steps of the City Hall in Cherbourg, and this was like 8pm on the 26th June. As I recall his name was Finlay. We had in my own organisation only three Medal of Honour winners and two of those people were awarded the Medal of Honour, the nation's highest award as you are aware, for combat in an operation to take Fort du Roule.

Fort du Roule commanded completely Cherbourg and the success of ever utilising Cherbourg as a harbour. It took a little bit more time to do than the Regimental Commander desired. It took a day and a half, because of an underground bunker as big as a small city - railroad tracks, a number of terraced 88 guns as well as weaponry that the German used, and it required a sergeant - Hurst was his last name - from E company of my battalion to lower charges by way of a rope into the apertures to silence the gun that was firing onto the main railroad terminal area. My own particular part in that operation:-

I was on, I believe, the Avénue de Paris - it is or was the main street that leads on down on the railroad terminal and to the docks for the steam ships. This was a major harbour of course, and the Germans on the 23rd of June, as I understand it, were expecting the fort to be captured and knowing the importance to the United States or the Allied armies and navies, decided to make it impossible or to render it useless. They took all of the heavy equipment they could - box cars, locomotives, cranes - whatever heavy equipment they could find - strung it across the entrance into the main terminal, and then dynamited or exploded it in some manner. They also - the ships that were in the harbour - they scuttled them. I can vividly recall crawling across this tangle of steel, and on the outer edge there was a dog tank trap which, as you know, is just a large ditch, in order to get to the beaches. Truthfully, the last pill box as far as I was concerned and when I say the last, it's not the last to fall, but the furthest point on the Cherbourg Peninsula that a pill box was placed, fell to 3rd Platoon of G Company which I commanded. I was unfortunate enough to have one of the privates who was in my unit go on top side in order to lower as a remembrance the Swastika flag that the Germans had flown. It was just a short period of time. I did not have with me what we refer to as a 'walkie talkie' - they weren't any good. They weren't as good as those you can buy for $4 or $6 now in a toy store. If you got anyone on it would be some tank outfit and we really didn't have communications. I can recall sitting down to clean my rifle when some fire was directed on the pill box. I thought it was a counter-attack. The gentleman who had gone top side - this soldier - he came stumbling down the steps. He was shot four times by the 4th Division who was attacking the pill box while we were in it. That is just one of the, you know, mistakes and lack of communication. We did not know and nor did they, who they were and they didn't know who we were. A sergeant by the name of Lepley, about the best soldier I've ever known. He fought in three wars. He climbed through the aperture in which a gun was placed facing the sea and tried to make his way back through that tangle of metal to say, 'Hey quit shooting. You know you're shooting at American troops.' But he didn't come back and so another fellow and myself we did the same thing and that time the fire lifted and we were able to get out this American soldier who had been wounded. And as I understand it with regard to Cherbourg, it took about two weeks for the British engineers, the American engineers - whoever were responsible - not necessarily to clear the scuttled ships but to clear the port and that shortly thereafter in landing the American troops without putting them on landing craft, and were able to dock at one time something like twenty-five vessels and numerous landing craft, and it was a tremendous job on the part of those people who had to make the clearance."

From the ferry terminal continue to the roundabout with the Britannia-like figure and follow green signs to CAEN.

This will take you to the dual carriageway that leads all the way to Caen paralleling the beaches. Originally the N13, it now bypasses the main towns and villages along the route with clearly signed exits to the D-Day sites to be visited. At times it becomes a non-toll Autoroute, the A13 (e.g. as it bypasses Bayeux), and occasionally is signed as the N2013! It is also signed as the E46.

The events of 1944 seem to have low priority and attract little civic attention in Cherbourg but if staying in or visiting the town you should turn left off the N13 signed *Centre Ville* over two bridges to the

TOURIST OFFICE. 2 Quai Alexandre III, near the Avant Port.

Tel: (0)2 33 93 52 02. E-mail: tourisme@ot-cherbourg-cotentin.fr Website: www.ot-cherbourg-cotentin.fr

They will supply a list of events (there are often sailing, windsurfing and other nautical competitions in the summer) and make accommodation bookings.

Conveniently placed by the Gare Maritime on Allée du Pres Menut is the ***Hotel Mercure**. 84 rooms. Tel: (0)2 33 44 01 11. E-mail: H0593@accor.com

On the way out of Cherbourg, en route for Itinerary One, is the **Hotel Campanile, la Glacerie.** 54 rooms. Tel: (0)2 33 43 43 43. E-mail: cherbourg.laglacerie@campanile.fr, and the **Ibis**, Rond Point André Malraux. 71 rooms. Tel: (0)2 33 44 31 55. E-mail: H21160@accor.com

In the town itself there is a wide choice of individual (such as the **Ambassador**, 22 Quai de Caligny, 40 rooms with safe parking nearby. Closed 19 Dec-6 Jan. Tel: (0) 2 33 43 10 00) E-mail: ambassadeur.hotel@wanadoo.fr and the popular **Hotel/Restaurant La Régence**, 42-44 Quai de Caligny. Attractive façade, 21 rooms. Good views. No lift. Closed 22 Dec-15 Jan. Tel: (0)2 33 43 16. E-mail: laregencecherbourg@wanadoo.fr

There are also several group-owned hotels and a large variety of attractive restaurants. Pick up a town plan to direct you to these and to the *Hotel de Ville.*

GOLIATHS being examined by US soldiers.

GOLIATH miniature tank, Fort du Roule Museum.

MUSEUM & MEMORIALS
Memorial and Plaque, Hotel de Ville/Map Ch1, 2.

On the town hall, Place de la République, Cherbourg, there is a **Memorial Plaque to Sergeant William F. Finlay** 39th Regiment, US 9th Division, who was the first US soldier to enter the town hall on 26 June 1944 and who died in action in Germany on 1 April 1945, aged 20. Also in the square is a **Memorial to Civilians** who were deported or shot by the Germans, surrounded by a rose called 'Resurrection'.

Plaque to Sgt Finlay, Cherbourg Town Hall.

Fort du Roule Liberation Museum (Lat & Long: 49.63027 -1.61403) Tel: (0)2 33 20 14 12. E-mail: mairie@cherbourg.fr Website: https://www.cherbourg.fr
To visit the fort from the N13 out of the ferry terminal, turn left at the second traffic lights signed to Fort du Roule and drive up the winding road to the top of the 112m high Montagne du Roule.

On a clear day it is worth a visit simply for the spectacular panoramic views over Cherbourg from the terrace. This **Museum**, housed in a military fort built between 1852 and 1857, underwent extensive renovation and improvement for 1994, with access by lift from the town (look out for signs from the Thémis roundabout area, entering the town on the N13). It has 17 rooms covering 800 square metres on two floors. At the entrance there is a **Plaque to Gen Joseph Lawton Collins**, 1896-1987, who directed the final assault on Cherbourg from this site and a **NTL Totem**, *Objectif un Port.*

Entry is through a reception area with snack facilities and WC and a collection of guide and history books for reference. The exhibition area is on two floors and using contemporary ephemera, artefacts, uniforms and arms, newspaper articles, letters and personal memories it covers human and military themes such as life on the home front and in occupied France, evacuation, rationing, the Hitler Youth Movement, concentration camp life, propaganda, resistance and execution, the landings and the liberation, the Red Ball Express Route and PLUTO. There is a cinema showing original American footage and a film about Children of War. Original maps, posters, photographs, record of Free French forces, well-documented story of the Battle for Cherbourg. There are changing temporary exhibitions.
Open: May-Sept 1000-1200 and 1400-1800, every day except Sun pm/Mon am. During the winter Wed-Sun 1400-1800 or by appointment. Tel: (0)2 33 20 14 12.

Remnants of Atlantic Wall Defensive Bunkers
In the harbour area there are many examples still to be seen of massive German bunkers. For details of the Atlantic Wall remains in and around Cherbourg, see *Cherbourg Sous l'Occupation* by André Picquenot, published by Ouest, France.

PLUTO
The **P**ipe **L**ine **U**nder **T**he **O**cean, qv) was laid from the Isle of Wight to Cherbourg (in four pipe-lines), and connected to underground pipes across the UK to Ellesmere Port. On French soil the lines ran for hundreds of miles close behind the advancing armies with interspersed pumping stations to keep the petrol flowing with more lines being laid later, including fourteen across the Channel to Boulogne.
From Cherbourg follow signs to Caen and join the N13/E46.

NOTE: On this road, which by-passes all the main towns along the route from Cherbourg to Caen, are the start points for all the Main Itineraries in this book (with the exception of Itinerary 5 which runs on from Itinerary 4 on the D514 coastal road).

Approach Two

DOVER-CALAIS-CAEN

Calais

When you are travelling from Calais to Normandy with modern motorways it can take up to 4 hours even at 80mph. The D-Day deception plan involved persuading the Germans that there was a good chance that the landing would take place around here and so German forces were held in readiness in the area. Therefore imagine the problems facing the Germans if they had to move forces to Normandy and how long it would take them to do it. Even without the damage caused by repeated heavy bombing of roads and bridges a normal military convoy travelling on clear roads without being strafed on the way would be lucky to average 12mph. Thus the 'Calais Deception' meant that German forces held around here would take several days to reach Normandy if needed.

THE CHANNEL CROSSING
DUE TO THE UNCERTAINTY OF THE EFFECT OF BREXIT ON DEPARTURE TIMES ETC PLEASE CONSULT THE RELEVANT WEBSITE/TEL NO.

P & O Ferries. From Eastern Docks, Dover, approached from M2/M20.
Reservations/Prices/Sailing Times - Tel: 08716 645645. Website: www.poferries.com. Crossing Time - 90 minutes. Check-in 30 minutes before.
Eurotunnel. From Eurotunnel Passenger Terminus, Folkestone-Cheriton, approached from Exit 11A from the M20. Reservations/Prices/Sailing Times - Tel: 08705 353535. Website: www.eurotunnel.com
Journey time -35 minutes. Check-in 30 minutes before.

FROM PORT TO CAEN
French Driving Regulations - See Approach One.
As the complete journey from Calais can now be made on the Autoroute system, this is the quickest method of reaching Caen for those living in the south-east of England.
Approximate time, without stopping for refreshments, and taking the most clearly signed route to Caen (over the Pont de Normandie): **3 hours 30 minutes.**
Motorway Tolls. This route is quite expensive, the **Pont de Normandie** toll alone being 5 Euros. The alternative routes are via **Pont de Tancarville** or **Pont de Brotonne** (see **Michelin Map** 231 (1:200,000).
Motorway Stops. These are called *Aires*. At the least they provide parking, toilets and a picnic table. The most sophisticated have petrol stations, shops and restaurants. They are signed well ahead with the distance to them and symbols showing the level of facilities. At the motorway toll booths you may pick up a free plan to the SANEF Autoroute system which shows these stops (you have to ask for it). There are also WCs here.

It is advisable to keep your tank topped up with fuel as off the main routes petrol stations are few and far between and have short opening hours. There is an increasing use in petrol stations (especially at motorway stops) of chip and pin cards.

KEY ROUTE WORDS TO LOOK OUT FOR ON ROAD SIGNS ARE IN SEQUENCE: A16/A26
PARIS; A16/E15/E402 BOULOGNE; A28 ROUEN/LE HAVRE; A29/A13, E46 CAEN
Set your mileometer to zero
From the Ferry Port, follow blue motorway signs A16/A26, direction Paris/Reims.
After 4.6 miles Boulogne and Rouen are also signed and the motorway forks.
Fork right on the A16/E15/E402.
After 8.5 miles, the entrance to the Channel Tunnel is signed at Exit 42b. Petrol is signed at Aire des Deux Caps in 10 kms.
If arriving via the tunnel, deduct 9 miles from the following mileages.

By-pass Boulogne and continue direction Rouen-Amiens A16-E402.
After some 14.5 miles Exit 38 to the WW2 CWGC Canadian Cemetery, Leubringhen is signed. In it are buried 3 soldiers whose Memorial is passed later.
At 57 miles the Département of the Somme (the WW1 battlefield covered by *Major & Mrs Holt's Battlefield Guide to the Somme* and *Major & Mrs Holt's Concise Illustrated Battlefield Guide to the Western Front – South*) is entered.
At 63 miles the Battlefield of Crécy is signed.
At 72 miles the motorway forks.
Fork right following the Rouen/Le Havre A28-E402 signs.
At some 108 miles DO NOT TAKE THE A29/E44 SIGNED TO AMIENS, Exit 7.

N.B. At some 113 miles by taking Exit 9, direction Neufchâtel-en-Bray on the D928, after .5 mile on the right is a well-tended **Canadian Memorial** to Robert Edison Andrews, Theodore Pattibone, Colin Carey White, 17th Duke of York's R Can Hussars, 31 August 1944. They are all buried in the Canadian CWGC Cemetery passed earlier (**Lat & Long: 49.72581 1.42582**).

At 114 miles Caen is signed.
At 120 miles the motorway forks. *Fork right following the Caen A29-E44 signs.*
At 130 miles the motorway forks. *Continue towards Le Havre/Caen A29-E44.*
At 140 miles Exit 9 to Yvetot-Est leads to the **Pont de Brotonne** (no tolls) on the D131.
At 167 miles Exit 6 to Bolbec leads to the **Pont de Tancarville** on the A131.
At 172 miles the **Pont de Normandie** is reached (Toll Euros 5.00).
The spectacular **Pont de Normandie** with superb views over the mouth of the Seine was opened in January 1995. Its design by architects C. Lavigne, F. Doyelle and M. Lechevalier, and designer M. Virlogeux, was a technological leap, its 184 staying cables providing incredible wind stability (able to withstand gusts of over 300 kph). Until the 890m Tatara Bridge in Japan came into service in 1999, its 856m central span was the longest in the world. The towers are 215m high and weigh 20,000 metric tons. It cost 2 billion French francs and 1,600 people were involved in its construction. Their names are engraved on the bridge pier. At night this stunning bridge becomes magical, lit up with blue and white lights designed by Yann Kersali who also lit the Champs Elysées and the Golden Gate Bridge.
There is access for walking across the bridge for the wonderful view over the Seine Estuary and the River towards Rouen **[it is absolutely forbidden to stop your car on the bridge to take photos]** from both the Calais and Caen directions. There is an **Exhibition Room** on the Calais side which has boards telling the story of the bridge, photos, a model and a film about the building of the bridge.
Open: daily 0900-1900. No entrance fee. Tel: (0)2 35 19 24 50.
Guided visits are available by appointment. Fee payable. Tel: (0)2 35 24 64 90.
There is also a **bar, restaurant and cafeteria, l'Armada**. **Open daily**. Tel: (0)2 35 53 28 02. Next to it is a souvenir shop with films, books, posters, postcards etc about the bridge. Near the toll building is The Engineers' Garden, with a 8.5m model of the bridge. The names of famous visitors to the bridge, other great bridges and places of interest in Normandy are featured here.

Extra Visit to 6th Airlanding Brigade Memorial, Berville-sur-Mer. (Lat & Long: 49.42817 -0.36143). Round trip: 10 miles. Approximate time: 25 minutes

On crossing the bridge, immediately take Exit 3 from the motorway and at the roundabout take the D580 signed Alencon, Le Mans, then the D312 direction Berville. Pass through Fiquefleur and continue through picturesque countryside with superb views over the Seine Estuary to the left, to the centre of Berville. The memorial is on the lawn in front of the school (next to the Mairie).

The commemorative Plaque, mounted on a rock, was unveiled on 7 June 1997 during an impressive ceremony attended by Veterans of the 1944 6th Airborne Division and of the Piron Brigade, members of today's 6th Airborne, and many local dignitaries. Elements of 6th Airborne liberated the town in their progression from Bénouville to Ranville and on to the mouth of the Seine.

Return to the bridge and rejoin the Approach Route.

Continue on the A29 and follow signs to Caen on the A13-E46.

You are now passing through the picturesque *Pays d'Auge* (see **Tourist Information** at the end of the book).

Continue to Exit 29b (some 212 miles).

Extra Visit to Memorials to 5th, 7th, 12th & 13th Para Battalions, 6th AB Division, Putot-en-Auge (Lat & Long: 49.21785 -0.06737) and Commandos Memorial, Tree of Liberty, Dozulé (Lat & Long: 49.23272 -0.04016) Round trip approximately 6 miles. Approximate time: 30 minutes

Take Exit 29b and turn back over the motorway on the D400 to the junction with the N175. Turn left and continue .5 mile to the junction with the D49, turn right signed Putot-en-Auge. Continue to the Information Board by the Mairie.

The **Information Board and Map** chronicle the Liberation of Putot on 18/19 August and the subsequent fighting around by **6th AB Div** under Maj-Gen R.N. Gale, **5th Para Bde** under Brig Nigel Poett and **4th SS Bde** under Brig P. Luard. Battles for the Station, the *Mairie*, the *Manoir* and the village houses, for Hills 13, 115 and 134 were fought by the 7th (Somerset) Para Bn, the 12th (Yorkshire) Para Bn, the 13th (Lancs) Para Bn, 46th RMC and 48th RMC. It was inaugurated on 6 June 2007 by Maj Jack Watson, MC, of the 13th (Lancs) Para Bn, with the Mayor of Putot. Jack died, age 94, on 14 April 2011 and on 6 June 2011 a Plaque to him was inaugurated on the *Mairie*. In the local churchyard there are 31 CWGC graves from these battles of 19/20 August 1944 and one Pilot of the RAFVR of 13 June 1944.

Return to the N175, turn right and continue into the bustling town of Dozulé to the Gendarmerie on the right. On the opposite corner on rue de Verdun is

The **Memorial** to **Commandos** and **Oak Tree** which commemorate Dozulé's liberation on 21 August 1944 by No 48 Cdo supported by Nos 46 & 47 Cdos in a night attack.

Return to the A13, direction Caen.

At 220 miles take the Périphérique Nord.
At 223 miles is the exit to Caen Centre.
At 226 miles is Exit 7 to the Mémorial Museum.
Exit and follow signs to the Mémorial, on Esplanade Dwight-Eisenhower in the la Folie Couvrechef district. It is well signed.

■ *No. 12. Mémorial: Un Musée Pour la Paix (A Museum for Peace), Caen/ approx 227 miles/1 hour +/Lat & Long: 49.19787 -0.38379 /RWC*

Not surprisingly, after their June and July 1944 suffering, the Caennais [the citizens of Caen] wished their magnificent new museum to be a symbol for peace. It was opened on 6 June 1988 by President Mittérand, in the presence of French and Allied veterans, 150 children of Caen, ten from the USSR, ten from Hiroshima and ten from each of the thirteen countries who fought in Normandy in 1944, whose official representatives laid thirteen symbolic memorial stones in the forecourt. The countries involved were Britain, USA, Canada, Belgium, Greece, Czechoslovakia, Poland, Holland, Norway, Luxembourg, East and West Germany and France. Outside the museum there are two **Normandie Terre-Liberté (NTL) Totems**, describing the martyrdom of the town and its citizens during the bombardment and bombing that preceded their liberation. The latest research puts the civilian casualties at some 3,000.

6th Airlanding Bde Memorial, Berville-sur-Mer.

Memorial to 3 soldiers of the 17th Duke of York's Royal Can Hussars, Neufchâtel-en-Bray. (See page 37).

The vast building (70m (230ft) long, 55m (180ft) wide, 12m (40ft) high) is on three levels and as well as a cinema to seat 170 houses the following:

The Main Hall. Reception area, renovated in 2008 for the 20th Anniversary, self-guided headphone facilities, well-stocked shop, ticket office, cloak rooms, rest area, telex which constantly records any acts of war throughout the world, a World War II Typhoon.

First Floor. Historical journey with milestones of history on a huge cylinder, from ancient times to the present day, with particular emphasis on the pre-war years, the occupation, World War II, the landings, the resistance and the reconstruction. There are several films, including original World War II material and finally a film whose subject is 'Hope' for freedom and human rights. Major exhibitions are regularly mounted.

D-Day Landing and Battle of Normandy

An important new area was opened in Spring 2010.

There are also **Cafeteria, Restaurant,** *bureau de change,* redesigned children's play area and ample parking facilities. The museum uses the most up-to-date audio-visual and computer technology and was funded by fund-raising committees, notably in the USA, and in Britain, Canada, Norway, Germany, and France, supported by the City of Caen and the *Comité du Débarquement.*

Around it is a Memorial Valley, which is approached over a Bailey Bridge. The American Garden has a pool and waterfall, below which is a wall with commemorative stones to the States/Units which took part in the Landings. There is also a Canadian Garden and a Gingko Biloba tree planted by the Dalai Lama on 17 April 1997 and the unique Nobel Peace Prize Gallery which also features the Red Cross, the League of Nations and the United Nations. On 5 June 2004 Prince Charles inaugurated the beautiful British Garden whose centre piece is a Fountain of Spirits, commemorating all those who lost their lives. In the garden are an **RAF Memorial and Plaques** with the badges of all the Divisions which took part in the Landings and the Battle for Normandy, and a striking **Naval (RN and MN) Memorial**. The beautiful engraved glass Memorial was designed by Rear Admiral Frank Grenier (Retd), an ex-submariner, now a distinguished glass engraver. It was commissioned by the 'Friends of the British Garden' whose Chairman is Admiral Sir Desmond Cassidi who served as a sub-lieutenant on HMS *Ramillies* in June 1944. The blue tinted Memorial has cameos of many naval functions including towing PLUTO, Beach Master, barrage balloon, the Mulberry Harbour etc.

The Garden can also be approached past the **Monument to Non-Violence** (in the shape of a revolver with a knotted barrel) and the new **Cold War Exhibition Hall**, made to look like a nuclear shelter. This impressive, highly technical museum is a must, but requires at least two hours for a thorough visit.

Open: daily (except 25 December and 1-14 January) from 0900-1900 (1800 in winter). Tel: (0)2 31 06 06 45. e-mail: resa@memorial-caen.fr. Website: www.memorial-caen.fr Entrance fee payable. Reduction for veterans, children and groups. **All-day visit passes** available which includes a **guided tour of the Landing Beaches,** also tours which include overnight accommodation and start at Caen or Bayeux railway stations.

Rejoin the Périphérique/N13/E46

• End of Approach 2

NOTE: On this road, which by-passes the main towns along the route behind the D-Day Beaches from Caen to Cherbourg, are the start points for all the Main Itineraries in this book (with the exception of Itinerary 5 which runs on from Itinerary 4 on the D514 coastal road). Thus you can move rapidly from the start of one itinerary to another. Coming from Calais you may choose to reverse the order of the Itineraries and it may be convenient to start with Itinerary 6.

From this point you may choose first to visit the city of Caen itself and the important *Mémorial de Caen* Museum.

Caen

Caen was the ambitious D-Day objective of the 185th Infantry Brigade Group of the 3rd British Division, which was not achieved on 6 June. It was not taken by the Allies until 9 July. It was a fearsome and costly period for the citizens of Caen.

The Mémorial, Caen

Air raids continued spasmodically throughout the month of June and into the next, until the dreadful climax of Operation CHARNWOOD 7-9 July. It was the final battle for Caen, preceded by a literally murderous attack on the night of 7 July by Lancaster and Halifax bombers.

Monsieur Poirier, the deputy mayor whose D-Day memory appears below, estimated that there were more than a thousand planes and that the raid lasted 45 crushing minutes. The dead and wounded reached unbearable and untreatable proportions, and many were buried, alive and dead, in the shattered buildings.

During 8 and 9 July the Germans withdrew and in the afternoon of 9 July the French-speaking Canadians of the 3rd Canadian Division entered Caen from the west and the British 59th and 3rd Divisions from the north. They offered cigarettes and chocolates to the citizens, who came out of their ruins, waving their battered *Tricolores*. 'The women kissed them, the men saluted them, but with dignity, without mad exaggeration. We have all suffered too much for our dearest ones to acclaim excessively those who have been forced by the necessity of war to do us so much harm,' commented an exhausted Monsieur Poirier.

Many Allied 'liberators' were appalled at the carnage and destruction as they entered the shattered city. Some seemed oblivious to the extent of the damage.

Monsieur Poirier, who had received the first German officer to enter the town on 18 June 1940, was now greeted by a British officer. They shook hands at length, both had tears in their eyes, and they had a long conversation about the basic needs of the Caennais. Finally, the officer asked if Monsieur Poirier could direct him to a good hotel where he could get a hot bath. 'Brave Major H', commented the deputy mayor, and explained that three-quarters of the city was razed to the ground. Although the worst was past, the fighting raged around the city until, on 15 August, after sixty-five days, the bloody battle for Caen was over.

A D-DAY MEMORY

Monsieur Poirier, *Maire-Adjoint*, responsible for the passive defence of Caen and the efforts of the citizens to survive June-July 1944.

(Permission to reproduce extracts from his moving and graphic account, (reprinted with other, anonymous memories by the *Mairie* of Caen in 1984) has been given by the Documentation Centre of the *Mémorial* Museum of Caen.)

"6 June I was woken up at about two in the morning by the dull, distant yet deafening sound of a bombardment. What is it? There's no doubt whatsoever.

Something's up on the coast. Is it the coastal batteries firing? Are they far off bombs? Could it be the landings? Aeroplanes prowl and sirens sound the alert. It is the 1,020th alert. It's never going to end ... I get up and report to my Passive Defence Command Post in the Central Commissariat's shelter. I call up the sectors, who in turn call their outposts. Everyone's at their post. The wakening population besieges the bakers ... It's the landings we've all been waiting for!

The Boches are taking off. Already! Really one has to smile - we're imagining that it's all going to happen without any pain. About 7 o'clock some bombs drop beside the station. I'm informed of one killed and two wounded. The morning passes calmly, but in the distance is still the bombardment of hundreds of artillery pieces from allied war ships. I lunch hurriedly, because I sense that something new is about to happen.

English planes prowl ceaselessly above the town and at 1300 a large formation of bombers release their bombs on the centre of the town. It is the first air raid of such unprecedented violence. The Caennais are stunned. An unbelievable number of bombs fall

Inauguration of 6TH AB Div Memorial Board, showing Maj Jack Watson with Nicole Asmant and the Mayor of Putot-en-Auge. (See page 38).

Memorial and Oak Tree to Commandos who liberated Dozulé. (See page 38).

Naval Memorial, British Garden, Caen Mémorial.

Monument to Non-violence, Caen Mémorial.

The Mémorial,
Caen.

Memorial to 3rd
BR Div, below
Caen Château.

Plaque to 3rd Can Div, Place de l'Ancienne Boucherie. Caen.

Memorial to Raising of Tricolore &
Caen's Liberators, Pl Mgr des
Hameaux.

D-Day Memory contd from page 41

... my sectors report to me on my special telephone, but already three lines are cut ... Red Cross emergency teams rush to the stricken regions. There are many dead and wounded, and general consternation at the suddenness of the attack. A crowd of terrified people flock into the Command Post and the shelters in the Town Hall cellars. They bring in the wounded and I send them to Bon-Sauveur [a convent], and already atrociously mutilated bodies are brought in... The raid only lasted about ten minutes but the damage is enormous. The Monoprix shop is in flames and there are more than ten homes on fire in the centre.

At 1625 another short raid, but as violent as the 1300 one. Bombs fall in the rue de Caumont, annihilating the annexe to the *Préfecture* ... old St Etienne is hit ... rue de Carel, the bus depôt for Courriers Normand, and all the coaches in it ... the undertakers where we had stored 500 coffins 'our supply for serious emergencies' - reduced to ashes. We won't have a single coffin to bury the dead. Two wards receive fifteen or so one- and two-ton bombs, burying eight nuns and thirty patients under the debris: one of the Sisters and five patients are killed outright. The St Jean Hospice is destroyed. An ambulance driving over the Vaucelles bridge is hit by a bomb, the young Red Cross driver killed and her body thrown into the Orne. Our No 1 first aid post takes a bomb which totally destroys it. Dead and wounded everywhere. Already the Red Cross and other voluntary workers are insufficient for the task. There aren't enough ambulances, not enough stretchers, two first aid posts are out of action. In spite of prodigious acts of devotion, the medical corps cannot look after or operate quickly enough on the wounded that are being constantly brought in.

The fires multiply, a quarter of the town is in flames... During the entire evening we hear the roar of aeroplanes. Doubtless they are observers who are coming to take stock of the results of the raids. The teams of helpers work relentlessly in the rubble to pull out buried survivors who are calling out.

There are so many sad victims that we won't be able to save because of lack of adequate tools and lack of enough helpers."

Caen Memorials. The subject of the bombing of Caen and the subsequent civilian casualties was treated in Antony Beevor's 2009 controversial book, **D-Day: The Battle for Normandy.** Many Memorials exist today as a tragic reminder of the civilian suffering - Caen is known as a 'Martyr Town' – as well as for its Liberation. The Caennais are faithful in their memory to their own dead and to their liberators. Each 6 June and 9 July ceremonies of remembrance and thanksgiving are held, when allied veterans and war widows are warmly welcomed. In 2010 some 50 Memorials/Plaques were identified for us by Thibault Revel, working with *Normandie-Mémoire*, and Julia Quellien. The complete list may be obtained from *Normandie-Mémoire*, 88 rue St Martin, Caen. Below are listed a selection of the most important/accessible memorials. It is advisable to pick up a city plan from the **TOURIST OFFICE** at Place Saint-Pierre (near the Castle) Tel: (0)2 31 27 14 14. Email: tourisminfo@ville-caen.fr Website: www.caen.fr/tourisme **Lat & Long: 49.183860 -0.361425.** The best times for driving through Caen, normally an extremely busy city, beset with many one-way systems, are Sundays and Mondays.

1. **Plaque to 3rd Can Div, 3 July 1944,** Place de l'Ancienne Boucherie. **Lat & Long: 49.184246 -0.37486**

2. **Memorial to Raising of 'Le Drapeau Francais'** & **Caen's Liberators**, Place Mgr des Hameaux. **Lat & Long: 49.18201 -0.37377**

3. **Plaques to 1st Can Soldier Killed in Caen, 18.7.44**: **Bombardier Everitt Ivan Hill**, [age 23, buried Bretteville-sur-Laize CWGC Cemetery], Bvd Bertrand. **Lat & Long: 49.17978 -0.36577**

4. **Memorial to 3rd BR Div who liberated Caen 9 July 1944**, below the Château. **Plaque to French Jewish Soldiers**, on wall of Synagogue opposite. **Lat & Long: 49.18537 -0.36075**

5. **Calvary with Joined Hands to Renaissance of Caen**, Top of Rue de la Délivrande. **Lat & Long: 49.19607 -0./36021**
6. **Monument/Plaques to *Déportés & Fusillés*, Victims of Racial Persecution**, Place de la Résistance; Remains of **Crucifix & Plaque to the Suffering of Caen**, in l'Eglise St Jean. **Lat & Long: 49.18098 -0.35650**

Tourist Information, *Caen*

Consult the **TOURIST OFFICE** (see above) for current information about events. Caen is a thriving city with many cultural and commercial events - notably the annual *Foire de Caen* in September at the *Parc des Expositions*. In the centre is a variety of theatres, cinemas, department stores and speciality shops, bars, restaurants and hotels, e.g:

***Mercure** centre, near Bassin St Pierre, rue de Courtonne. Attractive design. 129 rooms. Tel: (0)2 31 47 43. E-mail: H0869@accor.com 88. Website: www.mercure.com

***Moderne**, Blvd Maréchal Leclerc. Best Western. Centrally located. 40 rooms. Tel: (0)2 31 86 04 23. E-mail: info@hotel-caen.com website: www.bestwestern-moderne-caen.com

***Holiday Inn**, Place Foch. Centrally located. 88 rooms. Tel: (0)2 31 27 57 57. E-mail: holiday-inn-caen@wanadoo.fr website: www.caen-hotel-centre.com

Plaques to E.I Hill, 1st Can Soldier Killed in Caen, Bvd Bertrand.

IBIS Caen Centre, 6 Place Courtonne. 101 rooms. Tel: (0)2 31 95 88 88. E-mail: H1183@accor.com website: www.ibishotel.com

There are also several conveniently sited hotels off the *Périphérique* (N13 ring road), e.g:
***Novotel Cote de Nacre**, Ave. Côte du Nacre. Outdoor swimming pool. 126 rooms. Tel: (0)2 31 43 42 00. E-mail: H0405@ accor.com website: www.novotel.com
Convenient for the *Mémorial* are the hotels in Caen-Hérouville, e.g:
***Mercure Hérouville St Clair**, 2 Place Boston. 88 bedrooms with ensuite shower room. Refurbished 2010. No lift. Pleasant restaurant and bar. Tel: (0)2 31 44 05 05. E-mail: H5712@accor.com website: www.mercure.com
Campanile, Hérouville. Bvd du Bois. Small, but well-equipped rooms. Family run. 66 rooms. Tel: (0)2 31 95 29 24. E-mail: caen-herouville@campanile.fr website: www.campanile-caen-nord-herouville-saint-clair.fr
Ibis Hérouville St Clair. 4 Quartier Savary-Bvd Grand Parc. Small rooms but attractive décor. 89 rooms. Tel: (0)2 31 95 60 00. E-mail: H0605@accor.com website: www.ibishotel.com

ALL THE HOTELS LISTED FOR CAEN ARE OPEN ALL YEAR ROUND

AUX SOLDATS JUIFS
DES ARMÉES ALLIÉES
TOMBÉS POUR LA LIBÉRATION
DE LA FRANCE EN JUIN 1944

A LA MÉMOIRE
DES VICTIMES JUIVES DE LA
BARBARIE HITLERIENNE

03 JUIN 1984   03 SIVAN 5744

Plaque to French Jewish Soldiers, Synagogue wall.

*Calvary to Renaissance of
Caen, rue de la Délivrande.*

Memorial to Déportés, Fusillés, Victims of Racial Persecution, Pl de la Résistance.

*Memorial to the
Victims of Racial
Persecution, Pl de
la Résistance.*

*Plaque to Suffering of
Caen by Remains of
Crucifix, Eglise St
Jean.*

concrete wall on their seaward side. There was no opposition as they crossed the sand, but Brigadier General Theodore Roosevelt, the assistant divisional commander who accompanied the first wave, quickly realised that the Division had landed in the wrong place - 2,000 yards south of where they should have been.

An instant decision was needed: whether to try to correct the mistake by somehow signalling to the following waves out at sea or to accept the situation and continue the operation right there. Roosevelt chose the latter. Cane in hand he strode up and down, exhorting men to get up and off the beach and to move inland. It was a wise decision and one which won him the Medal of Honour. The intended landing place was far more heavily defended than the spot where they had actually landed and though German artillery and small arms fire did sporadically harass the 4th Division as they poured ashore, casualties were very light. Because the landing troops had no need to attempt to find shelter behind beach obstacles, as their comrades were having to do 15 miles to the east on OMAHA, the assault engineers were able to get to work on clearing the shore which they had completed by 0930.

It is unwise to be dogmatic about casualty figures since they are frequently manipulated for propaganda purposes by both sides in a conflict. However, by the end of the day, best estimates suggest that some 23,250 troops had come ashore and only 210 were killed, wounded or missing, less than one-third of those who died in the rehearsal on Slapton Sands.

THE TOUR

• **Itinerary One** starts at Ste Mère Eglise, looks at the 82nd and 101st Airborne Divisions' drop zones, the US 4th Infantry Division's landing at UTAH Beach and the German defensive batteries, ending near Montebourg.

• **The Main Route:** Ste Mère Eglise - Plaques to Gen Gavin & 505th PIR, Airborne Museum and Plaques, C47, Church and Stained Glass Memorials, Com Déb Sig and Mayor Renaud Memorials, Pump, 505th PIR Plaque rue de la Cayenne, Town Hall - Memorials and Kilometer Zero, US Cemetery Marker No 1; La Fière - 'Iron Mike' Statue and *Table d'Orientation*; Gavin's Foxhole; Chef du Pont - US Cemetery Marker No 2; 508th PIR Memorial; Les Forges - US Cemetery Marker No 3; Hiesville - General Pratt Memorial; Ste Marie du Mont - *Musée de l'Occupation, Musée de la Libération*; Signs, SGW; 101st AB Plaque; Exit 2 – Lt Winters Statue, Danish Memorial; UTAH Beach - Museum, US Memorials; St Martin de Varraville - Leclerc and *Comité du Débarquement* Monuments; Batterie de Crisbecq; Batterie d'Azeville; Perrette – 365th Fighter Gp Memorial; Quinéville - 365th Fighter Group Memorial, *Musée de la Liberté Retrouvée*; Montebourg - 4th Div Memorial.

• **Planned duration,** without stops for refreshments or **Extra Visits** or **'N.B.s': 6 hours 45 minutes.**
• **Total distance: 40 miles.**

• **Extra Visits** are suggested to Cauquigny - Chapel and Memorial Plaques; Amfreville – De Glopper MoH and 507th PIR Memorials; Gourbesville – 90th Inf & 82nd AB Divs Memorial; Picauville – ALG 8 Marker, 508th PIR, 9th USAAF, 82nd/101st AB & C47 Memorials; Hiesville - Gen Taylor's 101st AB HQ and Monument to 101st AB Hospital; Hemez – Massacre Memorial; Ecausseville - WW1 Dirigible Hangar.

• **N.B.s** The following sites are indicated: Neuville-au-Plain – 'D'Coy 2nd Bn 505th PIR Memorial; La Londe – 1st USAAC Airfield (A6) Marker; euzeville-au-Plain - Crew of a C47 and 506th PIR; Amfreville – "Timmes' Orchards" Memorial Complex, 'Lazaret von Amfreville Feb-June 1944, Lt Heisler PlChef du Pont Churchyard – Capt Rex Combs & 508th PIR Plaque; Orglandes – US 9th & 90th Divs Memorials, Ger Cem; Néhou – Gen Patton's HQ; L'Angle – Zane Schlemmer, 508th PIR Mem; Beuzeville-la-Bastille, R. Douve – 508th PIR Bridge, Chemin O.B. Hill; Brucheville – US 36th Fighter Gp, ALG 16 Marker; Brécourt Manor - Easy Coy (Band of Brothers) 506th PIR Memorial; Le Buisson – Gen Collins HQ, 1st US Command Post; UTAH

Beach – US Naval Reserve Memorial, Meeting of 4th US Div & 101st AB Div Plaque; The Chapelle de la Madeleine; Foucarville - Ger POW Camp Memorial.

• Ste Mère Eglise/0 miles/60 minutes/RWC/Map It1-1/Holts Map R1-14/Lat & Long: 49.40399 -1.31397

> **N.B** If coming from Cherbourg on the N13, by taking (just before reaching the Ste Mère exit) the D15E1 to the left some 1.5 miles to Neuville-au-Plain, a **Plaque to Coy 'D' of the 2nd Bn, 505th PIR, 82nd AB** (**Map It1-A, Lat & Long: 49.42978 -1.33033/GPPIt1-1/1**) may be seen on the Château wall opposite the Church. It was erected by the 82nd AB C-47 Club Quincy Bde in 2005.

See below for directions if coming from the Bayeux direction.

The approach into Ste Mère from the N13 is the same whether coming from direction Caen or Cherbourg. After taking the Ste Mère exit follow the D67 signed to the town.

It leads to a large sign on the left which proclaims '**6 Juin 1944. D.Day. 505th Airborne. H Minus. Gen J.M. Gavin**' and a crest. In front of the board is a bronze **Plaque** which summarises the story of the 505th's actions on D-Day who liberated Ste Mère Eglise at 0430 hours, listing individual units. Behind it are 5 fir trees. (**Lat & Long: 49.40399 -1.31397**).

Behind is the ** **Hotel le Sainte-Mère** (Logis de France). 41rooms. Tel: (0) 2 33 21 00 30. Email: hotel-le-ste-mere@wanadoo.fr.

Follow the road into the town along rue Général de Gaulle.

On the right at No 16 is **Static Line**, an antique militaria emporium. Tel : (0)2 33 41 02 42. www.staticline.military.com

On reaching the main square, Place 6 Juin, turn right onto rue Eisenhower and park in the car park opposite the church.

On places of historical interest around the town are numbered **Information Panels**. The other sites in Ste Mère Eglise are best visited on a **Walking Tour** (see below). There is a variety of **restaurants, snack bars** and souvenir/book shops in the town. The local speciality is the cheese *Petite Sainte Mère Eglise.*

Ste Mère owes much of its fame to an American called John Steele. Steele was a paratrooper of the 505th PIR of the 82nd Airborne Division and shortly after 0130 hours on the morning of 6 June he, and some thirteen thousand other airborne soldiers, jumped out of over 880 transport planes flying over Normandy. Steele fell onto the church steeple in Ste Mère Eglise, slid down it and then with his parachute caught on a flying buttress hung there for all to see. His story was told in the film, *The Longest Day*. But there is more to the story of Ste Mère Eglise than the adventures of John Steele.

The Germans arrived in the town on 18 June 1940. There was no fighting and over the next four years, despite the occupation of their houses and the huge swastika flag that flew outside the town hall, the inhabitants learned to live with their invaders. As 1943 wore on the number of soldiers billeted in the area began to decrease and there was little other than high prices to remind citizens that there was a war on. Sometimes an occasional Allied aircraft would drop leaflets.

Early in 1944 German anti-aircraft gunners - Austrian and mostly old - moved in, parking their wood-burning trucks in the square but behaving well and without any apparent enthusiasm for fighting. Lieutenant Zitt was put in charge of the town and through the mayor, Alexandre Renaud, requisitioned stores and labour to build field defences.

On 17 April the Germans turned their attention to putting up anti-airborne landing poles and ordered that all radios be handed in to the town hall. There were to be severe penalties for listening to the BBC. Lieutenant Zitt began to demand more co-operation from Monsieur Renaud, which the mayor stoutly resisted and then on 10 May all the Germans, except the anti-aircraft gunners, left. They had been moved to the Cherbourg Peninsula.

Everywhere, though, there was activity, and there were always soldiers passing through the town, including Georgians and Mongols of very Asiatic appearance. At the end of May the town was briefly fortified and then, once again, became quiet. Following Rommel's inspection of the

Cotentin Peninsula all the weapons and fighting soldiers had been moved forward towards the beaches. Only the Austrians remained, quite at home and causing no trouble.

On the evening of 5 June yet another of the frequent Allied air-raids began, and a large house in La Haule park, opposite the church, where the Museum now is, caught fire. The mayor and the villagers formed a long line from the village pump, passing buckets of water from hand to hand to throw upon the flames. As they struggled to pass the buckets quickly enough, paratroopers began to fall like human confetti amongst them. At least one paratrooper fell into the burning house.

The Germans shot at the Americans as they fell and ordered the French to go back into their houses. The Austrians, having no stomach for a fight, remained for about half an hour and then departed, leaving a few active soldiers here and there with only the machine gun on top of the church still firing. Just a few yards from the gun John Steele hung from the corner of the steeple pretending to be dead so that no one would shoot at him. After two hours he was cut down and taken prisoner, probably the last prisoner taken before active resistance in the town ceased at 0430 hours. The town had been liberated, the first town in France to be so. As the paratroopers gathered in the square and the sun began to rise, silence reigned.

The task of taking the town had been that of the 3rd Battalion of the 505th PIR commanded by Lieutenant-Colonel Edward C. Krause. Following a good drop on and around their planned dropping zone, DZ'O', the colonel ordered his own men to enter Ste Mère Eglise by stealth, using knives and bayonets and, where necessary, grenades. The tactic worked. The Germans were taken by surprise. At 0930 hours the enemy counter-attacked from the south with two companies of infantry and some armour. Most of the 2nd Battalion under Lieutenant-Colonel Benjamin H. Vandervoort, which had established a defence line north of the town, moved back to help. The Colonel broke an ankle in the drop but, using a stick as support, continued to command his battalion. The Germans then launched a simultaneous attack from the north onto the remnants of the 2nd Battalion which numbered forty-two men. When the attack and counter-attack sequence finally ended, some eight hours later, only sixteen of the forty-two men had survived. Both colonels were awarded the DSC for their conduct during the capture of Ste Mère Eglise, the medals being pinned on them in July by General Bradley himself. General Gavin was awarded the DSC at the same ceremony.

Soon after midday German artillery fire started to fall on the centre of the town and it continued sporadically all day and into the night. It began to look as if Liberation would exact a heavy price in civilian casualties and damage to property - a higher price than Occupation.

Intense local fighting continued in the Communes around Ste Mère Eglise, but on the afternoon of 7 June American tanks arrived from UTAH Beach. The beachhead was truly secure and the link-up between air and ground forces was complete.

WALKING TOUR.

On the wall of No 4 rue Eisenhower is a bronze **Plaque to Pfc Clifford A. Maughan,** Mortar Sqn 'F'Coy 505th PIR who parachuted in the garden of the house at 01.45 on 6 June.

At No 6 is the **TOURIST OFFICE.** Tel: (0)2 33 21 00 33 E-mail: ot.stemereeglise@wanadoo.fr. This has reasonable opening hours and helpful staff. Here you may hire (with a Euros 250 deposit) a GPS with a leaflet entitled **Open Sky Museum** which guides you around 10 points of interest around Ste Mère Eglise and area. At each stop you can hear commentaries, see slideshows, videos, etc.

Plaque to Col Robert Murphy, Ste Mère Eglise.

On the corner of the wall of No 8, the **Bar au Domino** Tel: (0)2 33 41 33 92, is a bronze **Plaque to Col Robert M Murphy** 1924-2008, 'a great friend of Ste Mère Eglise', erected in October 2009.

Continue along Rue du Général Eisenhower.

Beside the Museum is **Le Normandy Bar & Pizzeria**, Tel: (0) 2 33 21 25 25. Closed 15 Nov-10 Feb.

ITINERARY ONE MAP: US AIRBORNE OPS & UTAH BEACH LANDINGS

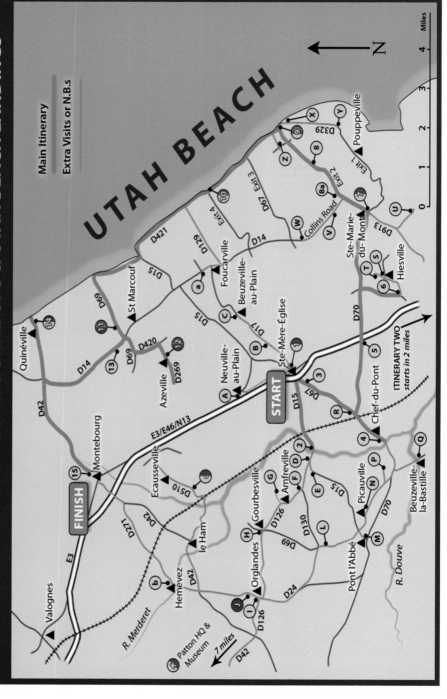

UTAH BEACH

Main Itinerary

Extra Visits or N.B.s

N

0   1   2   3   4   Miles

Valognes

R. Merderet

Patton HQ & Museum

7 miles

D42

E3

FINISH

(15)

Montebourg

Ecausseville

le Ham

Hemevez

(b)

Orglandes

J

I

D126

D24

D42

D271

D427

D510

E3/E46/N13

Gourbesville

H

D126

Amfreville

G

D130

D69

Pont l'Abbé

M

L

E

F

D

2

Picauville

N

P

D15

D70

Beuzeville-la-Bastille

Q

R. Douve

Quinéville

D14

D42

D69

D420

Azeville

D269

(14)

(11)

(13)

St Marcouf

(12)

D69

D15

Neuville-au-Plain

A

B

D17

Ste-Mère-Église

1

START

D15

3

Chef-du-Pont

5

R

4

ITINERARY TWO
starts in 2 miles

C

Beuzeville-au-Plain

a

D129

D15

Foucarville

Exit 4

D421

(10)

D67 Exit 3

Collins Road

W

D14

V

(8a)

Exit 2

Ste-Marie-du-Mont

D70

(7)

U

D913

Hiesville

S

T

6

Z

8

9

X

Y

D329

Pouppeville

Exit 1

The Sherman tank and C47 hangar, US Airborne Museum, Ste Mère Eglise.

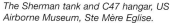

Com Déb Sig Monument, Ste Mère Eglise.

Kilometer Zero, the Mairie.

Plaque to 505th PIR, rue de la Cayenne.

Plaque to Tprs Leonard & Laws, 505th PIR, rue des Ecoles.

On it is a small **Plaque to Two Troopers, Jack Leonard** and **Bill Laws** of No **1 Coy 505 CP** killed here on 6-7 June 1944. **(Lat & Long: 49.40783 -1.31915)**. It was unveiled in 2005. Bill Laws is buried at St Laurent (qv).

Return to the Square and walk up rue Cap du Laine.

• Town Hall Memorials/Flag/Kilometer Zero/Holts Map R1,2,3,4,5

Outside the town hall is the pink marker stone of **Kilometer Zero**. The Kilometer Zero marker stones were erected by General de Gaulle's Government in 1946. They follow the path of General Leclerc's Free French 2nd Armoured Division and can be seen on roads 'from Chad to the Rhine'. One famous stretch leads to Bastogne, another traces an historic path through Reims, Verdun and Metz on the N44 towards Strasbourg. The 'Flame of Freedom' emblem, which decorates the markers, was also used on Free French postage stamps. Behind Kilometer Zero is the **Memorial** to the twenty-two civilians of Ste Mère Eglise (including a World War I veteran) who died in the battle of June 1944, and to the left and right are small plaques commemorating the liberation of the first town in France. To the right and rear of the marker stone is a **Memorial Stone** erected in tribute to Generals Gavin and Ridgway and 'all the gallant liberators of the town'. Inside the town hall is the great Stars and Stripes, the first US flag to be raised in liberated France. It was also the first to fly over Naples in October 1943. In addition there is a painting by a German soldier portraying the parachute drop of 4/5 June.

KILOMETER 0/KILOMETER 00/'FIRST TO BE LIBERATED'/FIRST TO LAND

The visitor may be somewhat confused by rival claims along the Landing Beaches.

For instance, which is the historical beginning of Liberty Highway - Kilometer 0 outside the town hall at Ste Mère Eglise, or Kilometer 00 at UTAH Beach? Both *Communes* proudly claim that their marker (known as a *borne* in French) is the rightful monument, and countless discussions and newspaper articles have argued their respective cases for many years.

Both have a case. Chronologically Ste Mère Eglise was the first town to be liberated - by the Americans - when Lieutenant-Colonel Krause, commanding 3rd Battalion of the 505th PIR 82nd US Airborne Division, hoisted the Stars and Stripes there at 0430 hours.

Geographically UTAH Beach, between Exits 2 and 3, was the first section of French soil to be occupied by the Americans landing from the English Channel.

Bayeux (14 June) claims to be the first city to be liberated, Courseulles (6 June) the first port. The café at Pegasus Bridge (qv) and Bénouville *Mairie* make the earliest claims of all - to have been liberated on 5 June, before midnight, but that is presumably using French local time which was one hour behind the time used by the Allies during the landings. However, John Howard's watch, broken on landing in his glider (the first to land), firmly fixes the time as 0016 hours on 6 June. In 2010 much debate took place about who was the first Allied soldier to land from the air. Up to that time general opinion was that John Howard's glider was the first to arrive but that year the Dead Man's Corner Museum (qv) claimed that an American pathfinder paratrooper landed at 0015 hours. In 1948 the 101st Airborne Division Association published *Rendevous with Destiny* their 'official' history in which they say that a Major Culp and a Major Pedone timed the moment that a Captain Lillyman was the first to jump out of the lead aircraft – it was 0015 hours. In 1979 Devlin's *Paratrooper!* claimed that Lillyman **landed** at 0015 rather than **jumped** as in the earlier account, so for those who are 'first minded' it is now a matter of working out how long Captain Lillyman took to land! Former Prime Minister Gordon Brown asserts in his book, *Wartime Courage*, that Lt Noel Poole, leading an SAS team of three in Operation Titanic, a plan to cause confusion behind German lines, landed west of St Lô at 0011. You pays your money, you takes your choice!

As visitors drive into the small seaside resorts along GOLD, JUNO and SWORD beaches, they will be greeted many times by a 'Welcome' sign that proudly claims 'First town/village to be liberated, 6 June 1944'. You will often be driving along 'Avénue de la Libération' or a street named after the individual Allied commander who led the invasion force in that area.

The rivalry indicates the pride and joy of the occupied French people on being liberated, plus a certain amount of Gallic exuberance, and should be accepted as such by the somewhat puzzled visitor.

Return to the Square and rejoin your car.

Follow signs to D17/Camping/College of St Exupéry along Rue du 505 Airborne. Pass the ** **Hotel du 6 Juin** (11 rue des Clarons, Tel: + (0)2 33 21 07 18. E-mail: hotel6juin@wanadoo.fr 8 rooms. Welcoming. Closed 1 Nov-31 Jan) on the left. *Continue to the fork.*

N.B.1 By forking left a **Marker to 1st US Army Air Corps Airfield in France (A6)**, La Londe (Map It1-B/Lat & Long: 49.41864 1.30307/GPPIt1-1/2) may be reached after about a mile. The Airfield (12 June-25 July 1944) was protected by the 552nd AAA AW Bn (MBL), commanded by Lt Col Benjamin W. Wakefield (qv). The Memorial was erected in June 1979.

N.B.2 By continuing some 1.25 miles on the D17 to Beuzeville-au-Plain, opposite the *Mairie* is a **Memorial to the Crew of a C47 of 439th TCG and 17 Paratroopers of the 506th PIR of 101st AB,** all of whom are named on the memorial, inaugurated on 6 June 2000. (**Map It1-C Lat & Long: 49.43116 -1.28573/GPPIt1-1/3**) Beside it is a small **Plaque** recording (in French) how the plane, No 66, flew at the head of its formation, was pierced by anti-aircraft fire and crashed violently into a hedge and exploded. The plane burnt with such intensity for 3 days that no-one was able to approach it and the crew and parachutists were all killed. On board the Company HQ plane was Lt T. Meehan III, Commanding 'E' Coy of 506th PIR who was carrying maps, documents and plans which were vital to the troops at the beginning of the Landings. The story of 'Easy' Company is told in Stephen Spielberg and Tom Hanks's *Band of Brothers*. The 'Forced Landing Association' who researched the crash site found in the ashes 'crickets' (qv), rings, a watch with its hands fossilised at 0112 hours, unopened parachutes and a helmet, as thin as a sheet of paper.

Thomas Meehan was a promising and popular young officer. As he boarded the C47 he passed this note to a friend to deliver, 'Dearest Anne, In a few hours I'm going to take the best company of men in the world into France. We'll give the bastards hell. Strangely, I'm not particularly scared. But in my heart is a terrific longing to hold you in my arms. I love you Sweetheart-forever. Your Tom.'

Fork right. After some 100 metres on the right by the sports field is

• US Cemetery Marker Number One/.5 mile/5 minutes/Map It1-1/Holts Map R6/Lat & Long: 49.40989 -1.31255

The commemorative stone is one of three marking the first three US cemeteries, all of which will be visited on this tour. There were some 3,000 soldiers buried here and their units are listed. By 10 June there were eight battlefield cemeteries in the American sectors, but shortly afterwards the graves registration organisation began to concentrate the burials in five places - St Laurent, Blosville, Ste Mère Eglise, La Cambe and Orglandes. In March 1948 they were either re-interred into the one National Cemetery at St Laurent or sent home to America. The sports field behind the marker was where a set was built for making the film *The Longest Day* and actor Red Buttons played the part of John Steele on a recreated steeple.

Return to the Square and drive out of Ste Mère Eglise by returning to Rue Général de Gaulle. Turn right in the direction of the Town Hall.

N.B At this point by continuing straight on past the Town Hall for 1.5 miles to Neuville-au-Plain the visit to the **Plaque to Coy 'D' of the 2nd Bn, 505th PIR, 82nd AB (Map It1-A, Lat & Long: 49.42978 - 1.33033/GPPIt1-1/1)** may be made if not done before.

SGWs to 82nd AB Div, Ste Mère Eglise Church.

The famous pump.

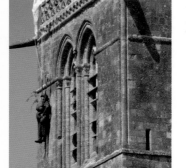

The Church, Ste Mère Eglise, with an effigy of John Steele on the steeple.

US Cemetery Marker No. One, Ste Mère Eglise.

Detail of the Table d'Orientation below 'Iron Mike', showing the bridge, the river and the stuck Sherman.

'Iron Mike', la Fière.

Turn left on the D15 direction Chef du Pont. Just after the bypass bridge, fork to the right on the D15 and continue direction Pont-l'Abbé signed Mémorial des Parachutistes crossing the Carentan-Cherbourg railway line, to the River Merderet. Stop in the large parking area to the right.

• 'Iron Mike' US Parachutist Monument/505th, 508th PIR, Deglopper Plaques/Table d' Orientation, la Fière/3 miles/15 minutes /Map It1-2/Holts Map R27/Lat & Long: 49.40115 -1.36333

The Merderet is very wide here and it was flooded in June 1944 (as it still can be in times of heavy winter rains - as in January 1999 and 2010). From the bridge ahead a 500-yard-long causeway crossed the flooded area. The Americans actually seized this causeway - one of their prime objectives - on D-Day, with a mixed group of 400 paratroopers from the eastern side led by Colonel Roy Lindquist of the 508th and a patrol of the 2nd Battalion of the 507th from the west. But German opposition was so strong they had to let it go at the end of the day. General Ridgway ordered it to be retaken and on the morning of D+3, following a massive artillery bombardment, the Americans attacked again. Despite intense German resistance, and a Sherman tank being stuck on the causeway, the Americans, urged on at the very front by Generals Gavin and Ridgway, and supported by artillery support and direct fire from a platoon of tanks, secured the crossing.

General Ridgway believed in leading from the front. (He was to display that attitude again during the Market Garden Operation in Holland during the delay north of Son). His view was that 'the place of a commander is where he anticipates the crisis of action is going to be, and it was obvious to me that these causeway crossings were the spots of greatest hazard'. In his opinion it was the presence of divisional and battalion commanders urging their men on that ensured the capture of the causeway. So intense was the fighting at la Fière that it was, he said, 'the hottest sector I saw throughout the war'. There is a series of bronze **Plaques to Coy A, 505th,, 2nd AB, 80th AB Antiaircraft, 508th PIR and PFC Charles Deglopper MoH, and a bronze Memorial book**.

The handsome bronze statue of an American paratrooper, known as '**Iron Mike**' (after St Michael, the patron Saint of the Airborne) was unveiled on 7 June 1997 by Major-General Kellogg, Commander of the 82nd Airborne, who jumped with his men in the commemorative drop that day. It bears the legend (in English on the front and in French on the back) 'A grateful tribute to the American Airborne Forces of D-Day 6 June 1944.' The statue is a replica of one that stands in the US Army Infantry School at Fort Benning in the U.S.A. Below the statue is a magnificent bronze **Table d'Orientation,** draped in a parachute, showing the crossing and the stuck Sherman.

On the 65th Anniversary an **Information Panel, 'The Battle of la Fière Causeway'** was inaugurated.

Charles N. Deglopper, Private 1st Class, C Company 325th Glider Infantry, 82nd Airborne Division was awarded the **Medal of Honour** for his actions here on 9 June when he volunteered to support his comrades by fire from his automatic rifle while they attempted to withdraw through a break in the hedgerow, 'scorning a concentration of enemy automatic weapons and rifle fire, he walked from the ditch into the road in full view of the Germans and sprayed the hostile positions with assault fire'. Although soon wounded, he continued to fire whilst his comrades reached a more advantageous position and established the first bridgehead over the Merderet. When his body was later found it was surrounded by dead Germans and the machine guns that he had knocked out. Deglopper is buried in Maple Grove Cemetery, Erie County, New York.

On the bridge is a blue and white sign *Voie Marcus Heim* and a sign to the Deglopper Memorial.

Marcus Heim. Major commemorative ceremonies were held in Normandy on the 40th and 50th anniversaries of the landings. In 1984 the Germans were not invited to attend and after much discussion with its former allies the French government decided that they would not be invited to the 50th anniversary either. Nevertheless, a *Bundeswehr* platoon commanded by Major Heim held a small ceremony of remembrance at the German cemetery at la Cambe on 4 June. It was not an official occasion, explained Major Heim, 'We are here on our holidays'.

Extra Visit to Chapel of Cauquigny (Map It1-D/Lat & Long: 49.40298 -1.37043/GPPIt1-1/4,5,6,8); De Glopper MoH Info Board (Map It1-E/Lat & Long: 49.40192 -1.37602/GPPIt1-1/9); Amfreville - 507th PIR Memorial Park (Map It1-F/Lat & Long: 49.40527 -1.38610/GPPIt1-1/7); Gourbesville 90th Inf Div/82nd AB Div Memorial (Map It1-H/Lat & Long: 49.42071 -1.40981/ GPPIt1-2/3); Picauville - Airlanding Ground A8 Marker (Map It1-L/Lat & Long: 49.39276 -1.41881/GPPIt1-2/6);9th USAAF Transport Memorials/C47 Engine (Map It1-N/Lat & Long: 49.37933 -1.39964/GPPIt1-2/8).
Distance to Chef du Pont: 10 miles. Approx time: 1 hour 30 minutes
The main itinerary may be rejoined at Chef du Pont, missing out US Cemetery Marker No Two
Cross over the bridge on the D15.
Note how exposed this crossing is.
Take the first turning right into the small square.
To the right is a sign, Square Capitaine Rae, 507th PIR. Below it is a **Plaque in Homage to the Men of 3rd Bn, 325th Glider Inf Regt, 82nd AB Div,** 9 June 1944. The lower Plaque commemorates the opposed crossing of the causeway over which you have just driven, that was carried out by the 3rd Bn of the 325th GIR on 9 June. An earlier attempt by the 1st Bn had failed and the 3rd Bn's assault was personally urged by both Generals Ridgway and Gavin. Casualties were heavy and the causeway, already obstructed by the stuck tank,

proved almost impossible to cross. However the west bank was eventually taken and the follow-up force of the 507th PIR under Captain Rae exploited further inland, hoping to link up with the 2nd Bn of the 507th of Lt Col Timmes (qv) isolated on the west bank around Amfreville. They had passed through here on 6 June when the bridge was in US hands but it was later lost. The 3rd Bn, though so-named for simplicity, was actually the 2nd Bn of the 401st 'on loan' to the 325th - hence the note on the Plaque.

Ahead is an **Information Board** describing the fighting at the Chapel of Cauquigny and a **Plaque** paying Homage to its **Liberators**. Beyond, on the wall to the right of the entrance on the beautifully renovated Chapel is a **Plaque** to the **507th PIR**, 82nd AB, June 1944-June 9 2005. To the left is a **Plaque** erected in August 2007 to **Col Wayne W. Pierce, Vet of 325th GIR, 82nd AB,** 'Citizen of Honour of the Commune of Amfreville'. Inside the Church are photographs and the stories of Deglopper's and Rae's gallantry.

Turn round, return to the D15 and turn right, then fork left, still on the D15. On the right is

An **Information Board with photos of Charles Deglopper MoH**, his citation (for his action on the night of 8/9 June 1944) and flags, erected in June 2008 by the '*Association US Normandie Mémoire* in gratitude'.

Return to the fork and turn left on the D126 to Amfreville. On entering the village there is a beautifully maintained grassy mound on the right, 507th Memorial Park.

The main **Memorial to 507th PIR,** in the form of a grey *bas relief* paratrooper, is at the top of the mound, entitled 'The Beginning'. It lists the medals and decorations awarded to members of the regiment throughout their battles in Europe, including Pte George J. Peters who was awarded his MoH for an action on 24 March 1945 in Weasel (sic), Germany during which he was wounded and subsequently died. He is buried in the American Cemetery at Margraten. At the foot of the mound are two pillars: one entitled 'The Way' shows maps of the Normandy, Ardennes and German campaigns. The other describes how the Park exists through the generosity of many donors – members of 507th, family, friends and businesses. They were unveiled by the Mayor on 23 July 2002.

N.B.1. By continuing past the local *Poilu* War Memorial and bearing left following signs to 'Vergers Timmes ' then right on the rue de la Rosière and right again on the narrow and bumpy Route du Thiers, an impressive **Memorial Complex** is reached on the right. An **Information Board** with photos describes how, having gathered his men at Cauquigny (qv) Chapel, Lt Col Charles J. Timmes headed from there towards Amfreville and the sound of gunfire, but in the orchards around this monument he and his small band were surrounded by Germans. Meanwhile the Germans had attacked and retaken Cauquigny, forcing out the Americans, some of whom arrived here by the night of 6 June, making his total strength around 150, of whom some 40 were wounded. During the next three days Timmes and his men held out under terrible conditions against an enemy more than three times their strength until on the 9th they were relieved by the 325th GIR and elements of the 508th PIR who had re-taken the causeway at Cauquigny.
Beside it is a **Memorial to "Vergers Timmes"** ["Timmes' Orchards"], 6-9 June 1944, flanked by 'Honneur' **Plaques to the 325th GIR and the 508th PIR**. (Map It1-G/Lat & Long: **49.41279 - 1.37784/GPPIt1-1/10**).

N.B.2. On returning to rue de la Rosière, by turning right and continuing to the end of the road a **Plaque** may be seen on the wall of the house where **Lt Walter 'Chris' Heisler**, 507th PIR, was interrogated by the Germans after surviving the crash of his C47 on 5-6 June. (Lat & Long: **49.11263 -1.390206**). An **Information Panel** in Heisler Square in Nègreville was inaugurated on 5 June 2009 in honour of Heisler and the soldiers who died in the C47 crash when their parachutes failed to open because of the low altitude. The crash site is marked by a small **Memorial** up a track off the D418.

N.B.3 By turning left on the rue de la Rosière, a rare German **Plaque** may be seen immediately on the right on the wall of house No 26. It is In Memoriam to the **German 'Lazaret' [Hospital]** Feb-June 1944/GPPIt1-1/11.

Le Colonel
Wayne W. PIERCE
Vétéran du 325ème Régiment de planeurs
82ème Division Aéroportée

<< CITOYEN D'HONNEUR >>
de la commune d'Amfreville

- Août 2007 -

507e P.I.R   82e DIV.
Square
Capitaine R A E

-HOMMAGE-
Aux hommes du 3/325ème régiment de
planeurs de la 82ème Division Airborne
ex: 2/401ème régiment de planeurs de la
101ème Division Airborne
-9 juin 1944-

NUIT DU 8 AU 9 JUIN 1944
Le Sacrifice du Soldat de Première Classe
CHARLES N. DeGLOPPER
Classe«C», 1/325e Régiment d'Infanterie des planeurs
de la 82e Division Airborne
(«C Co, 1/325e Glider Infantry Regiment, 82e AB»)
<< Médaille d'Honneur du Congrès >>

LAZARET VON AMFREVILLE

FEB - JUIN - 1944

IN MEMORIAM

GPPlt1-2/1	Plaque to US 9th & 90th Divs, Orglandes Church
GPPlt1-2/2	Ger Cem, Orglandes
GPPlt1-2/3	Memorials to US 90th Inf & 82nd AB Divs, Gourbesville
GPPlt1-2/4	Sherman Tank, Gen Patton's HQ, Néhou
GPPlt1-2/5	Memorial to Gen Patton's HQ, Néhou
GPPlt1-2/6	Marker to ALG8, Picauville
GPPlt1-2/7	Memorial to US 90th Div, Pont l'Abbé
GPPlt1-2/8	Memorials to 9th USAAF TC, 82nd AB & 101st AB Divs, Picauville
GPPlt1-2/9	Memorial to Zane Schlemmer, Ferme Pierre Cottell, L'Angle
GPPlt1-2/10	Plaque to 508th PIR, Beuzeville Bridge
GPPlt1-2/11	Plaque to O.B. Hill, 508th PIR, Beuzeville

N.B. On the Local War Memorial in Chef du Pont churchyard is a **Plaque 'To our Liberators of the 508th PIR and to their Capt Rex Combs**, 1912-1976.' (Map It1-R/Lat & Long: 49.38716 -1.34251/GPPlt1-3/1).

On the right immediately before the bridge over the railway is **The Hotel/Restaurant Le Normandie**. Tel: (0)2 33 41 88 13. 7 rooms. Choice of menus, speciality - grills on wood fire. Open every day, all day, July-Sept. Closed Sun night and Mon.

Continue to where that road crosses the River Merderet. Stop on the east bank.

• 508th PIR Memorials, Chef du Pont/7.7 miles/10 minutes/Map It1-4/Holts Map R15,16/Lat & Long: 49.377250 -1.353221

There is a **Memorial Stone** on the right and a Memorial Garden and **Plaques** opposite on the left, constructed and donated by the **508th Association**. In the Memorial Garden there is a **Stone to 'Our friend, O.B. Hill, founder of the 508th PIR Association'** (qv).

The bridge is 100 metres further on and there is a blue **NTL Totem** signboard on the left describing the action and a further sign, *Marais du Grand Fossé*. The Bridge over the Merderet has been named after **Capt Roy Creek** of the 507th PIR and his men.

There were three drop zones for the 82nd Airborne Division all just west of Ste Mère Eglise (see Battle Map 3). Zone 'O', immediately alongside and to the west of the N13 as it leaves Ste Mère Eglise towards Cherbourg, was the one where the first and most accurate drops occurred. The 505th Parachute Infantry Regiment and the 82nd's Divisional HQ came down in that area.

Zone 'N', the drop zone for 508th PIR, is about 2 miles north-west across the river from here, but the sticks were scattered along a 6-mile elongated path in that direction, with extreme elements fifteen miles away due north.

Drop Zone 'T', two miles north of Zone 'N', was almost empty, though 507th PIR, who were due to land there, achieved probably the best grouping of the division, but one mile due east of where they should have been. Their extreme elements were the farthest flung of all, from fifteen miles north of here to twenty-three miles south.

As part of their defensive measures the Germans had flooded the Cotentin area. The river here looked more like a shallow lake than the small stream you may well be looking at. Two of the division's three regiments, 507th and 508th, were across the other side of the water (see Battle Map 3). Their task was to control the lateral routes into the Cotentin by establishing a defensive line three miles west of the bridges over the Merderet. This was one of the bridges and it was supposed to be taken and secured by 505th PIR, the third divisional regiment which had landed pretty well on target three miles north of here alongside Ste Mère Eglise.

Unfortunately for the 82nd Airborne Division, particularly for the men west of the Merderet, they had dropped into the area defended by the German 91st Division which had been especially trained in anti-airlanding operations. In addition many men had fallen into the swamp lands caused by the flooding and under the weight of their equipment were drowned.

A D-DAY MEMORY

GOODY TOLD US THIS STORY IN STE-MERE-EGLISE

Trooper Howard ('Goody') Goodson. I Coy 3rd Bn 82nd Airborne Division. 505th Parachute Infantry Regiment. Dropped near Ste Mère Eglise.

"It was a very secret mission and at one time we were prepared to board the aircraft on 5 June and then they sent us back because of the weather and then on 6 June ... sometime around midnight of 5 June, we boarded the aircraft and took off for Normandy.... It was a full moon night when we left England. You could see the fighter aircraft all around the plane until we finally hit the coast of Normandy and all of a sudden it was just black. I thought it was cloud but it was smoke from German ack ack fire and I believe our plane was hit two or three times, it was shaking all over and I was scared to death.

We were wearing the authorised American jump suit which consisted of a jacket and a pair of pants with many many large pockets ... and we had a main chute and a reserve chute and about everything else you can imagine we carried into battle. We even carried land mines in on our persons, grenades ... the only place we could find to put our gas mask was the bottom part of a leg and it was the first thing we got rid of when we hit the ground. We were so heavily loaded that the crew chief on the plane had to come around individually and pull each man up. He couldn't rise up by himself. We had twelve men on each side I believe and we had a cable going through the aircraft and we used static line. When the red light came on it meant stand up and hook up and then we would wait for the green light to go on and when that went on the first in line on the door side went out. Each person should check the man in front but on the Normandy jump I don't think anyone checked anything we were all so ... in a big hurry to get out of the plane.

After I hit the ground and got my chute off ... on this jump everyone decided that we would get a piece of our parachute and that's the first thing I did ... I entered a very quiet area, I could hear battle going on in other places but where I was it was very quiet, no-one around me, so I ripped off a piece of my camouflaged parachute, put my gun together - we carried a bren/rifle that went in three pieces and was zipped up in a cloth bag ... and eventually I heard movement and I used my little cricket and it turned out to be a friend from my company called Pat and he was also the first person I saw in Sicily after I jumped. A group of us got together and advanced into Ste Mère Eglise where there was fighting going on and we were eventually taken over by our battalion commander, Colonel Krause. He set us up in a defence of the town."

Opposition to the paratroopers was considerable, yet the dispersion that made it impossible for them to gather in enough strength to achieve their objectives also made it difficult for the Germans to work out what was going on and thus to concentrate in order to take effective offensive action. In addition, there was confusion within the German command because two of the divisional commanders were away playing war games at Rennes when the invasion began. What is more, Lieutenant General Wilhelm Falley, commanding the 91st Division, was killed by paratroopers as he made his way back to his headquarters. Falley was in his staff car with two of his officers when he bumped into Lieutenant Malcolm Brannen and four men of the 508th. Oddly it was an encounter which would be paralleled by a similar incident on the opening day of the battle of Arnhem on 17 September 1944, when General Kussin, the town commander, speeding back to town to organise its defence, bumped into a patrol of 3 Para and was shot and killed by them. After Brannen had left, Corporal Jack Schlegel, one of Brannen's men, came upon the car and found a large swastika flag in it which he took away. In 1974 he presented the flag to the museum at Ste Mère Eglise.

The Americans headed for the obvious dry ground offered by the railway embankment (you crossed the line from Ste Mère Eglise and will cross it again on leaving here) and by mid-morning some 500 men had gathered near the bridge at la Fière 1.5 miles due north of here which the itinerary visited earlier. Several attempts were made at that time by elements of 505th and 507th

PIR to take the la Fière (Iron Mike) bridge, but these failed, and when General Gavin, the Assistant Divisional Commander arrived, he took seventy-five men and set off down the road you drove along, heading for this bridge.

Unfortunately a number of enemy soldiers had dug themselves in along the causeway in front of you, and on the west bank, and Gavin's force could not move them. Rumour had it that two enemy soldiers who had stood up intending to surrender had been shot, but it is not clear who shot them - their own side or Americans.

Meanwhile, the Divisional Commander, General Ridgway, had arrived at la Fière and decided upon another attack on the bridge there. Most of the men here were withdrawn, leaving a platoon to hold the ground. By good fortune a glider containing an anti-tank gun came down nearby and Captain Roy Creek, commanding the platoon, used the gun to hold off an enemy counter-attack but he could do no more than hold tenuously on to this eastern bank. Nevertheless Capt Creek's small force was the only unit along the entire invasion front that stood practically on the D-Day objective line by midnight 6 June. Over to the west, elements of the German 1057th Regiment were moving steadily towards the river and the bridges, here and at la Fi re, with orders to destroy all paratroopers in the area.

To the right, in a north-easterly direction along the line of the river, there is some high ground about 1.5 miles away known to the paratroopers as Hill 30. There Lieutenant-Colonel Shanley commanding a group of about two companies of men of the 508th PIR took up position and broke up repeated German attacks in this direction, thus saving Captain Creek's small force and denying the Germans use of this bridge as well as making a substantial contribution to the security of the men at la Fière. That is why the 508th memorial is here. Three of Shanley's men who stayed in isolated posts while Shanley was establishing his position, Corporal Ernest Roberts, Private Otto Zwingman and Private John Lockwood were all taken prisoner. Each was awarded the DSC. Zwingman was killed on 23 December 1944 while still a prisoner. He is buried in the American Ardennes Cemetery.

Return to Chef du Pont along rue du Capitaine Rex Combs(qv),signed 100 yards on the first building on the left hand side.

Combs, of 'A'Coy 508th, was with the group that liberated Chef du Pont on 6 June. Two days later he won the Silver Star for taking 42 German prisoners.

Continue and take the D70 east towards the N13 and Carentan. 100 yards before the D70 passes under the N13 there is a memorial marker on the right beside the road. Stop.

• US Cemetery Marker Number Three, les Forges/10.4 miles/5 minutes/ Map It1-5/Holts Map R17/Lat & Long: 49.38086 -1.29808

This is les Forges, the site of US Cemetery Number 3, the third of three large burial grounds established in Normandy by the Americans. It was opened in June 1944 and remained a cemetery until 1948. Then the men buried here were repatriated or re-interred in the National Cemetery at St Laurent above OMAHA Beach. There were 6,000 burials of soldiers from 9th Infantry Division, 79th Infantry Division, 1st Engineer Amphibious Brigade, 101st Airborne Division, 82nd Airborne Division, 746th Tank Battalion, 4th Infantry Division and 70th Tank Battalion. The Memorial was erected on 21 January 1958.

Around this area was Landing Zone 'W' for the 82nd. Drop zones were areas allocated to parachute troops and Landing Zones areas for gliders. Paratroop forces were generally given the task of landing in advance of glider-borne forces and of securing the landing zones in order to allow the gliders 'safe' landings. The Americans were using both Waco and Horsa gliders. The Horsa had a tendency to break up on hard landings and the US pilots christened it 'The Flying Morgue'.

By the evening of 6 June 1944 elements of the 8th Infantry from UTAH Beach had reached this point and established overnight positions here.

The tour now effectively leaves the area of the 82nd Airborne Division assault and enters into that of the 101st Airborne Division.

Continue on the D70 under N13 dual carriageway, direction Ste Marie du Mont to the crossroads with the D129. Turn right direction Hiesville. At the first junction continue on the D129 direction La Croix Pan. At the next junction stop at memorial on the left.

US Cemetery Marker No. Two, Blosville.

Memorial to the 508th PIR, Chef du Pont.

Memorial to O.B. Hill, Memorial Garden, Chef du Pont.

Causeway over the River Merderet in flood as it may have looked in June 1944, Chef du Pont.

US Cemetery No. Three, les Forges.

On 11 January 2011 the news was released by Maj Winters' family that he died on 2 January 2011, aged 92, after a long battle with Parkinson's disease. Sadly he will never see this tribute to him. Also he will not know if the current campaign to award him the Medal of Honour was successful. It was denied to him in June 1944 as the quota of 1 MoH to each division went to Lt-Col Robert G. Cole (qv) and Winters received the Distinguished Service Cross instead for his valour on 6 June at Brécourt.

The road you are travelling along, the D913, then becomes Bryant and then Jones Road. At this point there is an **Information Board** at Aire des Sources, and **Liberty Highway kilometer marker 10**. The road becomes Hinkel Road and, as it reaches the beach, Danel Road.

At the point where Jones Road becomes Hinkel Road, by a bridge over a small stream, La Petite Cricque Bau, is a memorial statue on the right. Stop.

• UTAH Danish Memorial/18.4 miles/5 minutes/Map It1-8/Holts Map S11/Lat & Long: 49.40318 -1.19619

This Memorial, raised in 1984 and designed by Danish architect Svend Lindhardt, commemorates the 800 Danes who took part in the landings. The Danes, mostly serving on board ships, were those who

The UTAH Danish Memorial.

had escaped from Denmark and were attached as individuals to British units. A number joined SOE and in April 1945 **Major Anders Lassen**, attached to the SAS Special Boat Service, won a posthumous **VC** in Italy. He is buried in the Argenta Gap CWGC Cemetery.

Continue down Exit 2 to the memorial area and museum where Danel Road exits from the beach. Park.

■ No. 4. UTAH Beach Museum/US Memorials/ 19.7 miles/1 hour/RWC/Map It1-9/Holts Map S2,3,4, 5,6,7,8,9,10,16,17/Lat & Long: 49.40318 -1.19619

It is helpful to walk down to the beach and to consider the basic story of what happened here before going into the Museum - which has been built around German blockhouse WN5. The area had been visited by Rommel early in May in line with Hitler's premonition about Normandy being a likely invasion target. When Rommel was pleased with what he found he often gave a concertina or mouth-organ to one of the soldiers putting up obstacles, in the hope that the soldier would play and encourage his comrades to sing, thus building morale. When he came here, however, he was not pleased.

He inspected the beach and the obstacles, and then demanded that Lieutenant Arthur Jahnke, in charge of blockhouse WN5, take off his gloves and show his palms. Jahnke did so and, on seeing the weals and scratches on the young officer's hands, which had clearly come from helping to put up beach obstacles, Rommel relented and told him that the blood he had spilled in putting up obstacles was as important as any he would spill in combat.

Just a week before the invasion General Marcks, LXXIVth Corps Commander, held a small parade in front of WN5 during which Jahnke was awarded the Iron Cross for service in Russia.

Early on the morning of 6 June Jahnke was in WN5, woken by the noise of aeroplanes and puzzled by the sound of gun fire coming from the direction of Ste Marie du Mont. He despatched a patrol to find out what was going on and to his surprise they returned in half an hour with seventeen American prisoners. The Americans told him nothing.

Then the air and naval bombardment began. Huge spouts of sand, pieces of concrete and clouds of dust filled the air. In little more than half an hour WN5 was ineffective. Their weapons, 50mm, 75mm and 88mm guns, were all out of action. Those men who had not been killed were dazed and shocked by the noise and brutality of the explosions.

Jahnke was wounded. As the noise lessened and the disorientated defenders looked out to sea they saw the approaching armada and, in the leading waves, floating tanks. The lieutenant tried to activate his own tanks, small wire-controlled tractors carrying explosives, called GOLIATHS, but they would not start. The devices, almost 5,000 of which were built altogether, were driven by a 703cc motor cycle engine and could move at 12 km per hour. Although in theory they had a range measured in kilometers the fact that they were wire-controlled limited their use - even if they started.

The Americans, encouraged by a 57-year-old General called Roosevelt, charged up the beach, engineers blew a hole in the sea wall and then, supported by their armour, they rushed WN5. Jahnke and his men surrendered. UTAH beach belonged to 4th Division. Roosevelt, who had once commanded the 1st Infantry Division, had been removed from active command and given a desk job. After much lobbying, he had got himself the appointment as second in command of 4th Infantry Division and, at 57, was the oldest officer to land with the assault troops. Sadly, he died of a heart attack on 12 July, in an orchard near Carentan. He never learned that he had redeemed himself and had been given command of 90th Division.

In 1987 Arthur Jahnke returned to WN5 and shook hands with another veteran of that 6 June - an American of the 8th Infantry Regiment who had led the charge ashore.

Force U for UTAH had launched its thirty-two DD tanks only 2 miles from shore, instead of the planned 4 miles, because of the bad weather. It was a fortunate decision and twenty-eight tanks made it to the beaches providing direct fire support to the infantry and helping the assault engineers to deal with obstacles. The costly lesson of Dieppe had been learned. By midday UTAH Beach was clear and the 4th Division was on its way inland across the causeways to link up with the airborne forces.

By the end of the day the 4th Division had achieved almost all of its immediate objectives. Over the beach had come 23,000 men and 1,700 vehicles. The causeways were secure and the beachhead firm.

The original Museum, which opened in 1962 and underwent a major refurbishment, modernisation and expansion in 1994, offered a splendid account of the events that took place here on 6 June 1944 and immediately thereafter. Funded by the local Ste Marie du Mont council, the region and veterans, it was built into and around German Blockhouse WN5, offering panoramic views over the sea, with landing craft, films using actuality footage, diorama, scale models, photographs, ephemera and artefacts, many donated over the years by veterans. By the old entrance is a **Plaque to 238th Combat Engineers**.

Opened in June 2011 is a complete renovation and expansion (to twice its present size) of the existing Museum incorporating the building of a new 1,000 sq metre hall and a hangar to house a full-scale, inter-active model of B-26 'Dinah Might'. Architect Nicholas Keleman's designs harmonise with the dunes, using much natural light and views over UTAH Beach. There are new exhibitions on the French during the occupation, the 101st Airborne, and the battle of the Band of Brothers at Brécourt Manor (qv). This important development aims to do justice to the extraordinary historical drama that was played out here in 1944 and to present it in a modern way for today's tourists, with many inter-active displays. It is financed by a Franco-American partnership, with the support of the Lt-Governor of Texas whose father landed at UTAH in June '44.

Veterans of the landings are asked to sign the Book of Honour (and should have complimentary entrance). Postcards, books and maps are on sale. To the right of the desk in the entrance is a **Plaque to 238th Combat Engineers**.

Open: daily April, May 1000-1800. June-Sept 0930-1900. Oct 1000-1230 and 1400-1800. 1-15 Nov, Feb and March 1000-1200 and 1400-1730. 16 Nov-31 Dec, weekends and school holidays 1000-1200 and 1400-1730. Closed Jan. Entrance fee payable. Reductions for children. Tel: (0)2 33 71 53 35. e-mail: musee.utahbeach@wanadoo.fr There are good parking, toilet facilities beside the museum. Outside the Museum is a **LEC Memorial** (qv).

The Wall of Liberty. This ambitious project to commemorate the names of 77,760 US Veterans on a wall in a Commemorative Garden has been put on hold while sorting out financial irregularities with the subscriptions.

'Thank God for the United States Navy!', said Maj-Gen Leonard Gerow, commander V Corps, to Lt Gen Omar Bradley on 6 June 1944 and finally, on 27 September 2008, a **US Navy**

Normandy Monument was inaugurated on the highest point overlooking UTAH Beach on land donated by the French. It is approached up **Voie Gen Dwight Eisenhower**, 1890-1969, Supreme Commander 6 June, as a **Plaque** to the right at the top proclaims.

Taking the form of a group of three 8-feet tall figures representing a Navy Captain, a sailor with a 5-inch shell and a member of a demolition team carrying a rifle, it was sculpted by Stephen Spears of Fair Hope, Ala. whose father served in the US Air Force. (He also sculpted the Doughboy statue to the 29th Inf Regt of US 1st Div in Cantigny, Somme, inaugurated on 28 May 2008.) On the base are the names of all Navy vessels that participated in the landings. It was felt that the role of the US Navy has never been fully recognised and the project was a matter of some urgency in view of the dwindling number of veterans. The Navy had assembled 15,000 US sailors on more than 1,000 combat ships, 87,000 on more than 3,500 landing crafts and 22,000 at bases in advance of D-Day. Their mighty firepower supported the Landings, after which they kept the troops re-supplied and shuttled the wounded to US hospital ships. Underwater demolition teams were pivotal – among the first to hit the beaches they cleared pathways through the deadly shore obstacles. At OMAHA these teams suffered 52% casualties. The Naval toll included 148 landing craft, a troop transport, 2 destroyers, a destroyer escort and a minesweeper and 1,068 sailors.

The idea of the monument was instigated by Cristy and Ray Pfeiffer of Historic Tours when Ray addressed the Naval Order of the USA (NOUS - a fraternal society of America's sea-services and others) on Pearl Harbour Day 2003 when he pointed out that there was no major D-Day US Navy Monument in Normandy. The NOUS took up the challenge, raised the required $500,000 and Stephen Spears sculpted the monument at his own expense. The NOUS, the Commune of Ste Marie du Mont and Historic Tours co-operated to co-ordinate the project.

The inauguration ceremony was magnificent and extremely moving, with speeches by Capt Gregory F. Street, USN (Retd) of NOUS, Henri Milet, the supportive *Maire* of Sainte-Marie du Mont, the Hon Craig Stapleton, US Ambassador to France and the Hon Gordon R. England, US Deputy Sec of Defence. Amiral Pierre-François Forissier, French Chief of Naval Staff who presented the *Légion d'Honneur* to the three UTAH Beach veterans who had made the journey to France: Capt Richard Zimmerman, CIC Officer USS Frankford, James Gaff, LCVP Coxswain and Chester Collins. The US Naval Forces Europe Band and a dramatic flypast of the *Groupe Aéronaval Embarqué* added to the drama of the occasion.

Opposite is the **Café and bar Le Roosevelt**, built adjoining a bunker on which is an **Information Board to the US Naval Amphibious Forces**, listing 41 men lost in the capture of the bunker, 6 June 1944. The landings involved 836,000 men, 220,000 vehicles and 75,000 tons of equipment.

This has evolved from a simple souvenir shop into a most interesting little Museum. Originally a fisherman's hut, it was used from 1942-44 as an office for the Todt organisation during the building of Atlantic Wall structures and the bunker built adjoining it was probably a telephone exchange. After the Landings at UTAH US 1st Eng Sp Bde Communication Group took it over and it was used as a communication centre for the US Navy from 8 June to 31 October to control the traffic between the fleet and the front. Signatures from various occupants – contemporary and modern – can be seen on the wall and the bunker has been recreated as a communications centre.

In the Café signatures of returning veterans cover the tables, the walls and the counter and there are some fascinating old radio sets, photos and other exhibits and mannequins, giving it a convivial 1940s atmosphere. A great place to have a warming *café-calva* on a cold and blustery day on UTAH Beach, it serves snacks and simple meals and sells postcards and souvenirs. Closed Dec-mid Feb. Tel: (0)2 33 71 53 47. E-mail: info@le roosevelt.com Internet access.

Around and about the museum the following memorials and objects may be found within walking distance and a smart new track leads to them.

NTL Totem, Sherman Tank, Landing Craft, US Anti-aircraft Gun.

4th Division Memorial Obelisk. Kilometer 00 - This marks the beginning of 4th Division's and Leclerc's 2nd Armoured Division's Liberty Highway which runs both into Holland and across France to the German border.

Through Normandy, markers can be seen every kilometer showing the distance from '0' at Ste Mère Eglise or '00' at UTAH Beach.

Plaque to 406th Fighter Gp, inside UTAH Beach Museum.

Sculptor Stephen Spears's fine 'Leadership' tribute statue to Lt "Dick" Winters, unveiled on 6 June 2012.

The Museum, UTAH Beach, with Bunker.

Artist's Impression of the new UTAH Beach Museum Extension

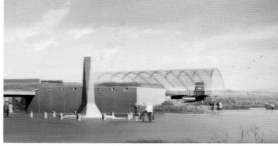

Rowe Road Marker at exit from beach.

40th Anniversary commemorative plaque, naming King Baudouin of the Belgians, Queen Elisabeth II, King Olav V of Norway, Grand-Duke Jean of Luxembourg, Queen Beatrix of the Netherlands, President Reagan, Prime Minister Pierre Trudeau of Canada and President Francois Mitterand.

Bronze plaque, Voie General Eisenhower, 1890-1969

Bunker System A. (See the Diagram 1: 'German Defences at Exit 2, La Madeleine, UTAH Beach). This carries the 24ft-tall polished red Baveno granite memorial obelisk to the American forces of VII Corps, who landed here and liberated the Cotentin Peninsula between 6 June and 1 July 1944. It was erected in 1984 by an agreement between the governments of France and America which included it as part of the permanent arrangement for commemoration, which already covered Pointe du Hoc and the St Laurent Cemetery. It bears the words 'Erected by the United States of America in humble tribute to its sons who lost their lives in the liberation of these beaches. June 6, 1944'.

Continue on the D421 past the large bunkers on each side of the road following signs to Quinéville on the D15 through Ravenoville Plage and back onto the D421 towards Quinéville.

At this point out to sea the Isles de Saint Marcouf can be seen. It had been suspected that the Germans had established a minefield control post on the islands and elements of the 4th and 24th Cavalry Squadrons under Lieutenant-Colonel E. C. Dunn landed there around 0530 on D-Day. Although no Germans were present, and no major minefield was discovered, a number of casualties were suffered from mines on the islands themselves.

Continue through Les Gougins and turn left by a German bunker onto the D69 signed Batteries d'Azeville et de Crisbecq. Continue to and stop at

• St Marcouf Batterie, Crisbecq/28.8 miles/30 minutes/Map It1-11/Holts Map Q3,4/Lat & Long: 49.479298 -1.295595

Beside the complex on the left is a **NTL Totem**. The entrance to the main complex is on the right of the road. There are formidable concrete remains here of control bunkers and gun emplacements. It is possible to climb on top of the central bunker to get a good view towards UTAH Beach. The works were begun in 1941 by the Todt Organisation and on 6 June the main armament in position was two 155mm guns. In addition there were three 21mm Skodas, six 75mm anti-aircraft weapons and three 20mm guns. An all-round defensive position was established with minefields, barbed wire and seventeen machine-gun posts. As part of the coastal defence organisation the battery came under the German Navy and the position was commanded by 1st Class Ensign Walter Ohmsen with a force of some 300 men. In the early morning of 6 June, following a raid in which some 600 tons of bombs were dropped around the battery without damaging it, a number of paratroopers of the 501st and 502nd PIRs, miles off course, landed nearby and twenty were taken prisoner. As daylight came the 155mm guns opened up on the invasion fleet off UTAH Beach, hitting a cruiser and sinking a destroyer as well as damaging others. In the return fire many guns were destroyed, though the casements remained intact, and, despite continued counter-battery work from the sea and local attacks by troops from UTAH Beach, the position held out until 12 June when men of the 39th Infantry Regiment entered the silent battery.

All the officers and NCOs had been killed or wounded. Ensign Ohmsen and seventy-eight men had withdrawn during the night. The damage that can now be seen is the work of US engineers who attempted to destroy the battery after its capture. The battery area covers 4 hectares and 19 dug-outs and shelters can be visited. Rest areas, hospital and kitchen are all furnished with contemporary artefacts. Entrance fee payable. **Open:** April, Oct, Nov: 1400-1800; May, June, Sept: 1100-1800; July, Aug: 1000-1900. Gift shop and WC. Tel: (0)6 68 41 09 04. E-mail: contact@batterie-marcouf.com/en Website: www.batterie-marcouf.com/en

Continue to the junction with the D14 and go straight over on the D69 signed Batterie d'Azeville. At the first junction turn left on the D269 and turn next right on the D269. Continue to the parking area on the left.

Beside the entrance is a **NTL Totem**.

• Batterie d'Azeville/30.5 miles/30 minutes/Map It1-12/Holts Map Q8/Lat & Long: 49.460793 -1.306827

The refurbished battery was one of the first parts of the Atlantic Wall to be constructed. It consists of four powerful casemates, 30 metres apart, linked by a 300 metre long network of concrete trenches, 150 metres of which were covered and used as ammunition bunkers, shelters and electric generators. Two of the enormous structures are uncharacteristically slab-sided.

The approaches to the position from the sea had been made almost impenetrable by the use of minefields and barbed wire thickened by one-man concrete shelters. The positions at both

Azeville and Crisbecq were still holding out on 8 June despite assaults by 1st Battalion 22nd Infantry preceded by artillery and naval gunfire. On 9 June Colonel Tribolet, commanding 22nd Infantry, decided to blank off Crisbecq with naval gun fire and to concentrate his efforts on Azeville. He discovered that the approach to the position from the west (that is from inland) had apparently been overlooked by the defenders who had not cleared the undergrowth for fields of fire and sent two companies in that way. They were able to pick their way through the wire and around the mines without being seen and opened fire on the nearest blockhouse with bazookas. Demolition teams laid three charges to blow up the blockhouse and a tank joined in, but none of the assaults caused serious damage to the concrete. The attackers were about to run out of explosives and be forced to withdraw when Private Ralph Riley, on the orders of his company commander, took the remaining flamethrower and set off to give the blockhouse 'one more squirt'. Having run through enemy fire, he reached the blockhouse only to find that the flamethrower would not ignite. Taking his life into his own hands, he turned on the oil jet and lit it with a match, aiming the burning stream at the door. By chance the flames reached some ammunition inside and explosions followed. Within minutes a white flag was displayed and the German commander surrendered with the entire garrison of 169 men. Riley was awarded the Silver Star. The capture of Azeville allowed the Americans to ignore Crisbecq and to push on to Quinéville.

Open: daily April, Oct and School Holidays: 1400-1800. May, June, Sept: 1100-1800. July and Aug: 1100-1900. Groups by appointment. Guided visits in English, French, German through 350m of underground passages, explaining the daily life of the 170 men stationed here and the course of the battle. Small boutique. Entrance fee payable. There is a pleasant picnic area and snack bar in the car park in the season. Tel: +(0)2 33 40 63 05. E-mail: musee.azeville@cg50.fr Website: www.sitesetmusees.cg50.fr.

Return to the junction with the D14 and turn left towards Fontenay-sur-Mer. Some 1,000 yards after the turning is a farmhouse on the left called 'de Perrette' and just beyond it a memorial marker.

• *The Perrette Airfield A7/365th Fighter Group Memorial 32.6 miles/5 minutes/Map It1-13/Holts Map Q2/Lat & Long: 49.48257 - 1.30739*

The US 9th Air Force Association in concert with friends in France has erected over a dozen memorials to commemorate its actions during the battle of Normandy. This one, marking the landing strip A7, used by the 365th Fighter Group, 9th USAAF, who were here from 28 June to 15 August, was dedicated on 21 September 1987 by a group of veterans who came over from America for the occasion. One of the P47 **Pilots, Harry Katoski**, who flew from here was killed on 26 July 1944 and there is a **Memorial** to him at Ste Pience, north of Avranches.

Continue through Fontenay-sur-Mer and turn right direction Quinéville at the junction with the D42. Continue to the sea and Museum parking on the right, Avénue de la Plage.

• *World War Two Museum/39th Inf Regt Memorial/ 36.5 miles/20 minutes/Map It1-14/Holts Map Q1/Lat & Long: 49.51502 -1.28695*

Taken over in 2019, renamed by enthusiastic collector, Jean-Paul Francois Herry (whose 12 year old father started his own collection after D-Day) and run with his son. Many new exhibits, including German figurines, ammunition cart, vehicles, uniforms and realistic maquettes. The cinema and realistic WW2 street, showing life under the Occupation have been retained. A blockhouse which forms part of the building may also be visited. In front of the museum is a **Liberty Highway marker** and a signboard telling the story of **Lieutenant Francis Vourch** and 5 other Frenchmen of No 10 Inter-Allied Commando who made a reconnaissance, named HARDTACK 21, of the area on the night 26/27 December 1943, and discovered and described one of the anti-tank obstacles, 'Element C', made of steel girders and weighing 2.5 tons, that was to form one of the main beach defences. They also took back with them samples of soil in waterproof bags, the information about Element C in particular, contributing to the success of the D-Day Landings. Vourch had also taken part in the Dieppe Raid with No 10 Commando in 1942. There is a **NTL Totem.**

Tel: + (0)2 33 95 95 or consult website for opening hours and fees. Website: www. worldwar2-museum.com Outside the Museum is a **Memorial to the 39th Inf Regt,** who took the Marcouf Battery and Quinéville, which was unveiled in June 2004.

The village was not taken until 14 June. Quinéville sits at the end of a ridge that runs west to east from Montebourg, and this high ground was seen by the Germans as essential for the protection of the route to Cherbourg and they established strong positions upon it. Equally, General Collins knew that the capture of the Montebourg-Quinéville Ridge was an essential prelude to an attack upon Valognes and thence Cherbourg. Establishing a firm position on the western end of the ridge, to the east of Montebourg which had yet to fall, he sent the 22nd and 39th Infantry along the crest of the ridge, west to east, and they fought their way in column of companies down to the nose and into the village with the support of an air strike by thirty six A-20s.

Return towards Montebourg on the D42

Pass on the right the Quinéville Militaria Collectables shop. Tel: +(0)2 33 40 31 20, and by it the **Hotel de la Plage,** 6 rooms. Tel: +(0)2 33 21 43 54. Hotel-de-la-plage-quineville@wanadoo.fr
Continue on the D42 towards Montebourg.

Pass on the left by the *Mairie* a sign to the left to the historic *** **Hotel/Restaurant Château de Quinéville.** Tel: + (0)2 33 21 42 67. E-mail: chateau.quineville@wanadoo.fr. French home of Stuart King James II. 39 rooms. Outdoor heated pool. 12 hectare grounds. Normandy specialities.
Continue towards Montebourg on the D42, passing the Abbey to the left, and immediately fork right on rue du Grand Clos into the Place de la 4ième Division.

• Plaque to the US 4th Infantry Division, Montebourg/41.2 miles/ 5 minutes/Map It1-15/Lat & Long: 49.49031 -1.37719

In the grass square is a stone **Monument**, the remains of the ruined XV Century Watchtower of the Fortress of St Marcouf les Gougins. On it is a **Plaque** to the soldiers of the **US 4th Div** who

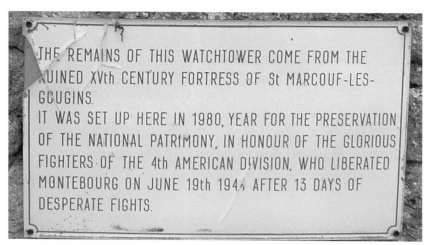

Plaque to US 4th Div, Montebourg.

The St Marcouf Batterie, Crisbecq showing bunker and gun-mounting platform.

The Azeville Battery main entrance.

Memorial to 365th Fighter Gp, Perrette.

Leclerc Memorial and Sherman Tank, St Martin de Varreville.

The immense WW1 Dirigible Hangar, Ecausseville. (See page 93).

hectares was bought from the National Navy by the Franco-American 9th USAAF Normandy Airfields Association (qv), who plan to open a Museum in it. A Friends of the Hangar Association was formed in September 2003 to maintain this extraordinary building, to work on the Museum and to organise guided visits.

Contact: Philippe Belin on +(0)2 33 54 01 02/Jacques Hochet on +(0)2 33 40 17 84 or *Mairie* de Montebourg on +(0)2 33 95 40 50. Visits on Tues, Thurs and Sat 1400-1800 or by appointment.

Continue on the D510 to the junction with D420, turn right and first left to the E3-E46 (old N13).

OR If **Cherbourg** has not been visited on Approach One, it can be visited now, via **Valognes.** Valognes was von Schlieben's headquarters (though on 6 June he was attending the War Games at Rennes) until the retreat to Cherbourg on 20 June. On that day, the 315th Infantry cleared stragglers in the area as they advanced towards Cherbourg.
Follow signs to Cherbourg along the old N13.

En route is the town of Tourlaville, in the cemetery of which are the graves of American Civil War casualties from the USS *Keersage* and the CSS *Alabama*.
For information on the Port, see the end of **Approach One**.

ITINERARY TWO

US RANGERS OPERATIONS & OMAHA BEACH

Background to Omaha and Pointe du Hoc

'Bloody OMAHA' is how most Americans who know refer to the more easterly of the American landing beaches. OMAHA was the critical beach and on the 4 miles of sands below its 100ft high frowning cliffs the Allied invasion came perilously close to failure. Once again, as with the paratroopers, it was the spirit and determination of small groups of GIs that won through.

During World War I groups of men from British villages, football teams and local clubs had volunteered together to fight. They had joined up together and, in the mass casualties on the Western Front, died together. Villages lost almost all their men at one stroke. Battalions that had been formed from such groups of friends were known as 'Pals Battalions'. On OMAHA the Americans were to have their own Pals Battalions and it is a story that had been overlooked in the popular history of the landings - until the making of Spielberg's film, *Saving Private Ryan*.

OMAHA BEACH LANDINGS

Assault Time:	0630 hours
Leading Formations:	116th Infantry Regiment (attached from 29th Division) and 16th Infantry Regiment of the 1st Infantry Division
US 1st Division Commander:	Major General Clarence R. Huebner
Bombarding Force C:	Battleships: USS *Texas* (flagship)
	USS *Arkansas*
	Cruisers: HMS *Glasgow*
	FFS *Montcalm* (French)
	FFS *Georges Leygues* (French)
	Eleven destroyers
German Defenders:	352nd Infantry Division and elements of 716th Coastal Defence Division
352nd Division Commander:	Lieutenant General Dietrich Kraiss

The Plan - OMAHA Beach Landings (See Battle Maps 5 and 6)

General Huebner's plan was to attack on a two-regiment front with the 16th Regiment on the left and the 116th Regiment on the right. In turn each regiment was to land two battalion teams on its own section of front with the task of clearing the beach obstacles and moving some two miles inland to secure the beachhead for follow-on landings. Almost 300 special assault engineers were to follow the leading waves of infantry in order to blow up the obstacles.

The set-piece plan had been prepared in great detail and perhaps reminded General Huebner of the way plans had been prepared for the highly successful American offensive at St Mihiel in 1918 in which he had taken part. The beach had been divided into eight sectors of different lengths beginning with DOG in the west and ending with FOX in the east. (See Battle Map 5). The infantry landings were to follow the air and naval bombardment at 0631 hours. The beach approaches were to be cleared by 0700 hours when for the next two hours another wave of infantry was scheduled to come ashore every thirty minutes. The plan continued in its detail - enemy strongholds to be neutralised by 0830 hours - artillery to begin landing at 0830. It was a plan that in its detailed precision had similarities to the one in September 1944 for Operation MARKET GARDEN which prompted the Pole, General Sosabowski, to complain, 'But what about the Germans?' Here, as in Holland, the enemy was not prepared to co-operate.

What Happened on D-Day

The effect of the weather on Force O for OMAHA was far worse than on Force U for UTAH because the 29th and 1st Divisions did not have the benefit of shelter at sea from the Cotentin Peninsula. The troops were loaded into their assault craft some eleven miles offshore, about twice the distance out that the British would use and against the latter's advice. Being so far out, the operation had to be done well before 0630 hours and it was, therefore, dark. Many craft got out of position, including those carrying the engineers, whose task it was to clear the beach obstacles.

Six thousand yards offshore twenty-nine DD (duplex drive) floating tanks were launched. Only two of these reached the beach. Many did not float at all, but went straight to the bottom taking their crews with them.

There were losses too among the LCVPs carrying the infantry. Ten were swamped by the heavy seas and sank. The men, loaded with almost 70lb of equipment each, had little chance of survival. Much of the intrinsic artillery to provide close-support for the infantry combat teams had been loaded on to amphibious DUKWs, but they proved to be top heavy and as a result they capsized, losing more than twenty guns.

As the leading waves of landing craft approached the beach they were off target, without their beach-clearing engineers, without supporting armour and short on artillery. The men, crouched down in the bellies of the LCVPs, had been there for three hours. They were cramped, cold and sea-sick and then, before they reached the shore, the enemy opened fire on them.

What happened on the beach is told in the battlefield tour that follows. Despite all difficulties, despite a situation that looked so desperate to General Bradley that he considered evacuating OMAHA, by the end of D-Day the Americans were on the cliffs above the beach and around the villages of Vierville and Colleville. They owed a great deal to the on-the-spot leadership of Brigadier General Cota, the Assistant Divisional Commander of the 29th Division who was awarded the DSC. That evening the first follow-up force, the 26th Infantry Regiment, came ashore to defend the bridgehead. However, the landing was behind schedule and only two of the five exits from the beach were secure. If the Germans were to counter-attack with armour within 48 hours, the beach might yet be lost.

THE TOUR

• **Itinerary Two** starts at St Côme du Mont, looks at the southern edge of the 101st US Airborne Division landing area and works eastwards over the area of the US Rangers operation to the 116th and 16th Infantry Regiments landings at OMAHA BEACH.

• **The Main Route:** St Côme du Mont - Dead Man's Corner Museum; Carentan - 502nd PIR Memorial, Town Hall and Memorials, Stained Glass Window in Church; Isigny - 29th US Division SGW in Church, 175th Inf & 747th Tank Bn Plaque, Com Déb Sig Monument; La Cambe - German Cemetery, Peace Garden and Exhibition; Grandcamp-Maisy - Heavy Group Bomber Command RAF Memorial, Rangers' Museum, Cdt Kieffer's House, Sergeant Peregory Memorial, Peace Statue; Pointe du Hoc - Rangers' Memorial, Bunkers; Englesqueville - 147th Engineer Combat Memorial; Vierville - Musée D-Day OMAHA, HQ 11th Port US Army Plaque, Floating Bridge remnants, US 5th Rangers, 29th Div Memorials; OMAHA Beach - National Guard, 121st Bn Assault Engrs, 58th Fld Armd Bn Memorials, Bunkers, 1st US Cemetery, Operation AQUATINT Memorials; St Laurent - Les Braves Sculpture, Com Déb Sig Monument; Le Ruquet - 2nd Infantry Division, Provisional Engineers Memorial, Bunker WN65; St Laurent - OMAHA Memorial Museum, AQUATINT Graves Churchyard, American Normandy Cemetery, Visitor Centre and Memorials.

Planned duration, without stops for refreshment or **Extra Visits** or '**NBs**': **7 hours** (+ 45 minutes if including the Visitor Center at the US Cemetery, St Laurent)

Total distance: 37.1 miles

• **Extra Visits** are suggested to Graignes - 507th PIR Memorial & Memorial Church to Massacre; Les Veys etc ALG A10 Airstrip & 50th Fighter Gp Marker; Brévands - Church SGW; Neuilly-la-Fôret - Airstrip A11 Memorial; Lison - US 56th Hospital Memorial; Cartigny l'Epinay - Col Warfield, US 115th Inf Regt Memorial; Les Jonquets - Airfield A5, 404th Fighter Gp Memorial; Tournières - Eisenhower's HQ Memorial; St Martin de Blagny - Airfield A5, 404th Fighter Gp & Lt Longmead Plaques; Colleville - Big Red 1 Museum, Memorials to 149th Tank Bn, 2nd Armoured Div/149th Tank Bn/Big Red One/5th Eng Sp Bde/20th & 299th Engs/146th Eng Combat Team/6th Nav Beach Bn/Bunker WN62.

• **N.Bs.** The following sites are indicated: Angoville-au-Plain - Medics of 501st PIR Memorials, SGWs in Church; Carentan – 502nd PIR & Col Robert Cole Plaque; 101st Airborne Division Memorial SGW in Church; Méautis - Airstrip ALG A17 & 505th Fighter Group Marker, 9th USAAF & Gen Roosevelt Plaques; les Vignets - 367th Fighter Gp Memorials; Cardonville - 368th Fighter Gp, ALG A3 Marker; la Grande Lande - 354th Fighter Gp, ALG A2 Marker; Grandcamp - Maisy Battery & 1,2,3,4,5,6, US Rangers & Gen de Gaulle Visit Memorials, Grave of Lt Cdr Kieffer; Criqueville-en-Bessin - Col Rudder/US Rangers Memorial; Englesqueville - Airfield A1 Memorial; Vierville - 81st Chem Mortar Bn Plaque and 'B' Bty 110th Fld Arty Bn Plaque; Formigny - US 1st & 29th Divs Plaque; Trevières - Local War Memorial, SGWs to 2nd US (Indian Head) Div, Plaque to 9th & 38th Regts, US 2nd Div.

NOTE: There can be some confusion in this Itinerary over the numbering of the N13 road. The original N13 goes straight through the towns en route and is sometimes used on the Itinerary. Following the construction of the dual carriageway by-pass road, the French should have renumbered it as the N2013 but it still appears on some sign posts as the N13. The newer dual carriageway N13 is also called the E46 and by-passes the towns.

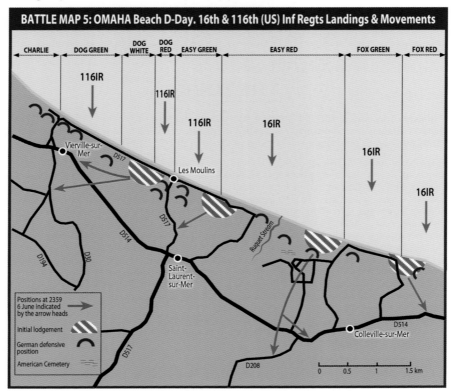

• St Côme du Mont/Holts Map R

The itinerary starts here as the natural progression from Itinerary One and in order to get an impression of the multiple waterway obstacles that faced the Americans en route to Carentan.

Exit the N13 - E46 on the D913 direction St Côme du Mont on the Route de la Voie de la Liberté.

N.B. By turning right over the motorway and taking the D913 towards Vierville, then after 1.25 miles turning right down the small road to Angoville-au-Plain and continuing to the Church, ahead between flags is a **Memorial** in Honour and Recognition of **Robert E. Wright and Kenneth J. Moore**, Medics of the 2nd Bn, 501st PIR, 101st AB for their humane and life-saving care rendered to 80 combatants and one child in this church, June 1944. **(Map It2-A/Lat & Long: 49.34896 -1.25327/GPPIt2-1/1,2,3,5).**

In front of the church is a small **Memorial** with the AB badge and the words 'Place Toccoa', Angoville au Plain. The Regiment was activated on 20 July 1942 at Camp Toccoa, Georgia, where the 506th, 517th and 295th Ord Heavy Maintenance Coy were also trained. Closed after the war, today there are **Memorials** to the Camp, to Col Robert F. Sink and to the Paratroopers and Units that trained here. Inside the beautiful little church is a colourful SGW by master verrier Jean Pierre Rivière, showing a descending parachutist, unveiled in June 2004. Two later stained glass windows show the Screaming Eagle's badge to the left and to the right a stunning SGW dedicated to **Robert Wright and Kenneth Moore.** It incorporates the Screaming Eagle and Indian Head badges, the Statue of Liberty, entwined through which is a blood red ribbon with the quotation from John 15:13, 'Greater love hath no man than this that he lay down his life for his friend.' Leaflets tell the story of how men of the 2nd Bn, 501st PIR found themselves isolated and surrounded by Germans after they parachuted into the village on 6 June 1944.

A D-DAY MEMORY
Madame Levigouroux, witness of the 6 June events, Angoville-au-Plain

'The Germans occupied the bell-tower as a look-out over the marshes. On 6 June a parachutist fell into a plane tree, another just beside our bull who didn't even budge. The parachutists were very numerous around the Grand Clos and the Vierville Road. At dawn bullets began to whistle. I was so afraid that I didn't want to open the curtains. Mme Sorel shouted to me from outside,

"But open up now, it's the Americans!"

Casualties mounted and CO Col Ballard sent his Adjutant, Lt Allworth, with the two Medics to the first aid post in the church. Wounded from both sides continued to pour in, plus one French child (M. Longeard, whose picture together with Robert Wright on 6 June 2002 is shown on the leaflet). Angoville changed hands three times but the aid station held fast. At one stage armed German soldiers burst into the church, but seeing their comrades being treated, quietly slipped out. The medics worked for 72 hours without rest or food.

Today the blood-stained pews and bullet marks still bear witness to this remarkable story but the ancient church is badly in need of repairs and upkeep that are beyond the means of the small congregation of a Commune of only 50 people. Please be generous with your donation. A booklet 'Angoville-au-Plain 6, 7 & 8 June 1944 is on sale for Ä3.00. It was published in June 2004 and describes pilgrimages to the church by both Wright and Moore. This is a most inspiring and moving story and Angoville is well worth a visit to pay tribute to their exceptional dedication and bravery.

Turn left following signs to Carentan on the N2013. Continue to the junction of the D913 and the turning to the right to St Côme. Stop in the parking area beside the Museum on the corner.

Set your mileometer to zero.

■ No. 5. Dead Man's Corner Museum, Paratrooper Militaria Emporium/ 0 miles/ 25 minutes/Map It2-1/Holts Map R32/Lat & Long: 49.32857 - 1.26841

Dead Man's Corner was chosen as the site for a Museum because of its historical importance. Its name dates from 7 June when in the American attack on Carentan the first tank to arrive at this crossroads was brought to a stop by the enemy and the Tank Commander was mortally wounded. His body hung outside the turret for several days. It is thought that his name was Lt Walter T Anderson of 80th Tank Battalion who were fighting in this area with the 3rd Battalion of the 2nd Infantry. Anderson is buried in the St Laurent Cemetery.

This beautifully presented Museum is in a sympathetically restored and converted house which in June 1944 had been requisitioned by the German 6th Paras under Major von der Heydte. On entry the visitor is immediately transported back to those momentous days passing from von der Heydte's command room to the first aid post of Dr Kartheinz Roos. One of the outstanding features of this Museum is the realism of the models in the dioramas which took over 1,000 hours to complete. Many of the faces were modelled from photos of actual participants in the drama that unfolded here.

Upstairs one moves from ship to tank to aircraft (don't forget to look up in the roof where a US Para is landing!). The showcases are brimming with personal belongings of some of the most important players in the 1944 drama: uniforms, weapons, packs and some moving personal items such as family photos, giving them an extra human dimension. The exhibits are largely the personal collection of Curator Michel de Trez, augmented by gifts and loans from American Veterans and their families. The two other driving forces of the Museum and the militaria emporium, The Paratrooper, that adjoins it are Belgian Michel De Trez, military publisher, film maker and manufacturer of authentic military uniforms and equipment (who worked with Spielberg on *Saving Private Ryan* and *Band of Brothers*) and Emmanuel Allain of Carentan who is also an expert on D-Day Militaria. Together they are working with CHC and other organisations to keep alive the memory of and to honour the Veterans of the Landings and the Battle for Normandy. Future plans include a fine statuary group of the bayonet charge of Lt-Col Robert Cole, MoH and Major John Stopka, DSC, of the 502nd PIR at 'The Cabbage Patch' (qv) when funds are available.

The Paratrooper is a veritable Aladdin's Cave for Militaria collectors with high quality souvenirs and artefacts for sale.

Outside exhibits include a French Chenillette and a German 88mm gun.

Open: Every day other than Sundays from 15 Oct-30 May. **Closed:** 24, 25, 31 Dec and 1 Jan. Entrance fee payable. Tel: +(0)2 33 42 00 42. E-mail: Carentan.101@orange.fr Website: www. paratrooper.fr

The road that runs past the house is called Purple Heart Lane.

At the end of D-Day the 101st Airborne Division had achieved most of its objectives, but around the locks on the outskirts of Carentan, which controlled the flood waters of the Douve River, the paratroopers were struggling against fierce resistance.

The High Command of the German 7th Army, responsible for the defence of the area, was still not certain that the main invasion had arrived. Reports coming in were confusing. The use of WINDOW had upset German radar and the Rupert dummy parachutists had fooled the Germans into believing that air drops had been made very far afield from the true DZs. The scattered drop also made life difficult for the defenders. Although some German forces, such as elements of von der Heydte's 6th Parachute Regiment, were fighting well, there was little co-ordinated resistance. It was small unit against small unit, often in contest over the possession of a village strongpoint or a road or railway bridge.

The N13 leading south from St Côme du Mont had been turned into a causeway by opening the locks on the Douve and flooding the fields. It was the obvious route to Carentan from the 101st Airborne landing areas and German resistance in St Côme was stubborn.

At 0430 hours on 7 June the 506th PIR with half-a-dozen Sherman tanks of 746th Tank Battalion advanced on the village from the direction of Vierville in the north-east. Attack and counter-attack followed, but by nightfall the Germans had not been moved. Over at the locks just above Carentan, after a day's fighting and following the initiative of Colonel Johnson, CO of the 501st PIR, who walked towards the enemy carrying a flag and suggested that they might capitulate, remnants of the 1st Battalion of the 6th Parachute Regiment surrendered - though not before some had been shot by their own officers for wanting to give up. However, enemy fire from Carentan prevented any exploitation south.

At 0445 hours on 8 June, behind a rolling barrage, a mixed force of the 101st Airborne Division under Colonel Sink attacked St Côme from the north-east. Some eight fierce actions followed, but when the Americans established a defensive line south of the village across the N13 at about 1600 hours the Germans withdrew to the west. Equipment abandoned in St Côme suggested that the defenders had been the young paratroopers of the 6th Parachute Regiment.

In concert with the attack from the east there had been an assault from the north in the area of Houesville by the 502nd PIR and it was there that General McAuliffe (the same General that would say 'Nuts' to the Germans in Bastogne) found Colonel Benjamin Vandervoort, the Commanding Officer of the 2nd Bn of the 505th, sitting in a wheelbarrow with his ankle in plaster directing the assault. It is a story depicted in the film *The Longest Day*. John Wayne played the part of Colonel Vandervoort.

Steadily over the next two days, the Americans linked up along the Douve and reorganised for a drive upon Carentan. Between St Côme and Carentan were four bridges over the four main waterways. West to east they are - the Jourdan, the Douve, the Groult and the Madeleine. Before Carentan could be taken the bridges had to be crossed.

On 7 June, Lieutenant General Omar N. Bradley, Commanding the American First Army, had decided to alter the priority task given to Major General J. Lawton Collins' VII Corps which had landed on UTAH (4th Infantry Division was part of VII Corps) The corps' objective was changed from the capture of Cherbourg to the linking up with V Corps on OMAHA, i.e. that the Corps' direction should shift to the south. The heavy resistance encountered, particularly on OMAHA, made it advisable to concentrate and co-ordinate the two American forces before the Germans could exploit the gap between the Beaches.

The key to the joining of the forces was Carentan, set squarely on the N13 and at the base of the Douve, and its canal system running to the sea. The Germans were aware of the town's importance and the German 7th Army Headquarters ordered 6th Parachute Regiment to 'defend Carentan to the last man.'

On 10 June glider and paratroop forces of the 101st Division began their move astride the N13 towards Carentan, scrambling over and under the bridges and paddling in rubber dinghies. The Germans countered with 88mm and machine-gun fire, supported by a brief air attack by two German planes, but the Americans pressed steadily on towards Bridge Number 4, the last one before the town.

Continue on the D974/N2013 towards Carentan, crossing the rivers, Jourdan, Douve, (and passing Kilometer Marker 10) Groult and Madeleine. The bridge over La Madeleine was Bridge Number 4. Continue to the roundabout with the D971.

N.B.1. By turning right here onto the D971 and continuing to the first house on the left, a black **Plaque** with the Screaming Eagle insignia may be found in the fence of the house. It notes that this was the **Command Post** of **Col Robert G. Cole** from which his **502nd PIR** launched their bayonet attack on the Cabbage Patch (qv). **Map It2-B/Lat & Long: 49.31226 -1.26139/GPPIt2-1/6).** Erected by the Assoc des Amis du 101st AB.

N.B.2. By continuing and going straight over at the next roundabout still on the D971 signed to La Haye du Puits (known to the GIs as 'Hooey Pooey'), then straight over at the crossroads and first right onto the small road, the D443 direction Méautis, continuing over the D903, a Marker will be reached on the left after some 3 miles. It is to **Advanced Landing Group A17 and the 505th Fighter Group, 9th USAAF**, built by **840th Air Engs Bn**, 16.08/15.09.44. **Map It2-C/Lat & Long: 49.28095 -1.29531/GPPIt2-1/7).** It was erected on 7 June 1989 by the people of Méautis in gratitude to those who gave their lives for its liberty.

N.B.3. By continuing another half a mile into the village and turning right at the crossroads the Church will be reached. In the churchyard is the local war memorial and on it is a white **Plaque** with gold letters to **Gen T. Roosevelt** (qv), who died in the Commune on 13 July 1944 (**Map It2-D/Lat & Long: 49.27931 -1.30132/GPPIt2-1/10).** There is another, more recent, grey polished granite **Plaque** to the General, 'Citizen of Honour of Méautis, on the wall of a house some 100 yards before the church in Place Gen Roosevelt.

ITINERARY TWO MAP: US RANGERS OPS & OMAHA BEACH

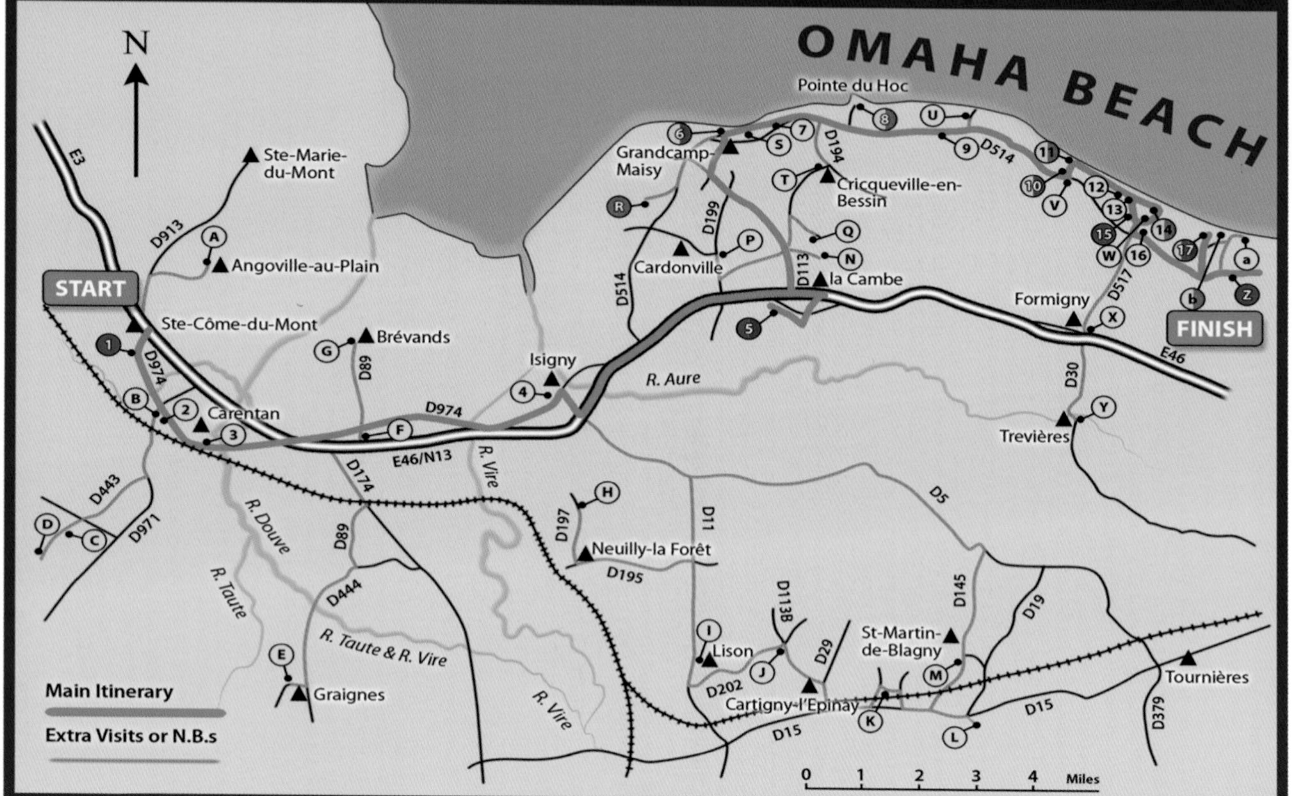

OMAHA BEACH

N

START

FINISH

Pointe du Hoc

Grandcamp-Maisy

Cardonville

Criqueville-en-Bessin

la Cambe

Formigny

Trevières

Tournières

St-Martin-de-Blagny

Cartigny-l'Epinay

Lison

Neuilly-la Forêt

Isigny

Brévands

Carentan

Ste-Côme-du-Mont

Angoville-au-Plain

Ste-Marie-du-Plain

Graignes

R. Aure

R. Vire

R. Douve

R. Taute

R. Taute & R. Vire

R. Vire

D514

D194

D199

D513

D30

D517

D5

D11

D195

D197

D174

D89

D974

E46/N13

D971

D443

D444

D913

E3

D29

D202

D113B

D145

D19

D15

D379

E46

0 1 2 3 4 Miles

Main Itinerary

Extra Visits or N.B.s

LEGEND: ITINERARY TWO MAP: US RANGERS OPS & OMAHA BEACH

MAIN ITINERARY

1. Dead Man's Corner Mus/Emporium, St Côme
2. 502 PIR/Col Cole MoH/Capt Hancock Silver Star, Cabbage Patch, Carentan
3. Com Déb Sig/101 AB SGW, Carentan
4. US 29 Div SGW/Com Déb Sig/175 Inf & 747 Tank Bn Pl, Isigny
5. Ger Cem/Exhibition, La Cambe
6. Heavy Bomber Gp Cmd RAF/Rangers' Mus, Grandcamp-Maisy
7. Cdt Kieffer's House & Grave/Sgt Peregory MoH/Peace Statue, Grandcamp-Maisy
8. Info Centre/Rangers' Mem/Bunkers, Pointe du Hoc
9. 147 US Combat Bn, Château d'Englesqueville
10. Mus D-Day OMAHA/HQ 11 Port US/Mulberry Section/6th Eng Sp Bde/5 US Rangers Bn/ 29 Inf Div/J.R. Sainteny, Vierville
11. Nat Guards/121 Bn Assault Eng/58th Armd Fld Arty/Bunker, OMAHA Beach
12. 1st US Cem, Europe, OMAHA Beach
13. AQUATINT Pl/Com Déb Sig/Les Braves Sculpture
14. 2 Inf Div/Prov Eng Sp Bde/Bunker, le Ruquet
15. OMAHA Mem Mus, St Laurent
16. AQUATINT Graves, St Laurent
17. Normandy American Cem & Mem/Visitor Center, St Laurent

EXTRA VISITS & 'N.B.s'

A. Moore & Wright, 501 Medics/SGWs/Camp Toccoa, Angoville-au-Plain

B. Col Cole Cmd Post/502 PIR, Carentan
C. ALG A17/505 Fighter Gp, Méautis
D. Roosevelt Pls, Méautis
E. 507 PIR/Massacre, Graignes
F. Airstrip A10/50th Fighter Gp, Les Veys
G. SGW, Brévands
H. Airstrip A11, Neuilly-la-Fort
I. US 56 Hosp, Lison
J. Col Warfield/US 115 Regt, Cartigny l'Epinay
K. Airstrip A5/404 Fighter Gp, les Jonquets
L. Gen Eisenhower HQ, Tournières
M. Airstrip A5/404 Fighter Gp/Lt Longmead, St Martin de Blangy
N. ALG A2/367 Fighter Gp, les Vignets
P. ALG A3, 368 Fighter Gp, Cardonville
Q. ALG A2/354 Fighter Gp, la Grande Lande
R. Maisy Bty, les Perruques
S. US Rangers/Gen de Gaulle, Grandcamp-Maisy
T. Col Rudder & US Rangers, Criqueville-en-Bessin
U. Airstrip A1/366 Fighter Gp, Englesqueville
V. 81 Chem Mortar Bn/B Bty 110 Fld Arty Bn, Vierville
W. Airfield E1/A21C, St Laurent
X. US 1 & 29 Div Pl, Formigny
Y. Lady of Trevi res/ 377 IR & Geo L Praz SGWs/9 & 38 Regts, US 2 Div Pl, Trevières
Z. Big Red 1 Mus, Colleville
a. 149 & 741 Tank Bns, Belhambra Club, Colleville
b. 1st Inf Div Mem/5 Eng Sp Bde/20 & 299 Eng/146 Eng Combat Bn/6th Nav Beach Bn/Bunker WN62, OMAHA Beach

BATTLE MAP 6: OMAHA Beach 6-8 June. 1st & 29th (US) Inf Divs Movements

Continue straight over the roundabout and stop on the right after some 400 yards by a memorial and flagpoles in front of a warehouse building (Agrial).

• 502nd PIR Memorial, the Cabbage Patch, Carentan/1.3 miles/5 minutes/Map It2-2/Holts Map R24/Lat & Long: 49.31092 -1.25650

The American attack petered out in the early hours after the leading company lost fifty-seven men out of the eighty that had begun the assault, and both sides, exhausted by their efforts, rested during the remainder of the night. So many casualties were suffered on the Causeway that it became known as 'Purple Heart Alley.' Taking advantage of the lull, Lieutenant-Colonel Robert G. Cole, commanding the 3rd Battalion 502nd PIR, led his men over Bridge Number 4 and then came under fire from a house in a field behind the warehouse (which was not built at the time). Calling down a smoke screen from the artillery, the Colonel told his men to fix bayonets and at 0615 hours on 11 June he and Major John Stopka led a charge upon the house from across the road and past where the memorial now stands which was then a cabbage patch. It was probably the first bayonet charge in France since the one led by Major Pat Porteous (qv) at Dieppe in 1942. Major Porteous won the VC for his leadership. Colonel Cole was awarded the Medal of Honor, the first man in the 101st to be so honoured, and Major Stopka received the DSC - sadly the Colonel was killed in Holland (without knowing about his award) and the Major at Bastogne. Major Porteous, who landed on SWORD beach with No 4 Commando, survived the war later becoming a Colonel and a friend of the authors. He died in October 2000. The **Memorial** reads: "11 June 1944. Here, in a cabbage patch, the decisive attack of the **502nd Parachute Infantry Regiment** of the 101st Airborne drove out the Germans and liberated Carentan."

At the bottom is an additional **Plaque**, headed **'Hancock Field', to Captain Fred A. Hancock** of the 502nd PIR, a **Silver Star** winner.

In 2009, the 65th Anniversary, the flower beds by the path to the Memorial were planted with superb ornamental cabbages and behind it was a dramatic floral 'Screaming Eagle'.

Continue towards Carentan. Immediately passing Kilometer Marker No 9.

There is a series of small **restaurants** to the right of the road between here and Carentan Station, e.g. on the right at No 55, the **'101st Airborne' Pizzeria & Saladerie**, Tel: + (0)2 33 42 18 22.

Continue and park if you can by the Town Hall (opposite the railway station on the right, which was renovated in 2008) or failing that in the main square by turning left.

In the Town Hall parking area is a **NTL Totem**: 'The Battle of the Marshes'.

• Carentan: Town Hall/Comité du Débarquement Monument/101st AB Memorials/Lat & Long: 49.30299 -1.24626; 101st AB Stained Glass Window, Eglise Notre-Dame, Lat & Long: 49.30527 -1.24313/ 2.1 miles/20 minutes/RWC/Map It2-4/Holts Map R20,21,22,23

The first contact between troops from UTAH and OMAHA, that is between the Vth and VIIth Corps, had been made near Brévands, (Map It2-G) east of Carentan, when men of 327th Glider Infantry Regiment met soldiers from the 29th (Blue and Gray) Division on the afternoon of 10 June. That contact was sealed when Carentan was cleared by an attack from the east by the 327th on 12 June. The German 7th Army's appreciation of the importance of Carentan led to a counter-attack on the town on 13 June along the railway from Baupte (some 5 miles due west of Carentan), by the 17th SS Panzer Grenadier Division supported by thirty-seven assault guns and what was left of the 6th Parachute Regiment.

The 101st Airborne Division was badly mauled, but, with support from the 2nd Infantry Division from OMAHA and a P47 strike by the American 9th Air Force, the town was held. General Maxwell Taylor recalled, 'The battle for Carentan lasted for three days during which I was constantly scuttling in my Jeep from one flank of the division to the other.'

The paratroopers then pushed out defensive lines to the south and south-west of Carentan and stayed there until they were relieved by the 83rd Infantry Division on 29 June. It was the last serious battle for the airborne division which was ordered back to the UK after the fall of Cherbourg.

It was not quiet in Carentan all the time though. On 20 June the representatives of units within the 101st Division had assembled in the *Place de la République* behind the town hall for a ceremony in which the Silver Star was to be presented to officers and men when German artillery fire hit the square - however, not before Colonels Sink, Johnson and Michaelis received their awards. The ceremony ended quickly. There was another one though on 7 July in Cherbourg. Then General Maxwell Taylor, the division's commander, was awarded the DSO by General Montgomery in recognition of the division's achievements. On 13 July the division arrived back in England.

Com Déb Sig Mon, Carentan Mairie.

In front of the town hall are a *Comité du Débarquement* Memorial, and at the base a Plaque commemorating the Screaming Eagles, presented by the 101st Airborne Association on their 'Heritage Tour' in 1973 and a **NTL Totem**. Inside the town hall are flags, plaques and souvenirs of US veterans' visits.

Behind the Town Hall is the **TOURIST OFFICE.** Boulevard de Verdun. Tel: (0)2 33 71 23 50. E-mail: info@ot-carentan.fr

Here a town plan and details of the town's hotels and restaurants are available. Note that Monday is Market Day and that many shops and restaurants are closed on Saturday.

Walk to the main square, Place de la République, past **Hotel du Commerce et de la Gare/Restaurant Escapade** on the left. It has a good variety of menus. Tel: (0)2 33 42 02 00. Closed Sat lunch.

At the far end of the square is the Pizzeria des Arcades, Tel: (0)2 33 71 22 40, which you will usually find open, pleasant, quick service and good atmosphere.

N.B. By walking to the Post Office at the far end of the Square and turning along rue des Prêtres, the Church of Notre-Dame is reached. In it there is a fine **101st Airborne Division Memorial SGW** on the right as you enter the main door (GPPIt2-3/8).

Return to your car and continue towards Isigny.

Opposite the station at 11c Boulevard de Verdun, is the **Hotel & Restaurant Auberge Normande**, Tel: (0)2 33 42 28 28. E-mail: auberge-normande@wanadoo.fr Attractive décor and liable to be open fairly late. Choice of menus from gourmet to reasonable.

Cross the River Taute (your French map may show it as the Douve!). Continue about 1 mile, over the traffic lights, to the roundabout.

Extra Visit to the 507th PIR Memorial (Lat & Long: 49.24115 -1.20214/ GPPIt2-1/8) and Memorial Church to Massacre at Graignes (Map It2-E/Lat & Long: 49.24407 -1.20625/GPPIt2-1/4,9,11). Round trip: 12.2 miles. Approximate time: 35 minutes

Take the exit direction St Lô, on the D174. Continue, passing Liberty Highway Markers 45 and 44 and the railway line. Turn right on the D89 signed Graignes. At the junction with the D444 fork right, signed Graignes and continue over a causeway across the marshes. Enter Graignes on rue du 11 juin 1944, ignore the signs to the Memorial and continue to the crossroads.

Here there is a **Memorial Marker to the 507th RIP [PIR]** on the right.
Continue, following signs to the Memorial and stop in the car park on the right in Place de la Libération 12 juillet 1944.

In the parking area is a **NTL Totem** and there are WCs.
Walk through the local cemetery to the preserved ruined church.

In the early hours of 6 June, the sleepy village of Graignes was astounded to see in the bright moonlight a cloud of young American parachutists dropping into the marshes that

6 JUIN 1944 - ANGOVILLE AU PLAIN - 6 JUIN 2004

EN L'HONNEUR ET GRATITUDE A
ROBERT E. WRIGHT
KENNETH J. MOORE
INFIRMIERS 2ᵉ Bn 501 PIR
101ᵉ AIRBORNE DIVISION
QUI ONT RECUEILLI ET SOIGNE AVEC
HEROISME 80 COMBATTANTS ET UN ENFANT
DANS CETTE EGLISE
EN JUIN 1944

IN HONOUR AND IN RECOGNITION OF
ROBERT E. WRIGHT
KENNETH J. MOORE
MEDICS 2ⁿᵈ Bn 501 PIR
101ˢᵗ AIRBORNE DIVISION
FOR HUMANE AND LIFE SAVING CARE
RENDERED TO 80 COMBATANTS AND A CHILD
IN THIS CHURCH
IN JUNE 1944

John 1:15

ROBERT WRIGHT ✦ KENNETH MOORE

Ici ce situait le poste de
commandement du Lieutenant
Colonel Robert G. Cole. C'est
d'ici que sous ses ordres le
502ᵉᵐᵉ régiment lança l'assaut
du Carré de choux.
Cette plaque est en l'honneur
des hommes qui se sont battus
pour notre liberté.

Colonel Robert G. Cole's
command post was situated here.
It is from this place and under his
command that the 502nd PIR
launched their bayonet attack on
"Cabbage patch".
This plaque is dedicated to the
memory of the men who fought
for our liberty.

Plaque offerte par l'Association des Amis de la 101ᵉᵐᵉ Airborne de Carentan

RUE
DU
507ᵉ RIP

MÉMORIAL
FRANCO – AMÉRICAIN

INAUGURÉ LE 12 JUIN 1949
PAR Mʳ DAVID BRUCE
AMBASSADEUR DES U.S.A. EN FRANCE

AU GÉNÉRAL
T. ROOSEVELT
CITOYEN D'HONNEUR
DE MEAUTIS
MORT AU COMBAT SUR CETTE
COMMUNE LE 13 JUILLET 1944
LA POPULATION
RECONNAISSANTE

IN MEMORY OF THOSE CITIZENS OF GRAIGNES
AND THE AMERICAN SOLDIERS WHO GAVE THEIR LIVES
IN DEFENSE OF GRAIGNES DURING THE PERIOD 6-12 JUNE 1944

EN MÉMOIRE DES VICTIMES
DE LA LIBÉRATION DE GRAIGNES

GPPIt2-1/1	Memorial to Place Toccoa, Angoville
GPPIt2-1/2	SGW to Parachutists, 6 June 1944, Angoville Church
GPPIt2-1/3	Memorial to Medics R.E. Wright & K.J. Moore, 2nd PIR, 101st AB, Angoville
GPPIt2-1/4	Ruined Memorial Church, Graignes
GPPIt2-1/5	SGW to Robert Wright & Kenneth Moore, Angoville Church
GPPIt2-1/6	Plaque to Col Robert G. Cole's Cmd Post, Cabbage Patch, Carentan
GPPIt2-1/7	Marker to ALG 17, Méautis
GPPIt2-1/8	Memorial to 507th PIR, Graignes
GPPIt2-1/9	Plaque unveiled by US Ambassador, 12 June 1949, Graignes
GPPIt2-1/10	Plaque to Gen T. Roosevelt, Méautis
GPPIt2-1/11	Memorial to Civilians and US Soldiers, Graignes
GPPIt2-1/12	Marker to ALG A10 & 50th Fighter Gp, Les Veys

Dead Man's Corner Museum and The Paratrooper Militaria Emporium.

Dead Man's Corner Para Museum Shop, St Côme du Mont.

Diorama of Von Heydte's Command Room, Dead Man's Corner Museum.

Memorial to the 502nd PIR at the 'Cabbage Patch', Hancock Field, Carentan.

Extra Visit contd

ringed Graignes on three sides. Many of them, weighted down with their 100lbs of combat gear, drowned. The survivors made their way towards the church, silhouetted against the dark sky, until, 48 hours later, 14 officers and 168 men had struggled into the village. They were men of the 507th Parachute Infantry of the 82nd Airborne, dropped from 8 to 15 miles south of their intended drop zone, plus a glider pilot, a C47 pilot and 2 soldiers of the 29th Division who had landed at OMAHA. On the morning of 7 June the Mayor of Graignes, Alphonse Voydie, held an emotional town meeting in the church attended by practically every man, woman and child in the village. They unanimously agreed to help the young Americans, even though they knew the risks - summary execution if caught - and, led by the Mayor and their priest, l'Abbé Leblastier, they searched the swamps for the equipment dropped in them. Soon the soldiers were equipped with machine guns, mortars and ammunition. Major Charles D. Johnson of the 3rd Battalion took command of the group and set up a command post and strong points around the village.

On 8 June they ran out of rations and the village greengrocer and café owner, 50-year-old Madame Boursier, organised a ration collection from the villagers. They prepared two meals a day and transported them to the men in the outlying observation positions and occasionally made the hazardous trip over mined roads by horse-drawn cart to nearby Saint Jean de Daye, held by the Germans, to fetch bread. Several of the youngsters of Graignes scoured the surrounding countryside to bring back valuable intelligence reports and guide the American patrols.

On 8 June came the first encounter between an Americans patrol and a truck filled with German grenadiers. Several Germans were killed, but, out-gunned, the Americans withdrew to Graignes. Later that day another patrol collided with a German field artillery unit, with the same result. Then Johnson sent a group under Lieutenant Francis E. Norton to blow a bridge on the road to Carentan. As the men set charges, a 12-year-old girl warned them of the approaching Boches. Waiting until several Germans were on the bridge, the Americans blew the charge, killing several of the enemy.

On 10 June another patrol encountered a German motorcycle patrol, killing all but one man, who returned to his base with the news of the American presence in Graignes. A medic, Captain Abraham Sophian, set up an aid station in the church to treat the wounded, with the women and girls of the village acting as nurses. On 11 June the citizens were attending 1000 Mass when the news of approaching Germans burst. After a short but bitter exchange of fire, the Germans pulled out, leaving behind many of their dead. It was a mere reconnaissance in force, and at 1900 hours the real gun and mortar attack began. Soon Major Johnson and Lieutenant Elmer Farnham and his assistant were killed during the two-hour bombardment. It soon became obvious that the American force was surrounded and just before dusk they were charged from all directions. Running out of ammunition, they attempted to pull out, in many cases only to run into the hands of the Germans. The small band that remained in the church were pinned down by their attackers. Most of the villagers managed to flee into the swamps, but Madame Boursier, the Abbé and a young Franciscan priest, Father Lebarbarchon, and two of the self-appointed nurses refused to leave the wounded. Infuriated by their own losses, the Germans dragged 12 captured American paratroopers into the village square, then transported them by truck to nearby Mesnil-Angot where they were shot or bayoneted. The Abbé and the Franciscan were also murdered. The next day another 12 Americans were killed in Graignes - as were the two 'nurses' - and thrown into the pond. Among them was the surgeon, Captain Sophian. Forty four of the remaining citizens of Graignes were arrested, 66 homes destroyed and 139 badly damaged in the German reprisals, leaving only two houses untouched. The eight-centuries-old church was blown up.

About 100 of the fleeing Americans eventually managed to reach their own lines, exhausted from their hair-rising near encounters with the enemy. After sleeping for 18 hours, they were fed, showered and issued with new uniforms and were back with their units and in the fighting again within 24 hours.

The ruined church has been left as a dramatic and moving reminder of the terrible events that took place here in June 1944. Under the vaulted roof are the **Tombs of Curé Albert Leblastier and Louis de Gonzague**, shot on 12 June 1944, and on the wall to the left is a **Plaque** commemorating the inauguration of the **Memorial by US Ambassador David Bruce** on 12 June 1949. Beneath it is a blue **507th PIR Plaque**. On the rear wall is an imposing marble **Plaque** bearing in gold letters the names of the **citizens of Graignes and the American soldiers killed 6-12 June 1944**.

From the memorial are incredible 360o views over the flat marshland and the Marais de la Taute which during wet winters flood spectacularly, giving the land the appearance it had in 1944. Below the church wall is a viewing platform of the *Parc Naturel Régional des Marais du Cotentin et du Bessin*.

Return to the roundabout with the N13 and rejoin the main itinerary.

Take the 3rd exit, crossing the dual carriageway N13 to the second roundabout and take the D974 exit signed Catz. Continue to the crossroads with the D89.

Extra Visit to A10 Airstrip & 50th Fighter Gp Marker (Map It2-F Lat & Long: 49. 30508 -1.17967/GPPIt2-1/12), Les Veys; Brévands Church SGW and RAF Grave (Map It2-G/Lat & Long: 49.333 -1.1833/GPPIt2-2/1) Round trip: 2 miles. Approximate time: 15 minutes. ■ No. 6 for details of new Museum

Turn right on the D89 signed St Pellerin and continue on the narrow road to a Marker by flagpoles.

The **Marker** is in memory of **ALG A10** and those who gave their life for Liberty. **50th Fighter Gp** 9th USAAF. Built by 826th Air Engs Bn. 25.06-16.08.44. Catz, Les Veys, St Pellerin, St Hilaire, Brévands. Erected 1989.

Return to the junction and go straight over on the D89. Continue to Brévands and enter the village. Turn left signed to the church and Le Port. Drive to the entrance of the church.

In the churchyard, to the left of the church, is the grave of **Sergeant Pilot R.F.C. Dean**, **RAFVR**, 17 November 1941 who had been flying a Spitfire on an 'opportunity targets' mission.. In the church, on the right-hand side, is a **SGW** with the caption, La Paroisse de Brévands Reconnaissante. Juin 1944. Forces from OMAHA and UTAH first made contact in the Commune of Brévands.

Return to the junction with the N2013 and turn left towards Isigny, rejoining the main Itinerary.

Continue towards Isigny.

On the left is ****Hotel/Restaurant Aire de la Baie**. 40 rooms. Tel: (0)2 33 42 00 99 is passed. The River Vire, marking the junction between La Manche and Calvados, is then crossed. *Continue into Isigny and stop near the church on the left.*

• *US 29th Division SGW/175th Inf & 747th Tank Bn Plaque, Isigny Church/9 miles/10 minutes/Map It2-4/Holts Map S19/Lat & Long: 49.31702 -1.10264*

This striking, modern **SGW** was unveiled on the 50th Anniversary. On the far outside wall of the church is a **Plaque** bearing the Divisional Insignia which describes how **175th Inf and 747th Tank Bn** led by Brig-Gen Norman Cota liberated the burning town of Isigny, thereby helping to link UTAH & OMAHA. Dedicated 4 June 2004, on the 60th Anniversary.

GPPlt2-2/1	SGW, Brévands Church
GPPlt2-2/2	Memorial to Airfield A11 & 474 Fighter Gp, Neuilly-la-Forêt
GPPlt2-2/3	Memorial to 56th Gen Hospital, Lison
GPPlt2-2/4	Memorial to Col Warfield, 115th IR, US 29th Div, Cartigny-l'Epinay
GPPlt2-2/5	Memorial to Gen Eisenhower's HQ, nr Tournières
GPPlt2-2/6	Plaques to 404 Fighter Gp, 9th USAAF & Lt Langmaid, St Martin-de-Blangy Church
GPPlt2-2/7	Memorial to Airfield A5 & serving Officers 404 Fighter Gp, les Jonquets
GPPlt2-2/8	Information Board re Lt Langmaid's crash site, St-Martin-de-Blangy Church
GPPlt2-2/9	Memorial to ALG A2, 354th Fighter Gp, la Grande Lande
GPPlt2-2/10	Memorial to US 367th Fighter Gp, les Vignets
GPPlt2-2/11	Memorial to ALG A3, 368th Fighter Gp, Cardonville

Next to the church is the **TOURIST OFFICE**. 1 rue Victor Hugo. Tel: (0)2 31 21 46 00. E-mail: isigny.tourisme@ccigi.fr

Walk a few hundred yards to the main square to

• Isigny Comité du Débarquement Monument/5 minutes/RWC/ Holts Map S16/Lat & Long: 49.31808 -1.10135

Beside the Monument is a **NTL Totem**.

The towns of Isigny, Bayeux and Caen, all off the N13 road behind the landing beaches, were D-Day objectives. None was taken on D-Day. Isigny was scheduled to be taken by 29th Division who were due to land in strength once a foothold had been established at OMAHA by the 1st Division. Major General Gehrhardt, commanding the 29th Division, was to take back under command the units attached to 1st Division for the landings and head for Isigny, while the 1st Division under Major General Huebner was to drive east to link up with the British at Port-en-Bessin.

When the Americans landed at OMAHA they had expected formidable fortifications and the less- than-formidable defenders of the 'ear-nose-and-throat' 716th Static Division. What they found were good quality troops of the 352nd First Attack Division. Instead of there being just four battalions of indifferent troops to overcome between Bayeux and Isigny, there were those, plus four from the 352nd Infantry Division.

Because of the difficulties on OMAHA, Major General Gehrhardt did not assume formal command of the 29th Division until 1700 hours on 7 June and that evening the task of taking

Plaque to US 175th Inf & 747th Tank Bn exterior wall, Isigny Church.

SGW to US 29th Division, Isigny Church.

The United States of America recognizes the selfless service and manifold contributions of General Dwight David Eisenhower, Supreme Allied Commander, 1944-1945. Near this site, General Eisenhower established the Supreme Headquarters' first command post on the European continent.

This plaque was dedicated by a United States Department of Defense delegation and the Eisenhower family on 6 June 1990 during the Centennial year of his birth and the 46th Anniversary of Operation OVERLORD.

Isigny was given to the 175th Infantry Regiment supported by the 747th Tank Battalion. In a remarkable night-time offensive the 29th Division cleared la Cambe before dawn on 8 June, though a mistaken attack by allied aircraft caused 20 'friendly' casualties, and that night, following a naval bombardment that destroyed 60 per cent of the town, moved unopposed into Isigny. Omar Bradley was so overwhelmed by the devastating effects of the naval fire, for which he had frequently pestered Admiral Ernest King, (C-in-C of the US Fleet), that he gathered the Admiral, General George Marshall (Chief of Staff of the US Army), General Henry Arnold (Commanding General of the US Army Air Forces) and General Eisenhower all together in the square to show them the damage. As they were sitting in open cars, it was, he said, an opportunity from which 'an enemy sniper could have won immortality as a hero of the Reich'.

Known by the Americans as 'Easy Knee', Isigny claims to be the birthplace of Walt Disney's forebears who were 'd'Isigny', i.e. 'from Isigny'

To the right is the Logis de France **Hotel de France**. Tel: (0)2 31 20 00 33, 18 rooms, and there are a couple of convenient **restaurants** nearby, notably the good value **Le Globe**, Tel: (0)2 31 51 96 70.

Return to your car, continue and take the right turn along Avénue de Versailles signed D-Day Le Choc/Toutes Directions/Bayeux/Grandcamp Maisy on the D5.

Extra Visits to Airfield A11 Memorial, Neuilly-la-Forêt (Map It2-H/Lat & Long: 49.28370 -1.09843/ GPPIt2-2/2)/US 56th Hospital Memorial, Lison (Map It2-I/Lat & Long: 49.241924 -1.054850/GPPIt2-2/3)/ Col Warfield, US 115th Inf Regt Memorial, Cartigny l'Epinay (Map It2-J/Lat & Long: 49.24852 -1.01829/GPPIt2-2/4)/Memorial to Airfield A5, 404th Fighter Group 9th USAAF, les Jonquets (Map It2-K/Lat & Long: 49.23693 -0.98297/GPPIt2-2/7)/General Eisenhower's HQ, Tournières (Map It2-L/ Lat & Long: 49.22713 -0.94841/GPPIt2-2/5)/Plaques to Airfield A5, 404th Fighter Group 9th USAAF & Lt Longmead, St Martin de Blagny (Map It2-M/Lat & Long: 49.24823 -0.94875/GPPIt2-2/6) Round trip: 31 miles miles. Approximate time 2 hours

Take the D5 direction St Lô then fork right on the D11 still following St Lô signs to Castilly. In Castilly turn right on the D195 to Neuilly-la-Fôret. In the village turn right on the D197, past the Mairie (with Plaque to Resistance worker Jean Picot 1944 and the local War Memorial) and continue on a winding road past the end of the village sign to a Memorial on the right with flagpoles.

Airfield A11. On the stone Memorial are **Plaques to 38th Signal Bn**, July 1944, **474 Fighter Group, USAAF, Squadrons 428, 429, 430, 1944 -1984**, and a **Plaque** presented by the Assoc Groupe Combattants 9th US Force Aérienne USA 1944. Beside the Memorial is an **Information Board**. The airstrip ran across the road here pointing north east.

Return to the D11. Continue, passing the turning to the left to Lison on the D88, and stop at the Monument on the left.

It is an Inox (stainless steel) **Sculpture** by local artist Zavier Gonzalez from St Jean de Savigny symbolising the Three Waves of the Invasion Force on a plinth of red granite from a local quarry with the inscription '**56th General Hospital** July 1944-45'. Senior citizens of Lison remembered the large field hospital staffed by some 400 American Medics which operated here for over a year and which also treated their civilian wounded. They wished, in the 60th Anniversary year, to commemorate it with this monument.

Continue some 500 yards on the D11 to the turning to the left on the D202.

NOTE In Lison there is a MLC Memorial by the *Salle des Fêtes*. By continuing on the D11 and then the D6 and turning left on the D54, St Jean de Savigny is reached where there is **Wall of Remembrance to the 29th US Inf Division**. By continuing on the D66 to Cérisy-la-Fôret a marble and granite **Memorial to the 2nd US Division** on Ave 2ième Division d'Infanterie can be seen. This was also designed by Zavier Gonzalez with the Division's distinctive Indian Head insignia.

Turn here and continue to the crossroads with the D113B. By the flagpoles is

Memorial to Col William E. Warfield, 115th Inf Regt. Gold letters on the polished marble Memorial describe how on the night of 9-10 June 1944 the 2nd Bn, 115th Inf Regt of US 29th Div engaged in combat with a unit of the German Army. Eleven officers and 139 men became casualties including their Commander, Col Warfield.

Turn right on the D113B signed to Cartigny l'Epinay and continue as it becomes the D29 to the junction with the D(N)15). Turn left onto the D(N)15 and second left on a small road over the railway, to the junction with the Memorial with flagpoles on the right by a stagnant pond at les Jonquets.

On the stone **Cairn** is a granite **Plaque commemorating Airfield A5, Fighter Group 404 USAAF and Squadrons 506, 507, 508, May-August 1944-1985** (when the Memorial was inaugurated). It lists the names of 15 Lieutenants and 2nd Lts, a S/Sgt, a Cpl and a Pfc. It seems curious that so many officers are commemorated.

Turn right and continue keeping right over the railway line to the D15. Turn left and continue for one mile. At the crossroads where the D15 bends sharp left, go straight ahead on the small road and continue to the Monument straight ahead.

General Eisenhower's HQ near Tournières. When the Franco-American 9th US Airforce Normandy Airfields Association (qv) located the site, the Eisenhower Foundation erected this Monument near the actual HQ. The original had been in a field which was part of a farm between Le Percas and Bailleul. The field was commandeered from the farmer who was totally excluded from the high security area, patrolled by MPs. The inscription reads, 'The United States of America recognizes the selfless service and manifold contributions of General Dwight David Eisenhower, Supreme Allied Commander 1944-1945. Near this site General Eisenhower established the Supreme Headquarters' first command post on the European Continent. This **Plaque** was dedicated by a United States Department of Defense delegation and the Eisenhower family on 6 June 1990 during the centennial year of his birth and the 46th Anniversary of Operation OVERLORD.'

[NOTE In Jullouville-les-Pins on the Gulf of St Malo is another Monument to Eisenhower's HQ in August 1944.]

Return along the D15 and take the first turning right, the D145, signed to St Martin-de-Blangy. Cross the railway line and stop on the left at the church.

In the porch is a **Plaque to A5, 404 Fighter Group 9th USAAF** listing the same 18 names as at the les Jonquets Memorial (qv), who 'Fell in Normandy for our Liberty".

Below is a small **Plaque to 'Langmaid, N.E.**, 07.06.1944' of 397 Fighter Squadron who was shot down by Flak over Bayeux. To the left is an **Information Board** with several photos and accounts of the moving story of the search for Lt Norman Langmaid's crash site.

Continue on the D145 to the D5 then to Isigny and pick up the main itinerary.

Rejoin the N13-E46 dual carriageway and continue to the La Cambe exit and follow signs to Cimetière Militaire Allemand on the D113.

• The German Cemetery/Exhibition/Peace Garden, La Cambe/15 miles/35 minutes/Map It2-5/Holts Map T18/Lat & Long: 49.34304 - 1.02598

The Cemetery. This was originally an American cemetery, with burials of both American and German dead. In 1947 the Americans were repatriated or re-buried at St Laurent. The following year the British and French War Graves organisations began bringing in German dead and in 1956 work began on concentrating all German burials in the area into six cemeteries. The German People's Organisation for the care of War Graves (*Deutsche Kriegsgräberfürsorge*) established, and continues to care for, this and similar cemeteries. (See War Graves

RANGERS

COMMANDANT PHILIPPE KIEFFER

09

June 7, 1944 next to the
Church in "Vierville-Sur-Mer",
B" Battery, of the 110" Field
Artillery battalion, was attacked by
Enemy artillery fire.
Severely disabling four Trucks
And two Howitzers,
Wounding many men
And killing
S/SGT John E. Montgomery,
This honors them

William A. Boykin III
Captain, Commanding

10

1944 – 1945

81st CHEMICAL MORTAR BATTALION

POUR LA LIBERTE   IN HONOR
DE NOS   OF THOSE WHO
SUR ONT DONNE   FOUGHT AND DIED
LEUR VIE   FOR FREEDOM

6 JUNE 1944
NORMANDY

NORTHERN FRANCE   RHINELAND
ARDENNES   CENTRAL EUROPE

12

IN HONOR OF
MEN WHO LIBERATED
OUR VILLAGE
7th JUNE 1944
May they never be forgotten

American D.Day

Return to your car and turn left signed Centre Ville. At the crossroads there is a sign to the left to the Rangers Museum, a route which you could drive, see above.

> **N.B.** By turning sharp right on the narrow road leading to the Town Hall which is then on the left in Place de la République, the splendid **Memorial to 1,2,3,4,5 and 6 US Rangers**, 6,7,8 June 1944, with a grappling iron below it, is reached. It was unveiled on the 55th Anniversary. To the right of the Town Hall is a **Memorial**, erected in 1989, recording that **General de Gaulle** addressed the citizens of Grandcamp here on 14 June 1944. **(Map It2-S/Lat & Long: 49.38769 -1.04115/GPPIt2-3/2,3).**

Continue on rue de la Liberation which becomes rue Commandant Kieffer to the narrow house just beyond the Church.

• Plaque on Cdt Kieffer's House, Grandcamp-Maisy/5 minutes/ 21.8 miles/Map It2-7/Lat & Long: 49.38816 -0.03575

The **Plaque** states that **Cdt Philip Kieffer**, French Green Berets Cdo No 4, 6 June 1944, lived here. *Continue to the junction with the D514.*

> **N.B.** To the left is the Town Cemetery. Here, at the back of the cemetery between two flagpoles, is the grave of **Commandant Philippe Kieffer 1899-1962,** who landed with his men of the 1er Bataillon de Fusiliers Marins serving with No 4 Commando on Sword Beach on 6 June 1944 (qv). He died after a long illness, age 63. **(Map It2-7/GPPIt2-3/6).**). Also buried here is **Flying Officer Nicholas Richard Peel, RAF,** 24 Nov 1941, age 22 (qv).

Memorial to French Units, Bomber Command, Grandcamp-Maisy.

Rangers' Museum, Grandcamp-Maisy.

Memorial to Sergeant Peregory MoH, Grandcamp-Maisy.

The Statue of Peace, Grandcamp-Maisy.

Plaque on Cdt Kieffer's House, Grandcamp-Maisy.

• Sergeant Peregory Memorial/Memorial Gardens/Statue of Peace/ 21.9 miles/10 minutes/Map It2-7/Lat & Long: 49.38799 -1.03141

The Monument and the Memorial Garden behind it were inaugurated on the 50th Anniversary. Medal of Honor recipient Sergeant Frank Peregory, 29th Division, is buried in the US Cemetery. On 8 June advance elements of the 3rd Battalion, the 116th Regiment were halted by the deadly fire of a German machine gun. Sergeant Peregory attacked the enemy with daring using grenades and his bayonet. He captured 35 enemy soldiers and opened the way for the leading elements of the battalion to advance and secure its objectives. Beside the Memorial a gigantic, 10m high, 12 ton, angel-like steel **Statue** representing **World Peace** and holding a dove of peace, was erected in 2004. It was sculpted by Chinese artist Yao Yan of the Statue of World Peace Foundation (whose object is to install many such Peace statues around the world, e-mail: yyimage@hotmail.com) and is his gift to the People of Normandy. The caption is in French and Chinese and explains the complicated symbolism incorporating V for Victory, W for World, Worship, Warm etc and the double 'O' symbolising Serenity and Calm.

On leaving Grandcamp there is a replica of the Town Hall **Rangers' Memorial.**

Continue on the D514, direction Vierville sur Mer/Pointe du Hoc to the turning to the right on the D194 signed to Criqueville-en-Bessin.

N.B. Up this road in Cricqueville-en-Bessin Church there is a **Memorial to Colonel Rudder and the American Rangers** (Map It2-T/Lat & Long: **49.37704 -1.00020/GPPIt2-3/7**) erected on the initiative of then Mayor Louis Devin, President of the Pointe du Hoc Committee. The key to the church may be obtained from the *Mairie* 150 yards east (when open!). A naval shell hit the church during the landings but the church was otherwise undamaged and it is said that its bell brought US soldiers to it to prayer. The Mayor also erected the memorial to the 354th Fighter Group (qv) visited earlier.

Continue, then follow signs to the left to Pointe du Hoc, stop in the large parking area as close to the Visitor Centre as possible.

■ No. 17. Pointe du Hoc/Ranger Memorial/Bunkers/Visitor's Centre/ 24.2 miles/35 minutes/ WC/Map It2-8/Holts Map T2,2a,3/Lat & Long: 49.39468 -0.98900

On 6 June 1979, in a ceremony attended by General Omar Bradley, the American Battle Monuments Commission took over responsibility for maintenance of this area. The French have selected 12 '*Grandes Sites*' which they are improving and promoting, one of these being the Federal Monument (a sign proclaims this at the entrance) of Pointe du Hoc. Opened in May 2004, it has a Visitor's Building with receptionist, WCs and parking area with a very long walk to the actual site and a signed walking route (suitable for wheelchairs) with 23 points at which there are bronze explanatory plaques. It is a joint Franco-American project which cost over 2 million Euros. There is an explanatory **NTL Totem** at the entrance and an **Information Board**. The area of craters and bunkers has been tidied, with mown grass and viewing platforms over some of the bunkers which give good views over the site and the landing beaches, though some of the atmosphere of an original battlefield has been lost. In the reception building are two bronze **Plaques** commemorating the feat of the **Rangers** and with their Roll of Honour, listing 81 names. The casualty figures in the two Plaques conflict. **Open:** 1 April-31 Oct every day 1000-1300 and 1400-1800; 2 Nov-31 March Fri-Mon 0900-1300 and 1400-1700. Closed 1 Nov, 25 Dec and 1 Jan. Tel: (0)2 31 51 90 70. E-mail: pointeduhoc@wanadoo.fr

The small road down which you have driven from the D514 is Rangers Road. In June 1944 it was much narrower and the entrance to the coastal area was controlled halfway down by a manned guard post. The area between the guard post and the sea, which is today the memorial area, was completely sealed off by barbed wire and sentries. The only way in was past the guard post. Allied intelligence had taken great pains to locate all coastal gun batteries that could menace the invasion, and a total of seventy-three in fixed emplacements had been identified. The most formidable along the American beaches was the six-gun battery at Pointe du Hoc, which was capable of engaging targets at sea and of firing directly onto UTAH and OMAHA Beaches. The guns were thought to be 155mm, with a range of 25,000 yards and, in preparing their bombardment plans, the Americans placed Pointe du Hoc on top priority. It was decided that the gun positions would be steadily bombed during May, with a heavier than average attack by both day and night three days before D-Day, and then again during the night of 5 June. The potential threat of the Pointe du Hoc battery was seen to be so great that the 2nd Ranger Battalion was given the task of capturing the position directly after H-Hour.

The battery position is set upon cliffs that drop vertically some 100ft to a very small rocky beach. In addition to the main concrete emplacements, many of which were connected by tunnels or protected walkways, there were trenches and machine-gun posts constructed around the perimeter fences and the cliff's edge. The German garrison numbered about two hundred - men of the static 716th Coastal Defence Division, mostly non-Germans.

The responsibility for the assault on Pointe du Hoc lay with General Gerow's V Corps and hence with the 1st Infantry Division and thence with the right-hand assault formation, the 116th Infantry Regiment attached from 29th Division. They were given two Ranger battalions under command to do the job.

The man commanding the Rangers was Lieutenant-Colonel James E. Rudder from Texas who at the last minute, when his Executive Officer who was supposed to be heading the assault was not fit to do so, determined that he would lead the assault himself. General Huebner protested at the idea, but Rudder said, 'I'm going to have to disobey you. If I don't take it, it may not go'. Rudder trained his men on the cliffs on the Isle of Wight, helped by British Commandos.

The position was out on a limb, separated from DOG Green, the nearest edge of the main OMAHA beach at Vierville, by four miles of close country. Between them was another prominent feature, Pointe de la Percée, which like Pointe du Hoc, jutted out into the sea (See Battle Map 6).

The plan called for three companies of 2nd Ranger Battalion to land below the cliffs, climb them and then make a direct assault on the battery. Meanwhile, a fourth company was scheduled to land on DOG Green (Battle Map 5) with the 116th Infantry and to move west to tackle fortifications at Pointe de la Percée in order to cover the flank of the main Ranger force here.

On D-Day the Rangers were late. The strong easterly tide had pulled them too far east, and in the morning light and confusion of the air and sea bombardment Lieutenant-Colonel James E. Rudder, commanding the 2nd Battalion, mistook Pointe de la Percée for Pointe du Hoc.

Walk along the James E. Rudder footpath to the Ranger Memorial at the edge of the cliff.

Over to the right the prominent feature jutting into the sea is Pointe de la Percée. Realising his mistake, the Colonel turned his small flotilla of seven British-crewed LCAs (three had already sunk in the heavy seas and the men were bailing out with their steel helmets in the ones which remained afloat), and moved in this direction, parallel to the shore and some 100 yards out. They came under the direct fire of those manning the trenches, and the Rangers turned inshore and landed some 500 yards away to your right, Rudder's boat being the first to hit the beach. There Colonel Rudder established his HQ, featured in a well known photograph showing the spread-out American flag. The Rangers headed for the cliffs. In a novel approach they had fitted DUKWs with firemen's ladders, but the small beach had been so cratered by the earlier fire support by the battleship *Texas* and others, that the vehicles could not reach the cliff. Rocket-fired grapples were tried, but the ropes, heavy with sea water, held many down, and so with ladders and daggers the Americans began to climb.

The responsibility for the defence of the area had been taken over by the 352nd Division, a full attack formation, following its move forward to the coast by Rommel in February 1944, but fortunately the troops here were those of the Coastal Defence Force. In anticipation of commando landings, the Germans had placed 240mm shells attached to trip wires at 100 yards intervals along the cliff, and the forward troops were amply supplied with hand grenades which they rolled down as the Americans climbed up. The area was in a state of great confusion. Minutes before the Rangers arrived eighteen medium bombers raided the German positions, driving the defenders underground and, as the attacking troops struggled to gain the top of the cliffs, they had direct and very effective fire support from the US destroyer *Satterlee* and the

The Pointe du Hoc with the Rangers Memorial on the clifftop.

Rangers' Memorial, Pointe du Hoc.

One of the bunkers, Pointe du Hoc.

Memorial to US 147th Engineers in the grounds of the Chateau d'Englesqueville with the owner M. Bernard Lebrec.

British destroyer *Talybont*. Only very stubborn or foolhardy defenders remained at the cliff's edge to take a personal part in the proceedings and, once on top, the Rangers, scattering small arms fire around them, worked quickly across the torn and smoking ground to the gun emplacements. When they got there they found that the guns had been removed.

Colonel Rudder then split his small command into two. One stayed where it was and prepared a defensive position while the other set off up the road, now called Rangers Road, to find the guns, which fortunately they did. Five of the six (one had been damaged by bombing and the Germans had removed it for repair) were hidden in an orchard at the back of the field where Rangers Road meets the D514. They were found by Ranger Sergeant Leonard G. Lomell, well camouflaged but unguarded and using thermite grenades, he destroyed them.

It was in this orchard that Gen Bradley set up his first command post on 9 June and was visited there by Gen Eisenhower for a lunch of C and K rations after he landed at Omaha on 12 June.

To this point, despite the difficulty of assault and because of the air and naval fire support, the Americans' casualties had been relatively light, probably thirty to forty, but later that day the 1st Battalion of the 914th Regiment began a series of counter-attacks that nearly wiped out the

Plaque to 11th Port HQ, Vierville Château.

Memorial to Jean Roger Santenay, OMAHA BEACH.

Memorial to US 6th Engineer Special Brigade.

Marker to 1st American Cemetery, OMAHA Beach.

'Flying Fortress' over OMAHA Beach.

OMAHA Beach and the 'Pals Battalion'

The general aspect of the memorial is that of a three-sided concrete box and a Plaque in English and in French thanks the people of Vierville for helping to build the Memorial and is dated June 1989. On opposite arms on the outside of the box are quotations from Winston Churchill and Charles de Gaulle:

'I am all for volunteers who come from some uplifting of the human soul some spirit arising in the human breast.' Winston Churchill 6 May 1947. *'Les armes ont torturé mais aussi façonné le monde honteuse et magnifique. Leur histoire est celle des hommes.'* Charles de Gaulle. [Weapons have tortured, but also shaped the shameful yet magnificent world. Their history is that of mankind.]

Inside the arms of the Memorial the story of the National Guard in 1917-1918 and 1940-1945 is told in English and in French and the whole structure has been built upon blockhouse WN72. The Germans had built two *Wiederstandsnest* (WN) 'resistance points' to cover each of the five exits from the beach. On D-Day this position's two casemates, one with a 50mm weapon and the other with a 75mm gun, enfiladed the beach left and right. The position was overcome by a Sherman DD of 743 Tank Battalion with assistance from the USS *Texas* shortly after mid-day. In the cliffs to the left of the memorial other bunkers can be seen. To the left (west) along the beach can be seen Pointe de la Percée. Where you are, however, is effectively the western end of OMAHA Beach and it stretches away to the right in a concave arc for almost four miles. Nowhere less than 100ft high, cliffs stand guard over the seashore and there are only the five exit gullies (the Americans called them 'draws') through to the heights above. You are standing at the entrance to the Vierville draw, D1 (DOG 1) with beach sector DOG GREEN ahead. By the National Guards Memorial is a **LEC Memorial.**

On the right hand side of the path down to the beach from the Memorial is another **Memorial** - to the **US 58th Armoured Field Artillery,** a unit equipped with 105 self-propelled guns. The 58th began supporting fire for the assault troops at around 0600 shooting from their LCTs but when they attempted to land on Dog White (some 500 yards to the right of where you now are) some three hours later, they lost three LCTs to mines and were stopped by beach obstacles. They eventually came ashore at Dog Red (by the *Com Déb Sig* Monument visited shortly) late in the afternoon. PFC John H Glass crewed one of the M7 Priest guns which sank, and in escaping left his kit inside. This was recovered after the war by Jacques Lemonchois who led one of the official wreck recovery teams and founded the Underwater Wrecks Museum (qv). Glass's story is told in the museum and his kit is on display. Glass survived and Lemonchois made contact with him.

Beside the 58th Memorial is a **NTL**. Below the National Guard Memorial is a **German Bunker** and below that remains of the **American Mulberry Harbour**.

Below the cliffs is a mixture of dunes, scrub and waterpools leading down to the beach road on the sea-side of which is a wall marking the edge of the beach some six feet below. The beach is broad and flat and at low tide a good 200 yards can separate the beach wall from the water's edge. Those 200 yards are clearly visible to anyone on the cliffs.

On 6 June 1944 there were many people on the cliffs and they were not, as had been thought, just the conscript mixture of the 716th Static Division, but a force hardened by the addition of trained combat soldiers of the 352nd Division. To compound the situation further, one of the battalions of the 352nd Division was just completing an anti-invasion exercise in the area and was therefore deployed correctly to counter a landing - a situation oddly akin to that at Salerno in September 1943 when, following a similar exercise, Kesselring's Panzers seemed to be waiting for Mark Clark's 5th Army to come ashore. The defensive positions were formidable too, though they tended to be bunched around the five draws. Estimates indicate that along the beach were eight big guns in concrete bunkers, thirty-five anti-tank guns in pillboxes and more than eighty machine-gun posts. Then there were the beach obstacles.

The thickening of the Atlantic Wall that Rommel had inspired was very evident at OMAHA. On the sand were log obstacles in three jumbled lines each about 20ft apart, carrying mines and shells, whose function was to prevent landing craft reaching the shore. Among and inland of them were metal hedgehogs producing a combined obstacle belt of some 50 yards thick which was totally submerged at high tide. From the beach wall to the bottom of the cliffs were mines and wire, particularly concentrated in the five draws and, sprinkled along the slopes as if from some ghastly pepper-pot, were anti-personnel mines.

The 1st Division's landing plan was simple. The beach was divided into two main sectors, DOG where you are now, and EASY to the east (to the right) - See Battle Map 5. On DOG would land the 116th Infantry Regiment under command from the 29th Division. Once a foothold had been established the 116th would revert to its division and clear the area to the River Aure beyond the N13 as far west as, and inclusive of, Isigny. On EASY Red and beyond the 16th Infantry Regiment were to land and then head east to link up with the British at Port-en-Bessin. Each regiment had attached to it supporting forces to help it in its task - two battalions of floating DD tanks to provide direct fire support against enemy fortified positions and two special brigades of engineers to clear beach obstacles ahead of the bulk of the landing craft carrying the infantry. The combined forces were known as RCTs (Regimental Combat Teams), i.e. the 116th RCT and 16th RCT. It was planned that by the end of D-Day the 1st Division force would have a bridgehead 16 miles wide and 5 miles deep. In reality by nightfall on the day the bridgehead was barely the length of the beach and averaged less than 1 mile deep with most units still below the cliffs.

At first, as the armada approached the shore, despite the swamping of the DD tanks almost as soon as they were launched, the loss of supporting artillery in the top-heavy DUKWs and the absence of the main force of the special engineers who had got out of position in the heavy seas, things seemed to be going well. The landing craft were not being fired upon. It was when the ramps were dropped for the men to go ashore that the enemy made his presence felt. The leading company of the 116th Regiment was Company 'A'. It came ashore below where the National Guard Memorial stands and a regimental account of what happened was prepared by survivors and approved by the Commanding General. John Slaughter (qv) gave us typed drafts of their accounts. Here are some extracts -

The first ramps were dropped at 0636 in water that was waist deep. As if this had been the signal for which the enemy waited, the ramps were instantly enveloped in a crossing of automatic fire which was accurate and in great volume. It came at the boats from both ends of the beach. Company 'A' had planned to move in three files from each boat, center file going first, then flank files peeling off to the right and left. The first men tried it. They crumpled as they sprang from the ship, forward into the water. Then order was lost. It seemed to the men that the only way to get ashore with a chance for safety was to dive head-first into the water. **(Pvt Howard L. Gresser)**

A few had jumped off, trying to follow the SOP, and had gone down into water over their heads. They were around the boat now, struggling with their equipment and trying to keep afloat. In one of the boats, a third of the men had become engaged in this struggle to save themselves from a quick drowning. **(Pfc Gilbert G. Murdock)**

That many were lost before they had a chance to face the enemy. Some of them were hit in the water and wounded. Some drowned then. Others, wounded, dragged themselves ashore and upon finding the sand, lay quiet and gave themselves shots, only to be caught and drowned within a few minutes by the on-racing tide. **(Murdock)**

But some men moved safely through the bullet fire to the sands, then found that they could not hold there; they went back into the water and used it as cover, only their heads sticking out above it. Others sought the cover of the underwater obstacles. Many were shot while doing so. Those who survived kept moving shoreward with the tide and in this way finally made their landing. **(Murdock and Pfc Leo J. Nash)**

They were in this tide-borne movement when Company 'B' came in behind them. **(Pvt Crosser)**

Others who had gotten into the sands and had burrowed in, remained in their holes until the tide caught up to them, then they, too, joined the men in the water.

Within 7 to 10 minutes after the ramps had dropped, Company A had become inert, leaderless and almost incapable of action. The Company was almost entirely bereft of Officers. Lieutenant Edward N. Gearing was back where the first boat had foundered. All the officers were dead except Lieutenant Elijah Nance who had been hit in the head as he left the boat, and then again in the body as he reached the sands. Lieutenant Edward Tidrick was hit in the throat as he jumped from the ramp into the water. He went on to the sands and flopped down 15ft from Pvt Leo J. Nash. He raised up to give Nash an order. Him bleeding from the throat and heard his words: 'ADVANCE WITH THE WIRE CUTTERS!' It was futile, Nash had no wire cutters. In giving the order, Tidrick himself a target for just an instant, Nash saw machine-gun bullet cleave him from head to pelvis.

German machine-gunners along the cliff directly ahead were now firing straight down into the party. Captain Taylor N. Fellers and Lieutenant Benjamin R. Kearfoot had come in with 30 men of Company 'A' aboard L.C.A. No. 1015, but what happened to that boat team in detail will never be known. Every man was killed; most of them being found along the beach.

In those first 5 to 10 minutes when the men were fighting in the water, they dropped their weapons and even their helmets to save themselves from drowning, and learning by what

Plaque to 121st US Assault Engineers, OMAHA Beach.

Memorial to US 58th Armd Fld Arty Bn, OMAHA Beach.

Plaque to the AQUATINT Commando Raid, OMAHA Beach.

Sculpture, Les Braves, OMAHA Beach.

OMAHA Beach 1944.

they saw that their landing had deteriorated into a struggle for personal survival, every sergeant was either killed or wounded. It seemed to the others that enemy snipers had spotted their leaders and had directed their fire so as to exterminate them. A medical boat came in on the right of Tidrick's boat. The Germans machine-gunned every man in the section. **(Nash)**

Their bodies floated with the tide. By this time the leaderless infantrymen had foregone any attempt to get forward against the enemy and where men moved at all, their efforts were directed toward trying to save any of their comrades they could reach. The men in the water pushed wounded men ahead of them so as to get them ashore. (Grosser and Murdock) Those who reached the sands crawled back and further into the water, pulling men to land to save them from drowning, in many cases, only to have them shot out of their hands or to be hit themselves while in these exertions. The weight of the infantry equipment handicapped all of this rescue work. It left many unaided and the wounded drowned because of it. The able-bodied who pulled them in stripped themselves of their equipment so as to move more freely in the water, then cut away the assault jackets and the equipment of the wounded and dropped them in the water. **(Grosser, Murdock and Cpl. M. Gurry)**

Memorial to US 29th Division, OMAHA Beach.

Within 20 minutes of striking of the beach, Company 'A' ceased to be an assault company and had become a forlorn little rescue party bent on survival and the saving of the lives of the other men.

The tactical story of OMAHA Beach, the casualties and the bravery are usually associated with the 1st Division, because their General commanded the landing. In a sense they get the glory, yet the heaviest casualties on this bloody beach, indeed anywhere along the whole invasion coastline, were taken here on DOG Green, just below where you stand, by A Company of the 1st Battalion of the 116th Infantry Regiment of 29th Division, a 'Pals Battalion' from Bedford, Virginia. It is this part of the OMAHA landing that opens the film *Saving Private Ryan*.

The 29th Division was a National Guard Division. The nearest British equivalent would be a Territorial Division, but the British geographical recruitment net was much wider than the American one. The Americans were pals and many had been since childhood. The leading companies of the 1st Battalion were A, B and D, recruited and based respectively around the Virginian towns of Bedford, Lynchburg and Roanoke.

A D-DAY MEMORY

JOHN SLAUGHTER TOLD US HIS STORY AS WE WALKED ON THE BEACH WHERE HE LANDED

Sergeant John R. Slaughter who landed with D Company and who returned to OMAHA in 1988 to share in the unveiling of the 29th Division Memorial

"We landed in column of companies. 'A' Company about 0630, B Company some ten to fifteen minutes later and D Company about 0710, though we probably all were late. We hit the eye of the storm. The battalion was decimated. Hell, after that we didn't have enough to whip a cat with.

The small town of Bedford lost twenty-three men on D-Day. It's a town of 3,000 people. Twenty-two of those men were from A Company of the 116th Regiment. There were three sets of brothers in A Company. Raymond and Bedford Hoback were killed. Raymond was wounded and lay on the beach. Then when the tide came in he was washed out to sea and drowned. They never found his body. He was carrying a Bible and it washed up upon the sand. The day after D-Day a GI found it. It had Raymond's name and address in Bedford inside and the soldier mailed it to the family. On the Saturday (D-Day was a Tuesday) the family got a telegram that Bedford was killed and then on Sunday they got another one saying that Raymond was too. There were two Parkers killed. Then Roy and Ray Stevens who were twins, Roy was wounded and Ray was killed."

It was because of family tragedies like this, in particular the loss of 5 Sullivan brothers who were serving on the same ship, that the policy was adopted to remove from the active front remaining close family members when two members of that family had been killed in action. This fact was the inspiration for the Steven Spielberg film. His story was based on an actual family - the Nilands from Buffalo New York, six of whom, four brothers and two cousins, were on active service. Three of the brothers were in Normandy and one of the cousins also jumped at Ste Mère Eglise. When Fritz Niland was asked to identify the body of his brother he was shocked to find it was not the brother he had been told was killed and that he had therefore lost two brothers. They were Sergeant Robert J. Niland of the 505th PIR, 82nd Airborne, killed on 6 June, and 2nd Lieutenant Preston T. Niland of the 22nd Infantry, 4th Division, killed on 7 June. They are buried in the American Cemetery at St Laurent (qv). A third brother was declared missing in the Pacific (but happily was found as a POW after the war).

A D-DAY MEMORY

WE SAT WITH LEE ON THE CLIFFS ABOVE OMAHA AS HE TOLD US THIS STORY

Pte Lee Ratel. 18 years old. 16th Infantry Regiment, 2nd wave, Never in action before. A replacement. Landed on OMAHA Beach.

"It was waist deep when we went in and we lost, I'd say, probably one third between getting off the boats and to the edge of the water and then probably another third between there to the base where you get any protection at all, because it was straight down and they were zeroed in there. They're very, very good defensive soldiers, but they're not trained the same ... they're trained to think how they're told to think and Americans are more independent, they can think on their own resources and this makes a lot of difference in a battle. Most, except myself, were seasoned men, they knew what to do ... there were landing craft blown up in the water, lying in the water, they never got in ... direct hits ... bodies of men who didn't even get into the sand and there were a lot of them lying on the sand ... there was crossfire from pillboxes ... the beach here cost an awful price in men, good men ... it was a job that had to be done and we were allotted to it. That's it. You do what you have to do."

Fritz Niland was then withdrawn from active service. He survived the war, but after returning home was never again able to go upstairs as he could not bear his brothers' empty bedrooms. He became a dental surgeon. Coincidentally the Niland cousins - who both attended the premier of *Saving Private Ryan* - went to school with Charles Deglopper (qv), the only 82nd Airborne Medal of Honor recipient (for his action at the bridge at la Fière, qv.)

In September 2008 *The Bedford Boys: One American Town's Ultimate D-Day Sacrifice* by Alex Kershaw was published, telling the human story of these sons of Bedford from their schooldays and basic training to their deaths on 6 June 1944.

Further east, at the next draw, designated D3 (there was no D2) and known as les *Moulins* where DOG sector became EASY, the two other battalions of the 116th landed on either side of the exit. There was less opposition on the beach, and smoke, from grass and buildings set on fire by the naval bombardment, produced a screen that saved many lives. On EASY Red though, the 2nd Battalion of the 16th Infantry Regiment of the 1st Division were suffering the same fate as the 1st Battalion of the 116th on DOG Green, having landed opposite the Colleville draw, E3. The minefields claimed many victims and the Americans, without the specialised armoured vehicles developed by the British for clearing beach obstacles, were confined to single-file movement through the mined areas. This led to slowness in getting off the beaches and a log-jam of men and material, excellent targets for enemy fire from strong points, unaffected by the pre-assault bombing which had been dropped too far inland.

The Americans come in for much criticism over the planning for the OMAHA assault. In particular the following are singled out:

1. The decision not to use the British-developed specialised armour was foolhardy in view of the lessons of Dieppe.

2. The assault plan was too 'clockwork' and in particular ignored British advice about when and where to launch assault craft.

3. The frontal assault went against British advice, with rumours that a bloody victory in a Presidential election year would not only re-elect the President but also reaffirm the nation's pledge to deal with Germany before Japan.

Later the British, in particular Montgomery, were to have their share of criticism for being too slow in breaking out from the Normandy beachheads - Monty had already been accused of being slow, first when following up Rommel after El Alamein and second when fighting across Sicily. Much of the criticism would come from the Deputy Supreme Commander, the same officer who had said that it would be too dangerous to use the 82nd and 101st Airborne Divisions on the Cotentin Peninsula. We have the benefit of hindsight to aid our assessments of both viewpoints.

Immediately across the road opposite the National Guard Memorial is a small bronze **Plaque** mounted on the wall. It reads (in French) - 'An anti-tank wall blocked this exit from the beach at Vierville. It was destroyed 6.6.44 about 1700 by assault engineers of **29th Div USNG, 121 Battalion,** Company C, 3rd Peloton, 9th Escouade'. They used satchel charges containing 20lbs of plastic explosive.

Landing on EASY Red with the 16th was veteran war photographer Robert Capa (qv) who had covered the Spanish Civil War and the Italian and North African campaigns. Capa kept his camera shooting as he made for the shore between dead bodies and German obstacles, eventually dropping down on the sand to escape the constant small arms fire, only to be strafed by a mortar bombardment. Capa stood up and ran to a landing craft. He had shot 106 pictures and he wanted to get them back. The three rolls were rushed to the office of *Life* for whom Capa was working, and the darkroom technician in his eagerness to develop the films quickly, dried them too fast and melted the emulsion, ruining all but twelve frames. Those twelve frames are today the most evocative and familiar of the whole invasion operation. What Capa said when he learned what had happened is not recorded. There is a memorial stone to Capa at the entrance to the War Correspondents Memorial (qv) in Bayeux.

Perhaps the most telling comment made on D-Day was by Colonel George Taylor of the 'Big Red One' who, on seeing what was happening on the shore, shouted, "Only two kinds of people are staying on this beach - the dead and those who are going to die. Now let's get the blazes out of here." [It is doubtful that he actually said 'blazes'.]

There is an **MLC Memoria**l here.

Continue along the beach. To the right is the

• First American Cemetery in Europe Marker/30.1 miles/5 minutes/ MapIt2-12/Holts Map T13/Lat & Long: 49.372610 -0.885193

By house No. 156 the Memorial marks the site of the first US battle burials on Continental Europe. The 2nd Platoon of the 607th Graves Registration Coy who landed on D+1 set up a cemetery site on the bluff but it was soon discovered to be under enemy sniper fire. As they had been instructed not to make any burials on the beach itself (as it would have a demoralising effect on new troops landing) they bulldozed a trench in the sand at this site, then known as St Laurent Cemetery No 2. At midnight on 10 June, after 457 bodies had been interred they removed them to St Laurent No 1 (today's US Normandy Cemetery).

Continue to the small plaque in the wall to the left just before the Com Déb Sig.

• Operation AQUATINT Plaque/30.4 miles/5 minutes/Map It2-13/ Holts Map T14/Lat & Long: 49.37104 -0.88065

The **Plaque** commemorates an unsuccessful **British Small Scale Raiding Force Commando raid** of 1942 by eleven men commanded by Major Gus March-Phillips. The idea was to land in the dark and to take a prisoner but the Germans were probably on the alert following the raid on Dieppe which had taken place less than a month earlier. The team was transported by MTB making the final approach in a small collapsible boat. Once ashore a firefight began and shouts were heard from the shore, presumably hailing the boat. However one of the MTB's motors was damaged by a bullet and it lay offshore for a while. When she attempted to go in-shore again she was fired on by German patrol vessels, and with the beach illuminated and under machine gun fire, efforts to pick up the landing party had to be abandoned. By monitoring German radio broadcasts it was learnt that Major March-Phillips had drowned while trying to swim out to the MTB and Sergeant A. Williams and Private R. Leonard were shot by the Germans on 13 September. All three are buried in the churchyard of St Laurent-sur-Mer which is visited later on this itinerary. The other members of the force were taken prisoner and some later escaped.

Continue to the Com Déb Sig Monument.

• Comité du Débarquement Signal Monument/Les Braves Sculpture/30.5 miles/10 minutes/Map It2-13/Holts Map T15/Lat & Long: 49.37055 -0.87972

On the sides of the Monument are panels to 1st Infantry Division and 116th Infantry Regimental Combat Team of the 29th Infantry Division. The monument marks the junction between DOG and EASY sectors and is at the bottom of Exit D3, les Moulins. A **NTL Totem** also tells the story here. On the beach below is a 9m high stainless steel sculpture by Anilore Ban (website for more details: www.anilorebanon@wanadoo.fr) weighing 15 tons called *Les Braves*. The central pillar represents The Rise of Freedom and it is flanked by the Wings of Hope and Fraternity. The Euros 600,000 for the statue was donated by M et Mme Jean Paul Delorme. It was inaugurated on 6 June 2004.

Along the beach wall on rue **Bernard Anquetil** (*fusillé*, 1916-1941) are **Information Panels** describing the symbolism of the sculptures and the Landings here.

Continue along the Beach, signed to le Ruquet, on a road that can be very busy in the season.

On the right is the modern unrated **Hotel-Restaurant La Sapinière**. Pleasant, accommodating restaurant. Large terrace and garden. 5 rooms. Closed Nov-beginning of March. Tel: + (0) 2 31 92 71 72. E-mail: sci-thierry@wanadoo

Continue to the memorials and bunkers on the right.

• 2nd Infantry Division/Provisional Engineers Special Brigade Memorials/Bunker WN65, le Ruquet/33.1 miles/15 minutes/Map It2-14/Holts Map U1,2,3/Lat & Long: 49.36432 -0.86355

The beach here is EASY Red and the exit which runs uphill past the obvious bunker is E1. The American official history records this as the St Laurent exit and mistakenly calls the river Ruquet, the 'Ruguet'.

The bunker was designated WN65 - *Wiederstandsnest* 65. The WN defences were generally the smallest structures, usually manned by one or two squads though not always with heavy weapons. When several WNs were combined for defence of a greater area the arrangement was called a *Stutzpunkt* (strong point) and had a 'garrison' of about platoon strength, plus a local reserve, though none of this form were found along the beaches (the defences in the area of the Leclerc Monument were probably the nearest to a *Stutzpunkt*. Larger combinations, such as that around Cherbourg, were known as *Verteidigungsbereiche* (defensive areas).

Thanks to the determined efforts of the 37th and 149th Engineer Combat Battalions the 16th Infantry were able to move off the beach here relatively quickly and it became the main exit for

Plaque to the 467th AAA AW Battalion (SP) and gun, Bunker WN65 at Exit E1.

Bunker WN65, the St Laurent draw, (Exit E1) le Ruquet, OMAHA Beach.

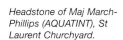

Bunker WN65, June 1944. (Compare with picture above.)

1940s Family Scene, OMAHA Musée Mémorial.

Headstone of Maj March-Phillips (AQUATINT), St Laurent Churchyard.

Entrance to OMAHA Musée Mémorial.

OMAHA on D-Day. E Company of the 16th, with the help of the 37th, three of whose men won the DSC that day, took the bunker in a fight that left 40 Germans dead. Serving in the 149th were twin brothers Jay B. Moreland and William W. Moreland, both of whom were killed on D-Day. They are commemorated on the wall in the Garden of the Missing in the American Cemetery. Following its capture, the bunker was used by the Provisional Engineer Special Brigade Group as its HQ on D-Day and there is a plaque on the bunker recording that fact and giving a list of the units in the Brigade.

Over the gun port is another **Plaque** to the **467th AAA AW Bn (SP)** [who] landed here am 6 June. Dedicated by the survivors of the Bn June 6 1994.' It was a self-propelled Anti Aircraft Artillery Air Warning Bn.

In front of the bunker is a black monolith **Memorial to the 2nd Infantry Division** which was part of the follow-up force on 7 June and on the heights behind and to the left of the bunker can be seen the fir trees that form the boundary to the American National Cemetery.

Below the Memorial is a **NTL Totem** describing how on 7 June the Engineers built an airfield, ELSA21, on the flat ground between Le Ruquet and Les Moulins, the first airfield on liberated territory. By 1900 hours that night it was in use to evacuate the wounded. Gen Eisenhower, who crossed the Channel on the Destroyer *Thompson*, landed at OMAHA on 12 June, noticed that the airfield was still being bulldozed. The **Memorial to ELSA21 (E1 A21C)** is described later in the Itinerary but may be reached by foot or small car by continuing up the narrow road behind the Bunker.

Return to the Comité Monument and turn left uphill.

To the right is the pleasant **Restaurant l'Omaha.** Tel: (0)2 31 22 41 46.
E-mail: l-omaha@wanadoo.fr with good choice of menus.
To the left is the modern, unrated **Hotel-Restaurant D-Day House**. Tel: (0)2 31 92 66 49.
E-mail: jj.gaffie@wanadoo.fr Open all year.

Continue to the museum on the right.

• OMAHA MUSEE MEMORIAL, 6 JUIN 1944/34.2 miles/20 minutes/ Map It2-15/Holts Map T16/Lat & Long: 49.36713 -0.88185

Now much enlarged, with new dioramas, this private Museum has a chronological presentation of the events from the occupation to the landings, including Operation AQUATINT. There is an impressive display of guns, uniforms and military vehicles from the campaign. Among its well-presented exhibits and documents are many personal items including some moving photos of the 'Bedford Boys' killed on DOG Green Beach and an audio-visual presentation. In the car park is a Sherman Tank, a 155mm 'Long Tom', a landing craft and an **NTL Totem**. There is an attractive boutique.
Open: 15 Feb-15 March 1000-1230 and 1430-1800, 16 March-15 May 0930-1830, 16 May-15 Sept 0930-1900 (July and Aug 0930-1930). 16 Sept-15 Nov 0930-1830. Entrance fee payable. Tel: (0)2 31 21 97 44. Email: musee-memorial-omaha@wanadoo.fr Consult website: www.musee-memorial-omaha.com for changing information.

Continue uphill to a turn to the left on Rue du Val.

N.B. By turning left here, then forking left and left again signed to 'La Plage, La Sapinière', a **Memorial** to **Airfield E1,A21C** is reached. Beside it is an **Information Board** about the Airfield which was operational from June 8 1944, constructed by 834th Air Eng Bn, 9th Eng Command, 9th USAAF and used by 9th AF Service Command. (**Map It2-W/Lat & Long: 49.36129 -0.86723/GPPIt2-3/11**).

Note that you can reach the Bunker at Le Ruquet, La Sapinière and the beach from this site by continuing down the narrow road.

Continue to the D514 crossroads.

On the left is the **Hotel-Restaurant La Cremaillère**. Tel: (0)2 31 22 44 22.

N.B.I. By continuing straight over on the D517 to the crossroads in Formigny just before the N13 [with a splendid 100 Years Memorial on right], there is a small **Tourist Office** Building to the right. On the wall of the *Mairie* to the left there is a **Plaque** to **US 1st and 29th Divisions,** with their divisional insignia, who liberated the village on 7 June 1944. (**Map It2-X/Lat & Long: 49.33277 -0.89960/GPPIt2-3/12**). It was dedicated on 3 June 2006 by two veterans of each Division.

N.B.2 By continuing under the motorway on the D30 a **LEC Memorial** may be found by the bridge over the Aure River en route to Trevières Church (some 4 miles from D514.) Beside the Church is **Trevières War Memorial.** (Map It2-Y/Lat & Long: **49.30771 -0.90379/GPPIt2-4/1**). The face of this striking bronze female figure wearing a *Poilu's* helmet was damaged by a shell during the Battle of Trevières in June 1944. It was, of course, the village First World War Memorial. The citizens decided to keep the damaged figure as a reminder of the dreadful suffering that Normandy had to undergo for her liberty. A small Plaque to the right shows the statue in her pre-war glory and explains the story in French and in English. At a ceremony on 23 October 2004 a replica of Edmond de Laduedrie's 1921 statue, called **'The Lady of Trevières'**, was unveiled in the fine **National D-Day Memorial** in Bedford, VA, that had been dedicated by President Bush. At the same ceremony the *Légion d'Honneur* was presented to US 29th Div Veteran, Bob Slaughter (qv), to former military Nurse Evelyn Kowalchuk and to the Mayor of Bedford. The small town of Bedford was chosen as the site for the National D-Day Memorial as proportionally it sustained the US nation's highest D-Day casualties. In the church behind the altar are two **SGWs, to the left Saint Michael, commemorating the memory of the officers and soldiers of the 377th Inf Regt, 95th Inf Div, Men of America, Friends of France, and to the right St George, In memory of Geo L Praz and the American friends of Trevières** (GPPIt2-4/2).

On the wall to the right of the entrance to the *Mairie* (opposite) is a **Plaque to the 9th and 38th Regiments of the Second Infantry Division (GPPIt2-4/6)** who took part in the battle of Trevières 8-10 June 1944. It was erected by the 2nd Infantry Division Association Monument Foundation on 6 June 1989. There are strong links between the Association and the citizens of Trevières and there have been several pilgrimages here by veterans and their families. Inside the *Mairie* is the Divisional History of the 2nd 'Indian Head' Infantry Division, whose motto is 'Second to None'. In the words of a survivor, the Battle of 'Trevières was a tough nut to crack'. The attack by 9th and 38th Regiments began at 1200 hours on 9 June on this important German HQ, with its carefully prepared positions. By the end of the day the 38th had entered the town, but it was not until the end of 10 June that they cleared Trevières after a house-to-house battle. 2nd Medical Battalion Clearing Station at St Laurent quickly established a collecting station near the town to evacuate the casualties of the fighting.

Turn left. After 200m turn left by the War Memorial and continue down the small road to the church.

• AQUATINT Graves, St Laurent Churchyard/35.0 miles/10 minutes/ Map It2-16/Lat & Long: 49.35947 -0.87818

To the right on entering the churchyard are the CWGC graves of: **R. Lehnigen**, who served as **Private R. Leonard**, Pioneer Corps Commando, age 42, personal inscription *"Die Internationale wird die Menschheit sein"*, he was a Sudetenland Czech who had escaped to England and had been on the Dieppe Raid; **Major G.H. March-Phillips**, DSO, MBE, Royal Artillery, Commando, age 34, personal inscription, "A gallant, beloved husband, 'He that loveth, flyeth, runneth and rejoiceth: He is free'", and 609816 **Sergeant A.M. Williams**, The Queen's Royal Regiment, Commando, age 22, personal inscripton, "R.I.P." Beside March-Phillips' grave is a marble slab with one of his poems, "If I Must Die", written in 1941, "." All took part in the **AQUATINT Raid** (see above) of 12 September 1942.

Return to the D514 and continue following signs to the American Cemetery. Turn left onto the approach avenue. ■ **No. 7.**

Immediately on the left is the charming ***Hotel-Restaurant Domaine de l'Hostréière**, based on an old farmhouse, with 19 well-designed modern bedrooms, heated outdoor pool/sauna, massage, Internet connection. Quick lunches available. Closed 1 Dec-30 April. Tel: (0)2 31 51 64 64. Fax: (0)2 31 51 64 65. E-mail: hotelhostreiere@wanadoo.fr

Continue, following signs to the car park and stop at the top as close as possible to the new Visitor/Interpretation Center.

NOTE. Regular visitors should note that the cemetery should now be approached through the **Visitor/Interpretative Center** and that the old Reception Center is now closed, though it is possible to go directly to the cemetery. If making a thorough visit to the Center a further 45 minutes should be added. This poses something of a dilemma to those, especially tour groups, on a tight schedule and a difficult priority choice may have to be made or a decision to omit

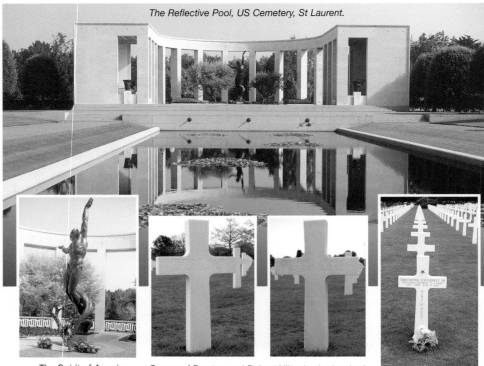

The Reflective Pool, US Cemetery, St Laurent.

The Spirit of America statue.

Graves of Preston and Robert Niland, who inspired the 'Private Ryan' story.

Grave of Brigadier General Theodore Roosevelt, MoH.

something else. Some regular visitors find the exterior of the building somewhat austere and severe and the security measures rather forbidding. This is belied by the very emotional personal stories that are featured through photographs, documents and excellent film footage.
In the area of the old car park was a **NTL Totem** which bore the lines,

Visitor
Look how many of them there were
Look how young they were
They died for your freedom
Hold back your tears and be silent.

Follow signs to Visitor Centre (and signs to WCs/restrooms situated to the left).

• The Normandy American Cemetery and Memorial, St Laurent/ 37.1 miles/45(+45 more if including the Visitor Center) minutes/ WC/Map It2-17/Holts Map U4,10/Lat & Long: 49.35658 -0.85297

Open (Visitor Center and Cemetery): 15 April-15 Sept 0900-1800; 16 Sept-14 April 0900-1700. **Closed** Christmas and New Year's Day. Flags are lowered half an hour before closing time when recordings of 'Retreat' and 'To the Color' are played. There is no admission charge. Visitors go through a security check on entering the Visitor Center. Tel: (0)2 31 51 62 00. Website: www.abmc.gov

Visitor/Intrepretative Center (completely renovated early 2019)

This is not a museum in the received sense of the word. Most of the artefacts and uniforms are reproductions, meant to illustrate their actual 1944 appearance, as the soldiers received them, but a more than adequate sense of what happened here in WW2 is experienced through the films and the exhibits.

Inaugurated on 6 June 2007, this 30,000 square feet building, which cost some $30million, was designed by the Smith Group of Washington with exhibition designers Gallagher & Assocs of Bethesda, Maryland. The historical consultants were Brig-Gen John S. Brown, USA (Retd), Russell F. Weigley, PhD and History Assocs Inc. It has three specific goals:

The Visitor Center, US Cemetery, St Laurent.

1. To provide an effective and efficient facility that architecturally complements the cemetery with style and dignity and which deepens the cemetery visit experience.

2. To develop appropriate messages to increase the visitor's appreciation of the magnitude and significance of the Normandy operations and the sacrifices involved in victory.

3. To expand public awareness of the ABMC's services, facilities and objectives with regard to honouring America's War Dead. The Center is on two levels and throughout both there are meaningful quotations by WW2 generals, soldiers and politicians inscribed on large panels. There is a clear intent to acknowledge the role of the individual.

On the entry level is a reception desk with helpful staff, the Superintendent's office, a Next of Kin (who are escorted to the headstone) reception room and four computers on which visitors can search for casualty information (in English and French) which increasingly has background information on unit, decorations etc. of personnel buried in ABMC cemeteries worldwide. Incidentally, since WW2 all American war dead have been repatriated at Government expense, although the names of the missing are inscribed on memorials. Up until then the next of kin had the choice to bury their loved ones with their comrades near where they fell (as Gen Patton's family chose to do in the Luxembourg ABMC Cemetery) or to have them repatriated.

Panels describe the history and philosophy of the ABMC, and then take three important themes: Competence (planning, training, logistics and equipment); Courage (experiences on the battlefield from various roles such as parachutist, medic, resistance operative etc which describe the battles); Sacrifice (the ultimate sacrifice, lives changed forever, families left to mourn…). Each theme is illustrated with moving personal stories, portrait photographs and exhibits.

Downstairs the lead-up to war is illustrated with the flags of the Allies who participated in the Normandy Campaign. Themes include the Deception Plan, Allies, The Airborne, Life Behind the Lines, Resistance, Medical FacilitiesÉ There are several films/videos, the principal one being 'Letters', shown on the hour and half hour and lasting 16 minutes in an auditorium that seats 154 and has disabled facilities. Another called 'Beyond the Beachhead' uses contemporary film and sound. Two other short films, 'On their Shoulders' (featuring three soldiers buried on site) and 'Let's Go' (about Eisenhower's decision that put the plans for the landings in motion). There is an interactive computer programme called 'Advancing Inland'. Finally, in the Hall of Sacrifice, a quiet and serene area where one hears the names of all those buried or commemorated in the cemetery who are listed here, are twenty life-sized portraits, placed at the visitor's eye level with brief biographies.

The overall impression one gets from a visit here is that real people fought, suffered, showed courage and fear and made the ultimate sacrifice for our liberty during the Landings and the

Battle for Normandy. They had grieving families, they included women, brothers, fathers and sons, some were awarded gallantry medals, some survived but were scarred for life.

The exit leads to the path that overlooks the beach, with the graves to the left.

Cemetery Area

The cemetery was built and is maintained by the American Battle Monuments Commission (qv). **The ABMC ask that, as this is a place where the dead are honoured, all visitors should show respect during their visit, therefore quiet voices are preferred and appropriate dress (no bare torsos, swimming suits); no picnics, no dogs outside the car park.**

The architects for the memorial features were Harbeson, Hugh, Livingston and Larson of Philadelphia, Pennsylvania, and the cemetery was dedicated on 18 July 1956. The site was chosen for its historical importance - overlooking the OMAHA beaches - and includes the area of one of the original battle cemeteries used during the landings. It covers 172.5 acres, all beautifully landscaped and tended, which were donated by the French people 'without charge or taxation'. The park is a horticulturist's joy, with many species of trees, bushes and shrubs which are rare and unusual to the area, such as evergreen oaks, pines, cedars, roses, heather and holly. The beds and lawns are immaculately tended, with the avenue of trees leading to the memorial shaped and trimmed.

It contains 9,387 headstones, 307 of whom are unknown and whose white marble crosses or Stars of David (of which there are 149) bear the inscription, 'Here rests in honoured glory a comrade in arms known but to God'. On the known graves are inscribed the rank, unit, name, date of death and home state of the serviceman or woman commemorated. The headstones are set out in straight lines, perpendicular, horizontal and diagonal, which form a dramatic geometric pattern on the immaculate emerald green grass, whichever way the eye looks. Each casket was draped with the American flag as it was lined up for burial. The flag was then sent to the family.

Medal of Honor recipients' headstones are lettered in gold. This is America's highest award for gallantry, the equivalent of the British Victoria Cross. The most famous here is that of **Brigadier General Theodore Roosevelt** (Plot D, Row 28, Grave 45), who died of a heart attack on 12 July 1944. His medal was awarded for 'his valor, courage and presence in the very front of the attack [on 6 June at UTAH] and his complete unconcern at being under heavy fire inspired the troops to heights of enthusiasm and self-sacrifice... He thus contributed substantially to the successful establishment of the beachhead in France.' Beside him lies his youngest brother, **Lieutenant Quentin Roosevelt**, a World War I aviator who died in France on 14 July 1918, and who was reinterred here when the cemetery was made.

There are forty other pairs of brothers, 33 of whom lie side by side, including the Nilands (qv) in Plot F, Row 15, graves 11 and 12. Eight other pairs of brothers are buried here, but in different rows, and a father and son, Colonel Ollie Reed (Plot E, Row 20, Grave 19) and Ollie Reed Junior (Grave 20). Cousins Paul A. Lepisto and Tauno J. Lepisto lie together (Plot E, Row 18, Graves 8 and 9).

Two other **Medals of Honor** recipients of the Normandy campaign buried in the cemetery are: **Tech Sergeant Frank Peregory** (qv) of the 116th Infantry Regiment, 29th Division, whose story we tell where it happened, at Grandcamp Maisy on 8 June, and **1st Lieutenant Jimmie W. Monteith**, Jr. of the 16th Infantry, 1st Division whose act of conspicuous gallantry took place on 6 June on OMAHA. Monteith landed with the initial assault waves under heavy fire. Without regard for his personal safety he continually moved up and down the beach reorganizing men for further assaults, which he then led. He then went back to lead two tanks on foot through a minefield and then rejoined his company. He continued to attempt to strengthen links in his defensive chain under heavy fire until he and his unit were completely surrounded and he was killed by enemy fire.

There are also some women Red Cross personnel and WACs (Mary Bankston Pfc, D-20-46; Mary Barlow Pfc, A-19-30; Dolores Brown, Sgt, F-13-19; Elizabeth Richardson, Red Cross, A-21-5. Elizabeth was a 'Doughnut Dolly', giving out coffee, doughnuts, chewing gum, newspapers from a bus that drove among military units. She died in a plane crash on the way to a Red Cross meeting on 25 July 1945.) Also buried here (Plot G, Row 14, Grave 12) is **Major Thomas Howie**, 29th Div, who motivated his troops with the cry, 'I'll see you in St Lô' as they battled to liberate the town. He was killed on 17 July, one day before the liberation. His troops laid his body on the bonnet of the leading jeep as they drove into the town and then laid it on the rubble of Ste Croix Church under the American flag to receive a military salute from all those who passed. Today there is a fine **Memorial** to him to the east of St Lô at the roundabout with Rue du Maréchal Leclerc and the N174 from Vire.

The servicemen and women resting here were re-interred from temporary cemeteries (e.g. at Ste Mère Eglise, la Cambe and OMAHA Beach - now marked by memorials). 14,000 others of their comrades were repatriated at government expense. This impressive cemetery receives more than 1 million visitors each year - not only veterans or their families, but local French people. It was the setting for the beginning and end of the film *Saving Private Ryan.*

Other features are:

Time Capsule. Embedded in the ground on the right-hand side just inside the old entrance, the time capsule, dedicated to General Eisenhower, contains sealed reports of the 6 June 1944 landings. It is to be opened 6 June 2044.

Memorial. This area consists of a semi-circular colonnade, with stone loggias at each side which are engraved with vivid battle maps, picked out in coloured enamel and designed by Robert Foster of New York. Ornamental urns at each side flank a 22ft-high bronze statue of *The Spirit of American Youth Rising from the Waves,* sculpted by Donald de Lue of New York.

In 1987 the American Veterans' Association donated a memorial bell which tolls every hour and at noon. It is reminiscent of the memorial bell in the church of Belloy on the Somme, donated as a memorial by the parents of the American poet Alan Seeger, who fell in July 1916. They both toll for Americans who gave their lives in France. Every hour the carillon tolls the time and plays two US patriotic songs at random.

Garden of the Missing. Behind the memorial, the garden's semi-circular wall bears the names of 1,557 missing with no known graves, who came from 49 of the 50 States that make up the Union. An asterisk against a name means that the person has since been identified, two of the eleven, Jay and William Moreland (qv), were twin brothers. The garden is planted with ornamental shrubs and roses.

Reflective Pool/Stars and Stripes. To the left of the memorial is the rectangular reflective pool with water lilies and, beyond it, two enormous flagstaffs. The American flag flies proudly from each of them, raised each morning, lowered each evening. A reflecting pool is often a feature of American memorials as in the Lincoln Memorial in Washington DC where the pool stretches to the WW2 Memorial and the Washington Monument.

Orientation Tables. Continuing past the memorial, one reaches the first orientation table, overlooking OMAHA Beach, with a map pointing to features on the nearby landing beaches. From here one can descend a deceptively gentle-looking path down to the beach itself. (It seems very long and steep on the way up.) It is well worth the effort as from the bottom one can look up at the formidable cliffs and the sites of the heavily defended German positions which faced the Americans as they landed.

On the way down, a second orientation table shows the Mulberry Harbour designed for OMAHA, washed away in the storm of 19 June.

Chapel. Along the central pathway is the non-denominational chapel with a fine ceiling mosaic designed by Leon Kroll of New York.

Statues of United States and France. At the end of the main axis beyond the chapel are two granite figures sculpted by Donald de Lue representing the two countries.

• *END OF ITINERARY TWO*

• *OR CONTINUE WITH THE EXTRA VISIT.*

GPPlt2-4/1	WWI Memorial, Trevières
GPPlt2-4/2	SGW to US 377th IR, 95th Inf Div, Trevières Church
GPPlt2-4/3	Plaque to 741st Tank Bn, Club Belambra, Colleville
GPPlt2-4/4	Poster, 'Big Red I' Assault Museum, Colleville
GPPlt2-4/5	Plaque to 2nd Armd Div & 149th Tank Bn 'Hell on Wheels', Club Belambra, Colleville
GPPlt2-4/6	Plaque to 9th & 38th Regts, US 2nd Inf Div, Trevières
GPPlt2-4/7	Plaque to US Tank Exit Road, Club Belambra, Colleville
GPPlt2-4/8	Plaque to 2nd US Armd Div ('Hell on Wheels'), Club Belambra, Colleville
GPPlt2-4/9	Memorial to 'Big Red One', overlooking OMAHA Beach
GPPlt2-4/10	Chaplain Andrews Display, 'Big Red I' Assault Museum, Colleville
GPPlt2-4/11	Memorial to 56th Eng Sp Bde on WN62, overlooking OMAHA Beach

Orientation Table, US Cemetery, OMAHA Beach beyond.

Extra Visits to Big Red One Museum (Map It2-Z/Lat & Long: 49.34704 -0.85093/GPPlt2-4/4,10), US 149th Tank Bn, 2nd Armoured Div 'Hell on Wheels' and US 741st Tank Bn Plaques, Belambra Club (Map It2-a/Lat & Long: 49.35900 -0.84033/GPPlt2-4/3,5,7,8); 1st Infantry Div Memorial (Map It2-b/Lat & Long: 49.35839 -0.84922/GPPlt2-4/9); 5th Eng Special Bde Memorial/20th & 299th Eng Plaques/146th Eng Combat Bn & 6th Naval Beach Bn Plaques/Bunker WN62/OP/(Map It2-b/GPPlt2-4/11/Holts Map U6). Round trip: 3.5 miles. Approx time: 45 minutes

Return to the main entrance to the cemetery and turn left. Continue to the museum on the right.

Assault Big Red One Museum. All the exhibits in this interesting small Museum are original and many were found on OMAHA Beach by the enthusiastic and knowledgeable proprietor, Pierre-Louis Gosselin, who also conducts tours of the Landing Beaches. Outside are the remains of a rare 'Element C, Belgian Gate' beach obstacle found on Fox Green sector in August 2007. Known as 'Cointet' Gates, they were originally used, to little effect, by the Belgians in May 1940 to halt the German advance south of the Wavre. Inside is a rare collection of helmets and uniforms, many the gift of relatives, written and photographic

GPPIt3-1/1	Plaque to 2nd Bn SWB, Aure Bridge, Vaux-sur-Aure
GPPIt3-1/2	War Reporters' Memorial Garden, Bayeux
GPPIt3-1/3	Memorial to Base B8 & 145th FFL, RAF, Sommervieu
GPPIt3-1/4	Plaque to FO Richard Rohmer, 430 Sqn RCAF, Petit Magny
GPPIt3-1/5	Memorial to Airfield A13 & 846th US Air Eng Bn, Vaucelles
GPPIt3-1/6	Memorial to Photographer Robert Capa, Bayeux
GPPIt3-1/7	Marker to ALG B7, Martragny
GPPIt3-1/8	Marker to ALG B7, nr Martragny
GPPIt3-1/9	Memorial to 20 RAF Airfields, Esquay-sur-Seulles
GPPIt3-1/10	Plaque to US 1st Inf Div, Tour-en-Bessin
GPPIt3-1/11	*Table d'Orientation* Gen Montgomery's TAC HQ, Blay

N.B.1 By continuing to the crossroads with the D516, turning right signed to Arromanches on the D516 turning left to Vaux-sur-Aure at next crossroads and continuing to the bridge over the river a **Plaque** to the **South Wales Borderers** may be found on the bridge over the Aure. **(Map It3-A/Lat & Long: 49.3029 -0.70307/GPPIt3-1/1)**. The Plaque describes the liberation of the bridge by the 2nd Bn SWB at 2350 hours on 6 June 1944. The village, twinned with Nagasaki, is extremely picturesque.

N.B.2 By returning to the last crossroads, going straight over on the D153 to the crossroads with the small road Bois de Pouligny, then turning left on a small road with a dead end sign, the Manoir du Petit Magny is reached. On the gateway is a yellow **Plaque to 430 Sqn RCAF's 'Waiting Room'**. **(Map It3-B/Lat & Long: 49.29841 -0.67590/GPPIt3-1/4)**. Hundreds of missions were flown from Airstrip B8 (Sommervieu, visited next), including an operation on 17 July when **Flying Officer Richard Rohmer** of 430 Sqn spotted Fld Marshal Erwin Rommel in his Horch staff car near Livarot. He called in Spitfires by radio who attacked the car, severely injuring Rommel and taking him out of the war.

N.B.3 By returning along the small road to the junction with the D153, turning left and then left at the crossroads on rue Jacques Cartier in St Sulpice and continuing for approx 600 yards a **Memorial to Base B8** may be found. **(Map It3-C/Lat & Long : 49.29830 -0.65866/GPPIt3-1/3)**. The splendid black polished granite **Memorial** is to Airfield B-8, Sommervieu, constructed by the REs soon after D-Day. It was the base for 400 Sqn (Bluebird Spitfires) and 414 & 430 Sqns (Mustang Is), part of 39 Rec Wing. The Memorial actually commemorates 145th Free French Wing of the RAF, 19 August 1944.

Return to the Eisenhower Statue.

N.B.4 From the Eisenhower Statue take the D613 direction Caen and at the roundabout go straight over on the D613 (avoiding the N13). At the crossroads with the D35 turn left and continue to the Memorial on the left. It is to **20 RAF** Airfields built and used by the RAF for the reconquest of the Liberty of Europe. **(Map It3-D/Lat & Long: 49.25436 -0.62475/GPPIt3-1/9)**. The Memorial is in the shape of an arrow, with a Map showing all the Airfields at the end, the words VAUSSIEUX MARCAGNY on the top and '268'on the tip.

N.B.5 By continuing on the D35 to the small crossroads, turning right on the rue de Vaux, continuing to the first right turn, turning right and continuing to the road junction opposite the entrance to the Chateau in Martragny, a **Marker to ALG B-7 (Map It3-E/Lat & Long: 49.25100 -0.60215/GPPIt3-1/7)** is found. It was in service by the RAF from 19 July-3 Sept 1944.

N.B.6 By turning right onto the rue de l'Ormelet and continuing some 0.7 mile a **Marker to B-7** 1944 is to be found in the bank on the left. **(Map It3-F/Lat & Long: 49.24926 -0.61775/GPPIt3-1/8)**. The Marker is in the form of a boulder.

Take the ring road, direction St Lô on the D572.

Almost immediately to the sharp left is the road to the *****Château de Bellefontaine** (breakfast but no restaurant, elegant salon, simple bedrooms), 20 rooms. Open 2 Feb-31 Dec. Tel: (0)2 31 22 00 1. E-mail: info@hotel-bellefontaine.com

> *Continue, passing the railway station then the* ****Hotel Campanile***, 46 rooms. Excellent buffet meals. Tel: (0)2 31 21 40 40, e-mail: bayeux@campanile.fr on the left, over the traffic light and along Boulevard Fabian Ware (named after the founder of the Commonwealth War Graves Commission) following signs to the Musée Mémorial to the Museum parking area on the right.*

■ No. 11. Musée Mémorial de la Bataille de Normandie, Notts Yeomanry, Military Police & 2nd Bn Essex Regt Memorials/1.2 miles/30 minutes (add 25 minutes for the film) /RWC/Map It3-2/Holts Map A12,13,13a/Lat & Long: 49.27301 -0.7110

In the parking area is a blue **NTL Totem.** The Museum was closed from October 2005 until its reopening in June 2006 during which time it was completely revamped. Gone is the complete collection of J-P Benamou (qv) which formed its basis and in its place comes a new collection of materiel and arms. This is displayed in 2,000 modernised and redesigned square metres with space for temporary exhibitions. After an Introductory section, 'The world at the beginning of June 1944' and 'The 6 June 1944', the week by week story of the Battle for Normandy from 7 June to 29 August 1944, interspersed with thematic displays (Gen de Gaulle at Bayeux, The Resistance, the destruction of the bridges, Allied airstrips, Medical Services, Rommel's accident and the attempt on Hitler's life, Broadcasts, The Engineers, The Liberation, The Reconstruction etc), is told. Space is also devoted to War Correspondents and to Bayeux's Annual War Correspondents' Prize held in the 1st week in October. An International Jury presides over 4 categories: Written accounts; Photos; TV and Radio, for prizes of Euros 7,600. Exhibitions of photos, films and debates are open to the public.

One interesting exhibit is the original model of the *Voie de la Liberté* Marker (qv) designed by French artist, Francois Cogné. They stretch from Ste M re Eglise to Bastogne.

In 2010 the Gen de Gaulle Museum in Bayeux closed and the exhibits were moved to a special exhibition space in this Museum, covering the years 1934, 39, 40, 44 and 46. It also includes a Resistance sector and Jewish POW uniforms, and a model of *la Combattante* (qv).

A 25 minute film, alternately shown in French and English, completes the picture (times vary from season to season). There is also a documentation section. An entry/exit at the side gives direct access to the new boutique, although the Museum should still be entered from the front.

Although the Museum, now owned and administered by the *Mairie* of Bayeux, addresses many of the same themes as its predecessor, its approach is more "*pedagogique*' (educational) and exhibits are chosen so as not to cause offence.

Open: 1 May-30 Sept 0930-1830. 1 Oct-30 April 1000-1230 and 1400-1800. Entrance fee payable (except for Veterans, Service personnel in uniform and local schoolchildren).
Tel: + (0)2 31 51 46 90. Fax: + (0)2 31 51 46 91 E-mail: bataillenormandie@mairie-bayeux.fr
Website: www.mairie-bayeux.fr WCs and snack-dispensing machines and ample free parking, which should also be used for the Cemetery and Memorial.

Outside are a number of once well-restored vehicles, guns, and some sadly deteriorating tanks (including a Hetzer SP anti-tank gun, a Sherman tank, a Churchill AVRE, and a 40mm Bofors gun).

For the assault on Bayeux, the Sherwood Rangers changed from support of the 231st Infantry Brigade to 56th Indep Infantry Brigade. Troop leader Lt Mike Howden of 'A' Sqn was the first person to enter the outskirts of Bayeux on the evening of 6 June in his tank. He was held up by a string of mines across the road and asked for Sapper support. As none was available at this stage, he was instructed to return to his squadron. It was decided by the Rangers' Inf, the Essex Regt, to remain on the outskirts of the town and the Sherwoods laagered their tanks on the site of what is now the Amazon Hotel on the ring road - disappointed not to be fulfilling Monty's plan to take Bayeux that night. After a short night they entered the town the next morning, 'A' Sqn in support of the Essex and 'B' Sqn coming in from the north of the town supporting the South Wales Borderers. 'C' Sqn remained in reserve at St. Sulpice. A machine-gun post to the south of the town set a house alight with its fire and the Bayeux fire-engine came clanging its bell, with a full crew in their shiny helmets, and put the fire out. This brought out a German machine-gun section - the only opposition encountered by the Sherwoods other than the odd sniper fire. It was because they were the liberators of the first city in Normandy, Bayeux, that the honour of erecting their memorial in the museum grounds was granted to them.

The Sherwood Rangers went on to Tilly-sur-Seulles where they have another memorial. There, on 9 June their most famous son, the war poet **Keith Douglas**, 2 i/c of 'A' Squadron, was killed. He is buried in Tilly CWGC Cemetery. Douglas, from an early age both a rebel and a poet, enlisted at the outbreak of war, but, like other undergraduates, his call up was delayed until July 1940. After four months of cavalry training, Douglas did three months at Sandhurst and five months' training with armoured cars in Gloucestershire with the 2nd Derbyshire Yeomanry, into which he had been commissioned - and whose collar dogs he insisted on wearing thereafter. Posted to the Middle East in June 1941 and, prevented by illness from joining his own regiment, he joined the Sherwood Rangers Yeomanry. His experiences in North Africa are vividly described in his book, *Alamein to Zem Zem*, and it was during this period that some of his most brilliant and enduring poems were written, establishing his reputation as probably the finest poet of the Second World War. In December 1943, after acquitting himself with credit in the North African campaign and becoming thoroughly attached to his adopted Regiment, Douglas returned with them to the UK. Preparing for the Normandy invasion, he continued to write poetry, as well as revising the manuscript of his book. In March he wrote an unfinished poem called *Actors Waiting in the Wings of Europe*. It includes the lines,

> Everyone, I suppose will use these minutes
> To look back, to hear music and recall
> What we were doing and saying that year
> During our last few months as people, near
> The sucking mouth of the day that swallowed us all
> Into the stomach of a war. Now we are in it.....

On 9 June a mortar fragmentation bomb exploded in a tree above him and Douglas was killed by a splinter so fine that there was no mark on his body. His loss to literature has been compared with that of Wilfred Owen during the First World War.

In September 1993 a **Memorial** was unveiled in the grounds to the **Notts (Sherwood Rangers) Yeomanry** and on 7 June 2002 a **Memorial** was unveiled to the **2nd Bn, the Essex Regiment ('The Pompadours')** in the newly-created Garden of Remembrance. It was designed and carved by David Dewey and initiated by Dennis Buston, a Chartered Surveyor. The project, which involved raising some £35,000, was carried out by the Regimental Association with financial support from a variety of benefactors. In the line of memorials is also a flat **Plaque** to the **Corps of Military Police** and a **MLC Marker** erected in 2004.

Leave your car in the museum car park and walk up the road towards the CWGC Cemetery. There is no parking at the Cemetery/Memorial and the area between them is now paved.

N.B. On the right is a stone **Memorial** to the famous WW2 photographer, **Robert Capa**.(qv) Behind it, approached over a small bridge, is the **Memorial Garden to War Reporters (Map It3-2/Lat & Long: 49.27382 -0.71204/GPPIt3-1/2,6).** The names of over 2,000 reporters and photographers who lost their lives reporting from a battlefield, world-wide, from 1944 are recorded on great stone slabs. They lead down to a grassy circle in the centre of which is a large stone with a quotation from Simone de Beauvoir, 'One may only taste freedom when others around us are free.' The Memorial Garden was funded by 'Reporters without Borders' and the town of Bayeux. There is an interactive terminal inside the Museum for more information.

• Bayeux Commonwealth War Graves Commission Memorial and Cemetery/30 minutes/Map It3-3/Holts Map A10,11/Lat & Long: 49.27441 -0.71409

On the same side of the road as the Museum is the **Bayeux Memorial to the Missing** with No Known Graves, designed by Philip Hepworth. It bears the names of 1,805 Commonwealth service men and women (1,534 from Britain, 270 from Canada and 1 from South Africa) who fell in the Battle of Normandy.

The Latin inscription above reads *'NOS A GULIELMO VICTI VICTORIS PATRIAM LIBERAVIMUS' (WE WHO WERE CONQUERED BY WILLIAM HAVE LIBERATED HIS FATHERLAND).*

HETZER tank destroyer in the grounds of the Museum.

Bofors 40mm anti-aircraft gun inside Bayeux Museum.

Battle of Normandy Memorial Museum, Bayeux.

Memorial to Notts (Sherwood Rangers) Yeomanry in the Museum grounds.

Memorial to 2nd Bn Essex Regt, Bayeux Museum grounds.

Plaque to Corps of the Military Police, Bayeux Museum grounds.

from a main base at Southampton and pipe laying began as soon as the routes across the Channel had been cleared of mines.

On 7 June 2004 Brig Gen G.S. Robison, Royal Marines, unveiled a grey *bas relief* stone **Monument** to the **Port Pétrolier**, representing **PLUTO**. It was the work of artist Pierre Courtois which was sculpted by Didier Poisson. It is to the left of the car park. The town boasts a tower built by Vauban (on the cliff above) in 1694 as defence against English and Dutch pirates. Later it became a magazine to supply the batteries at nearby Huppain and du Castel. Although damaged, the tower survived the invasion. Below it on the beaches, beside the hard, is a **Todt bunker,** facing out to sea, with a **Memorial Plaque to the No 47 (RM) Commando.**

> NOTE. From this point it is possible (but a hard slog, which will also leave your car in the wrong place) to trace the path of Capt Cousins and his handful of Royal Marines (qv) in their assault on the headland by climbing up the path past the Vauban tower and passing some bunkers en route. The easier route is described below.

On the jetty of the outer harbour is a *Comité du Débarquement* **Monument,** commemorating the landings, a **NTL Totem** and a dramatic statue to fishermen who have lost their lives at sea. On the cliffs overlooking the port there are gun emplacements and bunkers. These formidable positions were attacked by No 47 RM Commando on the afternoon of D+1, having worked their way, some ten miles, along the coast from Le Hamel carrying almost 90lb per man of weapons and supplies. Two of the strongpoints were taken with the help of a naval bombardment from HMS *Emerald's* 6in guns, rocket-firing Typhoons and artillery smoke. A German counter-attack, supported by flak-ships in the harbour, retook one of the hills, but at dusk the German commander and 100 men surrendered, though sadly the commandos' troop leader, **Captain T.F. Cousins**, (who is buried in Bayeux CWGC Cemetery) was killed. The commandos had captured a port which was to play an important role in maintaining the flow of vital supplies, and they had secured the junction between the British 50th Division on GOLD Beach and the US 1st Division on OMAHA Beach. By 14 June the port was handling more than 1,000 tons of supplies a day, much more than it had ever done in peacetime.

Along the coast to the east the remains of the Mulberry harbour at Arromanches can be seen on a clear day. **The Tourist Office, Bayeux-Bessin,** is round the corner on Quai Baron Gérard. Tel: (0)2 31 22 45 89. Website: www.bayeux-bessin-tourisme.com. Further along the Quai at no 12 is the ****Hotel Ibis**, opened in June 2008 with 62 rooms. Tel: (0)2 31 22 04 04. E-mail: h68565@accor.com

Today Port-en-Bessin is one of the premier fishing ports of France with between 10,500 and 12,000 tonnes of fish passing through its market and distribution system annually, one of the most modern in Europe. Its natural harbour, protected on each side by high cliffs made it a safe haven for the Romans, Saxons, and Normans - some of William the Conqueror's fleet was made here. In the 15th Century the two jetties were made. Damaged in the 17th Century by heavy storms, they were reconstructed in the 19th Century and the latest modernisation was in 1970. Christened by Françoise Sagan 'le petit Saint-Tropez normand', the port has been popular with literary, artistic and political personalities - from Seurat to Flaubert to Simenon to Presidents Félix Faure, Vincent Auriol and François Mitténand. It was in Port-en-Bessin that the scene in the film, *The Longest Day*, which purported to show the taking of the Casino at Ouistreham by Commandant Kieffer and his men, was actually shot.

There is a wonderful fish market here on Sunday mornings along the quay with its variety of interesting shops, patisseries and restaurants. Sunday lunch is very popular and it is advisable to book. A list of recommended restaurants may be obtained from the Tourist Office.

Drive along the Quay Baron Gérard past the Tourist Office and the Ibis Hotel to the end of the Quay. Keep left and follow signs left to 'Ibis Parking'. Stop at the end of the rue René Hommet. Walk up the grassy path leading uphill and walk some 150 yards towards the flags or flagpoles.

• Memorial to Capt Cousins, 47 RM Commando, Eastern Headland/ 10.7 miles/25 minutes/Map It3-9/Lat & Long: 49.34656   -0.74968

Unveiled by General G. S. Robison, Commandant General Royal Marines, on 7 June 2009, (he had unveiled the Western Headland Memorial on 7 June 2004 while Brigadier Commanding the Commando Training Centre – that Memorial is the next stop), the Memorial is on a granite slab beside what looks like a bunker but is apparently a post-war structure. On the early evening of 7 June Captain Terence Cousins led a party of 3 officers and 24 men up the steep path from the harbour through trenches, a wire fence and a minefield to attack a bunker which was holding them up, but was mortally wounded by a grenade. Despite determined resistance by the defenders the headland was secured. The story of this gallant officer, who had already been involved in the battle for the Western headland (qv), is told in full on the bronze **Plaque** on the Memorial. Also see www.47commando.org.uk Capt Cousins is buried in Bayeux CWGC Cemetery.

Many believe that Cousins' extraordinary feat of valour with his 25 Royal Marines was worthy of the Victoria Cross and Lt Col Phillips, his CO, did indeed recommended him for the award. The application was unsuccessful and Cousins received a Mention in Despatches, the only other posthumous award available. In 2002 the RM Veterans again mounted a case for a VC for Cousins, which was also refused. In 2004 Major General Julian Thompson wrote: "The operation by 47 Royal Marine Commando at Port-en-Bessin was one of the great feats of arms of any unit ... of any nation in the Second World War."

Return to the parking area by the PLUTO Memorial and drive back over the bridge along the one-way system. Take the second left following 'Toutes Directions', rue du Nord and turn right up a narrow road signed 'P' for Parking and 'Viewpoint 300m'. Continue to the viewpoint parking.

• Memorial Plaques to 47 Royal Marine Commando, Bunker, Western Headland, Port-en-Bessin/11.8 miles/10 minutes/Map It3-10/Lat & Long: 49.34956 -0.76102

Here, by the 6th Hole on La Mer Golf Course, there are a **Memorial and Plaques to 47 RM Cdo** giving a Roll of Honour of all those who died in the Assault on the Port and those who died in the Landings near Asnelles and a Board with an account of the battle itself and a Plan of Port-en-Bessin and the Port. Unveiled on 7 June 2004 during a splendid ceremony attended by many RM and Cruisers *Montcalm* and *Leygues* veterans, these are placed on top of a German Bunker. It is sited on the western headland above Port-en-Bessin, one of the Marines' objectives on D-Day which they fought bitterly to take and is one of the very few along the coastline from which a visitable 'contemporary' German view out to sea can still be obtained through the slit. It is the remaining one of eight concrete bunkers that together with machine-gun and mortar positions defended the headland. Fire from German flak ships in the harbour drove off the Commandos' initial assault, but following Capt Cousins' capture of the Eastern Headland, the Germans here surrendered the next morning.

Return to the one-way circuit and continue.

On the right is the **King Hotel**. 40 rooms. Tel: (0)2 31 21 44 44. E-mail: kinghotel@orange.fr At the junction with the D514 coast road turn left following signs to Longues or Arromanches on the rue du Croiseur Montcalm.

Immediately on the right is a **Plaque to the Cruiser *Montcalm*** next to the **Cultural Centre** and Tel: (0)2 31 21 92 33. Open Tues-Sat 1000-1200 and 1400-1900. Sun 1430-1900. Very helpful staff on cultural/commemorative events. **(Map It3-11/Lat & Long: 49.34360 -0.75485).**

Beside it is a **MLC Marker** (qv) [damaged in 2009] and a **Liberty Sequoia Tree**. The Free French vessel *Montcalm* was part of Bombarding Force C which supported the Americans on OMAHA Beach.

Continue to the next roundabout

Unveiling of Memorial to Capt Cousins, 47 RM Cdo, Eastern Headland, Port-en-Bessin.

Memorial to Capt Cousins, 47 RM Cdo, Eastern Headland, Port-en-Bessin.

47 RM Cdo Roll of Honour Plaques and Operational account, Western Headland, Port-en-Bessin.

View from 'RM' Bunker overlooking Port-en-Bessin.

Plaque to the Cruiser Montcalm, Port-en-Bessin.

Mémoire, Liberté, Citoyenneté Memorial, Port en Bessin.

Leave Arromanches eastward on the D514 coast road, following signs to Courseulles/ Cinéma Circulaire and stop in the parking area (for which there is a fee in the season) on the left just past the Statue of the Virgin Mary on the cliffs above the town.

• St Côme de Fresne Table d'Orientation/Bunker/RE Memorial/Free French Airforce Memorial/360° Film/21.6 miles/35 minutes/Map It3-15/Holts Map B16,17,18,19/Lat & Long: 49.33907 -0.61462

By the cliff edge are the remains of German bunkers which contained field guns which menaced GOLD Beach and were silenced by HMS *Belfast*. In the sea, the remains of the Arromanches Mulberry Harbour can be seen, and to the left below is Arromanches itself. This position, and Arromanches, were taken by the Hampshires before 2100 hours on D-Day, by which time the 50th Division bridgehead measured 5 miles by 5 miles.

No 47 RM Commando landed on your right on GOLD Beach, just below these heights, and swung around behind you going to your left, heading for Port-en-Bessin, a 10-mile march away, due west.

On the downward slope of the hill along the footpath towards Arromanches is a Memorial commemorating a Napoleonic naval battle off Arromanches in 1811 which was erected on the 100th anniversary. The **Table d'orientation** by the parking area gives excellent views over the remains of the Mulberry Harbour. Near it are traces of the radar station destroyed by allied airforce raids a few weeks before OVERLORD, including the truncated pyramid-shaped Würzburg radar mounting, gun emplacements and concrete shelters. It was the Würzburg that had been the focus of the Allied raid on Bruneval in February 1942. The raid was commanded by Major John Frost, later to find fame at Arnhem. There is a **NTL Totem** beside the site.

Walk towards the 360° Cinema to the memorial with the badge of the Free French Airforce.

The Memorial is headed **'Esplanade du Général d'Armée Aérienne Michel Fourquet'** (known as 'Gorré), the Commander of Groupe Lorraine, 'Leader of the Mission of 6 June 1944, 1914-1992'. The **RE Memorial** on the left. This is in the form of an obelisk with a bronze Plaque which gives the story of the RE's contribution to the invasion, surmounted by the Corps badge. Operation OVERLORD was an assault upon a defended coastline - defended not just by weapons but by obstacles. Therefore well forward in the assault forces had to be engineer units equipped to clear whatever devices the Germans had erected to impede the invasion - from the beaches onward. The Americans called these forces 'Assault' or 'Special' engineer formations. The British employed the Royal Engineers, all of whom were part of 1 (British) Corps, and for the landing the engineer units were split up and put under the command of the assaulting divisions. The Corps Engineer plan identified its tasks as follows:

On the beaches - obstacle clearance, construction of exits and subsequent beach organisation Operations inland - bridging, airfields and routes. The importance that the British attached to the engineers and to Hobart's Funnies (qv), which were operated by them, is well illustrated by the planned landing sequence given in the orders for the landing of 8th Infantry Brigade Group at la Brêche (visited later). It was:

A and B Squadrons 13/18 Hussars (DD tanks)
Eight gapping teams, each of two flail tanks, three AVREs,
one bulldozer and two obstacle clearing teams
The assaulting infantry.

The **360° Cinema** presentation uses an original 'Circorama' process employing 9 synchronised cameras to give a unique and moving account of the events of 6 June 1944. It has a good book and souvenir shop.

Open: Consult website www.arromanches360.com for current opening times. Entrance fee payable. Tel: (0)2 31 22 30 30. Email: contact@arromanches360.com

Continue on the D514 downhill.

360° Cinema, St Côme.

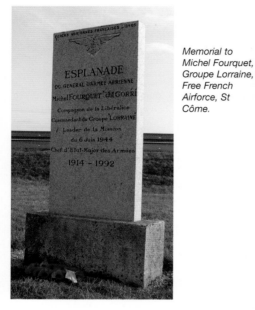

View over Arromanches from St Côme, showing the remains of the Mulberry Harbour.

Memorial to Michel Fourquet, Groupe Lorraine, Free French Airforce, St Côme.

Memorial to Royal Engineers, St Côme.

View over GOLD Beach from German Bunker, la Guerre.

N.B. On the wall of the Church of St Côme (Map It3-N/Lat & Long: **49.33781** -0.60468/GPPIt3-2/4) that is passed on the right is a **Plaque** commemorating the ringing of the bells as soon as the troops landed, despite the fact that the Church was damaged by the bombardment. In 2009 another **Plaque** was added stating that the bells were rung by the Sexton, A. Hamon, aided by inhabitants of the commune.

Continue to the crossroads with the D205 just east of le Hamel (Asnelles). Stop and walk 100 yards down the small road to the sea.

• D514/D205 La Guerre Crossroads & Bunker/22.6 miles/10 minutes/OP/Map It3-16/Lat & Long: 49.34023 -0.59549

At low tide there is a good view of the remaining Phoenixes of the Arromanches Mulberry, built to last a hundred days and still around after the Millenium. This was the eastern end of the Mulberry, the western was at Tracy. There is a typical German shore **Bunker** with deadly fields of fire across the open beaches, yet many of the German guns had limited traverse and this was to save countless British lives.

The Germans had assumed that the invaders would try to float over the beach obstacles and that therefore any landing would be made close to high tide. Thus they had arranged their arcs of fire to cover an area of the beach between the high water level and the sea wall. The landings, however, were made before half tide and thus not into the teeth of small arms opposition at the moment of landing.

The 1st Battalion Hampshires landed on the beach here and to the east, accompanied by DD tanks and Hobart's Funnies. With the armour ahead of them as they jumped from their landing craft, the soldiers of the Hampshires had the firepower to cover their movement across the sands. The German fire from le Hamel was heavy and the first three CRABS which flailed their way up the beach were bogged down or stopped by an anti-tank gun. A fourth CRAB beat its way into le Hamel giving cover for two companies of the Hampshires to bypass the village and to take Asnelles behind it. Even so it was not until after midday that the area was cleared. The enemy was able to hold out longer here because both the CO and the 2nd in Command of the Hampshires became casualties early on and, therefore, due to lack of central control, no requests were made for naval fire support against the strongpoints.

Continue on the D514 to the crossroads in the centre of Asnelles where the D514 meets the Rue de Southampton. Stop by the memorials on the left.

Memorial to 50th Northumberland Division, Asnelles. *Memorial to SW Borderers, Asnelles.*

• Place Alexander Stanier/50th Division, SW Borderers Memorials/ Gen de Gaulle Message, Asnelles/23 miles/5 minutes/Map It3-17/Holts Map B10,11,12,13/Lat & Long: 49.33972 -0.58575

The crossroads area is known as 'Place Alexander Stanier', in honour of the commander of the 231st Infantry Brigade of the 50th Northumbrian Division, Sir Alexander Stanier Bart (sic), DSO MC. At the small road 'Rue The Devonshire Regiment', there is a **Memorial** to the **Division**, the leading brigade of the 231st, and three battalions - the **2nd Battalion Devonshire Regiment**, the **1st Battalion Hampshire Regiment** and the **1st Battalion the Dorset Regiment**. The two assault battalions, the Hampshires and the Dorsets, received 'Normandy' as a battle honour. The Dorsets, landing off the beach here, were out of range of the German guns at le Hamel and, covered by the CRABS and working in conjunction with a variety of AVREs, were off the beach within the hour, having cleared three exits. It was as they moved south-west towards the high ground behind Arromanches, their main objective, that they met members of No 47 RM Commando and encountered opposition from entrenched elements of the 352nd Division. However, by nightfall they had reached Ryes, three miles inland. A **Memorial** surmounted by a metal Cross of Lorraine reproduces Général de Gaulle's **message** of June 1940. A black marble **Memorial** with inscriptions in English, French and Welsh to the **2nd Battalion the South Wales Borderers** who landed at Asnelles on 6 June 1944 was unveiled on 5 June 1994 by Brigadier Sir Nicholas Somerville Bt. [sic]. On special occasions the Welsh Dragon flies proudly above the Memorial.

From Place Alexander Stanier turn left in front of the Memorial to Nos Glorieux Libérateurs and at the first crossroads turn left down the small road to the sea. Stop in the car park.

• Bunker and Essex Yeomanry, 147th Field Regt RA Plaques, Asnelles/23.4 miles/10 minutes/Map It3-18/Lat & Long: 49.34188 -0.58416

Ahead is a significant **Bunker** on which are **Memorial Plaques to the Essex Yeomanry and the 147th (Essex Yeomanry) Field Regiment, RA.** The Essex and the Sherwoods came ashore at 0730 with Sherman DD tanks and Sextons, supporting the Hampshires and the Dorsets of 231st Brigade, and were given much trouble by this blockhouse which was eventually knocked out by Sergeant R. E. Palmer, using a 25-pounder self-propelled gun at 300 yards, in an action that won him the Military Medal. Oddly the Official History makes little of the participation of the Yeomanry regiments in the landings - the Essex are not mentioned at all, although they do have their own Memorial outside the Bayeux Museum (qv) - and in the various commemorative ceremonies held over the major anniversaries the Yeomans are frequently forgotten. The Sherwood Rangers lost eight DD tanks in the swim to the beach and another four during the day. There is a **NTL Totem** beside the Bunker.

Beyond the Bunker and along the beach to the left are the remains of a small **Anchor** embedded in the wall. It was used to tie up the landing barges which disembarked in the Mulberry at Arromanches.

Beside it is an **OP Board** which shows the units of 231st BR Bde who disembarked on GOLD Beach on 6 June, with a plan and an aerial view of the coast and coastal defences. An **Information Board** describes the Brigade's assault on Bunker, WN37 and tells how the Germans incorporated the adjoining Sanatorium (no longer here) into their defensive system, together with a minefield. The Sanatorium for TB patients operated from 1928 to 1938. On 6 June it was occupied by snipers and was eventually captured by the Allies at around 1600 hours.

It was about one mile to the east along this stretch of beach that No 47 RM Commando landed at 0825 hours, having boarded their LCAs some seven miles offshore. The fourteen LCAs headed in towards Arromanches and had to turn east towards their correct beach at le Hamel, losing four craft in the process. There was considerable confusion at the water's edge with burning vehicles, mined beach obstacles and a strong running tide, not to mention the intense German machine-gun and mortar fire, and the Commandos got mixed up with the Hampshires and the Dorsets who had landed further east at Asnelles and were working their way west. All of this delayed their departure for Port-en-Bessin until the late afternoon, otherwise it might have been taken on D-Day.

Return to the D514 and turn left, making particular note of the wet and marshy land between the road and the beach. At the small crossroads just after the sign indicating that you are entering Ver-sur-Mer, stop.

• KING Sector, GOLD Beach and Stan Hollis VC Memorial/26.4 miles/5 minutes/Map It3-19/Lat & Long: 49.34525 - 0.52802/OP

Stand at the crossroads.

The road to your left leading towards you from the sea was the exit road from King Sector of GOLD Beach (see contemporary and modern photos on page 182 and Diagram 4 on page 183). It was up this road that CSM Hollis with D Coy of the 6th Bn the Green Howards advanced on D-Day. The leading vehicle in the contemporary photo is a Cromwell tank, the second vehicle, a Sherman, is exactly at the crossroads where you are now.

Drive down the narrow road to a small brick building.

On 8 June 2006 a **Plaque** was unveiled on an old train hut on the beach as a **Memorial to CSM Stan Hollis**, the only man to win the **VC** on D-Day, and the men of the Green Howards who landed here with him. On that day Hollis mistook the hut for a German pillbox and fired an entire drum of ammunition from his Lewis gun into the building as his landing craft approached the shore. On landing the men discovered that it was 'only a bloody tram-stop'. In 2005 the bullet-scarred stone building still showing bullet holes for 6 June 1944, was put up for sale. On the Regiment's annual visit to Crépon, Brigadier John Powell, MBE, Col of the Regiment decided to purchase and renovate it as a tribute to Hollis. There are **Information Panels** beside the building explaining the significance of the hut with a photo of Hollis. The Memorial was unveiled by Hollis's son, Brian, together with two officers who landed here on D-Day, Major 'Bollo' Young MC, 6th Green Howards and Capt John Milton, MBE.

To the left is a **Sign commemorating the landing of Cdt Byrd on 1 July 1927** (qv). There is an Information Panel showing stops on the *Sentier de la Liberté*, a booklet describing which can be obtained in tourist offices of the Bessin, Seulles et Mer.

The German defences here were mainly sited along the line of the road or just south (inland) of it on the high ground. Thus they overlooked the wet and marshy land below, which was mined and traversed by an anti-tank ditch. It was here that Hobart's Funnies really paid off. Without them the infantry might have been stuck, floundering in the soft ground under the eyes of the defenders and without a scrap of cover. The weather was so bad that the DD tanks were not launched, and they and the Funnies were landed directly onto the beach. This assault, scheduled for 0725 hours, was the earliest of the British landings.

The main enemy position here was known as the Fleury battery (can be visited later) and consisted of four 150mm guns in concrete casemates on Mont Fleury (see Diagram 4). It was situated in what is now a new housing estate half a mile uphill from where you are and to the west of the exit. The casemates are still there today, though steadily being masked by new houses.

The assault of the 69th Brigade was led by the 6th Battalion Green Howards under Lieutenant-Colonel Robin Hastings. In his force for the landing he had a squadron of the 4th/7th Royal Dragoon Guards with DD tanks, two teams of AVRE and flail tanks (CRABS), one platoon of medium machine-guns of the 2nd Cheshire Regiment and a detachment of Royal Engineers. The front on which the force landed was some 900 yards long and, in addition to the Mont Fleury position, the Germans had half a dozen pillboxes with machine guns and at least one 105mm cannon. Colonel Hastings allocated different tasks to different companies within his battalion, though all had the general purpose of reaching the high ground of the Meauvaines Ridge on the skyline to the south of your present position. D Company was given the task of capturing Mont Fleury.

The Green Howards had boarded their transport ship, the *Empire Lance*, on 1 June and spent their time in physical exercise, cleaning their weapons, attending religious services on deck (General Montgomery's message to them, indeed to his whole force before the invasion, had said, 'Let us pray that "The Lord Mighty in Battle" will go forth with our armies...'), eating and sleeping. They also studied aerial photographs updated daily showing the beach obstacles. Their

Asnelles Bunker with NTL Totem.

Plaque to 147th (Essex Yeomanry) Fld Regt, RA, Asnelles Bunker.

Information Board and Anchor, Asnelles sea wall.

KING Sector GOLD Beach exit road today.

CSM Hollis VC Memorial Hut, GOLD BEACH, KING sector.

KING Sector GOLD Beach exit road on D+1

America - GOLD Beach Museum, Ver-sur-Mer.

Davis escape apparatus, America-GOLD Beach Museum.

Cet ancien hôtel "America" a été la résidence
des officiers d'État-major du 9ème "Beach Group"
de la Marine Royale britannique,
du 6 juin au 30 juillet 1944.
Ces officiers, sous le commandement
du Colonel J.R. Harper,
le baptisèrent "Gold Inn", "L'Auberge d'Or",
en référence au secteur "Gold",
comprenant les plages de Ver-sur-Mer à Arromanches,
dont ils controlaient le trafic maritime,
y compris celui du port artificiel "Mulberry".

Plaque on Old Hotel America, Ver-sur-Mer.

Plaque to Free French Sqns, Airstrip B3 Memorial.

___B 3___
LE 13 JUIN 1944
LES GROUPES DE CHASSE DE LA FRANCE LIBRE
ILE DE FRANCE ET ALSACE
340 ET 341 SQUADRONS FREE FRENCH
DE LA SECOND TACTICAL AIR FORCE - RAF -
ATTERRIRENT POUR LA PREMIERE FOIS
SUR LE SOL LIBERE DE LA PATRIE
POURSUIVANT LES OPERATIONS JUSQU'A LA VICTOIRE FINALE
SAINTE CROIX SUR MER LE 18 06 2000
CE SOUVENIR DE MEMOIRE EST DU A L'INITIATIVE DE L'ASSOCIATION POUR LA DEFENSE
ET LE DEVELOPPEMENT DE L'AERODROME DE CAEN-CARPIQUET

Airstrip B3 Memorial, Ste Croix-sur-Mer.

Plaque to Canadian Forces, Ste Croix-sur-Mer Church wall.

A LA MEMOIRE
DES SOLDATS CANADIENS
TOMBES POUR LA DEFENSE DU
TERRITOIRE LE 6 JUIN 1944
LA COMMUNE DE STE CROIX S/MER
RECONNAISSANTE

Consult website: www.goldbeach.org.uk for current opening times, entrance fees, latest news.

In the square is a **NTL Totem** and in the garden in the centre is an anchor from a 1944 battleship, recovered in 1985. To the left on House No 22 is a **Plaque** to the old Hotel America, residence of officers of the **Staff of 9th Beach Gp RM** from 6 June-30 July 1944. These officers under Col J.R. Harper called it 'The Gold Inn'.

Return to the D112, turn left, wiggling out of Ver and follow signs to Crépon. Continue half a mile to the junction with the rue du Calvaire. Turn left and continue onto the Route de Sainte Croix – an easily missed turn.

> **N.B. OP.** After some 800 yards (**Lat & Long: 49.32459 -0.52209**) the remains of **Bunkers** can be seen in the field to the right (**Map It3-22/Lat & Long: 49.32312 -0.52901/GPPIt3-2/7**). These are part of the **Mare-Fontaine Battery (WN32)** which had four H669 casemates with 100mm guns. One account suggests a duel between the battery and HMS *Belfast* with the latter firing over 200 shells without inflicting any serious damage.

Continue another 800 yards to the memorial and plaques on the left.

• Airstrip B3 Memorial and Plaques, Ste Croix-sur-Mer/29.5 miles/ 10 minutes/Map It3-23/Lat & Long: 49.31912 -0.51849).

They commemorate Airstrip B3, the first landing strip to become operational in Normandy on 10 June 1944. The distinction of being the first British squadron to land in France since Dunkirk is claimed both by 130 and 303 Squadrons. They landed at B3, Ste Croix-sur-Mer at 1200 hours on 10 June.

It was in use until 10 September by 144 Wing RAF/RCAF and 441, 2 & 3 Sqns RCAF. Around the **Memorial** are **Plaques** from 146 Typhoon Wing (who used it 10 June-4 September), from 340 & 341 Free French Sqns (13 June), 3210 Servicing Commando, RAF and the NVA. On the ground within the memorial wall is some original runway 'chicken wire'. Present at the unveiling was **Wing Cdr 'Johnnie' Johnson**, Britain's foremost 'Ace' with 38 scores. He died in 2001.

Continue into the village of Ste Croix on the C3 and stop opposite the church.

• Plaque to Canadian Forces, Ste Croix Church Wall/30.2 miles/5 minutes/Map It3-24/Lat & Long: 49.31319 -0.51012.

On the wall of the cemetery beside the church is a **Plaque to the Canadian Forces** who died here on 6 June 1944 in the defence of Ste Croix.

Take the D112a signed to Crépon. On entering Crépon turn right on the D65 to the figure of a seated soldier by the church.

• Green Howards Memorial, Crépon/32.2 miles/10 minutes/Map It3-25/Holts Map B29/Lat & Long: 49.31574 -0.55000

The figure on this magnificent **Memorial** is popularly supposed to be that of CSM Stanley Hollis, the only man to win a VC on D-Day, but although a plaque on the base of the statue tells the story of Hollis's VC, the figure is meant to represent **a Soldier of the Green Howards** on 6 June 1944 reflecting upon the events of the day. The men behind the idea of the Memorial were the then Colonel of the Regiment, Field Marshal Sir Peter Inge, and Ian Homersham, who with his friend James Butler, the sculptor (whose name can be seen inscribed on the figure's right foot), saw the project through. The whole project cost in the region of £100,000, which was greatly helped by a substantial donation by Sir Ernest Harrison the Chairman of Racal Engineering. On 11 November 1997 Sir Ernest also generously donated Stan's VC to the Green Howards' Museum and in return the Green Howards have renamed the medal gallery as the Harrison Gallery. The Memorial bears the legend, 'Remember the 6th June 1944', and is dedicated 'To the memory of all the Green Howards who fought and died in the Second World War'. Their names are listed in alphabetical order on the pleasingly designed wall behind the statue. The memorial was unveiled on 26 October 1996 by HM Harald V, King of Norway, Colonel-in-Chief of the Green Howards. The regiment's connection with the house of Norway dates back to 1875 when Alexandra, then Princess of Wales and a daughter of the Norwegian Royal Family, presented them with new colours. They then became known as 'The Princess of Wales's Own' and their cap badge, designed by Alexandra, incorporated the Cross of Denmark. In 1942 Alexandra's son-in-law, King Haakon VII - a Prince of Denmark who became King of Norway - became Colonel-in-Chief. He was succeeded by his son, King Olav V, and in February 1992 by King Harald, a great-great-grandson of Queen Victoria. The impressive unveiling ceremony was also attended by the Colonel of the Regiment, Brigadier F.R. Dannatt MC, Members of the Green Howards Association, the Corps of Drums of the 1st Battalion, many local dignitaries and Stan Hollis's son and daughter. Built on a site provided by the people of Crépon, the Memorial is one of the most beautiful in the whole Normandy area.

Beside the Memorial are detailed **Information Panels** about **Stan Hollis, VC,** 69th Inf Bde landings, and the capture of German Battery WN36A, Pavillon Farm and the Insignia of Units involved.

> **NOTE.** In the churchyard here are two RAF graves from 10 June 1944: **Aircraftsman 1st Class David D. Harris and Cpl Frank Olney.** They were both 23.

Return along the D65, signed Creully. In one-third of a mile on the left is

*** Chateaux & Hotels de France/Logis de France **Hotel-Restaurant Ferme de la Rançonnière.** Tel: + (0)2 31 22 21 73. E-mail: hotel@ranconniere.com. Website: www.ranconniere.com 35 rooms. Hotel open all year. Restaurant closed January. Picturesque traditional 13th Century Normandy manor house.

Opposite is an **Information Panel (Lat & Long: 49.31144 0.54719)** describing nearby **Airstrip B2** (qv) with many contemporary photos and the Depot set up in the Farm by 9th Beach No 2 Detail, RASC. In the large concrete hangar adjacent to the hotel a Base Post Office was set up.

Continue to the crossroads with the D12.

> **N.B.** By turning right here and continuing for 1.2 miles, turning right on the D87 and then first right into Bazenville, the Church is reached. In front of it is a fine **Memorial** in the shape of a Spitfire Wing, with an RAF Roundel. It commemorates **ALG B2** from which **403, 416 and 421 Sqns of RCAF** flew. There is also a **Plaque** to the exceptional Pilot, **Pierre Clostermann,** DFC + Bar, *Croix de Guerre, Légion d'Honneur,* who first flew from B2 on 15 June 1944, the first Free French pilot to land in France. Born in Brazil, Clostermann joined the Free French Airforce in 1942, flying all types of Spitfires. He made attacks on V1 sites on D-Day and in all made over 400 combat sorties. He died in 2006, age 85. Behind on the cemetery wall is a **Plaque to 83rd Gp Control Centre of 2nd TAC AF,** 7 June-10 August 1944. (**Map It3-Q/Lat & Long: 49.29879 -0.58757/GPPIt3-2/6.**))
>
> **N.B.** By returning to the D87 and turning right, the **CWGC Cemetery at Ryes** is reached after three quarters of a mile. (**Map It3-R/Lat & Long: 49.29979 -0.60126 /GPPIt3-2/9**). The first burials were made here just two days after the landings. The cemetery now contains 652 Commonwealth burials plus one Polish and 335 German graves.

Continue straight over, down the narrow road, and stop just before the bridge over the River Seulles. Look back to your right.

• *The Château at Creullet, Montgomery & de Gaulle Plaque/34.3 miles/5 minutes/Map It3-26/Holts Map B24/Lat & Long: 49.288864 -0.544735*

It was here at the Château, or 'Manoir', de Creullet on 9 June that General Montgomery parked his caravan and set up his Tactical HQ. He met Winston Churchill and Field Marshal Smuts in the grand salon of the Château on 12 June, de Gaulle on 14 June and King George VI on 16 June, when they came here after landing at Graye on JUNO Beach. However, shortly after arriving from Portsmouth, General Montgomery found that his caravan lacked one essential item - a chamber pot. An embarrassed ADC was sent to the château, and came back with a small white pot, decorated with pink flowers. On 22 June Montgomery moved to Blay, six miles west of

Green Howards
Memorial, Crépon.

Generals de Gaulle & Montgomery in front of the Château
gates, 14 June 1944.

Creullet Château
showing on right
Plaque commemorating
the meeting of Generals
de Gaulle &
Montgomery.

Detail, 4th/7th RDG Memorial,
Cruelly.

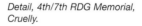

Memorial to the 4th/7th Royal Dragoon Guards, Creully.

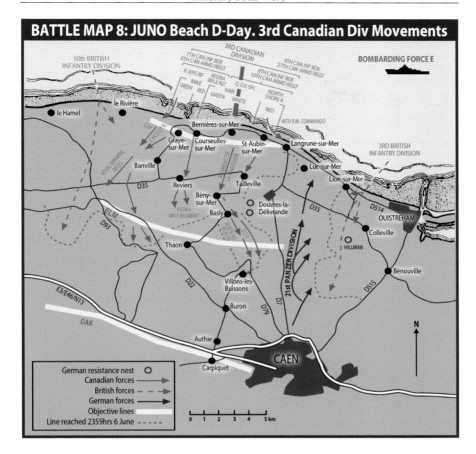

BATTLE MAP 8: JUNO Beach D-Day. 3rd Canadian Div Movements

Legend:
- German resistance nest ○
- Canadian forces ——▶
- British forces – – –▶
- German forces ——▶
- Objective lines
- Line reached 2359hrs 6 June – – – –

0 1 2 3 4 5 km

What Happened on D-Day - JUNO Beach Landings

During the night of 5 June, and early morning of 6 June, RAF Bomber Command hammered likely German defence positions along the Normandy coastline. At dawn the US Army Air Force took over and continued the attack until, as everywhere along the invasion front, the Royal Navy joined in. Off JUNO Beach were eleven destroyers and support craft adding their weight to the bombardment including two Canadian destroyers, the *Algonquin* and the *Sioux*.

The crossing for the troops at sea was rough and the time for the assault was put back by ten minutes because the heavy seas had delayed some of the landing craft, but despite considerable opposition from entrenched German positions relatively unaffected by the air and sea bombardments, the Canadians got ashore shortly after 0800.

By the end of the day they were practically everywhere beyond 'Elm', their intermediate objective line, and some tanks had crossed 'Oak', but, without infantry support, had withdrawn. General Keller's men had made the greatest gains of all on D-Day, in some places seven miles inland. On their right they had made contact with the 50th Northumbrian Division at Creully, but on their left was a dangerous gap between themselves and the British 3rd Division. Into that gap General Eric Marcks, Commanding the German LXXXIV Corps, ordered Major General Edgar Feuchtinger's 21st Panzer Division. South of Caen, that evening, the leading elements of 12th SS Panzer Division began to arrive. It was a critical moment.

THE TOUR

• **Itinerary Four** starts near Carpiquet Airport, Caen, covers the 3rd Canadian Division's actions on JUNO Beach and inland to Caen and ends at St Aubin.

• **The Main Route:** Carpiquet; Authie - Nova Scotia Highlanders Memorial; Buron – Highland Light Infantry and Sherbrooke Fusiliers Memorials; Villons-le-Buissons – Hells Corner, 9th Can Infantry Memorial, Airstrip B16, Norwegian Forces Memorial; Galmanche - 59th Div Memorial; Cambes-en-Plaine – 59th Div Memorial; CWGC Cemetery; 2nd Battalion the Royal Ulster Rifles Memorial; Anisy – Queen's Own Rifles of Canada Memorial; Anguerny – Fort Garry Horse & Queen's Own Rifles of Canada Memorials, Régt de la Chaudière Memorial; Basly - Maple Leaf Memorial; Bény-sur-Mer – Régt de la Chaudi re Memorial; Douvres – Radar Station Bunkers OP and Museum, Blockhouses, la Délivrande CWGC Cemetery; Bény – CWGC Can Cemetery, Cameron Highlanders Plaque; Reviers - Regina Rifles Memorial; Graye – Plaques to the Royal Winnipeg Rifles/Can Scottish; *Com Déb Sig* Monument, Churchill AVRE, Cross of Lorraine, Memorial to the Royal Winnipeg Rifles and Can Scottish, XXXIInd Dragoons Plaque; Courseulles - JUNO Beach Centre & Memorials, 85th RE Fld Coy RE 'Nottingham Bridge' Plaque; Sherman Tank, German Anti-Tank Gun, Memorials to de Gaulle's Landing, Can Scottish, Regina and Royal Winnipeg Rifles Regts and Destroyer *la Combattante*; Bernières - *Com Déb Sig* Monument, House of Q Own Rifles, Bunker with Régt de la Chaudière, Queen's Own Rifles of Canada, 5th Hackney Battalion the Royal Berks Regt, Plaques and Memorials, War Correspondents' Plaque; St Aubin - Bunker, Fort Garry Horse, 5 Fld coy RCA, 10 Can Armd Regt, North Shore Regt, No 48 RM Commando, Duclos Memorials.

• **Planned duration,** without stops for refreshments or **Extra Visits** or **'NBs': 7 hours**
• **Total distance: 31 miles**

• **Extra Visits** are suggested to: Carpiquet - Memorials to Maj Gauvin/Regt de la Chaudi re/Queen's Own Rifles/R Winnipeg Rifles/Fort Garry Horse, North Shore Regiment, Fort Garry Horse Plaque; Carpiquet Airfield - Memorial to Can Liberators, Bunker; St Manvieu – 5 Can Regts Marker; Norrey-en-Bessin - R Regina Rifles/1st Can Hussars Memorial; le Mesnil-Patry - Q Own Can Rifles & 1st Can Hussars Memorial; Putot-en-Bessin - R Winnipeg Rifles & 1st Can Scot Regt Memorial; Bretteville-l'Orgueuilleuse - R Regina Rifles Plaque; Rots - 46 RM Cdo Plaque, Regt de la Chaudière & Fort Garry Horse Plaques; Abbaye d'Ardenne - Can Massacre Site Memorials; Caen - Memorial to Stormont Dundas & Glengarry Highlanders; Thaon - Fort Garry Horse and Liberation Memorial; Fontaine Henry - La Chaudi re/Regina Rifles Memorial, Plaque on Church; Moulinaux – Pumping Station.

• N.Bs. The following sites are indicated: Cristot – 146th Bde, 49th Div Plaque; Brouay CWGC Cemetery; Château d'Audrieu Massacre Site & Dorset Regt Memorials; Secqueville-en-Bessin CWGC Cemetery; Communes of Thue & Mue – Liberators' Monument; Bretteville, CMEG Factory - Regina Rifles Plaque; Cairon, Rosel and Lasson - Can Liberation Memorials; St Contest – 59th Div Plaque; Mathieu – Harold Pickersgill Roundabout; Anguerny – Capt Gauvin Plaque; Colomby-sur-Thaon – Regt de la Chaudière Memorial; le Fresne-Camilly - Plaques to R Winnipeg Rifles & Can Scots, 7th Can Inf Bde and to Airstrip B-5; Cresserons – 22nd R Dragoon Guards, 30 Armd Bde, 79 Armd Div Memorial; Bény - ALG B4 Mem; Courseulles - King Geo V Plaque; Graye Church – Can 'Brothers', 8th King's Regt, 85th Fld Coy RE Plaques; La Br che de la Valette - C Sqn, Inns of Court Regt Memorial; Bernières – N Nova Scotia Highlanders Plaque; Church - E.W. Parker SGW, 14th Fld Regt RCA Memorial; 14th Fld Regt RCA Memorial.

• *CARPIQUET*

Take the D14/D220 Carpiquet/Authie exit from the N13, Caen Périphérique Nord.
Set your mileometer to zero.

Long Extra Visit to Carpiquet – Maj Gauvin, Regt de la Chaudière, Queen's Own Rifles of Canada, R Winnipeg Rifles, Fort Garry Horse Memorial (Map It4-A/Lat & Long: 49.18379 -0.44068/GPPIt4-1/1), North Shore Regiment Memorial (MapIt4-B /Lat & Long: 49.18404 -0.44642/GPPIt4-1/2), Fort Garry Horse Plaque (Map It4-B/Lat & Long: 49.18414 -0.44751/GPPIt4-1/3), Airfield Memorial to 'Our Canadian Brothers', Bunker (Map It4-C/Lat & Long: 49.18350 -0.45804/GPPIt4-1/7); St Manvieu - 3 Can Div Marker, (Map It4-D/Lat & Long: 49.18313 -0.48086/ GPPIt4- 1/5); Norrey-en-Bessin - R Regina Rifles & 1st Can Hussars Memorial (Map It4-E/Lat & Long: 49. 19726 -0.51375/GPPIt4-1/6); Le Mesnil-Patry - Queen's Own Can Rifles & 1st Can Hussars Memorial (Map It4-F/Lat & Long: 49.19441 -0.54608/GPPIt4-1/4); Putot-en-Bessin - R Winnipeg Rifles & 1st Bn Can Scot Regt Memorial, (Map It4-J/Lat & Long: 49.21084 -0.53876/ GPPIt4-2/1); Bretteville-l'Orgueilleuse - R Regina Rifles Plaque (Map It4-L/Lat & Long: 49.21195 -0.51458/GPPIt4-2/7); Rots - 46 RM Cdo Plaque (Map It4-P/Lat & Long 49.20834 -0.48488/ GPPIt4-2/8), Regt de la Chaudière & Fort Garry Horse Plaques (Map It4-P/Lat & Long: 49.21142 -0.47695/GPPIt4-2/5

Round trip: 16 miles. Approximate time: 1 hour 30 minutes.

Follow signs to Carpiquet back under the motorway, direction Airport, and continue on the D14 over the traffic lights on Avénue Charles de Gaulle.

Just before the second set of traffic lights, opposite the *Mairie* is a **Memorial to Major Gauvin** (qv) and his comrades of **the Regiment de la Chaudière, the Queen's Own Rifles, the R Winnipeg Rifles, the Fort Garry Horse**. The fine *bas relief* stone monument of a Maple Leaf and a Canadian helmet was erected by the Village of Carpiquet in gratitude and was inaugurated by Major Gauvin's wife on 7 June 2004.

Turn right at the traffic lights, direction Tilly/Caen-Carpiquet. Continue towards the next traffic lights. Just before, on the right, is the

Monument dedicated to the memory of officers and men of the **North Shore "New Brunswick" Regiment, 3rd Canadian Division** and the **People of Normandy** erected by the North Shore Veterans' Association in 1986. Beside it is a **NTL Totem,** with a comprehensive description of the action here by the Canadian 9th Brigade to take Carpiquet, and the fierce counter-attack of the 12th SS ('Hitler Youth'). It also describes the action of Operation WINDSOR in early July when the 8th Canadian Brigade led the assault with flame-throwing tanks, support from 21st Artillery Regiment, Typhoon fighter-bombers and the guns of HMS *Rodney*. The airfield was defended by a squadron of Panther tanks and a company of 12th SS Grenadiers. During the fighting, which lasted until 8 July, the Canadians lost 377 men, including 117 killed.

Continue over the traffic lights for about 100 metres to the ruin of a stone arch on the right.

On it there is a black marble **Plaque** to the **Fort Garry Horse** and below a brass plaque in memory of 4 July 1944 and expressing the homage of the Commune of Carpiquet to its **Canadian Liberators.**

Continue to Carpiquet Airfield on the D9 and park near the main building.
Follow signs to the Aero club and on the right by the entrance gate to the airfield is

A handsome **Memorial** surmounted by a Maple Leaf, erected on 8 July 1995 on the initiative of the Association for the Defence and Development of Caen-Carpiquet Airport. It was unveiled by the Canadian Ambassador and honours '**Our Canadian Brothers**' who fought to liberate this airfield. The Hell of Carpiquet. 4-8 July 1944. Prelude to the liberation of Caen'.

ITINERARY FOUR MAP: CANADIAN JUNO BEACH LANDINGS

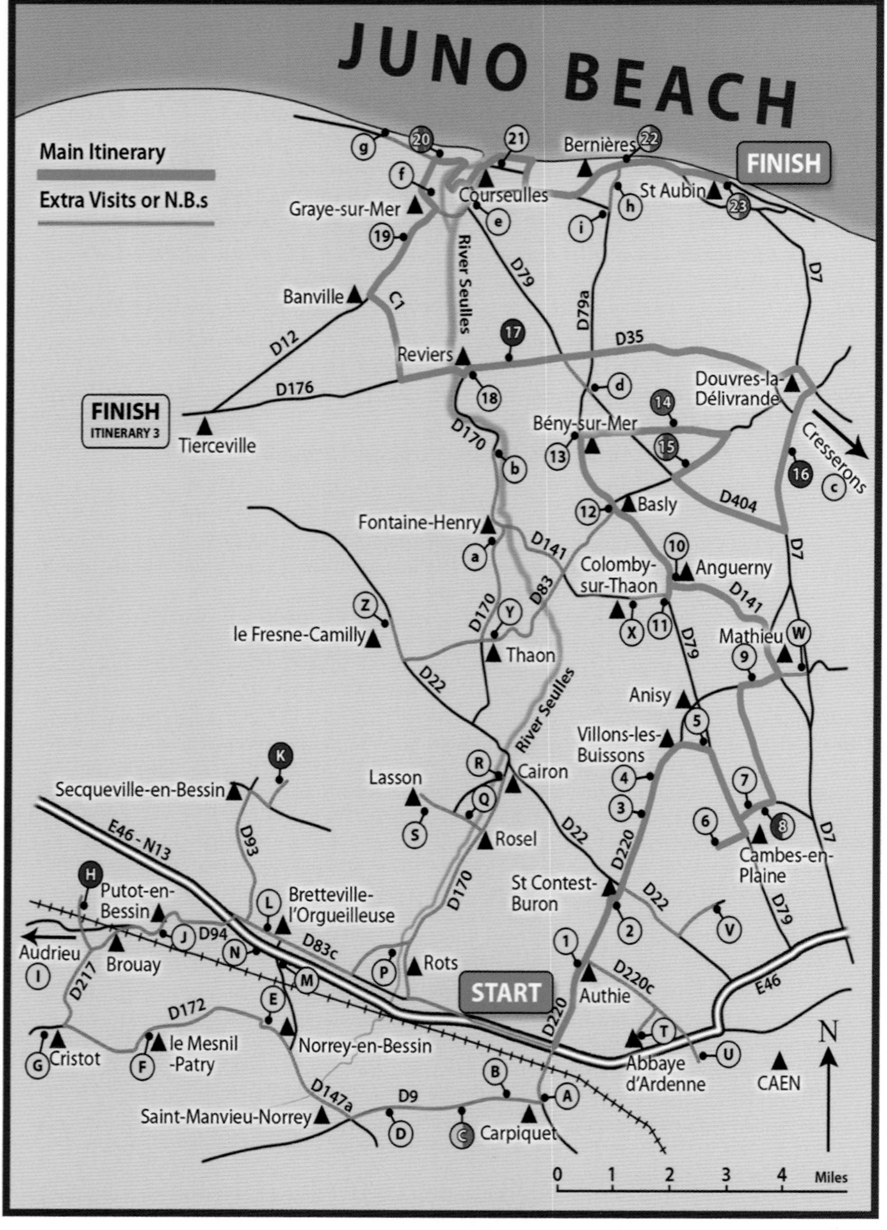

JUNO BEACH

Main Itinerary

Extra Visits or N.B.s

g 20 21 Bernières 22

FINISH

f

Graye-sur-Mer Courseulles St Aubin
e i h 23
19

Banville C1

River Seulles

D12 D79 D79a

Reviers 17 D35

FINISH
ITINERARY 3 D176 18 Douvres-la-Délivrande
Tierceville d 14 Cresserons
D170 Bény-sur-Mer 15 16
b 13 c

Fontaine-Henry 12 Basly D404
a D141 D7
Colomby-sur-Thaon 10 Anguerny
Z Y X 11 D141
le Fresne-Camilly D170 D83 79 Mathieu W
D22 Thaon 9

River Seulles Anisy 5

Villons-les-Buissons 4
Secqueville-en-Bessin K Lasson R Cairon 3 7
E46 - N13 D93 Q 6 8
S Rosel D22 D220 Cambes-en-Plaine
Putot-en-Bessin L Bretteville-l'Orgueilleuse St Contest-Buron D79
H J D94 N D170 2 V
Audrieu Brouay M P Rots 1 D220c E46
I D217 E START Authie
D172 T U N
Cristot le Mesnil Norrey-en-Bessin Abbaye CAEN
G F -Patry B d'Ardenne
D147a D9 A D220
Saint-Manvieu-Norrey D C Carpiquet

0 1 2 3 4 Miles

MAIN ITINERARY

1. N Nova Scotia Highlanders, Authie
2. HLI Can/Sherbrooke Fus, Buron
3. Hell's Corner/9 Can Inf, Villons-les-Buissons
4. Airstrip B-16, Villons-les-Buissons
5. Norwegian Mem , Villons-les-Buissons
6. 59 (Staffs) Div, Galmanche
7. 59 (Staffs) Div/3 BR Div/2 RUR, Cambes-en-Plaine
8. CWGC Cem/2 RUR, Cambes-en-Plaine
9. QO Rifles Can, Anisy
10. Fort Garry Horse/QO Rifles Can, Anguerny
11. Regt de la Chaudière/ Capt M Gauvin, Anguerny
12. Maple Leaf Can Liberators, Basly
13. Regt de la Chaudière, Bény-sur-Mer
14. Bunkers/Radar Station OP, Douvres
15. Mus/Bunkers/Radar Station, Douvres
16. CWGC Cem La Délivrande, Douvres
17. CWGC Can Cem/Cam Highlanders of Ottawa/ Toulouse Resistance, Bény-sur-Mer
18. Regina Rifles, Reviers
19. R Winnipeg Rifles/Can Scots, Graye
20. Churchill Tank/Com Déb Sig/Cross of Lorraine, R Winnipeg Rifles/Can Scots, Graye Cosy's Bunker, JUNO Beach Mus/Lt Col Blanchette/'Remembrance & Renewal Sculpture/Inuksuk Mon/La Combattante Pl/Nottingham Bridge, 85 Fld Coy RE, Courseulles
21. Sherman Tank:12 Fld Regt, RCA; 6 Can Fld Coy R Can Engs; 1 Can Para Bn;14 Can Fld Amb; 5 Fld Coy, R Can Engs Vets; Can Prov Corps; 13 Fld Regt R Can Arty; 19 Can Army Fld Regt (SP) RCA/14 Fld Regt RCA; RCEME/Ger KWK 39/Gen de Gaulle/1 Can Scots/Belg Volunteers/ 8 R Scots/6 R Scots Fus/6 Border Bn KOSB/ Regina Regt/La Combattante/R Winnipeg Rifles, Courseulles
22. Com Déb Sig/QO Rifles House/Bunker/1st Journalists/Inuksuk Mon/2 QO Rifles Can/Stormont, Dundas & Glengarry Highlanders/ 5 Hackney Bn R Berks/8 Beach Gp/Regt de la Chaudière/ Fort Garry Horse 10 Armd Regt/ 8 Bde, 3 Can Div/Map of Can Landings, N Nova Scotia Highlanders Pl, Bernières
23. Bunker/Fort Garry Horse/5 Fld Coy RCE/19 Fld Regt RCA/N Shore Regt/10 Can Armd Regt/48 RM Cdo/ Maurice Duclos, St Aubin

EXTRA VISITS & 'N.B.s'

A. Maj Gauvin/Regt de la Chaudière/QO Rifles/R Winnipeg Rifles/Fort Garry Horse, Carpiquet
B. N Shore New Brunswick/3 Can Div/Fort Garry Horse, Carpiquet
C. Can Liberators/Bunker, Carpiquet Airfield
D. 5 Can Regts of 3 Div, St Manvieu
E. R Regina Rifles/1st Can Hussars, Norrey-en-Bessin
F. Q O Rifles/1st Can Hussars, le Mesnil-Patry
G. 146 (W Riding) Bde, 49 Div, Cristot
H. CWGC Cem, Brouay
I. Massacre/Dorset Regt, Château d'Audrieu
J. R Winnipeg Rifles/1st Can Scot Regt, Putot-en-Bessin
K. CWGC Cem, Secqueville-en-Bessin
L. Regina Rifles, Bretteville l'Orgeuilleuse
M. Liberators Thue & Mue
N. Regina Rifles, Bretteville
P. 46 RM Cdo/Regt de la Chaudière/Fort Garry Horse/ Léon Gagne, Rots
Q. Can Liberators, Rosel
R. Can Liberators, Cairon
S. Can Liberators, Lasson
T. Massacre, Abbaye d'Ardenne
U. Stormont Dundas & Glengarry Highlanders, rue d'Authie, Caen
V. 59 (Staffs) Div, St Contest
W. Harold Pickersgill Roundabout, Mathieu
X. Regt de la Chaudière, Colomby-sur-Thaon
Y. Fort Garry Horse/8th Can Inf Bde, Thaon
Z. Airstrip B-5/121st Fighter Gp/R Winnipeg Rifles /7 Can Scots Inf Bde, le Fresne-Camilly
a. 1st Hussars/Regt de la Chaudière/13th RCA/RCEME/Can 'Heroes'/Lt d'Ouillamson, Fontaine-Henry
b. Pumping Station, Moulineaux
c. 22 R Dragoon Guards, Cresserons
d. ALG B-4/401,411, 412 Sqns RCAF, Bény-sur-Mer
e. King Geo VI, Courseulles
f. Can Brothers'/8 (Irish) King's Regt/85 Field Coy, RE, Graye Ch
g. C Sqn, Inns of Court Regt, la Brêche de la Valette
h. SGW to E.W. Parker, Regt de la Chaudière, Bernières Ch
i. 14 Fld Regt RCA, Bernières

The units involved are listed. To the right of the main airport building are the remains of a **Bunker,** the last vestiges of the 1944 Carpiquet Aerodrome fortifications. Inside the building is a **Bar/Café** and WCs.

Carpiquet Airfield became operational as **Airstrip B-17** in August 1944.

Turn left out of the airfield on the D9. Enter St Manvieu. Continue to a small road to the left, Chemin au Roy.

At the corner is a small, difficult to read **Marker to 5 Canadian Regiments of 3 Div** who regrouped in this hamlet before the Battle of Carpiquet, 4-8 July 1944. Prelude to the Liberation of Caen. Erected 4 July 1998.

*Continue to the roundabout. [**NOTE. St Manvieu CWGC Cemetery is 1 mile further on the right hand side.**] Turn right on the D147A signed to Bretteville. Continue to a right turn direction Norrey-en-Bessin, turn right on the D83 and then turn left on the D172. Continue to the Church in Norrey-en-Bessin. To the left is*

A beautiful polished pink granite **Memorial** with a gold outlined Maple Leaf and Regimental badges to the **Royal Regina Rifles** and the **1st Can Hussars**, 'In homage to our **Canadian Liberators**. 7 June 1944'. Below the silver-painted WW1 *Poilu* is a black **Plaque to Civilian Victims** of **Norrey-en-Bessin.**

Turn left, still on the D172, to Le Mesnil-Patry and continue to Place des Canadiens opposite the Mairie and before the modern church.

Here there is a large and handsome **Memorial,** with flags, to the **Queen's Own Rifles and the 1st Hussars,** with all the names of those killed on 11 June 1944 on bronze Plaques.

Continue on the D172 to the right turning on the D217.

> **N.B.** By continuing on the D172 to the church at Cristot there is a **Plaque** on the wall to **the** 146th (W Riding) Bde, **49th Div,** with its 'Polar Bear' insignia, next to the local war Memorial. They liberated Cristot on 16 June 1944. **(Map It4-G/Lat & Long: 49.19483 -0.57910/GPPIt4-1/8).** Airstrip B-18 was constructed at Cristot, completed by 25 July.

Turn right direction Brouay on the D217 to a crossroads.

> **N.B.1** By turning left at the crossroads on the small rue de la Limare, crossing the D94 and continuing under the railway some half a mile, **Brouay War Cemetery** is reached by the village church. **(Map It4-H/Lat & Long: 49.21428 -0.56286/GPPIt4-1/9)** The beautiful CWGC Plot, with an imposing entrance shelter, is above the local cemetery. It contains 377 burials, including 7 unidentified. Most of the burials relate to the fighting of June and July 1944.

> **N.B.2** By returning under the railway, turning right after the *Mairie* on the D94 and continuing some two miles, Audrieu is reached. It was here on 8, 9 and 11 June 1944 that 24 Canadians of the R Winnipeg Rifles and the Queen's Own Canadian Rifles and Pte W. Barlow of the 50th (Northumbrian) Div and Pte Evan Hayton of the DLI were massacred by elements of the 12th SS Panzer Division (Hitler Youth). The shootings took place in three groups on 8, 9 and 11 June in woods round the Château d'Audrieu (qv) where Cdr Gerhard Bremer, 12th Ger Reconnaissance Bn, had established his HQ. Brothers George and Frank Meakin of 9th Platoon, 'A' Coy the R Winnipeg Rifles, are buried in Bény CWGC Cemetery (qv), as is Hayton. Barlow is buried in the CWGC Cemetery at Hottot-les-Bagues. By continuing to the church and the *Mairie,* a **Memorial** to those **Royal Winnipeg Rifles** and others who were killed is on the opposite wall **(Map It4-I/Lat & Long: 49.20660 -0.59529/GPPIt4-1/10).** The handsome bronze Plaque, with the Roll of Honour of 'those who were murdered as POWs' at the Château, Near le Mesnil-Patry and at Le Haut du Boscq, was inaugurated on 8 June 1989 by Senator Col G. Molgat and 'Members and Friends of the RWR and Supporting Arms'. To its left is a **Memorial to Place du Dorset Regt** who liberated the town in 1944 **(Map It4-I//GPPIt4-1/11).** The Germans, having fled the Château, the Dorsets occupied it and were informed of the killings by the owner's daughter. Maj Lloyd Sneath of the Dorsets had served as an NCO with the R Winnipeg Rifles before being transferred to the Dorsets and to his dismay recognised some of his old comrades. Accounts of this sad incident vary enormously, as do the number of soldiers actually killed. Some accounts state that the shootings of the POWs were carried out by SS Kapitein von Reitzenstein as a reprisal for the wounding of Cdr Bremer during the allied bombardment on Audrieu. There is even a story that many years later a French translation of the official German 2nd SS History was suppressed. Today the adjacent **Château d'Audrieu** is an elegant luxury 4-star hotel with 25 bedrooms and 4 suites in glorious grounds owned by the Livry-Leve family. Outdoor swimming pool. Gourmet restaurant. Tel: + (0)2 31 80 21 52. E-mail: audrieu@relaischateaux.com. Website: www.relaischateaux.com/audrieu

Continue and take the first right immediately after the railway crossing on rue de Brouay, the D94. Continue to Putot-en-Bessin Church.

The Church at Putot-en-Bessin is classified as a *Monument Historique.*

Just beyond it in Place des Canadiens is

A large double **Memorial** with flags. On the left is a **Plaque and Badge to the Royal Winnipeg Rifles** with a poem by Paul Eluard. On the right is a **Plaque and Badge to the 1st Bn Can Scot Regt.** In front is an **Information Panel** describing the Liberation of Putot at the cost of 98 German losses, 256 Canadian, including 105 killed on the battlefield and 45 massacred at the Château d'Audrieu (qv).

Turn round and return to the D94. Turn right and continue under the N13 into Bretteville-l'Orgueilleuse. At the crossroads with the D83c turn right direction Rots on the rue de Bayeux.

N.B. By turning first left and continuing on the D93 to **Secqueville-en-Bessin**, the **CWGC Cemetery** (Map It4-K/Lat & Long: **49.23449 -0.50805/GPPIt4-2/3**) may be reached by continuing through the village, following green CWGC signs to a narrow metalled road to the left leading to the cemetery in open fields. This 'battlefield cemetery' contains 99 Commonwealth burials and 18 German. They are from July 1944.

Continue and take the third turning left just past the Mairie into the Place Canadien. Opposite the School is

Memorial to the Regina Rifles with **Plaques** in English and French and the Maple Leaf insignia. Below is a **Plaque** with the Regina Rifles Badge and the words *'Bretteville n'oublie pas'*. The group is surrounded with a chain and shells.

N.B.1 By turning right at the next crossroads onto the D83 and driving under the E46 to the roundabout, an impressive white **Memorial to Liberators of the Communes between the Thue and the Mue in 1944.** [The Thue and the Mue are two small rivers at the boundaries of the Commune.] It lists **the Liberating Units: 3 Can Inf Div, RCA, 2nd Armd Bde, 43rd Wessex Div, 15th (Scot) Div, 50th (Northumbrian) Div, 11th Armd Div, 31st R Tank Bde** and is situated in the centre of the roundabout with a beautifully landscaped approach path. Sculptor Muller de Schonger. **(Map It4-M/Lat & Long: 49.20681 -0.51104/ GPPIt4-2/6).**

N.B.2 By taking the 'Bayeux 12t' sign from the roundabout and entering the industrial estate, continuing to the road junction, going straight over and then turning left on rue du Commandant D towards the tall wireless mast and the CMEG Factory, a **Memorial** with a bronze **Plaque to the Regina Rifles (Map It4-N/Lat & Long: 49.20566 -0.51953/GPPIt4-2/7)** may be found by the factory entrance. The site was a linen factory in 1944 and here on 9 June D Coy of the Royal Canadian Rifles, commanded by Major Gordon Brown, withstood a fierce attack by the 12th SS Panzer Division *Hitlerjügend* who they repulsed at the cost of 51 killed and wounded. At the end of the battle only 2 officers and 40 men remained of the Company.

Continue round the square back to the rue de Bayeux/rue de Caen and continue on the D83c for 1.2 miles to a small crossroads. Turn left on the Chemin du Hamel in Rots signed to RM Cdo Stèle. On the left is

A Memorial Garden in the **Place du 46 RM Cdo, 11 June 1944.** On the wall is a splendid black marble **Plaque** with badge and a list of the fallen, with their ages.

Continue on the wiggly Chemin du Hamel to the T Junction with the Chemin de la Cavée. Turn right and continue to the small memorial garden on the right in Rots.

This is a beautifully landscaped paved garden. On the wall is a **Plaque to the Regt de la Chaudière**, 11 June 1944, with 7 names and the **Fort Garry Horse**, with their badges. There is an archway to 'Passage **Léon Gagne**, Canadian Sergeant'.

Continue to the T Junction with the D170.

At No 22 Route de Caen (the D83c) in Rots is the **Bar-Hotel-Restaurant Le Coup de Pompe**. 8 rooms. Open 1145-1430 and 1900-2030. **Closed** Fri and Sat evenings and Sunday. Tel: + (0)2 31 26 04 03. Website: www.coupdepompe.com. It has an amazingly good value 3 course lunch including drink with an excellent cold buffet. Opposite is **Le Bistrot Bar Brasserie.**

N.B. North of this point three local memorials thanking their Canadian liberators may be reached :
1. Rosel: On the left by the *Mairie* is the Local War Memorial with a **Plaque to the Canadians killed during the Liberation.** (Map It4-Q/Lat & Long: **49.22826 -0.45923/GPPIt4-2/9**). Opposite is a red British phone box.
2. Cairon: At the junction between the rue de Rots and the rue des Ecureuils, **a Monument to the Allied Liberators. (Map It4-R/Lat & Long: 49.23760 -0.45088/GPPIt4-2/4).**
3. Lasson: On Allée des Canadiens at the small crossroads is a cut out **Maple Leaf Memorial (Map It4-S/Lat & Long: 49.22960 -0.46540/GPPIt4-2/10).**

Return on the D170 to the T junction with the D83c. Turn left, continue and rejoin the N13 direction Caen. Pick up the main itinerary.

GPPIt4-1/1	Memorial to Maj Gauvin & Can Regts, Carpiquet
GPPIt4-1/2	Memorial to N Shore New Brunswick Regt, Carpiquet
GPPIt4-1/3	Plaque to Fort Garry Horse, Carpiquet
GPPIt4-1/4	Memorial to Can Q Own Rifles & 1st Hussars, le Mesnil-Patry
GPPIt4-1/5	Marker to 5 Can Regts of 3 Div, St Manvieu
GPPIt4-1/6	Memorial to R Regina Rifles & 1st Can Hussars, Norrey-en-Bessin.
GPPIt4-1/7	Memorial to 'Our Can Brothers', Carpiquet Airfield
GPPIt4-1/8	Plaque to 146th Bde, 49th Div, Cristot Church wall
GPPIt4-1/9	CWGC Cem, Brouay
GPPIt4-1/10	Plaques to R Winnipeg Rifles killed in massacre, Audrieu
GPPIt4-1/11	Memorial to Dorset Regt, Audrieu

Start the Main Itinerary by continuing to Authie on the D220.

On entering the town the white JUNO Itinerary sign with red lettering erected at the entrance to each town and village on the JUNO Routes and the typical 'twinning' sign (with North Baddesley, Hampshire) are passed. The road here is dedicated to **Henri Brunet,** 1902-1943, *Fusillé.* Brunet had a drawing office in Caen which the Germans used to produce plans of their defence works along the Atlantic Wall. Brunet passed details of the plans to the clandestine network named 'Turma' but was discovered and shot on 20 September 1942. The road name gives his death as 1943.

Continue to the memorial on the left opposite the Mairie.

• North Nova Scotia Highlanders Memorial, Authie/0.9 miles/5 minutes/Map It4/1/Holts Map H18/Lat & Long: 49.20650 -0.43139

This **Memorial** commemorates the **Nova Scotia Highlanders** who in fighting around the village on 7 June lost 84 men. It was in this area that 23 men were executed by the 12th SS (qv). In addition to the dead, the Nova Scotians lost 158 men wounded or taken prisoner. The Sherbrooke Rifles had 60 dead. 7 Citizens were also killed. Beside it is a **NTL Totem** describing the Canadians' progress from JUNO Beach to Buron on 7 June. Here in Authie leading elements of the Highlanders were attacked by Colonel Kurt Meyer's fanatical SS Units which pressed forward regardless of their losses. Below is a **Plaque to Civilian Victims,** erected on 7 June 2004.

Extra Visit to the Abbaye d'Ardenne Massacre Memorials (Map It4-T/Lat & Long: 49.196887 -0.415005/GPPIt4-3/5,7,9); Memorial to Stormont Dundas & Glengarry Highlanders (Map It4-U/Lat & Long: 49.19121 -0.39750/GPPIt4-3/4). Round trip: 4.5 miles. Approximate time: 40 minutes.

From the Highlanders' Memorial turn right on the rue de l'Abbaye, go straight over the next roundabout, passing rue du Col Charles Petch to the left. Turn right on the C301, signed Abbaye d'Ardenne and continue to the parking area beyond the Abbey entrance.

Meyer had taken over the Abbaye d'Ardenne, whose owners had been arrested the year before as members of the Resistance, as the HQ for his 25th SS Panzergrenadier Regiment of Fritz Witt's 12th SS (Hitler Youth) Panzer Division. He found its old tower an excellent vantage point from which to watch the Canadians moving inland from JUNO.

The severity of the losses was compounded by reports that Canadian prisoners had been shot by SS troops. These and other murders formed the basis for charges made against Meyer by a Canadian Military Court in December 1945. He was found guilty on three of five charges (on a charge of responsibility for twenty-three murders in the Buron area on 7 June 1944 he was acquitted) and sentenced to be shot. However, the sentence was commuted to life imprisonment and he was released in 1954 from a New Brunswick Penitentiary. He died of a heart attack seven years later. A chilling account of the shooting on 8 June of seven Canadian prisoners of war in the grounds of the Abbaye was given at Meyer's trial. They were called out one by one by name, led into the garden and shot in the back of the head. They had guessed what was to happen to them and each man had shaken hands with the others as his name was called. However, the shooting of prisoners was not confined to the SS and there is no doubt that many SS were killed in that way which thus accounts for why so few ever turned up in the prisoner-of-war cages.

The Veterans Affairs Canada Website, however, maintains that as many as 156 Canadian POWs may have been executed by the 12th SS Panzer Div.

By the entrance is a **Plaque in Memory of 27 Canadians** executed here (this includes the men shot in the nearby Château). In the grounds of the beautifully reconstructed Abbey there is a sad and dark little **'Canadian Garden'** (signed up a small path to the right of the main entrance) on the spot where the Canadians were shot on 7/8 June 1944. On the wall behind the **Memorial,** which names 18 massacred soldiers (6 of the 27th Can Armd Regt, the rest North Nova Scotia Highlanders), plus two others who died on 17 June, are poignant photos of sixteen of the tragic young men. The body of one of the latter two was found by soldiers of the Regina Rifles who liberated the Abbaye shortly before midnight on 8 July. Lt Williams was later buried in Bény-sur-Mer Cemetery (qv). The body of the other, LCpl Pollard, was not found and he is commemorated on the Bayeux Memorial (qv). The two men of the Stormont, Dundas & Glengarry Highlanders had been patrolling for disabled German tanks near Buron when they went missing. The Abbey had quickly filled with POWs captured during the fighting of 7 June. Ten of them were randomly picked and sent to the Château adjacent to the Abbaye, plus one more wounded soldier, Pte Hollis McKeil. They were shot in the Château gardens that evening.

After the Battle's brilliantly researched **D-DAY THEN AND NOW,** Vol 2, page 625, puts forward the theory that the massacre was in reprisal for the use by C Sqn, the Inns of Court (qv) on 8 June near Cristot of prisoners of the Panzer Artillerie Lehr Regt as human shields, with Oberst Luxenburger strapped to one of their tanks. This story probably originates with Kurt Meyer's own colourful memoirs.

Today the Abbey is the headquarters of the *Institut Mémoire* of Cultural Buildings and various cultural events are staged here. It is officially open to the public Tuesday-Sunday 1400-1800 and guided visits may be booked on weekend afternoons. Tel: (0)2 31 29 37 37. However the Canadian Garden can usually be visited.

Turn round, return to the roundabout and turn right direction Caen on the rue D'Authie, continue under the motorway to the crossroads with the Ave Pres Coty on the left.

Memorial to Stormont Dundas & Glengarry Highlanders ('Up The Glens'), among the First Allied Troops to enter Caen, erected June 1969.

Return to Authie and pick up the main itinerary.

Continue over the D126 on the D220 to the Place des Canadiens in St Contest-Buron.

Note that, confusingly, Buron and St Contest appear to be two separate villages on a map but their name is hyphenated and used for both locations.

• *Memorials to the Highland Light Infantry of Canada and to the Sherbrooke Fusiliers Memorials, Buron/1.8 miles/5 minutes/Map It4-2/Holts Map H19,20/Lat & Long: 49.21725 -0.42130*

The D220 road, down which you have driven, was a main axis for the Canadian forces moving inland from JUNO. It leads directly to the high ground at Carpiquet Airport three miles behind you which was the special visit at the start of this itinerary. Carpiquet was the objective of the follow-up, 9th Brigade Group. At the end of D-Day the Canadians had reached Villons-le-Buissons, 3½ miles north of here, and by around 0700 hours on 7 June the 9th Brigade, led by the North Nova Scotia Highlanders and the 27th Armoured Regiment (Sherbrooke Fusiliers), was advancing towards Buron. Just north of the village they came under fire from machine guns and anti-tank weapons, and a set-piece battle followed in which Canadians and Germans fought from house to house. It was not until midday that the village was secured. Meanwhile troops of the Highlanders and Sherbrookes not involved at Buron had pushed on to the edge of Carpiquet. The 9th Brigade was dangerously extended and, unknown to them, they were being watched by Kurt Meyer from the Abbaye.

At 1500 hours Meyer launched a counter-attack on Buron, hoping to drive to the sea in conjunction with 21st Panzer Division. Late in the afternoon the Canadians lost Buron and fell back to Villons-le-Buissons where they had begun the day. It had been a bloody struggle. The Highlanders had some 250 casualties and the Sherbrookes lost 21 cruiser tanks.

The battle for the high ground of Carpiquet was to be a long and hard one against fanatical troops of the 12th SS Panzer Division. It had been created in 1943 from elements of the 1st SS (Leibstandarte Adolf Hitler) Division and though it had not been in battle before it had a high proportion of experienced officers and NCOs from the Russian Front. The bulk of the soldiers were youngsters under 18 years old straight out of military fitness camps and full of Nazi ideology. In all, the division, which was initially commanded by Brigadeführer Fritz Witt, had about 20,000 men and 150 tanks. It was a formidable fighting force and it held on to Buron and Carpiquet for another month.

At 0420 hours on 8 July a combined five-phase British and Canadian assault was launched in the direction of Carpiquet, and once again the 9th Brigade advanced on Buron. As the second phase began the Highland Light Infantry of Canada and the Sherbrookes led off at 0730 hours and by 0830 hours were in the village. The 12th SS Panzer Division, now commanded by Kurt Meyer following Fritz Witt's death on 14 June, fought with the determination expected of them and it was not until early the following morning that the last SS man had been found and silenced. The Highland Light Infantry lost half of its attacking force in what had been its first real battle and it was to prove its bloodiest of the campaign with 262 casualties. The CO, Lieutenant-Colonel F.M. Griffiths, was wounded and later received the DSO for his actions on that day.

There are **Memorials to the Highland Light Infantry of Canada and to the Sherbrooke Fusiliers** here. The area is known as the Place des Canadiens, and the Highland Memorial was dedicated on 21 July 1969. The Sherbrooke Memorial explains the origin of the name: '...recruited from the city of Sherbrooke Quebec Canada'. The Maple Leaf is incorporated in the flagstones and the Canadian and French flags fly here.

Continue on the D220 to the D22 crossroads.

N.B. By turning right on the D22 and continuing about 1 mile to a roundabout and then turning left into the village of St Contest there is a black marble **Plaque** with badge and gold lettering to the Memory of the **59th (Staffs) Inf Div** who contributed to the liberation of this Sector, 8 & 9 July 1944. It was erected in 1994 on the churchyard wall. (**Map It4-V/Lat & Long:** 49.21432 -0.40157/GPPIt4-3/6.)

Continue on the D220 and head north towards Villons-les-Buissons. At the first road junction left, just short of the village, stop.

• Hell's Corner/9th Canadian Infantry Memorial, Villons-les-Buissons/3.1 miles/5 minutes/Map It4-3/Holts Map H22/Lat & Long: 49.23346 -0.41365

Here is the Memorial to the 9th Canadian Infantry (Highland) Brigade that fought so determinedly between here and Buron from 6 June to 8 July. It was dedicated on 8 June 1984. As the Canadian 9th Brigade cleared Villons they captured a German 88mm gun and a six-barrelled mortar, something that they had not seen before. The small road leading to the left is the rue des Glengarrians.

Continue to the small monument on the left and stop.

The unusual entrance to Cambes-en-Plaine CWGC Cemetery.

Memorial to 2nd RUR, Cambes-en-Plaine.

Plaque to Queen's Own Rifles of Canada, Anguerny.

Queen's Own Rifles of Canada Memorial, Anisy.

Plaque to the Regt la Chaudière, Anguerny.

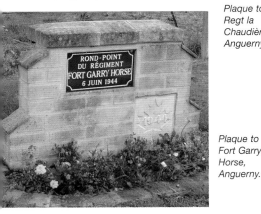

Plaque to Fort Garry Horse, Anguerny.

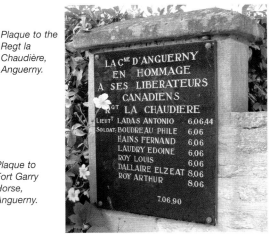

• Plaques to Fort Garry Horse and Queen's Own Rifles of Canada, Anguerny/9 miles/5 minutes/Map It4-10/Holts Map H32/Lat & Long: 49.26695 -0.40093

At the right hand corner is a **Plaque to the Rond Point du Regt Fort Garry Horse, 6 juin 1944** and on the wall opposite, to the right, is a bronze **Plaque to the Queen's Own Rifles of Canada**, unveiled on 5 June 1994.

Turn left on rue Queen's Own Rifles of Canada and continue past the church to the junction with the D141/D141A. Stop by the Mairie. On the left hand corner is

• Memorial to the Régiment la Chaudière, Anguerny's Liberators/ 9.2 miles/10 minutes/Map It4-11/Holts Map H29/Lat & Long: 49.26619 -0.40425

The black marble **Plaque** lists seven members of the regiment who died on 6 and 8 June 1944.

N.B.1 By continuing a further 80 yards one arrives at a green **Plaque to Square du Capitaine M. Gauvin** (qv). 6 June 1944. (**Map It4-11/Lat & Long: 49.26564 -0.40485/GPPIt4-3/2**). This was unveiled on the 60th Anniversary by the Canadian Ambassador. Michel Gauvin had led the Bren-carriers of the Chaudière during the Invasion and after the war became a diplomat and one of the founders of the Canadian Battlefields Foundation. He died in 2003.

N.B.2 By continuing on the D141 to the *Mairie* in Colomby-sur-Thaon in Place Poulbot, a **Memorial to the Regt de la Chaudière** (**Map It4-X/Lat & Long: 49.26525 -0.41129/GPPIt4-3/10**) may be found. In French it describes the long road which led to the Liberation of Europe from the Nazi yoke by the Regt de la Chaudière who liberated Colomby on 7 June 1944 and remembers the sacrifice of the Canadian soldiers, all volunteers, who died in Normandy in June 1944.

Turn right direction Basly on the D141A on rue Régiment de la Chaudière, 6 juin 1944. Continue to the junction with the D79 and turn right signed to Basly. Continue into Basly and stop at the memorial by the Church.

• Maple Leaf Memorial, Basly/10.6 miles/5 minutes/Map It4-12/Holts Map C30/Lat & Long: 49.27872 -0.42340

This was erected on 8 June 1991 by the citizens of Basly in gratitude to their Canadian liberators.

Extra Visit to the Fort Garry Horse, 8th Can Inf Bde and Liberation Memorial, Thaon (Map It4-Y/Lat & Long: 49.25834 -0.45482/GPPIt4-3/8), Canadian Memorial and Plaque, Fontaine Henry (Map It4-a/Lat & Long: 49.27459   - 0.45304/GPPIt4-3/1) and Moulinaux Pumping Station, (Map It4-b/Lat & Long: 49.28715 -0.45368/GPPIt4-4/2). Round trip: 7.5 miles. Approximate time: 1 hour.

Take the D83 signed Thaon and enter the village past the château on the right and follow the winding road through the village to some 200 yards before the Mairie. Stop at the memorial, Place de la Criée.

The **Plaque** on a small stone commemorates the liberation of the village by the **10th Armoured Regiment (Fort Garry Horse)** in support of the **8th Canadian Infantry Brigade** on 6th June 1944. It has regimental buttons as rivets on each corner – a feature of many of the Canadian Regimental Plaques. In the same way that it is unwise to be dogmatic about battle casualty figures, whether of men or equipment, it is unwise to assert that a particular place, house or person was 'liberated' at a specific time. The French remain enthusiastically grateful for their Liberation in 1944-5 and a vigorous internal contest has developed between claimants to being the 'first'. Failing the possibility of being a contender for a 'first' the next best thing is to have been liberated on D-Day, 6 June. Thaon says 'Thank you for Liberation on 6 June', while

---

official Canadian records suggest that it was not occupied until 7 June.

The village is just south of 'Elm', the intermediate objective, and in the general line of advance of the 9th Infantry Brigade Group on 7 June. The Régiment de la Chaudière, part of 8th Infantry Brigade Group, came ashore at Bernières on NAN White just before 0830 hours on 6 June, supported by two DD squadrons of the 10th Armoured Regiment (Fort Garry Horse). By midnight the Chaudières had reached Bény four miles north of here and there can be little doubt that elements of their brigade had entered Thaon, but the main body of the force spent the night north of the village, i.e. nearer the landing beaches. The 9th Brigade had followed the 8th onto the beach at Bernières and pushed on early on 7 June into the actions at Buron.

Continue to the crossroads with the D170.

> **N.B.** By continuing straight over on the rue du Fresne to the crossroads with the D22, turning right and continuing some half a mile to the junction with the C1 at le Fresne-Camilly, two black marble **Plaques** may be found on an old stone wall. **(Map It4-Z/Lat & Long: 49.26631 -0.48560/GPPIt4-3/11).** One commemorates the **R Winnipeg Rifles & Can Scots of 7th Can Inf Bde** who liberated le Fresne on 6 June 1944. It was erected by the JUNO Committee on 12 July 1994. The other shows the layout of **Airstrip B-5.** The Airstrip was built under enemy fire from 10-17 June and used by 121st Fighter Gp Typhoon Wing until 4 September 1944.

Turn right direction Fontaine Henry. Continue to the church and stop on the left.

In the parking area is a grey marble **Memorial** with a flagpole behind to **'The First Hussars, La Chaudière, Regina Rifles, 13th RCA and RCEME:** Fontaine Henry remembers.' On the side wall of the church to the left of the entrance is a well-weathered **Plaque** to the **Canadian Heroes who fell at Fontaine-Henry. 11 are listed by name.** In the church is a **Plaque to Lt Tanneguy d'Ouilliamson** (qv), killed in Indo-China, 1947.

Continue past the château on the right.

The 15th/16th Century Château here boasts the highest roof in France and the fact that it has never been sold. For visits apply to the owner, M. D'Ouilliamson. Tel: (0)2 31 80 00 42. E-mail: fonthenry@aol.com

Continue to the T junction and turn left on the D141 signed Creully/Courseulles to the junction with the D170. Turn right signed Reviers and just before the exit sign to Fontaine Henry turn right past house No 14. Stop at the first small house on the right and ask permission to see

The Pumping Station, Moulineaux. Note that it is in a field on private land. This stone structure was built to supply Airstrip B-16 at Villons-le-Buissons (qv). The signs *CARPE DIEM* and 'JULY 1944' can still be clearly seen on its walls.

Turn round and return to the junction with the D141 signed Colomby sur Thaon. Turn left and continue to the crossroads and turn left on the D83. Return to to Basly. Rejoin the main itinerary.

Continue on the D79 to Bény-sur-Mer. Stop in the Place de l'Eglise.

• Memorial to Régiment de la Chaudière, Bény-sur-Mer/11.5 miles/ 5 minutes/Map It4-13/Holts Map C32/Lat & Long: 49.29160 -0.43300

The inscription reads: '*Reconnaissance aux soldats Canadiens du Régiment de la Chaudière qui Libérèrent ce village 6 Juin 1944. Bény s/Mer. Aleppo'.* (Bény thanks the Canadians for Liberation on 6 June 1944). Canadians and French agree about Bény and HQ 8th Brigade actually signalled the Chaudi res at 1535 hours on D-Day: 'Understand you are in Aleppo'. 'Aleppo' was the codename for Bény.

Turn round and go past the church, turning left immediately on the Route de Douvres. Cross the D404 and continue on the C301 to Douvres-Tailleville. At the junction with the D219 go straight ahead signed Douvres. Continue to a cart track to the left. Stop.

Douvres-la-Délivrande CWGC Cemetery.

Headstones of two of the three Westlake brothers buried at Bény.

Entrance Canadian CWGC Cemetery, Bény.

Plaque to Toulouse Group of Deportés, Bény CWGC Cemetery.

Plaque to the Cameron Highlanders of Ottawa, Bény CWGC Cemetery.

• *Canadian CWGC Cemetery, Cameron Highlanders of Ottawa & Toulouse Resistance Plaques/Bény-sur-Mer/21.4 miles/30 minutes/ Map It4-17/Holts Map C25,26/Lat & Long: 49.30230 -0.45067*

This is the highest point for some miles around and there are two watch-towers from which excellent views may be obtained towards Courseulles and JUNO Beach. At the bottom of the left-hand tower is a **Memorial Tablet** to the **Cameron Highlanders of Ottawa**. Above it is a bronze leaf-shaped **Plaque** to *'Un Groupe de Toulousains Déportés Résistants Reconnaissants'*.

There are 2,049 graves in the cemetery, 2,044 of which are Canadian, including 335 officers and men of the 3rd Canadian Division who were killed on D-Day. Among them are **nine pairs of brothers - Blais, Boyd, Branton, Hadden, Hobbin, Meakin, Skwarchuk, Tadgell and White.** The **Meakin brothers, Cpl George and L/Cpl Frank,** R Winnipeg Rifles were killed in the massacre at Château d'Audrieu. Also killed in the massacre were Maj Frederick Edward Hodge, R Winnipeg Rifles and Pte Evan Hayton, DLI. There are **three Westlake brothers** - Rifleman T.L., of the Queen's Own Rifles of Canada age 33 and Rifleman A.N., age 26 of the same regiment, both killed on 11 June and buried side by side in Plot III Row D and **Private George**, of the Nova Scotia Highlanders, killed on 7 June who is in Plot VIII Row F12. The British and Commonwealth Forces did not at this stage have the same policy of trying to separate close relations as did the Americans (giving rise to the story of 'Private Ryan', qv). Also buried here is **Lieutenant Edward Frank Mantle** of the 5th Anti-Tank Regiment, RCA, killed on 2 August. His father, Major Alfred Mantle, was killed in the First World War on 26 September 1916 and is commemorated on the Vimy Memorial.

A three-year programme of headstone replacements throughout the cemetery has a completion date of 2011.

Unusually, in tribute to the French Canadians buried here, the legend on the War Stone is also in French on the back: *Leur nom vit pour les générations.*

Continue towards the village of Reviers and as the road enters the village there is a road junction to the left with a small memorial.

• *Regina Rifle Regiment Memorial, Reviers/21.9 miles/5 minutes/ Map It4-18/Holts Map C26/Lat & Long: 49.30131 -0.46182*

The small **Plaque** and stone are to the **Regina Rifle Regiment** who liberated Reviers on D-Day, mentioning Objective Line **ADEN**. They and their fellow regiment of the 7th Brigade, the Royal Winnipeg Rifles, moved rapidly off the beach at Courseulles and by mid-morning were two miles inland. The Reginas had the specific task of seizing the crossings over the River Seulles which lie at the bottom of this hill. By 7 June they were astride the N13 at Bretteville-l'Orgueilleuse, west of Carpiquet. The following morning they had a head-on battle with Meyer's 12th SS Division at Bretteville when one of the German Panthers got to battalion HQ, where it was knocked out by a PIAT (Projector, Infantry, Anti-tank). Although they were over-run they held their ground and the Germans withdrew.

Continue on the D176/35 following signs to Bayeux and immediately after crossing the River Seulles turn right towards Banville on the C1. In the village turn right onto the D12 signed Courseulles and continue to the turning left just before the river on the D112B. (Do not take the road to Courseulles).

N.B. By continuing on the D12 into Courseulles and turning right by the cemetery onto rue Charles Benoist (when the Château will be on the left) a small grey **Plaque** on the central door of the modest House No 5 recounts how **King George VI** stayed here on the night of 16 June 1944 (**Map It4-e/Lat & Long: 49.32944 -0.45732/GPPIt4-4/5**). There is parking in the square below by the Salles d'Exposition.

Turn left and follow signs to Centre Ville and Croix de Lorraine to the junction with the D112C.

> **N.B.** By turning right here and then first left, **Graye Church** (Map lt4-f/Lat & Long: 49.33006 -0.47111/GPPlt4-4/6) is reached. Inside the church is a marble **Plaque to 'Our Canadian Brothers'** who liberated Graye, from the grateful inhabitants. In the side Chapel on the right is a **Plaque to the 8th (Irish) Bn The King's Regt,** Liverpool, who landed on JUNO BEACH at Graye-sur-Mer on D-Day as a Beach Group in support of the Canadians. It lists the 10 comrades who fell and bears the slogan 'Erin Go Bragh' ('Ireland Forever'). On the right is a beautiful little brass **Plaque** with a *bas relief* frame showing figures of soldiers. It is to **85th Field Coy, RE** 'In Memory of the friendship between the villagers and the soldiers'.

Turn right at the War Memorial following the Croix de Lorraine sign. Continue on the D112C to, on the left,

• Plaques to the Royal Winnipeg Rifles/Canadian Scottish, Graye/ 25.7 miles/5 minutes/Map lt4-19/Lat & Long: 49.33355 -0.47150

Two bronze **Plaques** were unveiled on this renovated lavoir (communal washing place) on 5 June 1994 (D-Day + 50 Years) to commemorate Graye's liberation by these regiments, whose badges are on the Memorial.

Continue to the junction with the D514 coast road.

> **N.B.** By turning left here and continuing some half a mile to a sign to the right to La Brêche de la Valette, a **Monument to C Sqn, Inns of Court Regt** (Map lt4-g/Lat & Long: 49. 33743 -0.47792/GPPlt4-4/8), who landed here with their armoured cars on 6 June 1944 may be seen on the bank just before the turning. It is made of grey polished granite with gold lettering and has the motto, *Salus Populus Suprema Lex* (The Welfare of the people shall be the supreme law) and the words 'To the noble living and the noble dead'. On the reverse is a French caption which tells that the land for the Monument was given by the grateful citizens of Graye.
>   The Inns of Court (The Devil's Own) were the only armoured car unit ashore on D-Day, landing on JUNO. Their mission was to demolish bridges over the Orne and Odon. On 7 June they received a 'Friendly fire' attack by Thunderbolts, killing two officers and five ORs, at Jerusalem (near the CWGC Cemetery to the SE of Bayeux and on 8 June C Sqn was involved in an action with the Panzer Artillerie Lehr Regt, purportedly responsible for the Abbaye d'Ardenne massacre (qv).

At the junction go straight across towards the beach and a tank in the dunes, signed la Brêche de Graye/Croix de Lorraine along Avénue Général de Gaulle.

On the corner on the left is a **sign listing the VIPs who landed here,** including Gen Montgomery (8 June), Winston Churchill and Gen Smuts (June 12), Gen de Gaulle (14 June) and King George V1 (on 16 June).

• Graye Churchill Tank/Comité du Débarquement Monument/ Cross of Lorraine/R Winnipeg Rifles & Canadian Scottish Memorial, XXIInd Dragoons Plaque/26 miles/20 minutes/Map lt4-20/Holts Map B1,2,3/Lat & Long: 49.33707 -0.46903

By the *Com Déb Sig* Monument is a Churchill tank AVRE with a petard. Both are at the junction of the Green (left) and Red (right) sectors of MIKE Beach where the Royal Winnipeg Rifles came ashore together with elements of the 6th Canadian Armoured Regiment. They came to suffer 128 casualties, the second heaviest Canadian regimental casualties of the day. Accompanying the Canadians were the 1st and 2nd Troops of the 26th Assault Squadron Royal Engineers charged with clearing exits off the beach through the obstacles and the dunes. The leading AVRE touched down about 0755 hours, somewhat behind the DD tanks and assault infantry. Using flails and bridge-layers, the squadron began to work its way through the wire and the mines and between the bunkers whose remains can still be seen. Beside it is an **Information Panel** re 7th Can Bde with more information about the tank and a photo.

At this exit there was an anti-tank ditch and just south of it a flooded culvert connected to the

Memorial to Regina Rifle Regt, Reviers.

Memorial 'Lavoir' with Plaques to R Winnipeg Rifles & Can Scottish, Graye-sur-Mer.

Churchill AVRE with troop of French Scouts and Cross of Lorraine, Graye-sur-Mer.

Comité du Débarquement Monument, Graye-sur-Mer.

ICI LE 6 JUIN 1944
L'HEROISME DES
FORCES ALLIEES
LIBERE L'EUROPE

HERE ON THE 6th JUNE 1944
EUROPE WAS LIBERATED
BY THE HEROISM
OF THE ALLIED FORCES

Memorial to R Winnipeg Rifles and Canadian Scottish, Graye-sur-Mer.

initiative of some of the DD tank commanders, like Sergeant Leo Gariépy of B Squadron, who launched on their own initiative. Gariépy was probably the first to land.

The assault battalion here, east of the Seulles, was the Regina Rifles and A and B Companies hit the shore about 0800 hours. They were immediately fired upon from concrete strongpoints apparently unaffected by the pre-invasion bombardments. The following companies lost many men as their assault craft hit mined obstacles some 200 yards out to sea and the Canadians had a hard struggle to get ashore. Operating to a detailed plan in which Courseulles had been divided up into twelve zones of responsibility, the Reginas, helped by the tanks of the 1st Hussars, (6th Canadian Armoured Regiment), forced their way through and around the town.

In 1970 Jean Demota who owned the salvage rights off Courseulles recovered a **Canadian Sherman DD** from about three miles out at sea. Leo Gariépy had settled in France after the war and he, in conjunction with the Mayor of Courseulles, helped to raise money for the venture. Once on shore Canadian Army Engineers from Germany moved and restored the vehicle and in 1971 it was dedicated in the position it is in today. Leo Gariépy was present, although sadly he died a year later. The road behind the Sherman is named after him (Leo Gariépy, *Citoyen d'Honneur de Courseulles sur Mer. 1912-1972*. Gariépy is buried in Courseulles local cemetery). On the side of the tank is a row of regimental plaques: 12th Field Regiment, RCA; 6th

Sherman tank with, behind, Memorial to Gen de Gaulle's landing on 14 June 1944, Courseulles.

Plaque detail, 6th Fld Coy, Can Eng, Courseulles Sherman.

aque to the Combattante, Courseulles.

Plaque to 85th Fld Coy RE, Nottingham Bridge, Courseulles.

Canadian Field Company Royal Canadian Engineers; 1st Canadian Para Battalion; 14th Canadian Field Ambulance; 5th Field Company, Royal Canadian Engineers Veterans; Canadian Provost Corps; 13th Field Regiment Royal Canadian Artillery; 19th Canadian Army Field Regiment (SP) RCA; 14th Field Regiment RCA (erected in 1944) and above them RCEME. The tank was completely renovated in 2002.

NTL Totem

Plaque describing the action on JUNO Beach. German anti-tank gun KWK 39 used on 6 June 1944 and restored in 1994. Most of the coastal defence weapons were provided by the German Navy but large numbers of this pivot-mounted 5cm weapon (made by Krupp) plus its other tank variants, 39/1 and 40, were used. The KWK 39 was the main armament of the German battle tanks used during the advance on Moscow.

A Memorial commemorating de Gaulle's landing here on 14 June. On the rear is a bronze **Plaque** of the General's Appeal to Frenchmen of 18 June 1940 and a small bronze **Plaque** erected by Elisabeth de Miribel, the secretary to whom he dictated the Appeal, erected on 8 May 1993.

A Memorial on one side of the beach entrance erected on 6 June 1969 with **Plaques** to the **1st Canadian Scottish Regiment, Belgian Volunteers, the 8th Bn the R Scots, the 6th Bn R Scots Fus and the 6th Border Bn King's Own Scottish Borderers** who landed near this spot June 1944 as 44th Lowland Bde.

Plaques on the other side of the beach entrance to the **458 officers and men of the Regina Regiment** who fell from 1939 to 1945 and to the Flail Tanks of the 22nd Dragoons.

A Memorial to the French destroyer *la Combattante.* She was part of the supporting Bombardment Group and was built in 1942 at the Fairfields Yard in Glasgow. Her original name was HMS *Haldon* and she was loaned to the Free French Navy. On 23 February 1945 she was torpedoed east of Dungeness by the German Midget Submarine U5330. Sixty-five French and two Royal Navy sailors were lost.

Over the road in Place du 6 Juin is the ** **Hotel de Paris**. 27 comfortable rooms, some with sea view. Pleasant restaurant, bar and terrace. Fish and seafood specialities. Variety of menus and *à la carte*. Tel: + (0)2 31 37 45 07. E-mail: hoteldeparis-normandie@wanadoo.fr **Closed** 13/11-31/01.
    Walk some 200 yards to the east along the promenade to

'Little Black Devils', the Royal Winnipeg Rifles Memorial (Map It4-21/Lat & Long: 49.33571 - 0.45525) which is a huge memorial dagger, erected on 6 June 1964 by the Hon Roger Teillet, MP, Canadian Minister of Veterans' Affairs. After the Battle of Fish Creek during the North West Rebellion of 1869-70 in Canada the Sioux Indians, noticing the contrast of the dark green uniforms worn by the Winnipeg Riflemen with the red of the Mounted Police and the British, are said to have asked, 'Who are those little black devils?' The Regiment known generally as 'The Pegs', has the motto, *Hosti acie nominati* (Named by the enemy in battle). Another **Plaque** was unveiled on **'D-Day plus 50 years'** by the Mayor of Courseulles, J. de Mourgues, and Colonel the Hon Gildas Molgat CD, Senator. On the seafront side is a coloured regimental badge.
    Beside it is **La Crémaillère Restaurant** with superb cuisine, lovely sea view and warm welcome. Its hotel, 100 metres away, Logis de France Le Gytan, has 43 rooms. Tel: (0)2 31 37 46 73. E-mail: cremaillere@wanadoo.fr
    Continue along the Avénue de la Combattante and then on the D514 following signs to Bernières and Ouistreham.

N.B. As the road returns to the coast on entering Bernières, the Station de Sauvetage on rue R Berks Regt is passed on the left. On the wall is a **Plaque to the N Nova Scotia Highlanders** who landed here on 6 June. (Map It4-22/Lat & Long: 49.33524 -0.42442/GPPIt4-4/7).

Continue to the large clearing, Place du 6 juin, on the left, with a Comité du Débarquement Monument. Stop.

• Comité du Débarquement Monument/House of Queen's Own Rifles/Bunker, Plaques and Memorials Area/First Journalists Plaque/Inuksuk Memorial, Bernières/30 miles/40 minutes/Map It4-22/Holts Map C16,18,19/Lat & Long: 49.335051 -0.42299

The *Com Déb Sig* here was the first of these monuments erected by M Raymond Triboulet and the Comité du Débarquement along the Normandy landing beaches to commemorate 'Le Jour J'. The stones were designed by Yves-Marie Froidevaux, chief architect of Monuments Historiques. The 10 million francs required for the project were financed by the sale of allied wrecks. The foundation stone was laid on 6 June 1949 when Gen Montgomery placed a copper cartridge containing his speech beneath it. The Monument was inaugurated on 19 November 1950.

A D-DAY MEMORY

JOHN TOLD US THIS ANECDOTE DURING LUNCH IN DOUVRES

Sergeant Howard Roy (John) Clewlow. 13th/18th Hussars, Turret Gunner DD tank. Landed on SWORD beach.

We had to do this DD training in Yarmouth and then right to the north in Scotland to Fort George. We did practice landings in these DD tanks. The problem was ... it was a bit of a hairy scary thing. We were sometimes under the submarine command ... we had to have Davis escape apparatus ... if the tank sunk we had to put on the Davis escape apparatus, a bottle on our front, we had the bag on our chest, we had a nose-clip where we took the oxygen in. The submarine lieutenant there said, 'It's only to give you a bit of buoyancy, if you sink in these things, you'll go down so fast you'll get the bends.' I think it was in Yarmouth that they stuck us in a big tank, a big pit, and the water just flowed in and the water came up your body that quick ... you had to put the Davis escape apparatus on. The water went all the way over you and went up about twenty or thirty feet and you had to get out. If you couldn't swim you were a bit panicky.

DD tanks were compulsory. The regiment I was in did the charge of the Light Brigade and that was it, the charge of the Light Brigade came all again - officers with big moustaches and they all thought they were charging at Balaclava... DD tanks were a bit weird. All it was was a canvas screen and that kept the tank afloat. There were about thirty-two air pillows. The canvas screen came up - there was a mesh that kept it up. So all there was between you and the bottom of the sea was this canvas screen. The drive from the engine was transferred from two propellers at the back. You pulled a lever and it turned these two propellers and you went around 5 knots an hour and when you got heavy seas you really rocked...In training we lost about three crews up in Scotland, they went down in about three hundred feet of water and we never saw them again. It was a bit weird when you thought what might happen on D-Day, but we took it philosophically...

On D-Day there was a hell of a swell on ... we launched three miles out and the waves came up that high that we had to get out of the tanks and hold the canvas screen up, what a way to land... We were awash with water, we were sea-sick, we had the Davis escape apparatus on, we had the ear phones on, you'd got a mike, you'd got a Mae West on, you didn't know which to pull next.

The real panic came when the other stuff started to back up on us. We were supposed to be ahead of it but we were going that slow that the other stuff was catching up on us. If we got too close the landing craft just ploughed into you and sunk you. They didn't worry. Their idea was to get to the shore and if you were in the way that was just your hard luck. Being outside the tank instead of inside we could see these landing craft coming closer and the stuff was going over from the battleships, the fifteen inch shells, sixteen inch shells. The air force was flying around at about five hundred feet. You didn't know what to do and you were sick and you'd got all this gear on. People say, 'Were you panicky?' There was that much confusion you hadn't got time to feel frightened."

Memorials to the French destroyer, La Combattante, Courseulles.

German KWK 39
tank gun,
Courseulles.

a.

b.

c.

Plaques at JUNO BEACH Exit, Courseulles: a. (From
top to bottom) to 1st Can Scot Regt, Belg Volunteers
& Scottish Regts; b. 22nd Dragoons; c. Regina Rifle
Regt,

Memorial to
Royal Winnipeg
Rifles ('Little
Black Devils'),
Courselles.

Detail, 'Little Black Devils'.

La Maison de Queen's Own Rifles de Canada, today and as it was in 1944, Bernières.

First Com Déb Sig Monument, Bernières.

Bunker, showing 2 Plaques and Badge to 2nd Queen's Own Rifles of Canada & Memorial to Regt de la Chaudière, Memorial area, Bernières.

b.

c.

ques on Bunker, Memorial area, Bernières: a. 22nd Dragoon Guards Flail Tanks; b. 5th Hackney Bn, R Berks Regt 'o 8 Beach Gp; c. Stormont, Glengarry & Dundas Highlanders.

Memorials in Memorial area, Bernières to Historic Sites & Monuments of Canada and Fort Garry Horse.

This was the centre of the assault area of the 8th Canadian Brigade Group and the sector here is NAN White. The assault regiment was the Queen's Own Rifles of Canada and they had the largest D-Day casualties of any Canadian unit. The Germans had constructed a *'Wiederstandsnester'*, a resistance nest, with mutually supporting weapons and good fields of fire using concrete bunkers and connecting trenches.

The Queen's Own landed at about 0815 hours without tank support (it was too rough to launch the DDs), and some 200 yards east of its target - right in front of the *Wiederstandsnester*. The leading company lost half its strength running over the beach to the sea wall, but, thanks to the support of a flak ship which came almost to the beach, the Germans were so effectively silenced that only snipers were active when the Régiment de la Chaudi re began to land fifteen minutes later. The Canadians headed inland towards the D79 leading to Bény, but German 88mm guns and machine guns stopped the advance. The divisional commander, not aware of the hold-up inland, ordered the follow-up brigade, the 9th, to land at Bernières on NAN White, and by midday the whole area was packed solid with men and equipment. It was one huge traffic jam and the 9th could not get moving until around 1600 hours. Without the jam the 9th might have reached Carpiquet that night before the 12th SS, and the battle for Caen *might* have been quite different.

On the beach here a sapper bulldozer driver silenced one pillbox by driving up behind it and filling it with sand and on 8 June **Lieutenant Fairbrother RE** won the **George Medal** for moving ammunition during an air raid. It was awarded in November.

On the edge of the beach is the typical Norman house shown in many contemporary photos and film footage. Now known as '*La Maison de Queen's Own Rifles de Canada*' it bears a commemorative **Plaque** and along the wall are photos of the House in 1944 and the Canadians coming ashore.

In the square is the welcoming **Restaurant-Crêperie L'Estran**. You will find a tasty lunch here when many other restaurants have closed. Excellent galettes. Tel: + (0)2 31 37 19 48. Closed 2 weeks in Dec and Jan. Closed Mon except July/Aug.

From the Comité Monument walk 250 yards to the east along the promenade to the large German bunker.

There is a **NTL Totem** at the entrance to the draw. **The Bunker** is in an area called Place du Canada, [Bernières Memorial area.] (Lat & Long: 49.33566 -0.41990).

On the Bunker are:

Badge (showing the No 2) on top of Bunker of the **2nd Queen's Own Rifles of Canada.**
Plaque JUNO Remembrance Way No 1.
Plaque headed 'In Peace Paratus' which bears the lines, 'Stand for a moment and imagine what it must have been like when 800 men of the Queen's Own Rifles of Canada stormed ashore at this very spot on 6 June 1944. We will remember them!' It was unveiled by 'Members of the Regimental Family' on 6 June 1997. It bears the information that a book of remembrance is held in the Church of Bernières (qv).
Plaque in bronze to Queen's Own Rifles of Canada with a map of the Normandy campaign 6 June-18 August 1944 and European Operations 1944-45 and Rhineland Campaign 8 February - 27 March 1945.
Plaque to the Stormont, Dundas & Glengarry Highlanders who landed on 6 June aboard 7 large landing crafts, including LCIL 299, which was damaged and later served with the RN and USN.
Plaque to the 5th Hackney Battalion the Royal Berks Regiment and No 8 Beach Group who landed here with the assault troops.

In the Memorial area are:

Memorial to Le Régiment de la Chaudière. This mentions the CO of the Regiment, Lieutenant-Colonel Paul Mathieu DSO ED, and gives 0700 hours as the landing hour. The Official History says 'about 0830'. General Keller, the Divisional Commander, left his HQ ship HMS *Hilary* at

1145 hours and by 1435 hours held his first conference in France in a small orchard outside Bernières. It was erected by the *Commission des Monuments Historiques de Québec*.

Memorial to the Fort Garry Horse 10th Armoured Regiment unveiled in 1994.

Memorial with free-standing bronze Plaques erected in 1999 by the Historic Sites and Monuments Board of Canada to **8th Brigade, 3rd Canadian Infantry Division** showing a superb *bas relief* Map of the Canadian landings and progress, 6-9 June 1944.
    Return to Place du 6 Juin. Walk over the D514 to the road leading straight ahead.

The press had established themselves in the centre of Bernières even earlier - at 1030 hours - in the Hotel de Grave, now a private house, No. 288, the first on the left in the rue du Régiment de la Chaudière. There is a **Plaque** there to commemorate **'The first HQ for Journalists,** photographers and moviemakers, British and Canadian, from which the first reports destined for the press and the radio of the world were despatched.' To its right is a *bas relief* **bronze Plaque showing details of the Canadian Landings**. **(Lat & Long: 49.33420 -0.42256).** One thing in particular surprised the local inhabitants. The 'Tommies' spoke French.

N.B.1 Bernières Church may be reached by driving further along rue du Régiment de la Chaudière to the second crossroads and turning right. In it is **SGW to E.W. Parker, Regt de la Chaudière, 6 June 1944 (Map It4-h/Lat & Long: 49.33523 -0.4006/GPPIt4-4/9).** To the left of the entrance is the striking Memorial window, which incorporates a photo of Pte Parker and was designed by his son, Darren Parker of Leicester. (Unfortunately the Church is often kept locked other than during the weekly Mass on Sundays at 1100.)

N.B.2 By continuing along rue du Gen Leclerc and over the roundabout on the D79A, at the first junction to the right is a **Memorial to 14th Field Regt RCA. (Map It4-g/Lat & Long: 49.32794 -0.42506/GPPIt4-4/10.)** The moving legend reads, 'The shore nearby and the field you are facing saw the sacrifice of the following members of 14 Fld Regt RCA' and then lists 14 officers and men. It continues, 'Dedicated to the memory of those who fought without promise of reward or relief for the Liberation of Europe and the hope of a better world.' The Memorial, by sculptor Monchel of Trevières, was inaugurated on 6 June 2006. Beside it on 6 June 2009 a small sign was placed by the **Assoc Westlake Bros** (qv).

On the main road, just past the **Office de Tourisme** (and WC, into which the bus shelter gives uninterrupted views) is a striking symbolic male **statue** formed from large chunks of stone commemorating the **Inuit** Canadians, inaugurated on 6 June 2004.
    Continue on the D514 to St Aubin Plage keeping to the sea front and stop by the German bunker.

• Bunker and Memorials Area to Fort Garry Horse, 5 Field Coy RCE, 19 Field Regt RCA, North Shore Regt, 10th Can Armd Regt (Fort Garry Horse), No 48 RM Commando, Maurice Duclos, St Aubin/31 miles/15 minutes/Map It4-23/Holts Map C11,12,13,14,15/Lat & Long: 49.33254 -0.39492

The area to the east of here has no suitable beach for a major landing until la Brèche d'Hermanville is reached some four miles away. Therefore on this coast landed special forces such as commandos.
    No. 48 RM Commando were to land at St Aubin and to move east, while No 41 RM Commando were to land at Lion-sur-Mer and move west. They were to meet at Petit Enfer two miles east of Langrune, which was a German strongpoint.
    The North Shore Regiment of Canada under Lieutenant-Colonel D. B. Buell who landed here found that the German strongpoints were still in action despite the bombardment and it was thanks to their DD tanks, and AVREs using their petards, that they overcame the pillboxes. The 50mm gun in the bunker here put out of action some of the leading tanks but was eventually silenced by two tanks and a RM Centaur (a Centaur can be seen at Pegasus Bridge, Itinerary 5).

Plaque to 1st HQ for Journalists, Bernières.

Memorial to 48 RM Cdo, Civilian
victims and Maurice Duclos, St Aubin.

Inuksuk Canadian
Memorial,
Bernières.

Memorials area,
St Aubin.

It had some seventy empty shell cases inside it as witness to the determination of the defenders. About four hours after landing the beach was clear except for one strongpoint and a number of snipers. The Commandos struck out to Langrune two miles east where they were held up until the following day by stubborn German opposition.

There is a **NTL Totem** here which describes the charge of No 48 Commando over the rocks and through the waves under heavy shellfire and the fact that a misdirected British bombardment 'killed and wounded the assailants who were forced to withdraw'. To the left of the bunker are **Memorials** to the **Fort Garry Horse, 5 Field Company RCE, 19 Field Regiment RCA and North Shore Regiment,** listing their casualties; **Memorials** to **No 48 RM Commando, civilian victims and to Maurice Duclos,** a French secret agent code-named 'Saint Jacques' who landed here on 4 August 1940.

Duclos was an extraordinary man. He took part in the Narvik and Brittany Operations early in the war and escaping to England joined the personal staff of Gen De Gaulle. He made many secret trips to France, his first being here, by high speed motor boat and later by parachute into the Dordogne. In August 1944 he landed at Port en Bessin and fought with the Allied Special Forces in the Normandy Campaign. He had many decorations including the *Légion d'Honneur,* the MC and the OBE. He died in 1981 in Buenos Aires.

One hundred yards to the right of the bunker, in front of the *Syndicat d'Initiative* **(Tourist Office,** Tel: (0)2 31 97 30 41, E-mail: otstaubin@orange.fr) is a stone **Memorial** to the **10th Canadian Armoured Regiment, Fort Garry Horse,** erected in 1965. It was just below this point on the beach that a Thunderbolt crash-landed on D-Day and it was this beach that members of the 4th Special Service Brigade had later to clear up. Lieutenant-Colonel James Moulton remembered what it had been like:-

"It was a shocking sight. Many corpses, some of them badly dismembered, were lying among the rest of the debris of the assault ... among all this several French women were walking about picking up what tinned food they could find - incredibly they had small children with them."

• *END OF ITINERARY FOUR*

German Bunker with 50mm anti-tank gun enfilading the Beach, St Aubin.

ITINERARY FIVE

ALLIED COMMANDO OPERATIONS/ SWORD BEACH TO CAEN

SWORD BEACH LANDINGS - 3rd BRITISH DIVISION

Assault Time:	0725 hours
Leading Formations:	8th Infantry Brigade Group
	13th/18th Hussars DD Tanks
	1st South Lancashire Regiment
	2nd East Yorkshire Regiment
3rd British Division Commander:	Major General T.G. Rennie
Bombarding Force D:	
Battleships:	HMS *Warspite*
	HMS *Ramillies*
Monitor:	HMS *Roberts*
Cruisers:	HMS *Mauritius* (flagship)
	HMS *Arethusa*
	HMS *Frobisher*
	HMS *Danal*
	ORP *Dragon* (Polish)
	13 destroyers including HNMS *Svenner* (Norwegian)
German Defenders:	716th Infantry Division

The 3rd British Division had last been in action at Dunkirk, and most of its soldiers had since then only served on the Home Front. In a way it was similar in its battle experience to the 4th US Division that landed at UTAH Beach. In its training the Division had concentrated upon D-Day, and on the breaking of the Atlantic Wall which it identified with the moment of landing. That moment, because of the variation in the time of the tides between UTAH and SWORD, came one hour after the Americans and ninety minutes after dawn. Therefore the Germans were both alert to a seaborne assault and able to see the landing craft coming in.

The Plan - SWORD Beach Landings (Battle Map 9)

In formulating his plan for 1st British Corps, Lieutenant General Crocker was acutely aware that the 21st Panzer Division was in or around Caen. His eastern flank was well defined by the Orne river and canal and they were to be secured by the Special Service Brigade, plus 6th Airborne Division, but if the 21st Panzer Division reacted quickly and 12th SS Panzer joined them, he would be much inferior in armoured strength and likely to be thrown back into the sea. Thus it was important that the extreme eastern division, the 3rd British Division, should break through the defence crust and move rapidly inland in anticipation of an armoured counter-attack.

The plan of the 3rd British Division Commander, Major General T.G. Rennie, was to attack on a single brigade front on White and Red sectors of QUEEN Beach. The 8th Infantry Brigade Group, the first to land, had a number of tasks: to secure the landing areas; to relieve 6th Airborne Division at Pegasus Bridge; No 4 Commando to clear east to Ouistreham; No 41 Royal Marine Commando to clear west to the Canadians at Langrune; and 1st Special Service Brigade to move east across Pegasus Bridge. Following up was the 185th Infantry Brigade Group. Their task was to pass through 8th Brigade and to 'seize Caen' - the most ambitious aim of all.

What Happened on D-Day - SWORD Beach Landings

Naval Force S for SWORD gathered off the beach in the early hours of 6 June. Just before daylight a smoke screen was laid by aircraft between the ships and the coastal batteries at le Havre. In the morning gloom, thickened with smoke, four German E-Boats appeared, fired torpedoes and vanished. The *Warspite* and the *Ramillies* had narrow misses but the Norwegian destroyer *Svenner* was hit and sank. That was all that Admiral Ramsay's invasion fleet saw of the German Navy on D-Day.

The bombardment followed the pattern employed everywhere else, though SWORD probably had the most intensive attention of all of the beaches, and was concentrated on a strip 3 miles long and half a mile deep.

Despite the rough seas, the DD tanks of the 13th/18th Hussars and the LCT-borne 'Funnies' of the Engineer Assault Teams hit the beaches ahead of the LCAs of the infantry. Of the twenty-five tanks launched, twenty-one made the shore and these, together with the flail tanks of 22nd Royal Dragoons, gave immediate fire support to the infantry battalions.

Although the landing craft suffered considerable casualties from Teller mines on the beach obstacles, for almost five hours the landing sequence went pretty well to plan. The rising tide, however, reduced the beach to a width of 30 yards and this caused congestion and confusion so that follow-up landings had to be delayed.

The South Lancashire and East Yorkshire Regiments were off the beaches within an hour, though stubborn German resistance continued in la Br che, the centre of the landing beach, until around 1030 hours. The 185th Infantry Brigade began coming ashore mid-morning and passed through the 8th Brigade, but enemy resistance on the Periers Ridge, between Douvres and Bénouville, prevented rapid movement inland.

By the end of the day the 2nd Battalion King's Shropshire Light Infantry, part of 185th Brigade, whose task it had been to ride on the tanks of the Staffordshire Yeomanry into Caen on 6 June, were still four miles short. Another forty-three days would pass before Caen fell.

THE TOUR

• **Itinerary Five** starts at Langrune and covers the Commando actions and 3rd British Division's landings on SWORD Beach and movement inland, and finishes near Caen.

• **The Main Route:** Langrune - No 48 RM Commando, Colas 'Work of War' Memorials; Luc-sur-Mer – First Commando Raid 1941 Memorial; Lion-sur-Mer - No 41 RM Commando Symbolic Sundial & Plaque, 2nd Battalion Royal Ulster Rifles Churchill Tank, Roosevelt Quotation Memorial, No 1 RM Commando Square, Liberation and 77th Assault Squadron RE & 22nd Dragoons Memorials; la Brêche d'Hermanville – HQ Staff 9 BR Inf Bde Marker; RA 3rd British Division Sign and Memorials, S Lancs Regiment, 13th/18th R Hussars & 2nd/5th Yorks Plaques, Allied Pioneers, Gooseberry, Norwegian Matelot, Allied Sailors Memorial, AVRE Churchill Tank, Roger Wietzel Memorial; Colleville-Montgomery Plage - General Montgomery Statue, First British Graves/Anglo-French Forces, Naming of Colleville-Montgomery Memorials: Riva Bella/Ouistreham – Four Men of Kieffer's 4 Cdo Plaque; No 4 Commando, Cdt Kieffer and Ten Commandos Flame Memorial, No 4 Commando Museum, Atlantic Wall Museum, RN & RM Memorial, *Com Déb Sig* Monument, No 4 Commando Plaque; St Aubin d'Arquenay - 1st SS Bde, 6 Air Landing Bde and Civilian Victims Memorials/Colleville-Montgomery - HILLMAN Strongpoint, 1st Battalion Suffolk Regiment Plaque; Biéville-Berville – R Norfolk Memorial; Golfe de Caen – Allied Forces Memorial; Lebisy – 2nd KSLI Memorial.
• **Planned duration,** without stops for refreshments or **Extra Visits** or **'NBs': 4 hours, 15 minutes**
• **Total distance: 19 miles**

• **Extra Visits** are suggested to: Hermanville - Plaque to Well, CWGC Cemetery, 3rd Division & Medical HQ Plaques; Colleville-Montgomery Plage – 4 Cdo Monument, Bunker, Site of Bill Millin Statue; Ouistreham - Church SGW to the 51st Division and Commandos, Perier-sur-le-Dan 3rd BR Div Memorial; La Londe – 1st Suffolks Memorial; Epron – 59th (Staffs) Div Memorials.

• **N.Bs.** The following sites are indicated: Luc-sur-Mer - General Leclerc and his 2nd French Armoured Division Memorial; Hermanville – Harold Pickersgill Plaque; Colleville-Montgomery – Harold Pickersgill Plaque; Ouistreham - 13th/18th R Hussars Memorial.

From the end of Itinerary Four at St Aubin, turn right following the one-way system and left at the T junction on rue Maréchal Foch. At the second stop sign turn sharp left by the

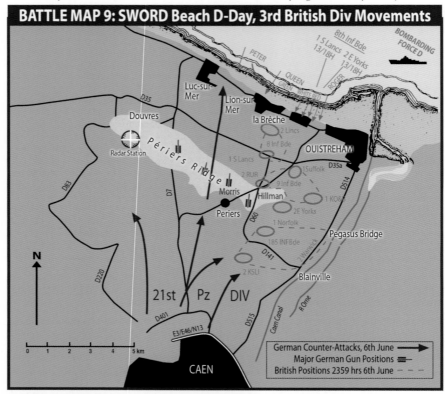

BATTLE MAP 9: SWORD Beach D-Day, 3rd British Div Movements

LEGEND: ITINERARY FIVE MAP: BRITISH SWORD BEACH LANDINGS

MAIN ITINERARY
1. 48 RM Cdo/Work of War, Langrune
2. 1st Cdo Raid/Lib Mem, Luc-sur-Mer
3. Churchill Tank/41 RM Sundial/Roosevelt Quotes/41 RM Cdo Pl, Lion-sur-Mer
4. Place 41 Cdo/Lib & RE/77 Assault Sqn RE/22 Dragoon Flail Tanks, Lion-sur-Mer
5. 9BR Inf Bde HQ Staff, la Br che
6. S Lancs RA Units/Pionniers/Gooseberry/2-5 Yorks/13-18 R Hussars/5 King's Liverpool Regt/Norwegian Matelot/Churchill AVRE/Allied Sailors/Chapelle, la Br che d'Hermanville
7. Roger Wietzel, Hermanville
8. Gen Montgomery Statue/Anglo-Fr Forces/1st Brit Graves/Naming, Colleville-Montgomery Plage
9. Four Men of Kieffer's 4 Cdo, Ouistreham
10. 4 Cdo/Cdt Kieffer, Ouistreham-Riva-Bella
11. Mus 4 Cdo, Ouistreham
12. Mus Mur de l'Atlantique, Ouistreham
13. RN & RM, Ouistreham
14. Com Déb Sig/4 Cdo, Ouistreham

15. 1 SS Bde/6 Airlanding Bde/Civilians, St Aubin d'Arquenay
16. HILLMAN (WN17)/1 Sussex, Colleville-Montgomery
17. R Norfolk, Biéville-Berville
18. Allied Forces, Golfe de Caen
19. 2 KSLI, Lebisy

EXTRA VISITS & 'N.B.s'
A. Gen Leclerc & Fr 2 Armd Div, Luc-sur-Mer
B. Mare St Pierre Well/CWGC Cem/2 BR Inf Div HQ/Medical Centre
C. Harold Pickersgill Pl, Hermanville
D. 4 Cdo Lib/Bunker/Site Bill Millin Statue, Colleville-Montgomery Plage
E. SGWs Cdos & 51 Highland Div, Ouistreham Ch
F. 13-18 R Hussars, Ouistreham
G. WN16 (MORRIS), Colleville-Montgomery
H. 3 BR Div(KSLI, 33 & 7 Fld Regt RA, R Sigs, E Yorks)/Lib Tree, Périers-sur-le-Dan
I. 1 Suffolks, Château de la Londe
J. 59 (Staffs) Div/Daniel Robinson MM/Local, Epron

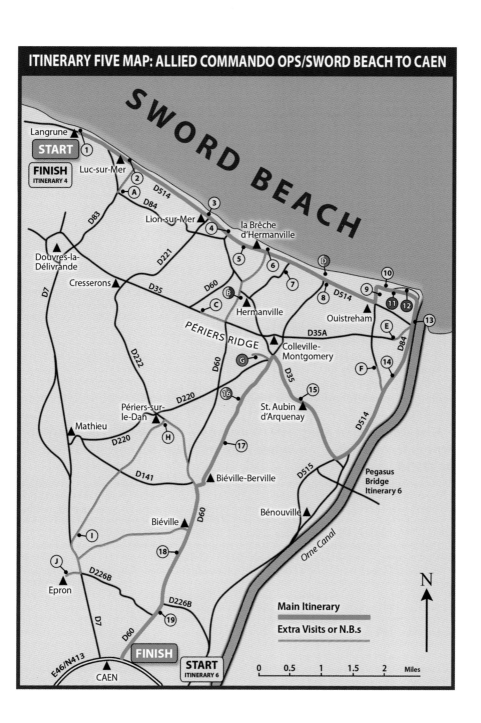

ITINERARY FIVE MAP: ALLIED COMMANDO OPS/SWORD BEACH TO CAEN

SWORD BEACH

Langrune
START 1
FINISH
ITINERARY 4
Luc-sur-Mer
2
A
D514
D84
3
Lion-sur-Mer
4
la Brèche
d'Hermanville
D83
D221
5
6
D
10
Douvres-la-
Délivrande
Cresserons
D35
D60
7
D514
9
B
8
11 12
D7
C
Hermanville
Ouistreham
13
PÉRIERS RIDGE
D35A
E
D222
D60
G
Colleville-
Montgomery
F
14
D84
D35
16
15
D220
St. Aubin
d'Arquenay
D514
Périers-sur-
le-Dan
Mathieu
D220
H
17
D141
Biéville-Berville
D515
Pegasus
Bridge
Itinerary 6
Bénouville
Biéville
D60
I
Orne Canal
18
J
D226B
Epron
D226B
Main Itinerary
D7
19
Extra Visits or N.B.s
D60
N
FINISH
START
ITINERARY 6
E46/N413
CAEN
0   0.5   1   1.5   2   Miles

basket ball court. Turn right at the T junction, passing a splendid Casino on the right. Continue and stop in the open space on the promenade of Langrune near the Tourist Office. Tel: (0)2 31 97 32 77. E-mail: tourisme.langrune-sur-mer@wanadoo.fr

Set your mileometer to zero.

• No 48 RM Commando/Work of War Memorials, Langrune/0 miles/ 10 minutes/Map It5-1/Lat & Long: 49.32537 -0.36998

This seafront road and the parallel one behind it had been strongly fortified by the Germans. The sea wall was covered in barbed wire and there were trenches running along this road, while the parallel one inland had inset concrete machine-gun positions. Lateral roads were blocked, the windows and doors of all the buildings were bricked up and there were connecting underground passages. Coming in on the parallel road from St Aubin, the Commandos enlisted the help of a naval bombardment and a Centaur tank of the 5 (Independent) RM Armd Spt Bty to help them break through to the seafront. The Centaur ran out of ammunition and was replaced by another. That blew up on a minefield. Further efforts involved an anti-tank gun and a Sherman tank, which was also immobilised. It was a bitter hand-to-hand battle, which was not won until late on 7 June, when thirty-one German prisoners were taken, but the Commandos had over 100 casualties. The **Memorial Stone** commemorates **No 48 RM Commando** on one side and on the other, under the coat of arms of Langrune and the *Croix de Guerre,* it carries the command *'Souviens-Toi* [Remember]'. In front and to the left of the memorial is a dramatic cubic **sculpture** made out of compacted debris of war with the caption, 'This is a not a work of arts. This is a work of war 1944-1994. Never again.' It was presented by the sculptor, Dominique Colas. Beside it is a **NTL Totem** to Langrune Fortified Town.

Continue on the D514 to Luc-sur-Mer. Pass the Casino.

It has a smart **Restaurant, l'Aile**, with panoramic view over the beach, Tel: (0)2 31 97 32 19] and **Tourist Office**. Tel: (0)2 31 97 33 25 E-mail: luc.sur.mer@wanadoo.fr

Stop at the eastern end of the sea front in Square Capitaine Tom Gordon Hemming.

Nearby is the **Hotel-Restaurant Le Beau Rivage** (renovated Logis de France. 20 rooms. Tel: (0)2 31 96 49 51. E-mail: mlefevre24@club-internet.fr)

• First Commando Raid, 1941/Liberation, Memorials, Luc-sur-Mer/ Petit Enfer/0.9 miles/5 minutes/Map It5-2/Lat & Long: 49.31919 -0.35250

This is the boundary between JUNO and SWORD Beaches, the town itself being in SWORD. It was to here that the small detachment of 21st Panzer advanced on the evening of 6 June to find the German defences intact, and it was the arrival of 6th AB Division's follow-up glider force that so stunned 21st Panzer's commanding general that by the time he recovered it was too dark to reinforce the advance. By the following day it was too late.

The **Memorial** asks the passer-by to remember *'le premier commando allié en Normandie, 28 Septembre 1941'* - the first allied commando raid on Normandy 28 September 1941. At the foot of the Memorial there used to be **a Plaque to 'Capitaine Tom Gordon-Hemming'**, after whom the square is named. The reference to Captain Hemming is a mystery because it does not seem that he was on the raid. He was certainly part of No 2 Commando employed during the Salerno landings in 1943 when 4th Troop, which Hemming commanded, took 35 prisoners. The raid referred to here was carried out on the night of 27 September 1941 by 5th Troop of No 1 Commando. Their intended landing place had been Courseulles but as they approached the shore their commander, Captain Davies, realised that they were heading for St Aubin and decided to go ahead anyway. As they landed, a machine gun fired at them and Davies led an assault over the sea wall. Two more machine guns joined in and the commandos had to withdraw. Two commandos were missing and one was wounded. However, there is some confusion about where this took place and whether a German bicycle patrol had been involved. Whatever the truth, the Memorial is here. It also commemorates the liberation of Luc on 6/7 June 1944.

> **N.B.** On the southern approach to the town (on the D83 coming from Douvres, or on the corner of Ave Foch coming from the seafront of Luc) in Place Gen Leclerc is a **Memorial** to **General Leclerc and his 2nd French Armoured Division** (Map It5-A, Lat & Long: 49.31108 -0.35565, GPPIt5-1/1).

Contine on the D514 to Lion-sur-Mer. At the roundabout at the entrance to the town stop in the car park to the left. Walk back to the tank and memorials.

• Churchill Tank, No 41 RM Commando Sundial Memorial, Roosevelt Quotes Monument/41 RM Commando Plaque, Lion-sur-Mer/ 3.3 miles/10 minutes/Map It5-3/Lat & Long: 49.30591 -0.32366

No 41 RM Commando landed here, having crossed the Channel in 'LCI(S)' - Landing Craft Infantry (Small) - and it was not until they had begun their far from comfortable journey that they found out their exact destination. At about 0845 hours they hit the sand some 200 yards out under intense mortar and shell fire and not exactly on target. Lieutenant-Colonel T.M. Gray, CO of No 41 RM Commando, sent part of his force to the east to make contact with the South Lancashire Regiment and part into the town. Three tanks brought up in support were quickly knocked out. Between 1600 hours and 1800 hours destroyers fired upon German positions in the town, but the defenders were still there the following morning. Just before a set-piece attack by the 5th Lincolnshires supported by the Royal Ulster Rifles and No 41 Commando, a raid with anti-personnel bombs by three Heinkels killed the Forward Observation Officer and wounded the CO and 11 members of the HQ staff. The attack was successful, however, and that evening No 41 Commando moved on to Luc-sur-Mer to join up with No 46 Commando.

There is a **NTL Totem** here and the spectacular **Memorial to No 41 RM Commando** is a symbolic sundial. The Churchill Tank was offered by General Sir Ian Harris who commanded 2nd Battalion The Royal Ulster Rifles. On a low **Plaque** is a quotation from President Roosevelt of 6 January 1941 outlining the four essential freedoms. There is also a **Plaque to 41 RM Commando**, who liberated Lion-sur-Mer, 6/7 June 1944, with a Roll of Honour of 30 names.

Continue through the town on the D514 and take the second turning left after the traffic lights (rue Marcotte) and at the next junction turn left and stop immediately by the car park on the right.

• Place du No 41 Commando, Map It5-4/Lat & Long: 49.30124 -0.31317 & Libération and Royal Engineer/22nd Dragoons Flail Tanks Memorials/Map It5-4/Lat & Long: 49.30357 -0.31673, Lion-sur-Mer/3.3 miles/15 minutes

The square has been named after the Commandos who landed here. The headstone-like stone nearby indicating 'Kiebingen 871 kms' refers to town twinning.

*Walk to the Promenade and turn left. Continue some 200 yards, passing the **Lion-sur-Mer Liberation Memorial**.*

The RE Memorial was unveiled by General Sir George Cooper GCB MC on the occasion of the granting of the freedom of Lion-sur-Mer **to the Corps of Royal Engineers** on 10 June 1989 to commemorate the part played by **77th Assault Squadron RE** in the liberation of the town 6 June 1944 and the continued links and a **Plaque** to **22nd Dragoons Flail Tanks** who landed here to clear the minefield at H-Hour on 6 June.

'Work of War' sculpture by D. Colas, Langrune.

Memorial to 41 RM Cdo, Lion-sur-Mer.

48 RM Cdo Memorial, Langrune.

41 RM Commando 'Sundial' and NTL Totem with Churchill tank in background, Lion-sur-Mer.

Memorial to 1st Commando Raid, Luc-sur-Mer.

er Bill Millin and friends on SWORD Beach, where he landed on 6
ne 1944.

3rd Division Insignia, with RA Memorial
and Statue of Le Matelot behind, La
Brêche.

*que to 2nd & 5th Bns, E. Yorks
gt, la Brêche d'Hermanville.*

Memorial to the Landings (with
the disputed text), la Brêche
d'Hermanville.

In memory of the 13th/18th Royal Hussars (QMO)
and their dedication to the liberation of Normandy on
6 June 1944

Plaque to 13th/18th R Hussars, la
Brêche d'Hermanville.

Svenner Anchor,
La Brêche
d'Hermanville.

As the troops and equipment poured ashore, the incoming tide reduced the width of the beach available and shore and exits became jammed. Orders were given to delay the landing of follow-up units, but, before the congestion could ease, accurate German artillery fire began to fall. It was a puzzle trying to decide how the Germans were working out where to aim their guns. Suddenly someone realised that they were ranging on the barrage balloons, which were being put up on the beaches against low-level aircraft attack. The balloons were quickly lowered. They were no loss. The only significant air attack came from eight aircraft the following morning. One was shot down and crashed 300 yards away to the right from the beach exit. Slightly right of centre, 1,100 yards out to sea, was the wreck of the French Cruiser, the *Courbet*. She had last helped the British by covering their evacuation from Cherbourg in June 1940. The old ship, without engine or guns, and filled with concrete, had to be towed across the Channel to be sunk as a Gooseberry blockship to provide protection for craft landing on SWORD Beach. There she proudly flew the *Tricolore* and the Cross of Lorraine, making her a favourite target for the Germans, ignorant of her helplessness. She was shelled, bombed and attacked by human torpedoes. German radio on 8 July claimed that their attacks had driven the *Courbet* ashore. The illusion of her importance was fostered by other Allied ships, which fired from directly behind her cover. Each of the five invasion beaches was provided with a temporary harbour named a

Gooseberry. The shelter was formed by sinking old ships in a line off the beach. Over sixty were sunk altogether. The majority were merchantmen, though a few warships were used - the cruiser *Courbet*, the British battleship *Centurion,* the cruiser *Durban,* and the Dutch cruiser *Sumatra*.

The order of landing of 8th Infantry Brigade Group from H-Hour at 0725 hours (se DIAGRAM 2, page 145) was:

1. A and B Squadrons of 13th/18th Hussars. DD tanks.
2. Eight Royal Engineer (77th and 79th Assault Squadrons) obstacle-gapping teams, each one made up of two flail tanks of 22nd Dragoons, three AVREs and one bulldozer.
3. Two obstacle-clearing teams, each of four flail tanks and four AVREs.
4. The assault infantry:
   QUEEN White - two companies of the 1st South Lancashire Regiment.
   QUEEN Red - two companies of the 2nd East Yorkshire Regiment.
5. At 0734 hours the HQ elements of the assault infantry plus their remaining two companies.
6. At 0810 hours HQ and C Squadron 13th/18th Hussars.
7. At 0825 hours the 1st Suffolk Regiment, the reserve battalion, plus 8th Brigade alternative main HQ.
8. At 1000 hours the 185th Brigade.

A D-DAY MEMORY

BILL TOLD US THIS STANDING ON THE BEACH WHERE HE LANDED

Piper Bill Millin. 1st Special Service Brigade. Lord Lovat's Personal Piper.

Landed on SWORD Beach.

"Lovat got into the water first ... I followed closely behind him ... he's a man about six feet tall and, of course, the water came up to his knees ... I thought it would be alright for me so I jumped into the water and it came up to my waist ... anyway I managed to struggle forward and then I started to play the bagpipes. I played Highland Laddie towards the beach which was very much under fire. At that time there were several ... three ... burning tanks, there were bodies, lying at the water's edge, face down floating back and forward. Some [men] were frantically digging in ... others crouched behind a low sea wall. No one could get off the beach. The road and the exits were under heavy fire. I made for cover at an exit ... a narrow road and I just got there behind a group of soldiers and they were all cut down ... about nine or twelve of them ... they were shouting and seeing me with the kilt and the bagpipes they shouted, 'Jock! Get the medics'.

Then I looked around and to my horror I saw this tank coming off a landing craft with the flails going and making straight for the road. I tried to catch the commander's attention ... his head was sticking out of the turret ... but he paid no attention and went straight in and churned all the bodies up. Then I saw Lovat and the Brigade Major standing at the water's edge. Everyone else was lying down. So I joined them. He [Lovat] asked me to play. That sounded rather ridiculous to me to play the bagpipes and entertain people just like on Brighton sands in peacetime. Anyway ... I started the pipes up and marched up and down. This Sergeant came running over, 'Get down you mad bastard. You're attracting attention on us'. Anyway I continued marching up and down until we moved off the beach."

Inevitably there was overlapping between the phases, but for over four hours the landings went to the timetable. Then, because of crowding on the beaches, a half-hour delay was ordered. However, despite the loss of the officer commanding the beach clearance who was killed on landing and over 50 per cent casualties to the armoured vehicles, nine beach exits were opened by 1130 hours. Meanwhile the German resistance on Periers Ridge (the strongpoint HILLMAN and the radar station at Douvres are on the ridge) was holding up movement inland, preventing the 185th Brigade from getting on towards Caen. There has been criticism of 3rd Division's performance following its successful landing. It has been suggested that their hearts and minds had been set on breaking the Atlantic Wall, and when that had been achieved relatively easily, the Division was left without a clear purpose. Troops accustomed to a defensive mentality in

England since Dunkirk favoured digging in instead of aggressive forward movement. The German resistance on the Periers Ridge, at the strongpoints named HILLMAN and MORRIS, leeched away the armour strength needed for the drive to Caen, where the 21st Panzer Division was gathering itself to strike. General Bradley, commanding the United States First Army, expressed himself as 'keenly disappointed' at the performance of General Dempsey's Second British Army. In September 1944, lack of drive of the ground forces was said to have been one of the reasons why the 1st AB Division was cut off at Arnhem. General Dempsey was again the Army Commander. *Walk back to the tank.*

The **Churchill AVRE Mark III** was presented to Hermanville on 6 June 1987 by 3rd British Armoured Division (it had originally come from the Imperial War Museum, Duxford). Seventy specially redesigned Churchill tanks came ashore from ten landing craft and cleared a 200m-wide lane through the beach obstacles for the assault troops. The Tank is a Memorial to all those who served and died here. In September 1998 the tank was moved from its original position by the main memorials and soldiers of 6 HQ Squadron 22nd Engineer Regiment spent a fortnight refurbishing it. Beside it is a **NTL Totem** telling the story of Major General Rennie's 3rd Infantry Division. *From the Churchill walk towards the beach on Avénue Félix Faure. Straight ahead is*

Memorial to the Royal, Merchant and Allied Navies, surmounted by a Celtic Cross and bearing a gold Anchor insignia. Unveiled on 6 June 2001 by Capt John Gower DSC RN Retd, Capt of HMS *Swift* of 23rd Destroyer Flotilla, it pays tribute to all the sailors who died in Normandy in 1944. *Return to the Churchill.*

Over the road is **La Chapelle de la Brêche d'Hermanville**, in which there is a colourful 4 metres high **SGW** which recalls the sacrifice of those who fought for the town's liberation. It depicts Christ on the Cross, surrounded by parachutes, aeroplanes and ships, with soldiers of June 1944 at his feet. The Chapel is often used for D-Day Landings and other exhibitions but is normally locked.

D-DAY MEMORIES OF ASSAULT ENGINEERS

Major C. H. Giddings, Troop Leader 629th Field Squadron
'On going on deck as we approached the Normandy coast the first thing I saw was a destroyer which had been mined going down by the stern - and at that moment a Sten gun was let off accidently on the mess deck and three men were unfortunately killed. Not an auspicious beginning.'

Major W. Carruthers, Troop Leader 3rd Troop 77th Assault Squadron
'As I was to follow the flails through the gap I asked my gunner to lay the log carpet in the gap, but this and the turret had jammed and I had to cut it loose - the log carpet fell in a heap and formed more of an obstacle than a road. While I was doing this there was a bang, flash, red lights, blue lights etc., and I found myself lying on the sand, having been hit by a hand grenade thrown from the house alongside the tank. I was assured later by the flail commander that the thrower had a 90mm shell all to himself in return.'

Lieutenant I. C. Dickinson Second in Command 3rd Troop 77th Assault Squadron
'For the work done on D-Day, 77th and 79th Assault Squadrons between them won two DSOs, four MCs, two DCMs and three MMs'.

Extra Visits to Hermanville: Mare St Pierre Well Plaque (Map It5-B, Lat & Long: 49.28741 -0.31232, GPPIt5-1/2), CWGC Cemetery (Map It5-B, Lat & Long: 49.28638 -0.30878, GPPIt5-1/3), 3rd Div HQ & Medical HQ Plaques (Map It5-B, Lat & Long: 49.28678 -0.31316, GPPIt5-1/4,5). Round trip: 2.5 miles. Approximate time: 35 minutes

Continue 50 yards to the D514, turn right and then left by the church, signed Hermanville on the D60B on rue du 6 Juin. Continue into the village following Centre Ville and at the church drive into the square. Stop.

On the left is a well with a **Plaque** which explains that this was the well of the Mare Saint

Churchill AVRE, la Brêche d'Hermanville.

Memorial to First British Graves, Colleville-Montgomery.

Memorial to Capt Roger Wietzel, nr La Brêche.

Memorial to Allied Sailors, the Beach, Brêche d'Hermanville.

Statue of General Montgomery by Vivien Mallock, Colleville-Montgomery

Memorial to Cdt Kieffer & No 4 Cdo, Colleville-Montgomery.

Memorial to S Lancs Regt, la Brêche d'Hermanville.

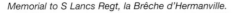

A L'AUBE DU 6 JUIN 1944
SUR CETTE PLAGE
DEBARQUENT LES
FUSILIERS MARINS FRANÇAIS
DU COMMANDANT
PHILIPPE KIEFFER
COMMANDO
BRITANNIQUE N° 4

Pierre which is mentioned in British Army records as having supplied 1,500,000 gallons of water to the British Forces between 6th June and 1st July 1944.

Turn left along the narrow road signed Cimetière Britannique. Continue to

Hermanville CWGC Cemetery in Place des Combattants 6 juin 1944. Before the entrance, on the ground, is the insignia of 3rd BR Div.

There are 1,005 burials in this beautiful cemetery, many of them from the 6 June actions in this area. There are 986 British, 13 Canadian, 3 Australian and 3 French. There is a pair of **brothers, Lieutenant Alan Law Davis,** 5th Battalion the W Yorks Regiment, age 24, Plot II Row O Grave 10, and **CSM Norman Clave Davis,** 5th Battalion the King's Regiment of Liverpool, age 28, Plot II Row O Grave 7, who were both killed on 6 June and *Croix de Guerre* winner the **Rev Peter Francis Firth, Chaplain First Class** to the Forces, age 33, killed on 7 June in Plot I Row J Grave 15.

Return to the square and continue 100 yards to the Mairie on the right – the right sort of building for a General!

On the left of the gatepost is a **Plaque** commemorating **3rd British Infantry Division HQ** set up here on D-Day and on the right a **Plaque** to an important **Medical Centre**.

> **N.B** By continuing straight on to the junction with the D35 and turning right and continuing to the third road to the right, a **Plaque** in memory of **Citizen of Honour Harold Pickersgill (Map It5-C, Lat & Long: 49.28265 -0.33259, GPPIt5-1/6)** who died in 1998, may be found under the sign 'Avenue Harold Pickersgill'. In 1943 Harold worked on the highly secret exercise PINWE - Problems of the Invasion of North West Europe - making detailed maps of the Normandy area. Much of the information for the maps was supplied by members of the French Resistance. In June 1944 he insisted on landing at la Brêche (part of the coast whose defences he knew so well from his secret work) with his old regiment, the Reconnaissance Corps, 3rd Division. The regiment established its HQ in the house of the Lebret family in the village of Mathieu, where they were pinned down by the German tank divisions that barred their way to Caen. During their prolonged stay in the village, Harold Pickersgill fell in love with the daughter of the family, Marie-Geneviève, who was to become his wife after the war, and the newly-weds settled down in Mathieu. In 1946 Harold was attached to the Graves Registration Service, based at Luc-sur-Mer, and worked as an administrative officer on the sad task of re-interring his dead comrades and burying them in the newly constructed war cemeteries. It was not until twenty years later that Harold found out that his own doctor, M Sustendal of Luc-sur-Mer, had been one of the principal informants for PINWE, for which he was decorated with the *Légion d'Honneur*. Always active in liaising between his old division and the local authorities for commemorative events, Harold himself received an MBE in 1984. When he died on 31 July 1998 at the age of 76, this Scot by origin but Norman by adoption, gave his body to medical research. A commemorative tree was therefore planted in his memory, with a Plaque beside it, opposite the *Mairie*. It was erected by the active HMS *(Histoire, Mémoire, Souvenir)* Association of Hermanville-sur-Mer, whose President is M J. Tirard. When the area was redeveloped a new Plaque was erected here. There is another Plaque to Harold Pickersgill at Mathieu at the roundabout with the D220 on the road to Anisy (qv).

Return to the D514 and rejoin the main itinerary.

Continue on the D514 for 0.2 miles to the traffic lights at the 'Place de la 3ième DIB' on the left and 'Boulevard du 3ième Division' on the right. Turn right and continue to the memorial on the left.

• *Roger Wietzel Memorial, nr la Brêche/5.3 miles/5 minutes/Map It5-7/Lat & Long: 49.29349 -0.29626*

It was from this spot that Roger Wietzel, the captain of the *Courbet,* took a sample of French soil on 7 June which he later presented to Gen de Gaulle.

Return to the D514 and turn right on rue Amiral Wietzel. Continue to the traffic light junction at Colleville-Montgomery Plage. Turn right on the D60A and stop in the square.

A D-DAY MEMORY

MAJOR (LATER COLONEL) PORTEOUS TOLD US THIS STANDING ON SWORD BEACH

Major Patrick A. Porteous, VC. RA No 4 Commando. Landed on SWORD Beach.

"0600hrs, 6th June 1944. Reached lowering position - grey sky - sea very choppy - ships of every shape and size as far as the eye can see.

As my landing craft hit the water, we took a large wave over the side. A foot of water swilling round our feet. Get pumping - Damn! The bilge pumps not working, so get bailing with tin hats. Difficult in very cramped conditions on board, especially as some men being sick. Still making water as every wave slops some more in. Approaching the beach all hell going on but anything preferable to this horrible boat. As the front ramps went down, she finally sank in three feet of water."

(Major Porteous won his VC at Dieppe)

• General Montgomery Statue, Anglo-French Forces/First British Graves, Naming of Colleville-Montgomery Plage Memorials/5.9 miles/10 minutes/Map It5-8/Lat & Long: 49.29043 -0.28213

In the square is the bronze **statue of General Montgomery** sculpted by Vivien Mallock (qv), to which the statue in Portsmouth (qv) is identical. It was unveiled on 6 June 1996 by Prince Michael of Kent and was presented to Colleville-Mongomery by the Normandy Veterans' Association. The *Commune* of Colleville donated the land on which the statue stands. At night the statue is illuminated.
Walk over the road.

To the left on either side of the road leading to the beach - Avénue du No 4 Commando - are two **Memorials**. One erected on 6 June 1945 commemorates the **First British Graves** of 6 June 1944, the Anglo-French forces of General Montgomery and Capitaine Kieffer of No 10 (Inter-Allied) Commando and the decision of Colleville-sur-Mer to change its name to Colleville-Montgomery. On the other side of the road is another memorial to **Commandant Kieffer and the French Forces of No. 4 Commando**.

Extra Visits to No 4 Commando 'Liberation' Memorial & Bunker (Map It5-D, Lat & Long: 49.29300 -0.28099, GPPIt5-1/7,2/1), Piper Bill Millin Statue (Map It5-D, Lat & Long: 49.29304 -0.28275), Colleville-Montgomery Plage. Round trip: 0.4 miles. Approximate time: 15 minutes

Return to the D514 and drive 100 yards to the junction with Ave du No 4 Commando on the left.

Turn left here past the Memorials and continue to the seafront. Turn left on Bvd Maritime and continue to the Memorial on the right.

The stone *bas relief* **Memorial** is to **No 4 Cdo,** including 177 French Commandos of 1st Bn French Marine Commando under Cdt Kieffer who landed here. Inaugurated in 1994, carved by Patrick Gheleyns, it vividly depicts the Commandos' landing and the heavy and fearful casualties they endured. *'Notre liberté fut a ce prix!'* is the inscription. In the top left hand corner is a **Plaque to the Royal Norfolks** and on the ground a bronze **Plaque** which relates how the French Commandos landed followed by Nos 3 and 6 and 45 RM Cdo. A new stone was added on 6 June 2004.

Opposite, incorporated into a house, is a large **Bunker** and beside it an **NTL Totem.**
Continue and take the next turning left on Ave de Bruxelles.

On the right in Place du Débarquement is a small **Tourist Office**, open during the summer months.

In the grassy area beside it is the site, chosen by Bill himself, of the **Piper Bill Millin** (qv)

Statue. The project to raise this statue was the initiative of an enthusiastic group of people led by President Serge Athenour and Catherine Nicolle, Deputy-Mayor of Colleville-Montgomery. Details of the campaign, interviews with Bill and the progress of the fund-raising can be seen on several websites by 'googling' Piper Bill Millin. See **STOP PRESS**, ■ *No. 8,* for photo and details.
Continue to the D514, turn left and pick up the main itinerary.

Continue on the D514 to the western edge of Ouistreham and at the cross roads turn left along Boulevard Winston Churchill.

• PLAQUE TO FOUR MEN OF CDT KIEFFER'S 4 CDO, OUISTREHAM/7.1 MILES/5 MINUTES/MAP IT5-9/LAT & LONG: 49.28906 -0.26436

In front of House No 40 is a **Plaque to Four Members of 1st Bn Fr Marine Cdo of Commandant Kieffer.** (They were killed fighting in this sector on the morning of 6 June '44.)

N.B. There are also two **Plaques** to three other of Kieffer's Commandos on House No 53, rue Pasteur, opposite the Casino.

Plaque to four of Kieffer's Commandos, Ouistreham.

Turn right following signs to La Plage, Casino and Musée.

At the small roundabout is the *****Hotel des Thermes Thalassotherapie Centre** (89 rooms, Thalassotherapy pool and treatments, **Restaurant Thalazur Riva Bella.** Tel: (0)2 31 96 40 40 E-mail: ouistreham@hotel-rivabella.com
Beside it is

• No 4 Commando, Kieffer Memorials, Ouistreham-Riva-Bella/7.4 miles/10 minutes/Map It5-10/Lat & Long: 49.29000 -0.2621

The central task of 1st SS (Special Service) Brigade was to land in the Ouistreham area, to clear the town and then to move on to link up with the airborne forces at Pegasus Bridge. The Brigade, under command of 3rd British Division, was made up of:

Brigade Commander. Brigadier The Lord Lovat, DSO MC
No 3 Commando. Lieutenant-Colonel P. Young, DSO MC
No 4 Commando. Lieutenant-Colonel R.W.F. Dawson.
No 6 Commando. Lieutenant-Colonel D. Mills-Roberts, DSO MC.
No 45 RM Commando. Lieutenant-Colonel N.C. Ries
No 1 and No 8 French Troops of No 10 Inter-Allied Commando. Captain Philippe Kieffer.

In addition, No 41 RM Commando (Lieutenant-Colonel T.M. Gray) also came under command but had an independent role at Lion-sur-Mer.

No 4 Commando landed at 0820 hours on QUEEN Beach Red sector and came under heavy fire, suffering about forty casualties. Lieutenant-Colonel Robert Dawson was wounded in the leg and in the head but No 4 Commando reached the D514 and set off towards Ouistreham, led by Philippe Kieffer. A local gendarme whom they met on route gave them details of German strengths and positions and after a fierce fight ending with grenades and bayonets, in which both sides sustained many casualties, Kieffer's men took the Casino, an action that was made much of in the film *The Longest Day.* The casino building itself had been demolished by the Germans in October 1942 and replaced with concreted gun positions which were taken on by a Centaur prior to the final assault. No 4 Commando then moved on towards Pegasus Bridge.

Lord Lovat, SS Brigade HQ and No 6 Commando landed on QUEEN Beach Red sector at 0820 hours, piped ashore by Piper Bill Millin. Artillery and mortar fire was considerable and three of their landing craft were hit. They moved rapidly inland, heading for Bréville to the east of

CAPTIONS FOR GROUP PICTURE PAGE ITINERARY FIVE – I, page 254

GPPIt5-1/1	Memorial to Gen Leclerc, Luc-sur-Mer
GPPIt5-1/2	Memorial to the Well of La Mare St Pierre, Hermanville
GPPIt5-1/3	CWGC Cem, Hermanville
GPPIt5-1/4	Plaque to HQ 3rd Br Inf Div, Hermanville Mairie
GPPIt5-1/5	Plaque to Medical Centre, Hermanville Mairie
GPPIt5-1/6	Plaques to Harold Pickersgill, Hermanville
GPPIt5-1/7	Monument to No 4 Cdo, Colleville-Montgomery-Plage

'Flame' Memorial to No 4 Cdo and Individual Memorials to Cdt Kieffer and his men, Ouistreham.

Pegasus Bridge, clearing two pillboxes on the way. As they approached the bridge they waved a Union Flag in order to establish themselves as 'friendly forces' and were met by Brigadier J.H.N. Poett, the Commander of 5th Parachute Brigade. 'We are very pleased to see you', said Nigel Poett. 'I am afraid we are a few minutes late sir,' was the reply. Lovat and his men then moved over Pegasus Bridge to the cheers of the paratroopers and attracted considerable fire from German snipers.

No 3 and No 45 RM Commando landed at 0910 hours and moved inland and across the bridges over the Orne river and canal. No 45 went on to Merville while No 3 formed a protection force at Ranville for 6th AB Division HQ.

By the end of the day the 1st SS Brigade had not occupied the high ground east of the Orne, but they had cleared Ouistreham and fulfilled their main task of linking up with the airborne forces. They had also found out that French civilians were not too enthusiastic about their shoulder patch, which said 'SS'. It was later changed.

On the dunes is a **Memorial** to the memory of **ten members of Kieffer's Commandos** and to **No 4 Commando**. It is a symbolic flame erected in 1984 on top of a German blockhouse cupola. At its base is a white *bas relief* **Memorial to Commandant Philippe Kieffer** and individual memorial stones with the names of his men.

Philippe Kieffer, age 40, joined the French Navy on 2 September 1939, serving on the battleship *Courbet* and taking part in Dunkirk. He then joined the Free French Navy and, as he spoke fluent English, acted as a translator and cipher officer. He founded the Naval Infantry Commandos which were attached to No 2 Commando during the St Nazaire Raid of March 1942. In 1944 Kieffer and the 177 men of his 1st BFM Commandos became part of No 4 Commando. During the 6 June operations 21 were killed and 93 wounded. Kieffer was soon wounded in the leg but refused to be evacuated for two days. He rejoined his Commando on 14 June, taking part in the breakthrough towards the Seine. He was the first man of the Free French Forces to enter Paris, at a time when his 18-year-old son, a recent member of the Maquis, was killed by the Germans. Kieffer who was awarded the *Légion d'Honneur*, the *Croix de Guerre* and the MC, died in 1962 and is buried in Grandcamp-Maisy (qv).

Continue to the junction, take the first left and turn left again.

On the right is the ** **Hotel Saint Georges**. 18 rooms. Restaurant. Tel: + (0)2 31 97 18 79. E-mail: saint-georges.hotel@wanadoo.fr

Continue to the Casino square and park by the Museum on the right.

By the Casino is the **Tourist Office**. Tel: (0)2 31 97 18 63. E-mail: office.ouistreham @wanadoo.fr website: www.ville-ouistreham.fr

Beside it is the **Bar-Brasserie-Crêperie/Saladerie L'Accostage**. Tel: + (0)2 31 97 05 23. Open every day and provides a good value snack/lunch when others may be closed. **Closed** Tuesday out of season.

The Casino has two **Restaurants: Le Doris**, with seaview and **Le Bistro** (Fri, Sat, Sun) with dancing/live shows, Tel: (0)2 31 36 30 01. Website: www.casinos-barriere.com Consult this site for any changes in opening hours/hotels/restaurants/commemorative plans.

• Musée du No 4 Commando, Ouistreham/7.8 miles/15 minutes/ Map It5-11/Lat & Long: 49.28853 -0.25921

The Museum, now signed as *Musée du Débarquement* as well as of **No 4 Commando**, was organised by a group of citizens of Ouistreham who wished to preserve the memory of the events of the landings here. It has exhibits of arms, uniforms, badges and souvenirs. There is a film of the landings. Outside is a propeller from a Wellington which was recovered from the sea. There is also a **NTL Totem** which describes how 123 houses and villas were demolished by the Germans in the construction of the impressive defensive system here.

CONSULT WEBSITE: https:/www.musee-4commando.fr for details of current opening times, news etc.

Continue past the museum and take the road 'Boulevard 6 juin' straight ahead signed Musée du Mur de l'Atlantique. 400 yards later stop by the large concrete building/museum on the left.

■ No. 15. Musée le Mur de l'Atlantique, Ouistreham/8.1 miles/25 minutes/Map It5-12/Lat & Long: 49.28723 -0.25268

This 52-feet-high concrete tower is the only major German work left in Ouistreham. It was a flak tower designed to control anti-aircraft defence of the harbour and was the German HQ in charge of the batteries covering the entrance of the River Orne and the Orne Canal. On 6 June the Franco-British commandos attempted to take the tower but were repulsed by machine-gun fire and stick grenades. It remained a threat until on 9 June Lieutenant Bob Orrell of 91st Field Company RE with three men placed explosive charges by the heavily armoured door which eventually burst open. The garrison of 2 officers and 50 men then surrendered. Since 1987 when it was fully restored the tower has been a museum in which one can see the generator room, the gas filter rooms, the machine gun emplacements, telephone exchange, radio transmission room and observation post. There are also many unpublished photographs and documents about the Atlantic Wall which employed over 2 million people in its construction. In September 1942 Hitler held a meeting with Speer (Minister for Armaments), von Rundstedt, Goering and others at which he specified a defensive coastal wall that would stretch from Norway to the Spanish border and consist of 15,000 strongpoints manned by 300,000 troops. In the grounds is a rare V1 and other interesting exhibits and a **NTL Totem.**

Open: daily from 12 February - 15 November 1000-1200 and 1400-1800 (from 1 June-30 September 0900-1900). Tel: (0)2 31 97 28 28 69.

*Continue straight on, and turn right on the coast road passing on the left **the Ferry Terminal**. Tel: 08 03 82 88 28. In the car park is*

• Royal Naval & Royal Marine Memorial, Ouistreham/9.2 miles/5 minutes/Map It5-13/Lat & Long: 49.28357 -0.24978

On 6 June 2000 a major omission was redressed when, during an impressive ceremony, HRH

Prince Philip, Duke of Edinburgh, unveiled a handsome 6-foot-high granite Memorial carrying accounts in French and English of the D-Day Operation, the Combined Operations badge and a kedge anchor. The Memorial was instigated by Maurice A. Hillebrandt, who served with Combined Operations, RN and who noticed that there was no Naval memorial along the landing beaches. With Lieutenant-Commander R.J. Brend, RN he formed a committee whose tireless efforts raised the necessary £18,000.

On the right is the conveniently sited ***Hotel Mercure Riva Bella**. Renovated. 49 rooms. Tel: (0)2 31 96 20 20. E-mail: H1967@accor.com

On the harbour wall to the left can be seen a '**Maginot Line' type cupola and remains of two pontoons.**

Continue to the large square with ample parking around which is a good choice of restaurants, newsagents and shops (Place Général de Gaulle).

This makes an ideal lunch stop and has a variety of hotels and restaurants in the vicinity, e.g.
** **Hotel Le Normandie**. 22 Rooms. Restaurant with seafood specialities. Tel: (0)2 31 97 1957. E-mail: hotel@lenormandie.com
** **Le Phare.** 19 rooms. Brasserie and pizzeria. Tel: (0)2 31 97 13 13. E-mail: hotelduphare@wanadoo.fr
La Broche d'Argent. 18 rooms. Restaurant and pizzeria. Tel: (0)2 3197 03 33. E-mail: labrochedargent@orange.fr
Le Channel. 10 rooms, traditional restaurant with grill. Tel: (0)2 31 96 51 69.

Extra Visit to Stained Glass Windows, Commandos/51st Highland Division, Ouistreham Church (Map It5-E, Lat & Long: 49.27661 -0.25850, Page 263 Round trip: 1 mile. Approximate time: 20 minutes.

From the square follow Centre Ville/12th Century Church signs. Continue to the church and park near the spendid Hôtel de Ville or La Poste.

In the church on the hill at the top are two beautiful **SGWs**. One is to the **Commandos**, offered by the Commando Association in memory of their dead and in recognition of the welcome of the people of Normandy. The other is to the **51st Highland Division**, the follow-up formation in I Corps that was to have bloody battles east of the Orne in the fight for Caen. It has a fine Highlander and regimental badges. The Division has a bronze Highlander statue at Château St Côme visited in Itinerary 6.

Return to the Place Général de Gaulle and rejoin the main itinerary.

Follow Autres Directions, then Caen and continue to the roundabout.

• Comité du Débarquement Monument, No 4 Commando Plaque, Ouistreham/10.2 miles/5 minutes /Map It5-14/Lat & Long: 49.270658 -0.255363

In the roundabout is a **Com Déb Sig Monument**, which until 1987 stood on the harbour at Ouistreham. At the back of the memorial is a **Plaque** to the **French** and **British Commandos of No 4 Commando**.

From the roundabout continue on the D84/D514 to the next roundabout.

N.B. By taking the first exit on the D514 and continuing over the next roundabout to the following roundabout (some half a mile) a red brick **Memorial** with metal **Plaque** is seen to the left. It is to the 13th/18th Royal Hussars (Map It5-F, Lat & Long: 49.27143 -0.26543, GPPIt5-2/2) and their dedication to the liberation of Normandy on 6 June 1944.

Continue straight over to the turning with the D35. Turn right and follow the rue du Gen de Gaulle into St Aubin d'Arquenay to a parking space on the right with flags, Place Boillet. In the corner is

4 Cdo Museum, Ouistreham.

Atlantic Wall Museum, Ouistreham.

Com Déb Sig Monument with 4 Cdo Plaque,
Ouistreham.

Inauguration of the RN/RM
Memorial, Ouistreham by
HRH Prince Philip on 6
June 2000.

• Memorial to 1st SS Bde, 6 Air Landing Bde and Civilian Victims, St Aubin d'Arquenay/13.00 miles/10 minutes/Map It5-15/Lat & Long: 49.26126 -0.28731

In the centre is the **Plaque to 1st SS Bde** and flanking it **Plaques to the Civilian Victims** and to **6 Air Landing Bde in OPERATION MALLARD.** MALLARD was the code name for the second lift of airborne troops into Normandy. The lead aircraft reached Normandy at about 2100 hours, just as the Germans were preparing to counter-attack into the gap between 3rd Canadian and 3rd BR Divisions. The presence of so many aircraft in the sky caused the German commanders to hesitate and by the time they decided to go ahead it was too dark to do so. MALLARD may well have prevented a dangerous situation developing with German armour between the two divisions.

    Continue on the D35 to the crossroads in Colleville-Montgomery. Turn left on the Grande Rue and continue to the first turning to the right, the rue de Caen.

CAPTIONS FOR GROUP PICTURE PAGE ITINERARY FIVE – 2, page 262	
GPPIt5-2/1	Bunker opp No 4 Cdo Mon, Colleville-Montgomery-Plage
GPPIt5-2/2	Memorial to 13th/18th Hussars, Ouistreham
GPPIt5-2/3	Memorial to 3rd Br Div, Périers-sur-le-Dan
GPPIt5-2/4	Bunker WN16 (Morris), Colleville-Montgomery
GPPIt5-2/5	Château de la Londe
GPPIt5-2/6	Memorial to 1st Suffolk Regt, Château de la Londe
GPPIt5-2/7	Memorial Sculpture to 59th (Staffs) Div & Civilian Plaques , Epron
GPPIt5-2/8	Memorial to 59th (Staffs) Div & Plaque to Daniel Robinson MM, 1921-1998, Epron
See below	SGW to 51st Highland Div, Ouistreham Church.

• Tribute to Allied Forces Monument, Golfe de Caen/17.8 miles/10 minutes/Map It5-18/Lat & Long: 49.22748 -0.33272

This truncated stone pillar with a bas relief showing the south coast of England and, across the Channel, Normandy, bears this legend, 'On this site and along a 2 mile front line towards the west where many soldiers died, the British Army fought for 34 days. The Memorial was erected by the village of Biéville-Berville as a tribute to all soldiers dead or still alive.' It was inaugurated 4 June 1994.

Continue in the direction of Caen. On the left is

• Memorial to 2nd Bn, King's Shropshire Light Infantry, Lebisy/19 miles/10 minutes/Map It5-19/Lat & Long: 49.21447 -0.34001

The **Memorial** marks the **German Front Line 6 June-9 July** and is in honour of the **2nd Bn KSLI** who liberated Bréville-Beuville and immediately attacked at Lebisey on the afternoon of 6 June 1944.

Continue to the Caen Périphique.

NOTE. At this stage the **CAEN MEMORIAL** may be visited if not already done on Approach 2.

• END OF ITINERARY FIVE

Memorial to 2nd
Bn KSLI, Lebisey.

SGW to 51st
Highland Div,
Ouistreham
Church.

Tribute to Allied Forces
Monument, Golfe de
Caen.

ITINERARY SIX

PEGASUS BRIDGE AND BRITISH AIRBORNE OPERATIONS

The Germans had begun to organise airborne forces in 1936. The Americans are said to have considered an airborne assault in 1918 at St Mihiel. The British began their airborne forces in 1940 at the instigation of Prime Minister Winston Churchill, and the early paratroopers were volunteers from No 2 Commando. The first British paratroop action was Operation Colossus on 10 February 1941 when 35 men of 'X' Troop No 2 Commando were dropped into the Italian Apennines. The commander of 'X' Troop was Major T.A.G. Pritchard who was, much later, College Commander at Sandhurst for one of the authors. In May 1943 6th Airborne Division was formed under Major General R.N. Gale and, with 1st Airborne Division under Major General R.E. Urquhart, comprised the Airborne Corps commanded by Lieutenant General Sir F.A.M. ('Boy') Browning. Within the organisation, and an integral part of it, was the 38th Wing of the Royal Air Force.

As early as August 1943 COSSAC had proposed the use of airborne forces in the invasion. At that time a direct assault on Caen was being considered. General Montgomery's appointment brought drastic changes to the plan. His idea was to seal each end of the sea assault using airborne troops. Their prime task was flank protection.

There were two types of airborne soldiers, classified according to the way in which they landed - by parachute or by glider. Thus there were two types of zones in which they would come down - *dropping* zones [DZs] for parachutists and *landing* zones [LZs] for gliders. Parachute troops can be widely dispersed by wind, which is a considerable disadvantage, while glider-borne forces can be more readily directed or aimed at small targets and can bring with them heavy equipment like field guns and small vehicles.

Gliders, however, are more vulnerable to obstacles such as the poles, known as 'Rommel's Asparagus', that the Germans were erecting on potential landing grounds along the French coast. Therefore, the mix of glider and parachute forces, and the tasks allocated to them, could decide the outcome of the airborne assault.

Six weeks before D-Day, over a three-day period, 6th Airborne Division carried out an airborne exercise. They did not know that it was a dress rehearsal for Normandy. On the 6th of June, owing to the shortage of aircraft, the Divisional Assault was done in two separate lifts, one early in the day called Operation Tonga and the other in the early evening, called Operation Mallard.

6TH AIRBORNE DIVISION LANDINGS – OPERATION TONGA

Drop Time:	0020 hours *coup-de-main* on Pegasus Bridge.
	0050 hours 3rd & 5th Parachute Brigades.
Leading Formations:	3rd and 5th Parachute Brigades of 6th Airborne Division.
6th AB Division Commander:	Major General R.N. ('Windy') Gale
German Defenders:	716th Infantry Division
716th Division Commander:	Lieutenant General Wilhelm Richter

The Plan - 6th Airborne Division Landings (Battle Map 10)

The airborne plan was scheduled to begin before the main landings, and in darkness, in order to achieve the maximum surprise. The earliest troops into Normandy were, where possible, to be paratroopers who would be less sensitive to obstacles than their comrades in gliders. The paratroopers were to clear landing areas for later glider landings. The tasks were distributed between two brigade groups on a geographical basis as follows:

5th Parachute Brigade Group (Brigadier J.H.N. Poett) comprising the 7th, 12th and 13th Parachute Battalions, D Company and two platoons of B Company of the Oxfordshire and Buckinghamshire Light Infantry and supporting arms and services was to:
1. Seize the bridges over the River Orne and the Caen Canal using six gliders manned by the Oxfordshire and Buckinghamshire Light Infantry and
2. Seize and hold the area of Pegasus Bridge and Ranville and clear the LZs north of Ranville for glider reinforcements. They were to land on DZ 'N' with elements of the 7th Parachute Battalion on DZ 'W'.

3rd Parachute Brigade Group (Brigadier James Hill) comprising the 1st Canadian Parachute Battalion, 8th and 9th Parachute Battalions and supporting arms and services was to:
1. Destroy the Merville Battery 11/2 hours before the first landing craft were due and
2. Destroy a number of bridges (e.g. at Varaville, Robehomme, Bures and Troarn) over the River Dives and thus prevent the enemy from attacking Ranville from the eastern flank.
They were to land on DZ 'K' and DZ 'V'.

In each case the airborne brigades would be spearheaded by pathfinders scheduled to drop at 0020 hours on 6 June. The main troops were due to come in about thirty minutes later.

What happened on D-Day - 6th Airborne Division Landings

The leading planes of 38th and 46th Groups of the Royal Air Force carried men of the 22nd Independent Parachute Company whose job it was to mark the dropping and landing zones. With them went the RAF Commander, Air Vice Marshal L.N. Hollingshurst, and on time the pathfinders jumped out into the night sky. One of the first to land was Lieutenant de Latour who featured in a *Picture Post* story on 22 July as the 'first' Allied soldier to land in France. On 9 September the same magazine carried a sad postscript - a picture of de Latour's grave with a temporary wooden cross. He was killed on 20 June, then a captain, and is now buried in Ranville CWGC.

At the same time as the pathfinders flew over their objectives the *coup-de-main* party of Ox and Bucks led by Major John Howard landed three of their gliders beside the Orne Canal bridge and two others near the bridge over the River Orne. In ten minutes both bridge were theirs.

Thirty minutes later at 0045 hours the main bodies of the para brigades arrived and then, less than three hours after that, gliders brought in the heavy equipment and General Gale, the division's commander.

By the end of the day both Orne bridges were in Allied hands, despite German counter-attacks, Ranville and the DZs were secure, a link-up had been made with Lord Lovat's Special Service Brigade from SWORD Beach, bridges over the River Dives at Troarn, Bures, Robehomme and over a tributary of the Dives at Varaville had been blown and the Merville Battery had been put out of action, despite a bad start. Only seven of over 260 parachute aircraft used in the assault were missing, but twenty-two of the ninety-eight gliders did not reach their LZs. Some never made it to France due to broken tow ropes, and many landed in the wrong place. Of the 196 members of the Glider Pilot Regiment involved in the operation seventy-one were casualties. Some of the drops were very scattered so that only about 3,000 of the 4,800 men who landed fought as planned. 6th AB Division had achieved its objectives, but it was thinly spread. The 6 June may have been the longest day for the men of the airborne forces but there was another one tomorrow and the Panzers were coming.

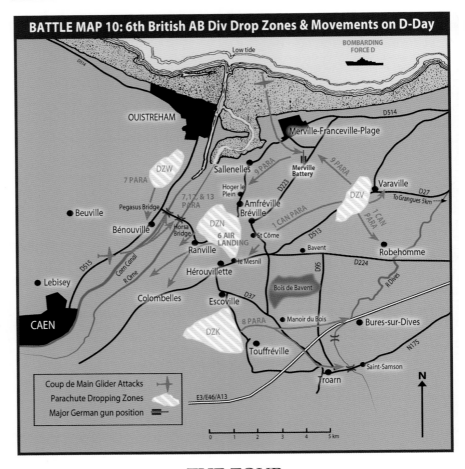

BATTLE MAP 10: 6th British AB Div Drop Zones & Movements on D-Day

THE TOUR

• **Itinerary Six** starts at the Caen *Péripherique*, continues to Pegasus Bridge and covers the British and Canadian Airborne and Commando Operations, ending at le Plain Gruchet.

• **The Main Route:** Bénouville - *Mairie* Plaque, 7th Light Infantry Bn, Para Regt, Café Gondrée, new Bénouville Bridge, Ox and Bucks Plaque, *Comité du Débarquement* Monument, Major Howard Bust, Glider Landings Markers, Centaur Tank, Cromwell Tank; Pegasus Memorial Museum - Old Pegasus Bridge, Bailey Bridge, Replica Horsa, Brig James Hill Statue, Den Brotheridge Memorial, *Coup de Main* Memorial; Horsa Bridge Glider Memorial; Ranville - CWGC Cemetery, Airborne Forces Plaque, 8th and 9th Para Regt Memorial Seats, 6th Airborne Division Cross; Churchyard - Den Brotheridge Plaque, Chapel - 6th AB Div, Edouard Gérard, 13th Lancs Bn, Can Para Corps, Plaques; Mill - Maj Strafford Plaque, Piron Brigade Memorial, 13th Para Bn Memorial, Scottish Para Seat; *Mairie* - General Gale Bust, original Liberation/13th Para Bn Plaque; Liberation/13th Para Bn Plaque; Amfréville - No 6 Commando Memorial, 1st Special Service Brigade Cross, No 3 Commando Memorial; Hoger - No 4 Commando, Colonel Robert

ITINERARY SIX MAP: PEGASUS BRIDGE & BRITISH AIRBORNE LANDINGS

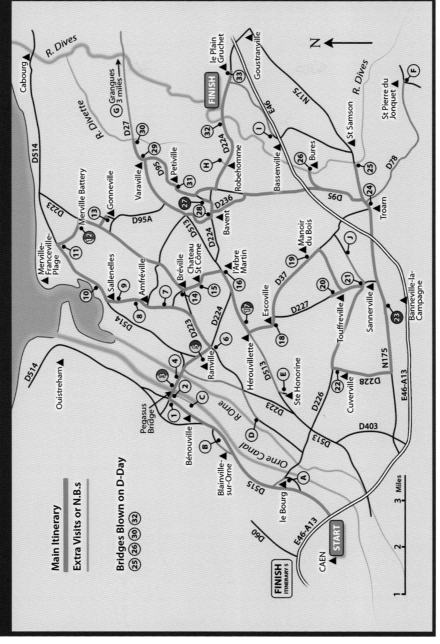

Main Itinerary

Extra Visits or N.B.s

Bridges Blown on D-Day
25 26 30 32

MAIN ITINERARY

1. *Mairie* Lib Pl/7 Lt Inf, Para Regt, Bénouville
2. Gondrée Café/Cromwell Tank/2 Ox & Bucks/*Com Déb* Sig/John Howard Bust/Glider Markers/New Pegasus Bridge
3. Pegasus Mem Mus/"Old" Pegasus Bridge/Bailey Bridge/Horsa/Brig Hill Statue/Brotheridge/*Coup de Main*
4. Horsa Bridge Glider Landings, R Orne
5. CWGC Cem, AB Cross,9 Para Seat, 8 Midlands Seat, Thanet Branch AB Assoc Seat/Chapel Mems: 6 AB, Edouard Gérard, 13 Lancs, Can Para Corps/Maj Strafford/ Piron Bde/Scottish Para Seat/Gen Gale Bust/13 Lancs, Ranville
6. 13 Lancs Lib Pl, Ranville
7. 6 Cdo/*Ferme des Commandos*/1 SS Bde/3 Cdo, le Plain, Amfréville
8. 4Cdo, Place Col Robert Dawson, Hoger
9. 4 SS Bde Hq, Sallenelles
10. Belg Edouard Gérard/Piron Bde, Sallenelles
11. 45 RM Cdo/Piron Bde/Civilians, Merville-Franceville
12. Mus/9 Para Bn/Col Otway Bust/3 Cdo/SNAFU Dakota, Merville Bty
13. 9 Para forming-up, Gonneville
14. 12 Para/12 Devons, Bréville
15. 9 Para Inf Bn/R Netherlands Bde/51st Highlander Statue, Château St Côme
16. 1 Can Para Bn/3 Para Bde/Square Brig James Hill, l'Arbre Martin
17. 2 (AB) Ox & Bucks/Allied Graves, Hérouvillette Cem
18. Brit Lib, Escoville
19. 8 Para Bn/Brig A Pearson, Manoir du Bois
20. Arthur Platt & W Billington, Touffreville

21. 3 Inf Div/Monty's Ironsides/Gp Capt Appleton/Lib, Sannerville
22. Middlesex Regt, Cuverville
23. CWGC Cem, Banneville-la-Campagne
24. 3 Para Sqn RE, Troarn
25. Maj Roseveare Bridge, R Dives, St Sampson
26. Capt Juckes Bridge, R Dives, Bures
27. Brig Mills-Roberts Grave, Bavent Churchyard
28. 1 SS Bde/Place A Lofi, Bavent
29. 1 Can Para Bn, Varaville
30. 3 Para Sqn RE/1 Can Para Bn, R Divette Bridge, Varaville
31. 3 Cdo/Brig Peter Young, Petiville
32. 3 Para Sqn RE & 1 Can Para Bn Bailey Bridge, R Dives, Robehomme
33. 1 SS Bde, le Plain Gruchet

EXTRA VISITS & 'N.B.s'

A. 2 Lincolns/Children Victims, le Bourg
B. 1 R Norfolks, Blainville-sur-Orne
C. 1st Bailey Bridge/17, 71, 263 Fld Sqns RE, Orne Canal
D. 1 RUR, Longueval
E. 5 Camerons, Ste Honorine la Chardonnerette
F. Massacre, St Pierre du Jonquet
G. Massacre, Grangues
H. 1 Can Para Bn/3 Para Bde & 1 Can Para Bde Seat, Robehomme
I. 9 Para Bn, Bassenville
J. 41, 46, 47, 48 RM Cdo, le Maizeret

Dawson Memorials; Sallenelles – 4th Special Services Bde HQ Memorial, Edouard Gérard Plaque, Piron Brigade Memorial; Merville-Franceville – 45 RM Commando, Allied Soldiers and Civilians, Piron Brigade Memorials; Merville Battery/Museum/9th Parachute Battalion Memorial, 3 Commando Plaque, SNAFU Dakota, Colonel Otway Bust; Memorial to 9th Para Bn Form-up Area; Bréville - 6th Airborne, 12th Para and 12th Devonshire Regt Memorial, CWGC Graves in Churchyard; Château St Côme – 51st Highlander Statue, Royal Netherlands Bde Plaque, L'Arbre Martin - 3rd Para Bde and 1st Can Para Memorials; Hérouvillette – Ox & Bucks Light Infantry Memorial; Escoville – British Liberators Memorial; Manoir du Bois - 8th Para Bn Memorial; CWGC Grave, Touffreville – Churchyard, Arthur Platt and Thomas Billington Memorial; Sannerville – 3rd Inf Div Memorial/Appleton Plaque; Cuverville – Middlesex Regt Memorial; Banneville-la-Campagne – CWGC Cemetery; Troarn – 3rd Para Sqn RE; Major Roseveare Bridge Memorial; Bures – Captain Juckes Bridge Memorial; Bavent Cemetery – Grave of Brigadier Mills-Roberts, 1st Special Service Brigade Memorial; Varaville – 3rd Para Bn RE & 1st Can Para Bn Plaque, Divette Bridge; Petiville – 3 Commando & Brig Peter Young Memorial; Robehomme – 3rd Para Bn Re & 1st Can Para Bn Bailey Bridge Plaque; le Plain Gruchet – 1st Special Service Bde Memorial.

• **Planned duration,** without stops for refreshments or Extra Visits: **8 hours 40 minutes**
• **Total distance: 47.4 miles**

• **Extra Visits are suggested to:** Hérouville – 2nd Bn Lincolns Memorial; St Pierre de Jonquet – Massacre Memorial; Grangues – Memorial to Crash and Massacre.

• **N.Bs.** The following sites are indicated: Blainville-sur-Orne – 1st Bn R Norfolks Memorial; Bénouville – 1st Bailey Bridge; Longueval – 1st RUR Memorial; Merville-Franceville Plage – site of 9 Coastal Guns; Ste-Honorine la Chardonnerette – 5th QO Cameron Highlanders Memorial; Le Maizeret – RM Cdo Mem; Robehomme – 1st Can Para Bn Plaque; Bassenville – 9th Para Bn Regt Memorial.

Take the Hérouville/Ouistreham/Car Ferry Exit 3a from the Caen ring road (Périphérique Est, E46).

Set your mileometer to zero.

Follow signs to Ouistreham and Car Ferry on the D515/D84. Continue on the D515 to the exit signed Colombelles D226.

Extra Visit to 2nd Bn Lincolns Memorial, Hérouville (Map It6-A/Lat & Long: 49.20670 -0.31825/GPPIt6-1/1). Round trip: 1 mile. Approximate time: 15 minutes.

Take the exit and follow the road round to the right, turn right at the bottom of the hill, continue to the crossroads with a stop sign. Turn right signed Autres Directions, then right again signed Ouistreham and continue to the Church.

On the Church wall is a **Memorial to the 2nd Bn the Lincolnshire Regt**, 32 of whom died in the Liberation of Hérouville, 8 July 1944 and a further 208 in battles in France, Belgium, Holland and Germany. Unveiled by the then-CO, Maj-Gen Sir Christopher Welby-Everard, KBE, CB, DL, 6 June 1990. There are also **Plaques to seven children** killed 'by the war' in December 1945.

Take the turn downhill on the small rue de la Fontaine, return to the D515 and pick up the main itinerary.

Continue on the D515 to the next exit, signed Blainville-sur-Orne on the D141.

N.B. By taking this exit, continuing straight over the roundabout, over the D515, turning right signed Centre Ville and continuing some .25 mile through the town, past the church on the left to a roundabout, to the right will be found a **Memorial to the 1st Bn R Norfolks (Map It6-B, Lat & Long: 49.23015 -0.29581, GPPIt6-1/2)**. It is a stone monument with bronze Plaques in English and French showing Blainville's recognition of its Liberation by the Norfolks on 7 June 1944. It is surrounded by a small, well-tended garden and trees. The main Itinerary may be rejoined by continuing on the D141 following signs to Bénouville.

Continue on the D515 and take the exit signed to Bénouville on the D514. Continue to the roundabout, Place de la Libération.

Some 600 yards north on the D35, at 18 Avénue de la Côte de Nacre, is **Le Manoir d'Hastings**, a traditional Normandy restaurant in a 17th Century Priory. Beside it is the ****Hotel La Pommeraie** with 15 rooms. Tel: + (0)2 31 44 62 43. E-mail: contact@manoirhastings.com

Turn right and park behind the Mairie. **Set your mileometer to Zero.**

• Bénouville/Mairie Plaque, 7th Light Infantry Battalion, Para Regiment Plaque/4.7 miles/10 minutes/Map It6-1/Lat & Long: 49.24313 -0.27795

On the *Mairie* is a **Plaque** commemorating it as the '**First Mairie to be liberated'.** Gallic enthusiasm insists that liberation came at 2345 hours on 5 June *'par les parachutistes anglais'*. However it must be remembered that French time is quoted which was one hour behind UK time. On the corner diagonally opposite the *Mairie*, at the foot of a religious stone memorial, is a **Memorial** with the word PAX at the foot bearing a **Plaque** in memory of **7th Light Infantry Battalion of the Parachute Regiment**. The 7th, the scheduled reinforcements for John Howard's men at Pegasus Bridge, were scattered by the strong winds and shot at by the Germans as they dropped but their CO, **Lt-Col Pine-Coffin,** using his bugler who dropped with him, rallied a force of about 200 and by 0300 established a defence perimeter around the bridge. Lt-Col R.G. Pine-Coffin, DSO, MC, commanded the 3rd Bn in N Africa and was famously portrayed in the film *A Bridge Too Far* defying the Germans with his umbrella on the Bridge at Arnhem.

Continue on the road (which is named 'Avénue du Commandant Kieffer') from the Mairie to the bridge. Park on the right in the café car park.

• Gondrée Café, Cromwell Tank, Pegasus Bridge, 2nd Ox and Bucks Plaque, Comité du Débarquement Monument, John Howard Bust, Glider Landings Markers/4.8 miles/40 minutes/RWC/Map It6-2/Lat & Long: 49.2426 -0.2751

The bridge over the Orne Canal was captured by the British airborne forces on D-Day, and subsequently named after the emblem of the Airborne Division. 300 yards away to the east is a

Infantry Division, guarding the bridge, several soldiers remember George Gondrée shouting loud encouragement. Within the first hours of D-Day, the Café quickly became a first aid post, with Thérèse who was a trained nurse helping the two doctors in the Café and Georges digging up 99 bottles of champagne which he had hidden in the garden. Much celebrating and 'reporting sick' went on. After the war the Café became a focal point for the veterans and their families and took the name of 'Pegasus Café', with the Gondrées and their three daughters, Georgette, Arlette and Françoise being a vital feature of every pilgrimage visit. The walls were covered with mementos and all veterans signed a 'Book of Honour'.

Following Madame Gondrée's death after the 40th Anniversary in 1984 there were many disputes among the family and with the *Comité du Débarquement* about the ownership of the land on which the cafe and adjoining museum were built (described in previous editions of this guide). In brief, after a campaign in the British press, this resulted in the Café continuing to be owned and run by Madame Gondrée's daughter Arlette (who as a child was in the Café on 6 June 1944,) – thus preserving the continuity of the Gondrée family – but in the closure of the museum and the removal of all the exhibits. Arlette has since rebuilt the museum as an annexe to the Café and has amassed a collection of exhibits. It now contains two large halls (which can be used for lectures or functions). The Café, which is a listed historic building, serves snacks and light meals and sells appropriate books and souvenirs. **Open: daily** 13 March – 12 November. Tel/Fax: (0)2 31 44 62 25.

Over the road is a **Centaur A27M Cromwell tank** of **5 (Independent) RM Armd Spt Bty**. It came ashore at la Br che d'Hermanville, where it was put out of action. It was recovered in November 1975, brought to the Pegasus Bridge area in June 1977 and was originally sited on the opposite bank.

Beside it is the **Brasserie les Trois Planeurs**. Closed during the winter on Tues, and Mon, Wed & Thurs nights. Tel: + (0)2 31 44 62 00.

> **N.B.** By walking some 300 paces up the path by Pegasus Café [Sentier GR 223/E0 Ouest walking trail] along the Caen Canal to the Château grounds on the right and a small bridge leading to a *lavoir*, there is an easily missed, small **Memorial Stone** in a brick surround on the canal bank **at the site of the first Bailey pontoon bridge** built in France, named 'London I', which commemorates the **17th, 71st and 263rd Field Squadrons RE.** It was completed by 0100 hours on D+3 and had a span of 220 ft. Another bridge, London II, was built across the river and was opened at 1230 at D+5. They were both 'Class 40' bridges. While the work was going on the REs had their HQ in the *Mairie* at Bénouville. **(Map IT6-C, Lat & Long: 49.239152 -0.277594, GPPIt6-5).**

To the right of the bridge is a fine painted Pegasus Bridge sign, renovated in 1996 by the Airborne Assault Normandy Trust.

Bust of John Howard & Glider Markers, Pegasus Bridge.

Centaur A27M Cromwell Tank of 5 Indep RM Armd Spt Bty, Pegasus Bridge.

Continue over the new bridge, drive to the Pegasus Memorial Museum, park in the car park and walk back to the bridge.

The original bridge was replaced in April 1994. The new bridge is essentially the same shape and design as the original but is longer and wider. On the bank of the Canal, known as the 'Esplanade John Howard', is a complex of memorials to the events of 5-6 June. On the side of the impressive new bridge is a **Plaque** to commemorate the action of the **2nd Battalion Ox and Bucks** who captured Pegasus Bridge in the night of 5-6 June 1944, erected by their heirs, the Royal Green Jackets, in recognition of the first Allied Unit victory on D-Day. On the bank is a German 50mm anti-tank gun where there was a Tobruk-type emplacement (a covered, protected gun position) in June 1944. Beside it is a *Com Déb Sig* **Monument** and an Orientation Table.

The bronze **bust of John Howard** was sculpted by Vivien Mallock (qv) and presented to the mayor and citizens of Bénouville by the Ox and Bucks Light Infantry Association and the Airborne Assault Normandy Trust in June 1995.

In the low ground behind are three **lectern-like Glider Markers**. They were unveiled in June 1977 by General Gale. They show exactly where each of John Howard's gliders landed, and give details of their crews (including Pilots S/Sgts Wallwork and Answorth) and passengers, and precise time of landing.

Face the Gondrée Café and take that direction as 12 o'clock.

From this point UTAH Beach, effectively the other extreme end of the invasion area, is 47 miles away in a straight line at 12 o'clock. Major Howard's glider PF800 landed at 0016 hours, where the first marker stands at 7 o'clock. It is 47 yards from the bridge. The leading section moved up, past where you are now standing, and threw grenades into a pillbox, which was located beside the bridge across the road from you at 3 o'clock.

Despite troublesome snipers in the woods, General Gale, Brigadier Poett, (who had dropped with the pathfinders at 0020 hours and was therefore the first general officer to land in Normandy) and Brigadier Kindersley (commanding 6th Air Landing Brigade) crossed the bridge (coming from 6 o'clock) on a tour of inspection around 0930 hours.

There were more snipers in the large building seen at 10 o'clock across the canal. It seemed likely that there was an artillery observation officer there too, because accurate mortar fire was coming down. However, it was thought that the building was a maternity hospital, and the paratroopers were forbidden to return the fire. To the right of the building, at 11 o'clock, there was a water tower, from which snipers were also operating, and, around midday, Major Howard agreed that one shot could be fired at the tower, using the 50mm German anti-tank gun on the riverbank. It scored a direct hit and everyone cheered. An even stranger sound was heard later, when Lord Lovat and No 6 Commando arrived, led by Piper Bill Millin (qv), en route to Amfréville, the village over the rise at 5 o'clock. He had piped them off from Spithead at 2100 on 5 June, and over the Ouistreham beaches at 0820 hours that morning, though he stopped playing as they crossed the bridge. For many years after the war Major Howard accompanied many student officers of the British Army's Staff College on their annual battlefield tour (including one of the authors). One of the innumerable stories which he told so well was of the two Italians that were taken prisoner near the bridge. Their job had been to put up the anti-glider poles in the fields. 'I didn't have the time to deal with prisoners,' he said, 'so I let them go. Do you know what they did? The silly sods went back to putting up the poles!'

A radio message was sent to John Howard to tell him that the river bridge had been captured intact and at almost the same time Howard learned that an inspection had shown that there were no explosives under the canal bridge. The first part of his task was complete. He ordered his men to take up defensive positions and despatched a patrol to secure the landing zones. Then he sent out the radio signal for success, 'Ham and Jam - Ham and Jam.' "As I spoke", he said, "I could hardly believe that we had done it."

Just before daylight three German tanks rounded the corner by the *Mairie*, at 12 o'clock, and headed slowly towards the bridge. The paratroopers' PIAT (Projector Infantry Anti-Tank) destroyed the first tank, which burst into flames and started exploding like fireworks. The noise it made probably persuaded the enemy that it was too dangerous to counter-attack until daylight.

Some time after this a German motor cycle and car approached at speed from behind you along the road. They were shot up by Lieutenant Tod Sweeney and his men on the river bridge, and crashed in the ditch between the bridges. An officer in the car turned out to be the bridge commander, Major Hans Schmidt, who asked to be shot, because he had 'lost his honour'. Whether his loss was related to 6th Airborne's capture of the bridges, or to the ladies' lingerie and perfume found in the car, was never established.

Brigadier Peter Young (he fought at Dunkirk, Dieppe and D-Day - he called himself the '3D' soldier', was later head of Military History at Sandhurst and founded the Sealed Knot in 1968) told us that in his opinion, 'Much of what passes for military history is little more than fiction'. While touring the Dieppe battlefield with the brigadier he told us that he had reassured his fellow Commandos as they crossed a wheatfield under German fire that they were quite safe as '6 feet of standing corn would stop a 303'. In the continuing struggle to achieve recognition as the 'first' to have done something or the 'first' to have been liberated some stories 'improve' with time. In a letter to the authors, Brigadier, later General, Sir Nigel Poett wrote, "Pegasus Bridge was the first engagement of D-Day. This is beyond dispute". That at least we can be certain of but it would be unwise to be dogmatic about timings.

Walk back to the Museum car park.

■ No. 16. Pegasus Mémorial Museum, Original Bridge, Bailey Bridge, Replica Horsa, Brig Hill Statue, Brotheridge Memorial, Coup de Main Memorial/5 miles/1 hour/RWC/Map It6-3/Lat & Long: 49.24208 -0.27185

After much debate the **old Pegasus Bridge** has now found a home in the grounds of the **Airborne Museum, Memorial Pegasus**, opened on 4 June 2000 by Prince Charles, Colonel in Chief of the Parachute Regiment. The Museum has become a well-loved place of pilgrimage to Para veterans and their families, many of whom donate precious items - uniform, documents etc.

The custom-built modern structure, whose roof is shaped like a glider, was sponsored by the *Comité du Débarquement*, the *Communes* of Bénouville and Ranville, the *Département* and the Region and it commemorates the actions around the Orne bridges, especially by 6th Airborne on 5/6 June 1944. In it are the main exhibits from the original Pegasus Museum plus many new items and models. One showcase, for example, is devoted to John Howard, including his famous red beret, another to the Medical Service. Another shows an Army Chaplain's kit.

There is a smart boutique with a good stock of books, maps and souvenirs. In the grounds is an **original Bailey Bridge** (one of 30 or so built by the REs in the area in 1944), rescued from a site near Falaise and inaugurated in March 2002. It stands beside the old Pegasus Bridge. The bridge is the 'original' one though perhaps in the way that someone who has had a face-lift still has their 'original' face. The bridge that was captured in 1944 was later widened by some 16 feet to accommodate the widening of the canal and the increased traffic, and in 1994 it was replaced by what is now the current bridge. On the bridge is **a Plaque to Lance Corporal Brian J. Mullen**, Sapper RE, No 4 Commando Intelligence Section. Corporal Mullen is buried in Hermanville CWGC Cemetery. On 5 June 2004 Prince Charles unveiled a unique full size replica **Horsa Glider** in the grounds.

Beside it are two small hangars - one with part of an original Horsa, the other a glider exhibition complete with John Howard's personal commentary. A **Memorial to Lt Den Brotheridge** was also unveiled.

In 2005 a **statue** by Vivien Mallock (qv) of **Brig James Hill, DSO, MC**, *Légion d Honneur*, US Silver Star, King Haakon's Norwegian Liberty Cross, was moved here from its original site at l'Arbre Martin (qv) to preserve it from vandalism. In Winston Ramsay's *D-Day Then and Now* the Brigadier told what happened when on landing he and his men were caught in a bombing raid. They flung themselves to the floor until the raid was over. "It was horrible. When, thank God, they [the aircraft] had gone, I raised myself on my arms and looked around ... I saw a leg in the

Pegasus Memorial Museum.

A 'Rupert' dummy from the Muse

Prince Charles in cockpit
of replica Horsa Glider
with James Wallwork,
first glider pilot to land
at 00.16, 6 June 1944.

Plaque to Lt Den Brotheridge,
unveiled on 5 June 2004, Museum
grounds.

Plaque to L/Cpl B.J. Mullen,
'Original' Pegasus Bridge,
Museum grounds.

Statue of Brig James Hill,
moved to the Museum groun

Coup de Main Memorial, with 'original' Pegasus Bridge, behind Museum grounds.

Gen Sir Richard Dannatt at the Inauguration of the Coup de Main Memorial, Pegasus Memorial Museum, 6 June 2009, Museum grounds.

Artist's impression from the Café side of the Coup de Main, Pegasus Memorial Museum.

Memorial to Horsa Bridge Glider Landings. River Orne.

middle of the road. I knew I had been hit, but when I took another look I saw it had a brown boot on and I knew it wasn't mine".

To mark the 65th Anniversary in 2009 a new **Coup de Main Memorial** was inaugurated on 6 June by Gen Sir Richard Dannatt, then Chief of the General Staff, dedicated to the men who landed in the gliders – flown by 12 men of the Glider Pilot Regt, and carrying Oxford & Bucks Infantrymen with supporting REs, medics from RAMC and a liaison Officer of 7 Para Bn.

The Memorial was set up by **'Project 65'** at the instigation of ex-RAF Station WO Barry Tappenden (son of Cpl Ted Tappenden, Maj Howard's Radio Operator) supported by Project Chairman Danny Greeno and Gen Sir Robert Pascoe, senior surviving officer of the Oxfordshire & Buckinghamshire Light Infantry, and with the help of friends of the Regiment. The six simple and dignified memorial stones stand beside the original Pegasus Bridge in the Museum grounds. Each stone shows the name of the RAF Halifax pilot, who tugged the gliders from Tarrant Rushton in Dorset, and the names of the 30 men in each of the six gliders. Four of those men took part in the unveiling ceremony: L/Sgt Tich Rayner, Pte Rocky Bright, Pte Stuart Watson, all of the Ox & Bucks, and Spr Harry Wheeler, RE.

Project 65 began its fund-raising in 2007. The main event involved a group of enthusiasts who embarked on a run of 65 miles from Tarrant Rushton to Pegasus Bridge on 4/5/6 June 2009. Not content with raising the money for the *Coup de Main* Memorial, Project 65 has a target of 500,000 euros which will be passed on to six of the main Service Charities. See their website: www.project65.net for their latest projects.

Tragically, **Capt Mark Hale** 2nd Bn Rifles, who organised a fund-raising team of rowers to cover 5,800 kms – the distance from Sangin to Pegasus Bridge - was killed by a bomb blast in Sangin, trying to help a wounded colleague, in August 2009.

Open: daily from 1 April-30 September 0930-1830, 1 October – 30 November and 1 February – 31 March 1000-1300 and 1400-1700. Closed 1 December – 31 January.
Entrance fee payable. Tel: (0)2 31 78 19 44. Fax: (0)2 31 78 19 42.
E-mail: memorial.pegasus@wanadoo.fr
Continue on the D514 to the pedestrian crossing before the bridge over the river on the left.

• Memorial to the Horsa Bridge Glider Landings/5.3 miles/5 minutes/ Map It6-4/Lat & Long: 49.24046 -0.26753

The **Memorial**, in French and English, tells the story of the capture of the bridge. It was erected by the Glider Pilots Association and was unveiled on 6 June 1989 by their President, Major Ian Toler. The bridge was then named 'Horsa' after the gliders used by the airborne forces. The enemy defending it had run away leaving their weapons behind. The first glider carrying the three platoons for the assault on the river bridge came down at 0020 hours about 190 yards away from it and, led by Lieutenant Fox, rushed it. Little more than a minute later Lieutenant Tod Sweeney's platoon landed some 400 yards away and he too led his men directly to their objective.

One of those who jumped into Normandy that morning was Richard Todd who landed just before 0100 hours. Both he and Lieutenant Sweeney told the same story about how they met each other on Pegasus Bridge on 6 June. Lieutenant Sweeney's version was, 'I met this chap on the bridge and he said, "Hello, my name is Todd and they call me Sweeney", so I replied, "Hello, my name is Sweeney and they call me Todd"'. Richard 'Sweeney' Todd went on to become a highly successful actor, notably in the role of Guy Gibson in *The Dam Busters*. He died on 3 December 2009, age 90. 'Tod' Sweeney, who won an MC in later fighting in Normandy and took part in the glider-borne assault over the Rhine at Hamminkeln in 1945, (both of which operations we studied with him on the ground). He stayed on in the Army after the war, retiring as a Colonel. He became the head of the Battersea Dogs' Home and the subject of a *This is Your Life* programme in the 1980s. He died on 4 June 2001, age 82.

A D-DAY MEMORY

TOD TOLD US THIS STORY WHEN HE VISITED US IN SANDWICH

Lieutenant H.J. ('Tod') Sweeney. 2nd Battalion Oxfordshire and Buckinghamshire Light Infantry. *Coup-de-main* group for the Orne river bridge.

'As the glider in which I was travelling broke through the clouds I saw clearly in the pale moonlight the River Orne, the Caen canal and the two bridges we had to capture - exactly as on the model we had studied so carefully over the last few weeks. The glider pilot called out, 'There's the bridge straight ahead, better strap up.' But I had one more task to carry out before I sat down and strapped up - to open the door for a quick exit. I struggled with the door for a few seconds and then it shot up. As it did so, to my horror, the glider made a final bank to the left and I found myself peering down at the fields and cattle 100ft below. Luckily my batman grabbed my belt and clung on to me until the glider righted itself and I was able to get into my seat. A minute later we were bumping over the fields of France towards the bridge over the River Orne. We had arrived, and for me and my platoon the invasion had started."

Continue to the roundabout.

N.B. By turning right on the D223, continuing past a large quarry on the right, then turning right signed Longueval, just after a right turn (rue Henri Davoisne) and by a pedestrian crossing, on the right is to be found a **Memorial to the 1st Bn the Royal Ulster Rifles, 6 AB Div** (Map It6-D, Lat & Long: 49.21674 - 0.28627, GPPIt6-1/4) who liberated the village on 7 June 1944 and who gave their lives in Normandy in the cause of freedom. 6 June-3 September 1944.

Take the D37 signed to Ranville. Take the next turning right on the rue de la Vallée and then immediately left heading for Ranville church. Drive just beyond the church to the Commonwealth War Graves Commission Cemetery. Stop on the left. There are a number of visits that can be made on foot:

• Ranville CWGC Cemetery & Mems; Chapel Mems to 6th AB Div, Edouard Gérard, 13th Lancs Bn, Can Para Corps; Piron Brigade; Maj Strafford Plaque and Scottish Para Seat/6.1 miles/45 minutes/Map It6-5/Lat & Long: 49.231108 -0.257772/OP

The capture of the Ranville area was the responsibility of the 13th (Lancashire) Parachute Battalion of Nigel Poett's 5th Brigade. First they had to improve and protect landing strips on DZ'N' in anticipation of the arrival of the glider waves at 0330 hours and of the 6th Airlanding Brigade at 2100 hours, and then move on to Ranville. Accompanying them, in order to remove the anti-landing poles and to prepare the landing strips, were sappers of the 591st Parachute Squadron RE, who dropped at 0030 hours. The first landing strips were cleared by 0330 hours and resistance by the 125th Panzer Grenadier Regiment of 21st Panzer Division was over by 0400 hours.

The cemetery was begun by Royal Engineers of 591st Parachute Squadron RE, who put up wooden crosses, which remained until after the war. Captain Davidson, the squadron second-in-command, was taken prisoner by the Germans and later rescued by the Commandos. By 21 June there were twenty-seven graves, left in the care of a 9-year-old French boy called Claude, who promised the Sappers that he would look after them. Today there are 2,563 burials, including 323 Germans. In it is buried Captain T.R. Juckes, MC who commanded 2nd Troop 3rd Parachute Squadron Engineers which blew one of the bridges over the River Dives, now named after him (see below). To the left of the War Stone almost in the centre of the cemetery is a **Stone Cross** bearing a bronze plaque with the emblem of the Airborne Forces on it and remembering simply, 'June 1944'. This was erected in September 1944 by Royal Engineers of 1st AB Division. The chains surrounding it are glider lashing chains and the shell-like supports are brake fluid casings. At the multi-denominational inauguration were the Count and Countess de Rohan-Chabot, whose paternal ancestor, Philippe de Rohan-Chabot, in 1840 organised the return from St Helena to Les Invalides of Napoleon's remains. Inside and to the left of the gateway is a **Memorial Seat to 9th Parachute Battalion**. On the other side of the gateway is a **Memorial Seat to 8th Midland Counties Parachute Battalion**, dedicated on 5 June 1988.

NOTE: There are Memorial Stones to both these battalions in the village of Annebault, some 6.5 miles to the west of Pont l'Evêque.

The **Seat** by the entrance to the local churchyard was presented by the **Thanet Branch of the Airborne Forces Association** in June 1986. It matches one they presented to the Airborne Cemetery at Oosterbeek in Holland.

Buried in Plot IIIA, Row L is the poet **Major William John Fletcher Jarmain**, of 193 Battery 61st Anti-tank Regiment, RA, 26 June. Like fellow poet Keith Douglas (qv) Jarmain served in North Africa. The night before he was killed he spent working through the records of his unit, assessing each man. Also like Douglas, he had a premonition of his death. Against advice he went on a recce into Ste Honorine la Chardonnerette (to the north of Ranville) and was killed by

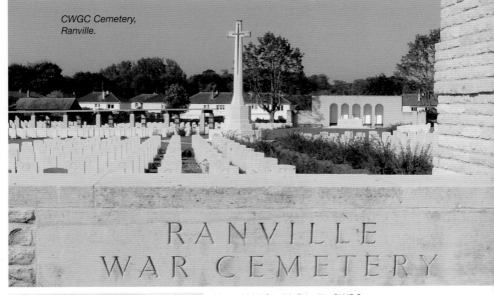

CWGC Cemetery, Ranville.

RANVILLE WAR CEMETERY

'June 1944 Cross', Ranville CWGC Cemetery.

Personal tribute on Headstone of Driver J. Wells, Ranville CWGC Cemetery.

Grave of Lt Brotheridge and Gondrée Plaque, Ranville Churchyard.

SGWs to 6th AB Div, Ranville Church.

Plaque to Belgian Edouard Gérard, Ranville Church.

Plaque to Piron Bde, Ranville.

Plaque to Luard's Own (13th Lancs Para Bn), Ranville Church.

Plaque to Maj Strafford, Ranville.

Plaque to 1st Can Para Bn, Ranville Church.

Plaques on Memorial Seat to Scottish Paras, Ranville.

a German mortar bomb. One of his best known poems - although written at El Alamein - seems appropriate to be read at his grave:

At a War Grave
No grave is rich, the dust that herein lies
Beneath this white cross mixing with the sand
Was vital once, with skill of eye and hand
And speed of brain. These will not re-arise
These riches, nor will they be replaced;
They are lost and nothing now, and here is left
Only a worthless corpse of sense bereft,
Symbol of death, and sacrifice and waste.

Those for whom the sacrifice was made do not consider it mere waste.

Also buried here are the men who were killed in the disaster and massacre at Grangues (qv). On 6 June 2009, the 65th Anniversary of D-Day, on the grave of **Driver James Wells**, RASC (IIIA.L.5) was a wreath from his brother saying that their mother's ashes had been interred within the grave. The ashes of the widow of **Serjeant H.W.S. Luxton**, Middx Regt, (VIII.F.10) who was killed at Cuverville (qv) on 18 July, have also been interred with him. In the grave beside him lies **Pte M. Philbin**, killed with him.

The **Rev Robert Edward Cape, MA**, Chaplain 4th class, age 30, killed on 25 June, lies in III.F.26.

On 19 April 2011 **Flt Lt Henry 'Lacy' Smith**, 453 Sqn RAAF, age 27, was buried in V.F.16. with full military honours. The wreckage of his Spitfire, shot down on 11 June 1944, was excavated from the mud in the Orne Estuary near Merville-Franceville in November 2010. His remains were in the cockpit.

Stand squarely in front of the main entrance to the cemetery and take that direction as 12 o'clock.

Next to the cemetery is Ranville Church. Opposite is a **NTL Totem**. The old ruined tower is to the left of the main building. Following the immediate shock of the invasion, the Germans reacted quickly. The town of Colombelles (known to the troops as 'steel city' because of its tall metal chimneys) some two miles away at 6 o'clock, became a forming-up area for German counter-attacks. On D+5 naval spotters were sent up the tower to direct the fire of HMS *Belfast* (now floating on the River Thames near Tower Bridge in London) onto Colombelles and the shells could be heard whistling overhead here. The Germans replied with 88mm artillery fire onto the church, which was badly damaged. The civilian cemetery was destroyed, and so the first soldiers' graves were dug in the field, which is now the CWGC Cemetery. To allow access to the graves from the church, a hole was knocked in the boundary wall. Today the hole is a gateway between the two. Around the inside of the wall on the far side of the church there are also 48 contemporary war graves, including one German and two French soldiers and **Lieutenant Den Brotheridge**, who was killed at Pegasus Bridge. Behind Brotheridge's headstone is a commemorative plaque placed by the Gondrée family acknowledging him as the first Allied soldier killed during the landings. In the cemetery is buried Bombardier H. Hall whose date of death is given as 5 June 1944, presumably because he - and so many others - were killed at sea or in the air on the way over the Channel.

In the Church is a side Chapel on the right with **SGWs to 6th AB Div**, showing the Pegasus Horse, 'In Memoriam, 1959' and to **St George**, Ranville 1960. On the wall is a brass **Plaque to Belgian Edouard Gérard** (qv) with a list of his decorations and a white **Plaque to Luard's Own, 13th Lancs Bn Para Regt** and a bronze **Plaque to the 1st Can Para Bn**.

The general area outside the church is known as the 'Place General Sir Richard Gale'. Immediately opposite the entrance to the CWGC Cemetery is a low wall on which is a map and a concise summary of the airborne operations in the area, erected by 1 Field Squadron RE which lists the units involved in the actions. In the field beyond the wall, which faces the *Mairie*, Sergeant Ken Routman of the 591st Squadron organised a football match against the 13th

Parachute Battalion on 9 June. The result is not recorded. Beside it is a stone tower on which is a **Plaque in memory of the Belgian Piron Brigade** which formed an 'Allied' element of the 2nd British Army together with a Czech armoured brigade, a Netherlands brigade and a Polish Armoured Division. Behind the tower is a **Memorial to Major Charles Strafford MBE** of HQ 6th AB Division, 1914-1993, erected by his comrades of the Airborne Forces and his many friends in France. Major Strafford, who lived for many years in Ranville (and had an excellent wine cellar, which we were fortunate to sample), was a knowledgeable and active member of the Association, has no grave - he left his body to scientific research. There is also a **Memorial Seat** to the **Scottish Paras**, erected by the Central Branch of the Para Regt Assoc. and unveiled by Gen Alastair Pearson on 18 October 1994.

Turn round, take first turning right and stop beside the Mairie on the left.

• *General Gale Bust, 13th (Lancs) Bn, Para Bde Liberation Plaque, Ranville Mairie/6.2 miles/5 minutes/Map It6-5/Lat & Long: 49.23178 -0.25703*

General Gale, the Airborne Division Commander, had arrived at about 0330 hours by glider and moved with his HQ to an area just to the west of the village of Ranville called le Bas de Ranville. On route he commandeered a white horse and many soldiers remember him riding it. Later it saved his life by being between him and a mortar shell. Le Bas de Ranville, which was being defended by the 12th (Yorkshire) Parachute Battalion, came under intense German counter-attacks, and when Lord Lovat's Special Service Brigade arrived at Pegasus Bridge at 1300 hours the leading Commando was diverted from its main task and sent up here. In the garden of the *Mairie*, in front of the Biblioth que (Library), is a striking **Bust of General Sir Richard Gale**, 1896-1982, sculpted by Vivien Mallock (qv). It was presented in June 1994 by the Airborne Assault Association and the Normandy Trust and was unveiled by Prince Charles during the 50th Anniversary commemorations. Below it is an old **Plaque** proclaiming that Ranville was the first village liberated at 0230 on 6 June 1944 by the 13th (Lancashire) Battalion the Parachute Regiment. This is the original of the plaque next visited, replaced because, when it was made in 1944, the badge upon it was painted, not carved, and therefore did not weather well. When the new plaque was erected, the old plaque was presented to the mayor and he placed it here.

Continue past the Mairie to the first crossroads in the village.

• *13th (Lancs) Bn Para Regt Liberation Plaque, Ranville/6.4 miles/5 minutes/Map It6-6/Lat & Long: 49.23088 -0.25420*

Here on the wall is the new **Liberation Plaque**, which has in *bas relief* an Airborne Division cap badge. Paratroopers re-visiting the area often discuss which was the first *Mairie* to be liberated, or the first house to be liberated, or the first village, or the first town, but the most enthusiastic conversation always centres around the first Frenchwoman they liberated. Whoever it was, and wherever, the ties between the local people and the British paratroopers remain very strong. The first Airborne Division pilgrimage here was led by Brigadier James Hill in June 1946 and the 29 June issue of *Illustrated Magazine* carried a full photographic report.

Turn left on the D223 following signs to Amfréville.

The road bisects DZ'N' on which the 5th Parachute Brigade and later the 6th Airlanding Brigade landed. The pathfinders of the Independent Parachute Company had had a scattered drop and were unable to set up their markers properly. One section operated its beacon thinking that DZ'N' was DZ'K' and attracted a number of 3rd Brigade units before the mistake was discovered. Therefore, as the Horsa gliders began to come in at 0330 hours, many pilots were unable to locate their correct strips or even be certain about which way they were supposed to land. One Sapper who was working on the landing strips remembered that "the gliders came from all directions ... some passed within thirty or fifty feet of each other going in opposite directions."

Bust of General Sir Richard Gale, Ranville library.

Plaque to Ranville, 'the first village liberated', and 13th Bn Para Regt.

Plaque to 13th (Lancs) Bn Para Regt, Ranville Liberation.

Memorial to No 3 Cdo, le Plain, Amfréville.

Memorial No 6 Cdo, le Plain, Amfréville.

Plaque to 'Ferme des Commandos, 6 juin 1944', le Plain, Amfréville.

seven days and nights reproducing the anti-tank ditch, the paths, the gun emplacements (with steel girders covered with sacking) and the minefield areas. In 1993 a marker was erected on Walbury Hill to mark the site.

The plan was complex. The battalion was to divide into two groups. The first, smaller, group, was to prepare a rendezvous for the arrival of the main body and also reconnoitre the battery. An attack by a hundred RAF Lancaster bombers was scheduled for 0030 hours and Otway wanted to know the resulting damage before launching his assault. The first group was to jump at 0020 hours and the main body at 0050 hours. The main body comprised most of the battalion, including 'B' and 'C' Companies. 'B' Company was given the job of breaching the first wire barrier and clearing a path through the minefield. 'C' Company was the assault force, while the remainder of 'A' Company was to hold a firm base from which the others could begin the assault. 'C' Company was to rush the gap in the minefield and split into four parties accompanied by sappers of 591st Parachute Squadron. Each party was to capture and blow up a casemate. The plan did not end there. Timed to arrive as 'C' Company made its charge through the battery defences, three Horsa gliders were to crash-land inside the perimeter. This party, named like John Howard's force at Pegasus Bridge, as a *'coup-de-main'*, consisted mainly of A Company personnel and a number of sappers. Then, if all else had failed, HMS *Arethusa* was standing by to pound the battery with her 6in guns at 0550 hours.

Otway trained his men very hard. He was sparing with his praise and quick to find fault. They rehearsed over and over again - all except the gliders. He could not get gliders to crash land into his dummy battery, so he arranged that the RAF would fly in low as the practice attacks went in. However, the fifty or so paratroopers of 'A' Company had to be retrained as glider troops. They flew over Salisbury Plain and practised accurate landings at Thruxton. Then, finally, the colonel declared himself satisfied and a few days later the battalion was sealed into its pre-invasion camp near Broadwell in Berkshire. There were over seven hundred men, ready, trained and anxious to go.

The first small group took off from RAF Harwell at 2310 hours on 5 June in Albemarles, and dropped accurately and to time at 0020 hours, despite the fact that the aircraft had an uneasy reputation for losing its tail in mid-air. The officer in charge of the rendezvous to which the reconnaissance group and then the main body were to report was Major Allen Parry and on landing he used his 'Ducks, Bakelite' (a whistle device that made a sound like a duck, and the British equivalent to the Americans 'cricket') to locate a friendly face. There was no one about, so he set off alone to the rendezvous, hearing, en route, the explosions from the Lancaster raid on the battery. It was well off target. Reaching the rendezvous Parry set up his Aldis lamp to guide in the paratroopers and waited for the main body. When they came the aeroplanes seemed to be spread out and as their engine noise faded away he began to flash his Aldis signal. But two hours after the drop only 150 men, including Lieutenant-Colonel Otway, had arrived. It was less than 25 per cent of those that had set out. There were no Royal Engineers and, apart from sidearms, they had only one Vickers machine gun and twenty Bangalore torpedoes between them. Otway decided to make for his objective and at 0250 hours set out, reaching the firm base area 500 yards from the battery at about 0420 hours. Parry, originally in charge of the rendezvous, was given command of the assault party and divided his allocation of fifty men into four units in imitation of the original plan. Now they would wait for the *coup-de-main* party. When that arrived as planned into the middle of the battery, then they would attack.

A D-DAY MEMORY

LES TOLD US HIS STORY AS WE STOOD IN FRONT OF THE BATTERY

Paratrooper Les Cartwright, 9th Parachute Battalion. Dropped for the Merville Battery.

'I think I should tell you first quickly who we were. Now we were the 9th Para Battalion. We were formed out of the 10th Essex Battalion and we were designated as a Home Counties Battalion therefore most of us came from the Home Counties - Middlesex, Surrey, Essex. That's who we were. The actual boys and myself, the Paras, the average age was 19 to 21. No older.

Our officers were a bit older. Our NCOs were a bit older, because 'Windy' (if I speak of Windy that means General Gale) - Windy had nicked a lot of NCOs from the 1st Division who had experience to put in amongst us so as to give us that bit of backing and a bit of experience. Anyway, the first thing we knew about this was we knew something was up, 'cos if you remember we had these little exercises and it always seemed to be guns we were after - up the hill and down the valley, and then one day a little while before Normandy they marched us out and we stopped at the Battalion and the Colonel told us what the job was. Well after that we went down on the plains and the Colonel found a position practically like this (the Merville Battery) and we built a battery and we attacked it night and day for a week. The idea was that first of all to drop would be our pathfinders, then some of the lads would drop and they'd make for the battery, make sure it was alright and then we get to the RV and we do the approach march which was approximately about a mile and a half across the fields. And then when we got here we had three gliders coming in with twenty paras in each who had volunteered to go in, those gliders, to actually crash land in the battery when we put the attack in. That was at the same time that one party came up here to the main gate. They would attack from that position. Well we were to come through and blow the wire in four positions. 'C' Company was the attacking Company. Then once through those four positions we had to take a gun each and blow it. And everything we done just dovetailed, and it was beautiful. We were so confident that we could do it, he'd brain-washed us too much. So anyway, a couple of weeks later, three o'clock in the morning, lights go on in the barrack room. 'Right - get up, get your kit - OUT'. And when we walked out on the square there were all these transporters. Into the transporters, and I think we drove around for about 8 hours, changing drivers here and there, and the last thing we knew there was all these tanks, all the barbed wire round it. In we went, they shut the gate and said, 'You stay there'. And we'd had a big mosaic made of the battery itself, and we had to study that and an officer could stop you any time and say, 'Where is so-and-so in the battery?' And if you didn't know, mate, you were back in there and you were stuck in there an hour, and you had to explain everything to him. So everybody knew exactly what the other chap was doing and exactly what was in there, and it looked a perfect plan. But come the night, 5 June, we took off just after midnight and we dropped just before one. It was a beautiful flight across till we hit the coast, and we hit the coast and you've never seen anything like it in your life. It was just like going into a firework display and the old duck was going five ways at once andeverybody was saying, 'Let's get out of this so-and-so thing'. Anyway eventually the Pilot says, 'Go', and puts the light on, and on our way we go. And as I dropped, obviously you look round and I could see other 'chutes coming down and I hit the deck and out of my 'chute, got my sten out, everything going, look round - couldn't see anybody. But there was one thing that got implanted in my mind - we must get to that RV. And the Colonel's orders were 'You were to have no private fire fights. You get to the RV AND THAT IS IT'. And I checked around a bit. I found the road that runs in front of the rendezvous. I didn't know which way to go - right or left - but I heard a fire fight going on up to the left so I thought I'd go up to the right. And I just got along the side of the road looking, and away in the distance I could just see this red light twinkling. And it was one of the officers got up the tree with an Aldis lamp and was flicking this right round in circles to bring the lads in. As soon as I saw that I knew where I was to get. I could see the tree across the fields and I saw a bod just in front of where I knew the RV was and I yelled the password out and he yelled it back and I looked at him and it was the Colonel. He was standing there waiting to bring the lads in. He tapped me on the shoulder and he said, 'Well done, lad. What company?' 'C Company.' 'Down there.' I went down there and ... I dropped down beside my Lieutenant (Jackson) and had a little word with him, you know. At the time I thought, well there don't seem many of us here, but you know most of us thought that but we didn't say it. 'Cos there's 100 of us in the company. It didn't look 100, but you didn't say anything because you didn't want to upset anybody. Any rate we was sitting there and we knew the timetable, knew we ought to be moving now. We ought to be moving and eventually the Colonel said 'Move', and it wasn't until years afterwards I found out that out of the 550 who jumped in our battalion, only 150 got to the rendezvous."

Things went wrong again. One of the three gliders broke its tow rope just after take-off, the second landed several miles east of the battery and the last one, although it actually flew over the battery, crashed in an orchard about 100 yards away to the south-west having been hit by anti-aircraft fire. The third glider did, however, distract the attention of some German machine gunners who had been causing casualties from their position outside the defended perimeter as well as intercepting a German patrol that was moving up to reinforce the battery. Otway decided to get on with the job. Without engineer support or any mine-clearing equipment it was a case of charging both the wire and the minefield. The paratroopers went forward firing their sten guns from the hip, using the gaps in the wire and minefield caused by the bombing and blowing two more gaps using the Bangalore torpedoes. At the main gate a small party opened fire, hoping to cause a diversion. The Germans fought well, coming out of their bunkers to counter-attack. It was a short and bloody scrap in which Allen Parry was wounded. The cost to the battalion was heavy - seventy officers and men killed or wounded. The battalion was down to eighty. The German garrison was reduced to twenty-two prisoners, all the rest were killed or wounded. When the fighting had stopped Sergeant Eric Bedford turned to one of his soldiers and said, "Blimey, Sid, here, take a look around. This is the 9th Battalion, mate. Looks more like the 9th Platoon to me." Bedford also laid claim to a 'first' - the first German flag captured in the invasion which he had found in Casemate 1. He stuffed it up his smock.

When the casemates were examined the guns were found to be old French 75mm weapons on wheels. The anticipated heavy weapons had not been installed. Nevertheless the guns were put out of action and the victory signal was made both by pigeon and by smoke flares just thirty minutes before 0530 hours when the *Arethusa* was due to begin her bombardment. The 9th Parachute Battalion had not finished its task, however. Now they had to head for the high ground around Amfréville. Otway led his men off and later in the day a combat group of the German 736th Grenadier Regiment regained Merville only to lose it the following day to an assault by two troops of No 3 Commando. Once again it was a fierce battle in the casemates and in the tunnels that linked the different bunkers, but the Germans were overcome. Almost immediately the enemy counter-attacked using self-propelled guns and drove the commandos out and back to Le Plain.

9th Parachute Battalion never collected all of its men. The initial drop which was supposed to have been contained within an area of 11/2 square miles was spread over 50 square miles. There were a number of reasons for this: the aircrews carrying out the drop were inexperienced, having only been formed into a Group (No 46) in January 1944: the leading aircraft of each formation did the navigating and signalled to the others when to drop so that single aircraft, when disorientated by trying to avoid flak on the way over, led groups of others to the wrong place, while others confused the Rivers Dives and Orne. Hundreds of men were dropped into the flooded areas of the Dives and many were drowned.

The main bunker contains the **Museum**, established on 6 June 1982, mostly due to the energy and enthusiasm of Gen Sir Nigel Poett, who commanded 5th Para Bde on D-Day. By the entrance is a **Plaque to No 3 Commando**. The museum contains a superb diorama with sound. At the back of it are toilets. On top of the bunker behind are three coloured plans of The Drop, The Assault and The Landing. As other bunkers are excavated, Information Boards in two languages and plans are attached to each.

Return to the T junction and turn right continuing in the original direction of travel to Descanneville. There turn right on to the D223 signed Bréville. Some 500 yards later turn left on the Chemin des Banques and continue to Carrefour du 9ième Bataillon.

• Memorial to 9th Para Bn Forming-up Area, Gonneville/14 miles/5 minutes/Map It6-13/Lat & Long: 49.26408 -0.18753

The red marble **Plaque** with faded gold lettering describes how on the night of 6 June 1944 the 9th Para Bn, reduced to 150 men and deprived of most of its weapons and equipment, but united behind its CO, Lt Col Otway, departed to assault and capture the Merville Battery.

Return to the D223, continue to the crossroads with the D37b in Bréville and stop before the crossroads and the Memorial on the right-hand corner opposite the Mairie.

Memorial to 9th Para Bn forming-up area, Gonneville.

• 12th Parachute/12th Devonshire Regiment Memorials, Bréville/
16.7 miles/5 minutes/Map It6-14/Lat & Long: 49.24045 -0.22597

To best understand the importance of Bréville and its high ground, the traveller is advised to consult Battle Map 10 and to ascertain the general direction of Amfréville/Le Plain/Hoger and the Château of St Côme.

During one of his inspection tours, Rommel had visited Bréville, planning his defence of the high ground from a viewpoint at the crossroads where you now are. That defence was formidable and, despite the best efforts of the commandos, paratroopers and 51st Highland Division, the Germans held on, giving ground reluctantly and at great cost to themselves and their attackers. Even by the start of Operation GOODWOOD on 18 July, some six weeks after D-Day, the British front line extended no further south than Bréville and GOODWOOD itself moved the line forward only to the southern edge of the Bois de Bavent, which is passed later on this tour.

The capture of the high ground on which Bréville and the other villages such as Le Plain, Hoger and Amfréville sit, was one of the tasks set for the 6th Airborne Division and General Gale allocated it to Brigadier James Hill's 3rd Parachute Brigade. The ground, and the bridges across the Orne which it overlooked, controlled German routes into the landing bridgehead from the east. It was vital, therefore, that it was quickly captured and then held.

On D-Day, after completing their primary tasks, the 9th Parachute Battalion (whose first task was to destroy the Merville Battery) and the 1st Canadian Parachute Battalion (whose first task was to destroy bridges over the River Dives) headed for the high ground. (See Map 10.) 9th Battalion got to Hoger, which you passed earlier, and the 1st Battalion reached le Mesnil, which you pass later. Meanwhile No 4 Commando dug in at Hoger and No 6 established themselves between Le Plain and Bréville. The Germans held Bréville. It was a patchy situation. The German defence was cellular, strong here and weak there, and this, combined with the independent nature of the specialist commando and airborne forces moving against them, produced a confused and irregular battlefield with opposing forces jumbled together.

The German formations in this area were the 346th and 711th Infantry Divisions and for three days after D-Day they mounted heavy counter-attacks against the lightly equipped airborne forces on the high ground. General Gale knew that his forces were tiring, and although the 1st

the **soldiers of all nationalities** who gave their lives in Sannerville in 6 June – 7 August 1944', in English, French and German

N.B. By continuing on the small road towards le Maizeret for .75 mile, you will come to a **RM Cdo Memorial** to Nos 41, 46, 47 and 48 (Map It6-J, Lat & Long: 49.18991 -0.20668, GPPIt6-1/3) erected on 8 June 1991.

Return to the D226 and continue straight over past the junction with the D227 to Cuverville. Turn left in the village at the main crossroads. Stop near the Mairie by the petrol station on the right in Place du 13 juin.

• Memorial to Middlesex Regiment, Cuverville/26.7 miles/5 minutes/Map It6-22/Lat & Long: 49.19200 -0.26359

The **Memorial**, which bears the Regimental crest, commemorates those who liberated Cuverville on 18 July 1944. It was inaugurated on the 50th Anniversary. The bodies of two of the Middlesex soldiers were brought to the town after the battle, Sgt HWS Luxton and Pte M. Philbin, and a Meeting Room has been named after them. The ashes of Sgt Luxton's widow were interred in his grave at Ranville Cemetery (qv) in 2007.

Continue on the D228 through Démouville to the junction with the N175. Turn left and continue to the CWGC Cemetery on the right.

• Banneville-la-Campagne CWGC Cemetery/29.8 miles/15 minutes/Map It6-23/Lat & Long: 49.176360 -0.229823

The cemetery, designed by Philip Hepworth, contains 2,175 burials - 2,150 British, 11 Canadian, 5 Australian, 2 New Zealand, 5 Polish and 2 unidentified graves. They are mostly from the fighting of mid July-end August 1944 when Caen was captured and the Falaise Gap was closed. Here, in Plot III, Row F, Grave 22, is buried the artist **Lt Rex Whistler,** age 39, Welsh Guards, 18 July 1944. Whistler was educated at the Slade School of Art and excelled in murals (e.g. restaurant of Tate Gallery), book illustrations and theatre designs. Taking a commission in the Welsh Guards Armoured Division at the outbreak of war he continued to work as a professional artist through his four years of service. He was killed by a mortar shell on his first day in action.

*Continue on the N175 (passing at the crossroads on the left the **Bar-Restaurant-Brasserie L'Epéron**. Tel: (0)2 31 23 32 10. Open every day) direction Troarn, going under the motorway. Continue to and cross straight over the roundabout.*

N.B. Immediately on the right is **Troarn Communal Cemetery** in which are the graves of **Pte H.W. Carter**, age 23, **Sgt John Davies**, age 22 and **Sgt John Iliffe**, age 26, all of AAC Para Regt, 6 June 1944.

In Troarn continue to the Syndicat d'Initiative on the right. Park in the square (named after Resistance hero Paul Quellec) behind the office.

• 3rd Parachute Squadron RE Memorial, Troarn/32.1 miles/5 minutes/RWC/Map It6-24/Lat & Long: 49.18206 -0.18244

On the wall of the **Tourist Office,** Tel: (0)2 31 39 14 22, is a **Plaque** erected by the population of Troarn in honour of the officers and men of **3rd Parachute Squadron RE** who, at dawn on 6 June 1944, on information obtained from the Resistance, destroyed the bridges over the Dives in order to protect the left flank of the landings.

At the far corner of the square by the *Mairie* is the Logis de France **Hotel-Restaurant Le Clos Normand**. 19 rooms. Open all year. Restaurant closed Sun evenings in winter. Tel: + (0)2 31 23 31 28. E-mail: leclosnormand@wanadoo.fr

Return to the N175. Continue downhill some 50 yards to the junction with the D78 on the right.

Memorial to 8th Para Bn, le Manoir du Bois.

Memorial to Brigadier Alastair Pearson, le Manoir du Bois.

Memorial to Arthur Platt & Thomas Billington, Touffréville.

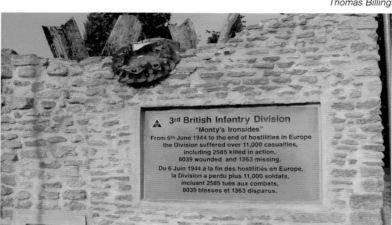

Memorial to 3rd Inf Div, Sannerville.

3rd British Infantry Division
"Monty's Ironsides"
From 6th June 1944 to the end of hostilities in Europe
the Division suffered over 11,000 casualties,
including 2585 killed in action,
8039 wounded and 1363 missing.
Du 6 Juin 1944 à la fin des hostilitiés en Europe,
la Division a perdu plus 11,000 soldats,
incluant 2585 tués aux combats,
8039 blessés et 1363 disparus.

Plaque to all nationalities killed 6 June-7 August 1944 in Sannerville.

En hommage aux soldats
de toutes nationalités qui ont péri
du 6 juin au 17 août 1944
dans cette partie de la Normandie

In homage to the soldiers
of all nationalities who prished
from 6 th of june to 17 th of august 1944
in this part of Normandie

Zum gedenken an die Soldaten
aller Nationalitäten
die vom 6.Juni bis zum 17.august 1944
in diesem Teil der Normandie gefallen sind

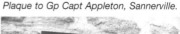

Plaque to Gp Capt Appleton, Sannerville.

A LA MÉMOIRE DU GROUPE CAPT
CHARLES APPLETON
CBE, DSO, DFC, CDG
COMMANDING OFFICIER
124 WING ROYAL AIR FORCE

ABATTU LE 12 AOÛT 1944,
A 38 ANS
AU MESNIL-GUÉRARD FRANCE
TYPHOON PILOT

Architect Philip Hepworth's serpentine path, Banneville-la-Campagne CWGC Cemetery.

Headstone of Lt Rex Whistler, Banneville-la-Campagne CWGC Cemetery.

Plaque to 3rd Para Sqn, RE, Troarn.

Memorial to The Middlesex Regt, Cuverville.

Extra Visit to the Memorial to the Massacre, St Pierre du Jonquet (Map It6-F, Lat & Long: 49.16900 -0.12424, GPPIt6-1/6). Round trip: 7 miles. Approximate time: 20 minutes.

Turn right on the D78 to St Pierre du Jonquet. Stop at the memorial at the crossroads with the D80.

The dramatic **Memorial** of figures tied to an execution post is to the memory of twenty-eight civilians shot for hiding British paratroops. It was unveiled on 15 November 1957. The bodies of 11 Unknown victims of the massacre are buried by the belfry in the nearby churchyard.

Return to the N175 and pick up the main itinerary.

Continue downhill to the bridge over the Dives at St Sampson.

• Major J.C.A. Roseveare Bridge Memorial, River Dives/32.9 miles/5 minutes/Map It6-25/Lat & Long: 49.18425 -0.16453

In the early hours of 6 June Major Roseveare, coming from the Manoir du Bois, drove down the D37 to the N875 junction in his jeep. At that time the D37 crossed a railway line before the town and the jeep ran into a barbed-wire knife rest guarding the crossing. The guard fired one shot at it and disappeared but it took twenty minutes to get free. At the N175 junction Roseveare's party met and shot a German soldier who roused the town. "We made the mistake of silencing him with a Sten instead of with a knife", said Roseveare. All the party then jumped into the jeep and trailer and Roseveare drove as fast as he could through the town. At about where the tourist office now is, in Major Roseveare's words, "The fun started, as there seemed to be a Boche in every doorway shooting like mad. However, the boys got to work with their Stens and Sapper Peachey did good work as rear gunner with the Bren. What saved the day was the steep hill down the main street. As the speed rose rapidly and we careered from side to side of the road, as the heavy trailer was swinging violently, we were chased out of the town by an MG 34 which fired tracer just over our heads."

When they got to the bridge at the bottom of the hill it was found to be unguarded but they discovered that they had lost their Bren gunner. Five minutes later they had blown a 20ft gap in the masonry structure. It was not yet 0500 hours. Roseveare ditched the jeep north of Troarn and the party navigated their way on foot to le Mesnil which they reached at 1300 hours. The bridge is now named the **Major J.C.A. Roseveare Bridge and the Memorial** was erected by the Commune on 5 June 1986 to commemorate the bridge crossing at dawn on 6 June 1944.

Return to Troarn and just before the Place Paul Quellec turn right and take the D95 direction Bure- sur-Dives. Turn right into Bures along rue du Capitaine Juckes, fork right at the village war memorial and continue downhill along rue du Port to the bridge over the River Dives.

• Captain Juckes Bridge Memorial, Bures/35.3 miles/10 minutes/ Map It6-26/Lat & Long: 49.20070 -0.16856

The **Memorial** commemorates the destruction of this bridge and the railway bridge to the north, by 2nd Troop, **3rd Parachute Squadron, RE** commanded by **Capt T. R. Juckes MC**. Juckes and his men arrived unopposed at the bridges at around 0630 hours and both were blown by 0930 after which they settled down for a well-earned breakfast. Sadly Capt Juckes was injured later in the campaign and died of wounds on 28 June 1944. He is buried in Ranville CWGC.

Return to the D95 and continue under the motorway direction Bavent. Continue to a left turn onto the D236 and in Bavent turn right to the church.

N.B. In the churchyard is the **Grave of Lieutenant David Haig-Thomas** of No 4 Commando, 'naturalist and explorer', who was killed on 6 June 1944.

Turn left opposite the church on the rue des Champs to large wooden gates on the left to the local cemetery extension. Stop. Walk into the top left-hand corner of the cemetery.

• Grave of Brigadier Mills-Roberts CBE, DSO & Bar, MC, Légion d'Honneur, Croix de Guerre, Bavent Churchyard/38.5 miles/10 minutes/Map It6-27/Lat & Long: 49.23228 -0.18342

The ashes of the Irish Guards commander of No 1 Commando Brigade who liberated Bavent on 17 August 1944 were interred here after his death on 1 October 1980. There is a seat nearby from Mrs Jill Mills-Roberts.

*Return to the T junction and turn right. Continue past the church and stop at the pond on the right, Place **Alexandre Lofi**, French Officer of No 4 Commando.*

Lofi, an instructor at Brest Naval College, escaped to England in 1940 and joined the Free French Forces. He fought with 4 Commando at the Casino at Ouistreham and later in Holland. After the war he had several senior naval appointments and died in 1992.

• 1st Special Service Brigade Memorial, Bavent/38.9 miles/5 minutes/Map It6-28/Lat & Long: 49.23004 -0.18975

The 40th Anniversary tribute board tells the story of the 'Liberators of Bavent and Robehomme' from their landing at Colleville to 17 August 1944.

Continue some 50 yards to the junction with the D236. Turn right and continue through the village to the crossroads with the D513 and turn right. Continue to Varaville and stop at the entrance to the village at the memorial on the right.

• 9th Para Bn & 1st Can Para Bn Memorial, Varaville/41.4 miles/5 minutes/Map It6-29/Lat & Long: 49.25164 -0.16237

The grey marble **Memorial** to **Col Otway's 9th Para Bn** and to **1st Canadian Parachute Battalion** was erected on the 50th Anniversary. At the bottom is a bronze plaque presented to Varaville by Canadian 1st Para Veterans and unveiled in June 1997. The town was taken by the Canadians following a fierce struggle on D-Day after the Germans, entrenched in the château, surrendered.

Nearby is the **Auberge de Varaville**, 1 Av de la Libération. Tel: + (0)2 31 91 25 07. E-mail: sarl.juliagui@hotmail.fr. Selection of menus. 3 rooms. Closed Sunday evening and Monday.

Continue downhill some 200 yards yards and turn right on the D27. Continue to the bridge over the Divette.

• Plaque to 3rd Parachute Squadron RE and 1st Canadian Parachute Battalion, Divette Bridge, Varaville/41.8 miles/10 minutes/Map It6-30/Lat & Long: 49.25415 -0.15472

The **Plaque** describes how the Sappers blew the original bridge over the Divette here at dawn on 6 June 1944.

Memorial to Maj Roseveare, Dives Bridge, Troarn.

Grave of Brigadier Mills-Roberts, Bavent churchyard.

Memorial to Captain Juckes, Bridge over the River Dives, Bures.

Plaque to 3rd Para Sqn RE & 1st Can Para Bn, Bridge over Divette, Varaville.

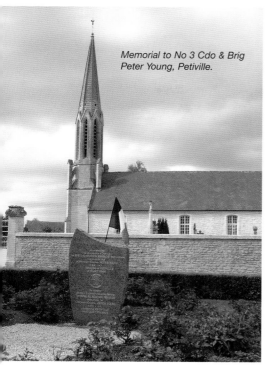
Memorial to No 3 Cdo & Brig Peter Young, Petiville.

Memorial to 9th Para Bn & 1st Can Para Bn, Varaville.

Memorial to 1st Special Service Bde, Bavent.

Plaque to 1st Special Service Bde, le Plain Gruchet.

Extra Visit to Grangues Crash/Massacre Memorial. (Map It6-G, Lat & Long: 49.26559 -0.05691, GPPIt6-1/10) Round trip: 9.5 miles. Approximate time: 35 minutes.

Continue on the D27 through Periers-en-Auge. Turn left on the D45B signed Grangues and continue (for what seems an awfully long time) along the narrow road to the church on the left.

Grangues Massacre Memorial

Beside the church is a large open parking area and just inside the churchyard on the right is a flat Memorial stone. Its caption is headed, 'In Memoriam 6 June 1944' followed by a list of 52 casualties. It summarises how two Stirling parachute transport aircraft (Nos EJ 116 and EF 295 of 620 Squadron RAF) were shot down close to Grangues Château near this site. The Stirlings had taken off from Fairford at about 2340 hours on 5 June. EJ 116 carried 14 men of 7th Para Battalion and 5 men from 6th Airborne Reconnaissance Regiment. The Paras were to secure the area around the River Orne and the Caen Canal bridges. The Recce Regt was to find and secure a tank harbouring area. EF 295 was flown by the distinguished RCAF pilot, Sqn Leader W.R. Pettit, OBE, DFC. It carried 15 men of 591 Para Sqn RE, including Major Andy Wood, the Squadron Commander, and 2 members of an advance party from HQRE, the Intelligence Officer, J.S. Shinner and Sapper Peter Guard. The 591 Squadron men had to clear the glider landing strips on the DZ of the obstruction poles and the Sappers were carrying bicycle inner tubes filled with plastic explosives for this task. The Stirlings made the wrong landfall and EJ 116 was hit and crashed in a field about 400 metres from the Château. All 6 aircrew and 19 parachutists were killed, the wreckage burning fiercely for a day because of the explosives it carried, during which time no-one dared approach it for fear of further explosions. EF 295 was approaching the coast and her parachutists had received the instruction 'Running in' when one of the explosive sausages she was carrying was hit by tracer and there was a blinding flash inside the cabin. Her engines were also hit. Four men, including Major Wood, were able to jump. He landed in the field next to the 4-gun Light AA battery at Gonneville-sur-Mer that had hit his plane and spent the next 20 hours in hiding. As the plane crash-landed and ploughed on for more than 100 metres, the 4 Aircrew at the nose and 4 parachutists were killed, most of the other occupants were badly injured.

The plane ground to a halt about 500 metres from the Château, which was occupied by the Germans, who were soon on the scene and rounded up the survivors. They were taken to a stable block and some primitive first aid was permitted for the injured. A wounded survivor, J.S. Stirling, describes how he was - perfectly correctly - interrogated and told he would be attended by a British RAMC Officer. Meanwhile the gliders were due to arrive from 0320 hours and two Horsas crashed in the grounds of the Château. One carried a party from 6th Airborne Division HQ, including Captain John Max (GSO 3) and five divisional HQ signals specialists. Captain Max and the co-pilot were killed in the crash, the remainder, including the pilot, Staff Sergeant D. Wright, were taken prisoner. The second Horsa came down vertically onto trees and all its occupants were killed. They included 3 men from division HQ and a Forward Observation party, consisting of an RA Officer and two RN telegraphists, who had been due to direct the fire of a cruiser offshore. A third Horsa landed with little damage in a field just to the north but the occupants have never been identified.

All French civilians in the vicinity had been confined to quarters so they could not witness what happened next. But from the evidence of a Red Cross worker in the Château, Mlle Thérèse Anne, it is clear that Staff Sergeant Wright and 7 of the Sapper survivors of EF 295 were shot. She was told there had been an attempted break-out and was shown the spot where the men were killed. The men were buried in a trench and were finally identified by a British medical team in 1945.

In all, 44 soldiers, sailors and airmen died or were mortally wounded and 8 survivors were shot. "These young men were all volunteers whose belief in the cause of freedom was such that they were prepared to give their lives in this dangerous mission. Let this peaceful place preserve a lasting memory of their names" are the very moving final words of the inscription. Grangues, a tiny, idyllic village with its XIIIth Century Church, is indeed a beautiful site for the memorial to this tragedy of war. The victims of the crashes and the massacre are buried in Ranville CWGC Cemetery. That they were able to be buried together was due to the fact that the owners of the Château had an Irish nanny who was so upset by what had happened that she went out and, using a wheelbarrow, collected all the bodies.

The Memorial was dedicated in June 1994 in the presence of about 400 people, including several relatives of those who died, who had not known until recently what happened to their men. The funds for it were raised by veterans of the units and next of kin involved in the incident.

Return to the bridge over the Divette.

Return to the 1st Can Para Memorial at the entrance to the village and turn left on the D95 to Petiville. Stop by the Mairie and church on the right.

• No 3 Commando & Brigadier Peter Young Memorial, Petiville/ 43.4 miles/10 minutes /Map It6-31/Lat & Long: 49.24173 -0.17531

The pink marble **Memorial** was inaugurated on the 50th Anniversary by a delegation of Commandos and veterans. It honours **No 3 Commando and Brigadier Peter Young** who liberated the town on 17 August. In the *Mairie* are a photograph of the Brigadier and a Commando dagger that were presented that day.

Continue, turning left on the D95 signed Bures and Troarn, bearing left at the fork on the D224 to Robehomme.

Continue to the junction with the rue des Sources on the left.

N.B. At this point by taking the rue des Sources on the D224, and following this some half a mile to Bricqueville/Robehomme, a **Plaque to 1st Can Para Bn** may be seen on the wall of house No 3, rue de l'Eglise behind the church and the local war memorial. There is also a **seat to 3rd Para Bde/1st Can Para Bde.** (Map It6-H, Lat & Long: 49.23090 -0.15409, GPPIt6-1/11).

Continue to the bridge over the River Dives.

• Plaque to Sappers of 3rd Parachute Squadron RE and 1st Canadian Para Battalion, Bailey Bridge over Dives, Robehomme/ 46.3 miles/10 minutes/Map It6-32/Lat & Long: 49.22581 -0.14116

The original Bailey Bridge, erected by the Sappers after they blew the original bridge at dawn on 6 June 1944, can still clearly be seen, painted green. The **Plaque** is on the small brick wall at the entrance to the bridge.

Continue to the crossroads with the D224A.

N.B. At this point the **Memorial to 9th Bn Para Regt** (Map It6-I/, Lat & Long: 49.21316 -0.13824, GPPIt6-1/8) may be reached by turning right and continuing for one mile on the D224A to just before the motorway bridge. It describes how on the evening of 17 August 1944 the Bn passed through Bassenville and cleared the enemy from Goustranville. The following night they attacked the railway station at Putot-en-Auge (qv).

Continue to the road junction in le Plain Gruchet.

• Memorial to 1st Special Service Bde, le Plain Gruchet/47.4 miles/5 minutes/Map It6-33/Lat & Long: 49.22473 -0.11865

The **Plaque** is on a white marker and commemorates a Brigade attack of 19 August by a force under Brig Mills-Roberts (qv) that included Nos 3, 4 and 6 Cdo, 45 RM Cdo and 1st Bn Commandant Keiffer's French Commandos. The force assembled here to infiltrate enemy lines through the night by an old railway track to attack the Auge hills between roads N175 and the D27.

N.B. There is another Brigade Memorial just to the east of Dozulé on the N175 (**Lat & Long**: 49.23272 - 0.04016.

• END OF ITINERARY SIX

ALLIED & GERMAN WARGRAVES & COMMEMORATIVE ASSOCIATIONS

The American Battle Monuments Commission

The Commission was established by the United States Congress in March 1923 for the permanent maintenance of military cemeteries and memorials on foreign soil. Their first task was to build cemeteries for the American dead of World War I.

After World War II, fourteen overseas military cemeteries were constructed, including the St Laurent Normandy Cemetery. They contain approximately 39 per cent of those originally buried in the region, the remaining 61 per cent were returned to the USA.

The ground on which each cemetery is built was granted by the host nation, free of rent or taxes. A white marble headstone marks every burial (Star of David for the Jewish, Latin cross for all others, whether they be Christian, Buddhist, agnostic or of any other belief). Memorials bearing the names of the missing, a non-denominational chapel and a visitors' room containing the register and visitors' book are standard in all cemeteries. All are open to the public daily.

The cemeteries are immaculately maintained by a superintendent (normally American) using local gardeners. He will supply photographs of the cemetery and the individual headstone for the next of kin and arrange for cut flowers to be bought locally and placed on the grave.

The Commission now maintains 26 permanent American burial grounds on foreign soil, in which there are 124,913 U.S. War Dead: 30,921 of WWI, 93,238 of WWII and 750 of the Mexican War. There are 25 separate memorials (3 of which are in the USA).

The first Chairman, in 1923, was Gen John J. Pershing and in 2018 Pres. Trump appointed David John Urban.

For full details of the Normandy American Cemetery and Memorial, the Commission's most-visited cemetery, see Itinerary Two above. Other Americans who died in Normandy are buried in Saint James south of Avranches on the N798 to Fougères. Called 'The Brittany Cemetery', it contains 4,410 burials and the names of 498 missing.

The Battle Monuments Commission offices are at:

UNITED STATES: Courthouse Plaza 11, Suite 500, 2300 Clarendon Boulevard, Arlington VA 22201. Tel: + 703 69666900.

FRANCE: 68 rue 19 janvier, 92 Garches, France. Tel: + (0)1 47 01 19 76

Their website home page is www.abmc.gov. Their Roll of Honour website is www.abmc.gov/searchww.htm and one may now search for the names of casualties buried in American Cemeteries at the Visitor Centre at the Normandy American Cemetery.

Canadian Cemeteries

The Canadian cemeteries at Bény-sur-Mer and Bretteville-sur-Laize are maintained by the CWGC and are described below. Although primarily Canadian they both include some British and other nationalities. Canadians are also buried in Bayeux (181), Ryes (21), Tilly (1), Hottot (34), Fontenay (4), St. Manvieu (3), Brouay (2), La Délivrande (11), Hermanville (13), Ranville (76), Banneville (11), St Charles de Percy (3), and St Désir de Lisieux (16).

B-15 Ryes
B-16 Villons-les-Buissons (Lat & Long: 49.23694 -0.41154 Map **It4/4**)
B-17 Carpiquet [existing Carpiquet Airfield Map **It4/C**]
B-18 Cristot
B-19 Lingèvres B-20 Demouville – not used
B-21 Ste Honorine-de-Ducy
B-22 Authie

Cheux. Plaque to Wing Commander Baker (D70)

Esquay-sur-Seulles. Memorial to 20 Airfields - 438, 439, 440 Squadrons RCAF (Lat & Long: 49.25436 -0.62475 **Map It3/D**)

Noyers Bocage. Typhoon Memorial (designed by M Triboulet, cost over £55,000), Plaques to 151 Pilots. (D875).

Monsieur Bréhin also researched the crash site of Pilot Officer Donald William Mason, Royal Australian Air Force, died 18 June 1944, and in March 1993 his body was re-interred at St Charles de Percy. The intact engine of his plane is in the museum at Tilly-sur-Seulles. In 2001 a plaque was erected to Flight Lieutenant Roy Crane (Honorary President of the Association, succeeding Monsieur Triboulet) in Mesnil-Hubert-sur-Orne (D25) where his plane was brought down in 1944 and dug up in 1991. During WW2 666 typhoon pilots were killed, average age 23. The dedicated Association continues to locate crash sites and make contact with pilots' relatives from the UK, Canada, Australia and New Zealand. Plaques and memorials are then erected in their memory. In June 2008 for example Monuments were inaugurated in Cheux to Wing Cdr Reg Baker, kia 16 June 1944 and in Mouen to Flt Sgt George Howard, kia 6 June 1944. See the website: www.asavn.net President's e-mail:president@asavn.net M Jacques Bréhin was awarded the Australian Medal in 2007 for his work.

AMERICAN WAR MEMORIALS OVERSEAS INC
Non-profit organisation whose mission is to document, raise awareness of and care for, private American gravesites and memorials where the US Government has no responsibility, liaising with local, national and international organisations.

Contact: Lil Pfluke. 6 rue du Commandant de Larienty 92210, St Cloud. Tel: (0)6 1173 1332 E-mail: info@uswarmemorials.org Website: www.uswarmemorials.org

MEMOIRE, LIBERTE, CITOYENNETE (MLC) FOUNDATION
Ancien Combattant Yves Hue, with connections with many Veterans' Associations, started an Association based in the *Mairie* of Bayeux whose main goals are to perpetuate memory, encourage respect and civic virtues and to preserve a fragile peace. As part of the Normandy 60th Anniversary programme, the Association actively encouraged the participation of young people in planting Sequoia trees, the symbol of the Anniversary commemorations, together with small 0.80m high white Memorials with a Plaque bearing the logo of the Association. Conceived with the help of teachers and pupils of the Laplace Lycée at Caen, it shows an Arc de Triomphe with the eternal flame burning and above it the statue of Liberty. What about the British and Canadians, one might ask?

Some 60 Memorials have been placed in Calvados, La Manche, the Orne and the Eure.

Contact: M Yves Hue, 4 rue de la Vergée, 14740 St Manvieu Norrey. Tel: (0)2 31 80 70 38. E-mail YvesHue@wanadoo.fr

ASSOCIATION WESTLAKE BROTHERS
Dedicated to the three Canadian Westlake brothers (qv) buried in Bény CWGC Canadian Cemetery, this organisation for young people of 8-22 is inspired by the Jewish Nobel Peace Prize winner and Auschwitz survivor, Elie Wiesel and dedicated to the Cause of Duty of Memory. Wiesel said, 'No justice is possible for the dead... but if we do not practise the Duty of Memory

they will die a second time". They lay flowers and wreaths on Canadian graves, take part in commemorative marches and many other acts of commemoration/
Contact: http://westlakebrothers.free.fr

GUILD OF BATTLEFIELD GUIDES

When we began our battlefield touring company over 40 years ago and then wrote our first guide books we were the only people running such tours. Since then battlefield touring has proliferated, with a wide variation in the quality of guiding. In 2002 Maj Graeme Cooper, a devotee and battlefield guide of the Napoleonic period, determined that a 'kite standard' should be created validating the capabilities of those who offered their services as guides. The Guild was duly launched on 28 November 2003 with Prof Richard Holmes as its Patron and the authors as Honorary Members. Sadly Richard died in May 2011. The current Patron is Lord Faulkner of Worcester. Its aim is to analyse, develop and raise the understanding and practice of Battlefield Guiding. It has since gone from strength to strength and the badge awarded to successful validation applicants is a mark of excellence and quality. The Guild has a magazine, *Despatches*, and regular events, the highlight being the Annual Dinner Weekend.

The coveted and respected Badge of an accredited Guide of the Guild of Battlefield Guides.

Contact: Guild Secretary: Email: secretary@gbg-international.com Website: www.gbg-international.com Tel: 07580 210440.

RELATED INTERNET SITES

There is an increasing number of sites about the Second World War. A search for the word 'D-Day' will bring up a large number of sites devoted to the Normandy Campaign. The most impressive is www.normandie44lamemorie.com For details of 75th Anniversary events see www.normandie-tourisme.fr. www.normandie44lamemoire.com

TOURIST INFORMATION

[For more Tourist Information, in particular how to get to Normandy via a Channel crossing and French motoring regulations, see the Approach Routes at the beginning of the book.]

N.B: CHANGING INFORMATION

Tourism is a transient industry! The reader must be aware that all tourist information is subject to frequent change.

Road numbers change as improvements are made, some roads morphing alarmingly from beginning to end so that one may start on an 'A' road and finish on a 'C'. Hotels and restaurants change management and sometimes standards, or simply close down. Museums change their opening times, admission prices, exhibits, or they, too, simply close down. Sometimes they do not open according to their advertised opening times. Therefore the visitor must take any tourist information given here as a guide and appreciate that it is as correct as possible at the time of going to press. Phone numbers are given where available so that visitors can phone ahead to confirm details.

It would not be appropriate in this book, which is first and foremost a guide to the D-Day Landing Beaches, to include a comprehensive account of the Province's rich history and culture. However, as the visitor will pass through areas redolent of its eventful past and productive present, he or she deserves at least a brief background to Normandy's culture, the better to enjoy the tour. It is also an area of outstanding natural beauty and delicious food - neither of which should be neglected.

NORMAN ARCHITECTURE

The routes one must follow to visit the Landing Beaches and Dropping Zones of the D-Day Invasion take the visitor past some outstanding examples of ecclesiastical, agricultural and manorial architecture.

The predominating style (many superb examples of which, thankfully, survived the fearful battering of the invasion) is known as *Romanesque*. The Normans created their own brand of Romanesque, which in Britain is known as Norman, and which can still be seen in many churches in Southern England.

It was a harmonious, geometric style, with zigzag decoration, square towers and narrow windows, which retained the rounded Roman arch. William the Bastard's Abbeys at Caen (L'Abbaye aux Hommes and L'Abbaye aux Dames) are High Romanesque, but the style was modified when, as 'The Conqueror', he carried it over the Channel to England.

On a simpler scale, the churches in many rural and littoral villages are fine examples of the style, e.g. at Secqueville-en-Bessin and Ouistreham. The distinctive, tall, wedge-shaped, tiled roof surmounting a square tower can be seen on old farmhouses and churches, throughout the Bessin. With their courtyards enclosed by high walls and turrets, the farms, still in daily use, seem like living pages from history books.

The restraint of the *Romanesque/Normand* period gave way to the exuberant, ornate Gothic era. Again, the Normans had their own version - *Gothique Normand*. The most glorious example in Calvados is the cathedral at Bayeux, but more modest churches are to be found at Bernières, Langrune and in many smaller towns.

The Renaissance left its architectural mark, principally on the church of St Pierre in Caen, with interesting examples of statuary and furniture scattered throughout the surrounding district.

Of the scores of picturesque châteaux in the areas covered by the Landing Beaches (most of which were used as German, then Allied, command posts) that of Fontaine-Henry, with its beautiful Renaissance wing and high, pointed slate roofs, is probably the most architecturally interesting. The local villagers sheltered in its cellars during the bombardments covering the invasion. Creullet Château, where General Montgomery pitched his caravan, is not open to the public, but is perfectly visible through the ironwork gates, and it is very close to Creully, whose sprawling, multi-period château was used by Allied broadcasters after the invasion. Their broadcasting tower can be visited by appointment with the town council, whose offices it now houses.

The beautiful creamy-coloured Normandy stone, quarried from the Caen area, and which was exported by the Normans to build their new castles and churches in England (notably Canterbury Cathedral and the Tower of London) is the building material used for many Norman towns and villages, even today. Some of the delightful villages bear a strong resemblance to Cotswold villages.

The most characteristic Normandy style, however, is the half-timbered, lath and plaster facade, akin to the English 'Elizabethan style'. It is much reproduced in modern pseudo-Norman buildings. It is the image that the visitor will most likely retain from his or her visit to Normandy.

The philosophical Normans approached the destruction of their buildings (an estimated 200,000 were damaged) in a practical way during the reconstruction. Many towns, in particular the devastated city of Caen, were rebuilt with wider roads more fitting to today's modern transport, better housing and office buildings and pleasant parks. Modern architects were able to leave their mark, too, on this ancient countryside. The new university building at Caen is considered an important example of modern style.

A building of note in the area is the impressive new *Mémorial* Museum at Caen. It was designed by architects Jacques Millet and Philippe Kauffmann, with artistic designer Yves Devraine, and was inaugurated on 6 June 1988 by President Mittérand.

GEOGRAPHY AND ECONOMY

The old province of Normandy is divided into administrative *Départements*, two of which include the sites of the June 1944 Landings:

CALVADOS (bordered by the River Vire to the south, the Eure to the east and by the *Département* of La Manche to the west). Its capital is Caen. It includes the area of the British action at Merville, the airborne landings near Ranville, GOLD, JUNO and SWORD Beaches, OMAHA Beach and Pointe du Hoc.

Calvados got its name in the 1790s, when the old provinces were divided into *Départements*. Resisting the description *Orne Inférieure*, the inhabitants preferred the suggestion of a Bayeux lady, who proposed that they should be named after the rocks lying off Arromanches - les Rochers du Calvados. They in turn had been named after one of Philip II of Spain's Armada ships, the *San Salvador*, which was wrecked on them.

Départements are further divided into *pays*, from the Gallo-Roman *pagi*. Those that concern our itineraries are:

Plaine de Caen. A rich agricultural plateau that grows sugar beet and grain, famous for its stone. Caen is now the eighth busiest port in France.

The Bessin. Bayeux (city of the Bacojasses) is its main town, Port-en-Bessin (where the British and American sectors met in June 1944) and Grandcamp are its main ports. Arromanches, on the tiny River Arro, is its most important resort, due now mainly to the remnants of its Mulberry Harbour and its museum. The ruggedly beautiful Pointe du Hoc, where the US Rangers landed, is its most picturesque site.

The Côte du Nâcre (The Mother of Pearl Coast). This runs from Ouistreham to Courseulles (SWORD and JUNO Beaches) with beautiful sandy beaches, where today it is difficult to imagine the terrible drama that was played out in June 1944. The small holiday resorts are very popular in the summer for their excellent seafood restaurants and water sports.

The bustling harbour, Port-en-Bessin.

LA MANCHE (bordered by Calvados to the east - between Carentan and Isigny - and to the north and east by the English Channel, which gives it its name.) The area which interests us mostly comprises the near-island of the Cotentin Peninsula.

La Manche includes UTAH Beach, Ste Mère Eglise and the US Airborne drop zones and Cherbourg, its main town and port. Cherbourg was provided with a hospital and a church by William the Conqueror and was often of importance during the 100 Years' War. Vauban recognised its potential as a large port but the main port was not opened until 1853, seeing its first transatlantic ship as late as 1869. It was taken by the Americans on 26 June 1944 and in late August its PLUTO (qv) was in operation. The taking of Cherbourg had been crucial to Montgomery's plan. Today it has an attractive pleasure port and is an important ferry terminal. The *Département* is famous for its thoroughbred racing and trotting horses.

'Piper Bill Millin' tee, OMAHA Golf Club.

GOURMET PRODUCTS AND SPECIALITIES

Both *Départements* share a climate similar to the south coast of England, although somewhat milder and sunnier. Their moistness contributes to their fertility and to the lush pastureland which feeds the cattle, which are the *Départements'* greatest asset. There are some six million head of cattle in Normandy, whose pedigree is proudly guarded. Dairy products include milk, cream and fabulous cheeses like Camembert, Petite Ste Mère Eglise, Livarot and Pont l'Evèque. The cream forms the basis of the rich *sauce normande*, served on seafood, chicken and pork chops.

The apple is also important in Normandy as it is the basis for its scrumptious cider (look for *cidre bouché* [mature bottled] or *cidre fermière* [home-brewed on the farm]). To drive through Normandy in apple blossom time is a visual delight. Calvados, distilled apple brandy, is the famous *trou normand*. This sharp liqueur is drunk in gulps between rich courses to clear the palate and then as a *digestif* finale to a good meal. Make sure your Calvados has been aged for 15 years, or it will take the skin off your throat - as many an Allied soldier found to his cost, sometimes fatally, in 1944. Other local specialities are: *Tripes à la Mode de Caen* (tripe cooked in the Caen style) which is an acquired taste, Courseulles oysters, Isigny mussels, butter and caramels.

Crêpes (pancakes) make a superb lunchtime snack. Savoury pancakes are called *galettes*, usually made with whole-wheat flour and come with a variety of delicious fillings: *Vallée d'Auge* (with cream and mushrooms), ham, cheese, onions, tomatoes, bacon etc. They are sold in Cr peries, often simple but attractive establishments. A *galette*, tossed green salad, crunchy *baguette* (long French loaf), Normandy cheese and a glass of *cidre bouché* make a perfect midday meal.

ATTRACTIONS OF THE AREA

Visitors to the Normandy Landing Beaches are coming to an area which is full of other attractions. There are safe, sandy beaches, casinos, tennis, horse-racing, fishing, sailing, wind-surfing, water-skiing, golf, horse-riding, delicious food and drink, fascinating history, culture, architecture from Romanesque to modern, handicrafts and beautiful, varied scenery - from the ever-changing coastline to the open wooded areas of the famous 'Bocage' (high hedges and ditches enclosing small fields, which were a great hazard to glider landings and tank progress in the battle for Normandy), the pretty villages, the colourful apple orchards. You may come to Normandy to study the D-Day Landings and fall in love with the country and its people.

BEFORE YOU COME

All these attractions add up to a very popular holiday area - not only with British and American battlefield visitors, but also with French holiday makers, especially from Paris, which is a short, easy journey away. It is, therefore, very important to book hotels or camping sites in advance during the busy summer season, which lasts from June to early September. These are the steps to take before travelling:

For French Tourist Information
Contact: https://about-france.com

Phoning to the UK from France: Dial 00 44, then drop the first 0 from your UK number

Phoning to Normandy from the UK: Dial 00 33 2 followed by the local number.

Phoning from one number to another in Normandy: Dial 02 followed by the local number.

Travelling by Road

French Driving Regulations/Motorway Tolls/Petrol – see Approaches 1 & 2

Travelling by Bicycle

Normandy, being relatively flat, is ideal for bicycle touring. There are now some organised cycle battlefield tours, e.g. www.crazyguyonabike.com. The site gives many details of preparations needed before undertaking such a tour and Americans **Beth and Ben Elderd**, experienced cyclists in Europe, offer the following advice lines: flying with your bike (www.crateworks.com) renting a bike (www.bikerentalsplus.com) clothes and panniers including spare parts www.thetouringstore.com documents and medical (www.iamat.org)

Lil Pfluke (herself a world champion cyclist and Founder of **American War Memorials Overseas** – www.uswarmemorials.org) organises interesting cycling tours. Tel: 0033 (0)6 1173 1332. website: fitnesstravelfrance.com

Bicycle hire info is available from all Tourist Offices. Gîtes, camping sites and *Logis de France* are the most bike friendly accommodations. It is vital to decide upon the type of bike that is needed and how you will keep it secure during the trip. A detailed packing list is also advised.

Travelling by Train

It is easily possible to visit Normandy by train.

Eurostar: London St Pancras/Ebbsfleet/Ashford-Paris Nord. Tel: 08432 186 186. www.eurostar.com
Paris St Nazaire – Caen/Bayeux. Tel: 08 36 35 35 35. www.voyages-sncf.com/-France

American, Canadian and other visitors flying into Paris are increasingly taking day trips to the Landing Beaches by taking the train to Caen or Bayeux. Once in Normandy many local Tour Operators will pick you up from the station.

Some Local Guided Tours of the Landing Beaches

Most major Museums offer tour guiding facilities

*The **Mémorial at Caen** arranges guided day tours and tours which include accommodation, plus a facility to meet and drop off at Caen or Bayeux railway stations. Tel: (0)2 31 06 06 45. On-line bookings at www.memorial-caen.fr

*Experienced bilingual guide Danielle Duboscq www.normandyours.com and son, Trevor Standefer, Tel: (0)6 30715577. Website: www.american-dday-tours.com E-mail: trevor.standefer@ gmail.com, a French-American who, as well as running in-depth tours of the American Sector, also caters for the British Sectors.

*D-DAY Academy (qv) '**1994 War Museum on Wheels' Tours** in authentic 1944 vehicles with expert guides. **Contact:** Dr J-P Benamou, Tel: (0)6 638 351 99. E-mail: JP.benamou44@gmail.com Website: www.ddaca.com

Tourist Offices

Known as *Offices de Tourisme or Syndicats d'Initiative,* they are to be found in all towns of any size. Follow **'i'** for information signs. Most of the useful tourist offices for Landing Beaches tours are noted as they are passed on the itineraries and are listed in a distinctive typeface. Important offices are:

Normandy Tourist Board: UK. For information on Normandy see their website www.normandy-tourism.org. Tel: 0117 986 0386. https://calvados-tourisme.co.uk/en/ E-mail: normandy@ european-marketing.co.uk

Calvados Departmental Office: 8 rue Renoir 14054 Caen. Tel: (0)2 31 27 90 30. E-mail: cdt@cg14.fr Website: https://calvados-tourisme.co.uk/en/.

La Manche Departmental Office: Maison du Département, 50008 Saint-Lô. Tel: (0)2 33 05 98 70. Fax: (0)2 33 56 07 03. E-mail: manchetourisme@cg50.fr Website www.manchetourisme .com.

These tourist offices will make hotel reservations, give information on local restaurants, events (e.g. festivals, sporting events, concerts, shows), places of interest (e.g. museums, markets, Calvados distilleries), guided tours and 'Routes'; *du Fromage* (cheese); *du Cidre* (cider); *des Moulins* (mills); *des Trois Rivières* (three rivers - l'Aure, la Drôme and la Tortonne), etc, all with well-signed itineraries.

Note that many tourist offices close during the French lunch hour other than in the high tourist season.

NORMANDIE MEMOIRE & Normandie Pass – See Commemorative Associations above.

Accommodation

Hotels/Restaurants
Those sited conveniently along the itineraries are listed in a distinctive **typeface** with their phone/e-mail numbers and basic details.

NOTE. Many French kitchens close firmly at 1400 hours after lunch, so it is advisable to start looking for a lunch stop by about 1230, especially outside the main tourist season or off the main tourist routes. Some Crêperies and Pizzerias, which now proliferate in France, may be open all day. A picnic (see above) is highly recommended when you are out for the day.

Lists are obtainable from the national or local tourist offices (see above). Book well in advance for busy holiday periods and in September when the Caen International Fair (*Foire de Caen*) takes place - check the precise dates with the tourist office. Details of the Hotels that lie conveniently along the itineraries are given as they are passed. The area is rich in hotels, which are graded as follows:

The tempting dessert buffet, Campanile Bayeux (see page 155).

MUSEUMS/PRESERVED BATTERIES

WAR CEMETERIES

GENERAL INDEX

Search also for relevant entries under 'group headings' of Aeroplanes; **Blockhouses/Bunkers/ Batteries; Brothers; Drop Zones; Massacres; Medal of Honor; Tanks etc.**